THE REMINISCENCES OF

Captain Louis Colbus
U.S. Navy (Retired)

INTERVIEWED BY

Paul Stillwell

U.S. Naval Institute • Annapolis, Maryland

Copyright © 2001

Preface

Above all, this oral history recounts the life and career of a destroyer man. As a junior officer, Louis Colbus served in the destroyer escorts Albert T. Harris and John R. Perry and on the staff of an escort squadron commander. As a mid-grade officer he was executive officer of the destroyer Basilone during Vietnam War combat service, commanding officer of the destroyer escort McCloy during a deployment with NATO forces, and a member of the team that developed the Spruance-class destroyers and Kidd-class guided missile destroyers. As a senior officer he commanded the destroyer Jonas Ingram and served as commodore of Destroyer Squadron Two. He had other tours of service, both at sea and ashore, but it was really his time in destroyer-type ships that defined him as a naval officer.

Captain Colbus's oral history is both informative and entertaining, because he has a knack for telling stories with zest and humor. But the reader should not be misled by his sometimes-zany, sometimes-irreverent approach, for he was truly serious about the business of being a naval professional. Even though he served through a time when the Navy changed dramatically, especially when Admiral Elmo Zumwalt was Chief of Naval Operations, Colbus adhered to the old values and traditions. He believed in smart-looking ships that were smartly operated. He also brought to the job a sense of panache, looking for the dramatic and seeking to share with others the enjoyment he felt from being part of the Navy, its ships, and its personnel.

From a historical sense, this memoir is valuable because of its candor about the people and situations Captain Colbus encountered during more than 30 years in uniform. And he does not spare himself in that regard, for his tells honestly of his own missteps. The sense of history is particularly evident when one compares the early years in small, fairly basic destroyer escorts to his tours on board the latest aircraft carriers. Though he was a dedicated surface warrior, he also describes his admiration for those with whom he served in the aviation portion of the Navy.

In the course of moving from the raw transcript to this final version, both Captain Colbus and I have done some editing in the interests of accuracy, smoothness, and clarity. At times various sections of the text have been moved from one place to another in order to improve the continuity of the narrative. He made use of his personal files to track down information useful for the editing of the transcript. In addition, I have inserted footnotes to provide further information for readers who use the volume. In going through the entire process of editing and footnoting, Captain Colbus has been most cooperative.

Ms. Ann Hassinger of the Naval Institute's history division has made a significant contribution through her diligence in the overall process of printing, proofreading, and overseeing the binding of the completed volumes.

Paul Stillwell
Director, History Division
U.S. Naval Institute
March 2001

CAPTAIN LOUIS COLBUS
UNITED STATES NAVY (RETIRED)

Personal Data

Born: 16 June 1931, Altoona, Pennsylvania

Married: 1 December 1961, to Mary Jo "Jody" Rierson. She died on 5 January 1994.

Children: Jonathan Colbus, born 24 April 1965
Joanna Colbus Washburn, born 26 August 1968

Education and Training

Bachelor of science in economics, University of South Carolina, Columbia, South Carolina, 1953

Graduate studies in economics, Pennsylvania State University, State College, Pennsylvania, 1953-54

Completed General Line School, Monterey, California, 1960

Completed the course at the Naval War College, Newport, Rhode Island; master of science in international relations, 1965

Completed the course at the Senior Officer Ship Material Readiness Course, Arco, Idaho, 1976

Dates of Rank

Ensign: 4 June 1954
Lieutenant (junior grade): 4 December 1955
Lieutenant: 1 April 1958
Lieutenant Commander: 1 February 1964
Commander: 1 July 1968
Captain: 1 May 1975

Chronological Transcript of Service

June 1954-June 1957	USS Albert T. Harris (DE-447)
June 1957-June 1958	Staff, Commander Escort Squadron 12
July 1958-November 1958	Staff, Commander Task Force 88

December 1958-January 1960	Aide and Flag Lieutenant, Commander South Atlantic Force
February-December 1960	Student, General Line School, Monterey, California
January 1961-February 1963	Executive Officer, USS John R. Perry (DE-1034)
February 1963-July 1964	Bureau of Naval Personnel, Washington, D.C.
August 1964-June 1965	Student, Naval War College, Newport, Rhode Island
July 1965-December 1966	Executive officer, USS Basilone (DD-824)
December 1966-May 1968	Commanding Officer, USS McCloy (DE-1038)
July 1968-July 1971	Destroyer Development Program, OpNav, Washington, D.C.
August 1971-November 1972	Commanding Officer, USS Jonas Ingram (DD-938)
December 1972-June 1975	Plans Officer, staff of Commander Carrier Division Six
July 1975-April 1976	Assistant Chief of Staff for Evaluation, Operational Test and Evaluation Force
April-September 1976	Student, Senior Officer Ship Material Readiness Course, Arco, Idaho
September 1976-August 1979	Commander Destroyer Squadron Two
September 1979-December 1982	Chief of Staff, Commander Carrier Group Eight
1 December 1982	Retirement from active duty

Awards

Legion of Merit
Meritorious Service Medal
Armed Forces Expeditionary Medal (two awards)
Vietnam Campaign Medal
National Defense Service Medal (two awards)
Sea Service Deployment ribbon (three awards)

Civilian Career

Fleet and lease manager/Public Relations, Hall Auto World
Senior analyst, Sonalysts
NavSea on-board representative, new construction, USS Wasp (LHD-1)
Business development, Creasy Electronics, Inc.
Foreign military sales proposal, SAIC/AMSEC
Business development, QED Systems, Inc.

Authorization

The U.S. Naval Institute is hereby authorized to make available to individuals, libraries, and other repositories of its choosing the transcripts of three oral history interviews concerning the life and naval career of the undersigned. The interviews were recorded on 30 August 1984, 31 August 1984, and 19 December 1984 in collaboration with Paul Stillwell for the U.S. Naval Institute.

The undersigned does hereby release and assign to the U.S. Naval Institute the rights and title to these interviews, with the exception that the undersigned retains the right to use the material for his own purposes, as he sees fit. The copyright in both the oral and transcribed versions shall be the sole property of the U.S. Naval Institute. The tape recordings of the interviews are and will remain the property of the U.S. Naval Institute.

Signed and sealed this 28th day of October 1998.

Captain Louis Colbus, USN (Ret.)

Interview Number 1 with Captain Louis Colbus, U.S. Navy (Retired)

Place: Captain Colbus's office at Sonalysts, Virginia Beach, Virginia, and his home in Virginia Beach

Date: Thursday, 30 August 1984

Interviewer: Paul Stillwell

Paul Stillwell: Captain, to begin at the beginning, could you tell me something about your early life: where and when you were born, your parents, and your childhood?

Captain Colbus: I was born in Altoona, Pennsylvania, and raised there. I graduated from high school in Altoona, then spent my first year of college in '49 at Penn State, where I became interested in the Navy, mainly in the NROTC.* I was lucky enough in my first year at Penn State to win an NROTC scholarship. At that time you matched your scholarship with admission to the school. It so happened that there was no "seat" at Penn State. There were 52 seats at 52 institutions, and all the seats at Penn State were filled.

My father was a Penn State graduate, class of '16.† Dad and I drove from Altoona to Washington, where we visited BuPers; it was my first look at the big Navy.‡ We walked in and had an interview with a man who would steer me to the school where I would match my scholarship with an open seat. We met this man at his desk and sat down. I wasn't overly impressed, because here we were on the second floor of BuPers, as we know it today.

Anyway, he looked at me and asked if I was related to Alvin Colbus, and, of course, we reared back. Here in this great Navy, how did this man pick out my cousin, who was an Army major during World War II? It turned out that this BuPers civilian had been the dean of men at Lycoming College and knew my cousin, who had attended Lycoming. It was one of the great coincidences that started me out on a great and fulfilling

---

* Pennsylvania State University is in the city of State College, which is in the center of the state, 44 miles northeast of Altoona. NROTC—Naval Reserve Officers Training Corps.
† His father was Haiman H. Colbus.
‡ BuPers—Bureau of Naval Personnel. From the early 1940s to the late 1990s the bureau was housed in the Arlington Annex, a building near the Pentagon and Arlington National Cemetery.

career in the Navy.

Paul Stillwell: Why did you want to get into the Navy?

Captain Colbus: Because I wanted to see the world, just as it was advertised. My dad had been in the Army, so I knew about it. But I had been to Atlantic City, New Jersey, a few times and had seen the ocean. To me it was more colorful, more romantic than a marching career. That's why I wanted the Navy instead of the Army.

Paul Stillwell: Had you had any exposure to the Navy, or was this all vicarious?

Captain Colbus: All vicarious, all vicarious, coming from an inland town such as Altoona. I did have one uncle, my Uncle Bill Colbus, who had been in the Navy in the First World War. He played baseball for USS Washington.* He boasted he had never been in the ship and never had been to sea until he was 76 years old. That was when I took him to sea in USS Jonas Ingram.† I was not influenced whatsoever, except I thought that would be an adventurous way to serve. It was something different, and I thought I would be adventurous.

The NROTC action officer at BuPers presented me with a list of schools that were available for a rising sophomore who would be a freshman in the NROTC program. I picked the University of South Carolina and had the greatest time of my life. It was the best choice I could have made. Again, luck, fate, whatever—I graduated there with still a year to go on my NROTC scholarship, and everybody encouraged me to continue school. I went back to Penn State and completed a year of graduate work. I was commissioned in '54, even though I received my B.S. in June of '53.

Paul Stillwell: Please describe some of the training you underwent in the program.

---

* USS Washington was an armored cruiser commissioned in 1906. In 1916 she was renamed Seattle and eventually served until being decommissioned in 1946.
† Colbus commanded the destroyer Jonas Ingram (DD-938) from August 1971 to November 1972. A later section of the oral history tells of Uncle Bill's visit to the ship.

Captain Colbus: All I can remember is Colonel Ferguson, who was the professor of naval science.* He was exactly what you would expect a Marine colonel to be—and what an influence he was on all of us! In fact, one of my classmates, Paul Hryskanich, just retired after 30-plus years.† I, too, retired with 30 years. I obtained a year and a half through reserve time, which I'd had before I went into the NROTC program. I guess I should mention that I joined the reserves when I was in high school. I went to boot camp and did all those things—again, for the romance of going to sea, even though I didn't get to sea as a seaman.‡ Back to Colonel Ferguson. He was a great man, a great influence, and really a fine man. What I most remember is the day he allowed me to command the drill team. He said, "All right, Colbus, have them remove their gloves."

I then directed 30 of my classmates, "Please remove your gloves."

That's when he took me aside. And I'll remember for the rest of my life what he said: "Colbus, in the military you don't have to plead for anything. You tell people what you want. You command people. Never say 'Please.'" And if you moderate that somewhat, that's a good rule.

In fact, one of the things that developed later on was when it was time to present kudos to shipmates, I would tell my shipmates what Colonel Ferguson had said: "We never thank people for the job they do. We don't plead to get the job done. However, for the manner in which you mates did that job, thank you very much for your spirit." Now you know how much Colonel Ferguson was a strong influence on all of us.

By the way, many of those South Carolina people from the year groups '53 and '54 stayed in the Navy. I can't give you a percentage, but I can give you the names of 25- and 30-year men. So it was a good time for us.

Colonel Ferguson was followed by Captain Anderson, who was a submariner, and I have to tell you how I met this skipper.§ I was taking—and don't laugh—a typing course. I never learned to type, and that was one of the quick courses. My best friend was Warren

---

* Colonel Edwin C. Ferguson, USMC, was professor of naval science at the University of South Carolina from 1948 to 1952.
† Captain Paul L. Hryskanich, USN, retired from active duty in July 1984. He was commissioned in June 1954.
‡ "Boot" is a slang term for a newly enlisted sailor or Marine. Recruit training is known as boot camp.
§ Captain William L. Anderson, USN, was professor of naval science at the University of South Carolina from 1952 to 1955. He had been the first commanding officer of the submarine Thresher (SS-200) when she was commissioned in 1940.

Rowlands, who went into the Navy and is now an FBI agent.[*] We had this beautiful woman in our typing class. I was then 21 or 22 years old, and I did all the things a young man should do. I carried her books, watched how she typed, discussed everything.

One day I was carrying her books, and she said, "I have to drop these off." We went right over to the NROTC building and took the books right into the office of the professor of naval science. He was a Navy captain submariner, and he was her husband! It was the first time, I guess, I'd really gotten in trouble. I had made a run on the new commanding officer's wife. He thought that was great. I was embarrassed, but we got over that. He had a daughter in school too.

Paul Stillwell: How regimented was the life of a midshipman at that time?

Captain Colbus: Compared to the Naval Academy, not very regimented; to today's midshipmen, very much so. Marriage was not permitted. We did comply with all rules and regulations. Our conduct was always under scrutiny, and I will tell a sea story that shows that. It was my Navy captain friend, the professor of naval science, who bailed me out.

At that time panty raids were very popular. Would you believe it if I told you I was sitting in the library studying one night when I saw a group going by, and I just went out and joined the group? We went over to the girls' dorm, and to this day I swear on my good honor that I was not what I was accused of afterwards—an organizer, an instigator. Anyway, I was standing around watching all this.

Our president was a retired CEC admiral named Smith; we called him "Snuffy."[†] Admiral Smith was standing there trying to keep the crowd quiet, and somebody grabbed his Panama hat and ran off with it. That's when all hell broke loose. Well, anyway, to make a long story short, a lot of reprimands went out; people were being expelled. The raiders, who were football players, actually got into the girls' dorm. I was accused of being

---

[*] Ensign Warren L. Rowlands, USN, was commissioned in June 1953.
[†] The university president at the time was Rear Admiral Norman M. Smith, Civil Engineer Corps, USN (Ret.). Born in 1883, he had served as Chief of the Bureau of Yards and Docks from 1933 until his retirement from the Navy in 1937.

one of the instigators, and I was taken to what I guess you'd call mast.[*]

My punishment was verbal from the college itself, because I convinced them that I didn't grab the president's hat, and that I wasn't an instigator. I wish I had been, but I couldn't control them that well. It was really the athletes and the big men on campus who did that. I was just a poor boy from up north. When I went in to see the captain, he read me the riot act, looked over his glasses, and chastised me properly: conduct unbecoming, misuse of leadership, he could expel me, etc. I was scared to death. As I was dismissed, he called me back, looked over his glasses, and said, "Louis, if you knew what I did at the Naval Academy in 1926, this is child's play."

Paul Stillwell: He had done his duty.

Captain Colbus: He had done his duty by kicking my rear end, and then he patted me on the back.

Paul Stillwell: Was there a kind of competitive spirit among members of the same class, compared with the Naval Academy?

Captain Colbus: No, I don't think so, because we sailed with those boys in the summertime, and there was quite a bit of envy. For instance, I think we earned $70.00 a month when on summer cruise, and we got the entire $70.00! The academy men also were paid $70.00, but they were allowed only $5.00 every two weeks, I think. So we had more money, we had much more freedom, and we were really looked down upon.

I think when NROTC men came into the Navy, they had an inferiority complex. If someone was a Naval Academy man, I was just an NROTC boy. They used to sing, "Take down your service flag, Mother. Your son's in the ROTC." I noticed, though, after about three years it really didn't make any difference. And today if you look at flag rank, it certainly doesn't make any difference. But in those days, yes, there was a difference. They lived Navy 24 hours a day, seven days a week. We drilled twice a week, and it was much

---

[*] Captain's mast is a sort of court in which the commanding officer of a unit listens to requests, awards non-judicial punishment, or issues commendations. Most often captain's mast is used for punishment of lesser offenses than those that merit courts-martial.

easier. Again, comparing it to today, NROTC had much more discipline. But comparing it then to what the Naval Academy midshipmen had, we were much looser and had an easier life.

Paul Stillwell: What percentage of your time in college would you say was devoted to the Navy?

Captain Colbus: We had three classes a week; we wore our uniforms twice a week. That's five hours' curriculum time, as they called it. And we had the Quarterdeck Society, which made us a closer group. The majority of the NROTC class was made up of northern men who had come south. Most of us were on a scholarship, because that's the way we were able to go to school. Affluent groups were few and far between in those days. Even the local NROTC students looked forward to that $50.00 a month stipend. That and the fact that the Navy was paying all our tuition and fees permitted most of us to attend school. We greatly appreciated NROTC and looked forward to a career in the Navy. It was a very, very favorable environment. Also, we were respected on the campus. You were really something special when you were an NROTC student at USC. That was true also at Penn State, where I spent a year.

Paul Stillwell: How did you finance that freshman year before you got the scholarship?

Captain Colbus: Well, I would have gone to school anyway. My dad had made arrangements. We weren't wealthy, but I had my way paid to school. My dad sent me my first year. He even provided me with a Packard car when I went off to school. I was living high off the hog.

Paul Stillwell: In your case it probably didn't make the difference.

Captain Colbus: The NROTC scholarship allowed other monies to buy the Packard. My grandmother wanted to send me to school to be a doctor. She had that all set up. What I was really going to do was be a lawyer, attend Dickinson College at Carlisle,

Pennsylvania, but I got into Penn State and then the Navy.

Paul Stillwell: What was your father's profession?

Captain Colbus: He was an engineer who had a small real estate and insurance company. He also worked at the engineering end of it, trading as the Altoona Rail and Machinery Company. He was a great one for going up in the Pennsylvania mines and dealing with the equipment used in that area.

Paul Stillwell: So you had concluded you definitely wanted to do something different from him.

Captain Colbus: Yes.

Paul Stillwell: What did you major in at South Carolina?

Captain Colbus: Economics.

Paul Stillwell: Why that?

Captain Colbus: I can't answer that. It just happened. I really didn't have any desire to be an engineer, had had no math, had had no physics or any technical discipline. That showed up later when I went to Idaho Falls in 1976 and was the poorest prepared student in the first class at the school out there.* That's another story.

Paul Stillwell: The Navy, of course, now puts great emphasis on engineering in NROTC. I gather there was not any sort of pressure then on a major.

Captain Colbus: No. The only thing we were told when we came in was that we couldn't

---

* This is a reference to the Senior Officer Ship Material Readiness Course, which Colbus discusses later in the oral history and refers to as "oily-rag school."

be in pre-law, pre-med, veterinary medicine, and a few other disciplines that I guess you'd call unusual professions. However, the majority of the students were in engineering. We did have our sociologists, psychologists, and other unusual pursuits in the Navy.

Paul Stillwell: What do you recall about the naval science courses themselves?

Captain Colbus: It was very difficult, because they were a whole new field, and here I'm speaking for myself. We studied all the subjects that one would expect; these subjects closely paralleled those at the Naval Academy. In fact, I think some of the books are still used. Steam engineering was all new to me. Gunnery wasn't that difficult. I guess the toughest thing was navigation. I remember that clearly. The navigation learning experience I use today. I was completely out of touch with reality until one day, all of a sudden, I saw it in three dimensions, and it just made sense.

Paul Stillwell: Are you talking about celestial navigation?

Captain Colbus: Yes. We would go out and stand on the building and shoot stars at night. It was the only science I thought I knew or had down pat, and I liked that very much. It was that type of environment—easy for the engineers, difficult for myself and sociologists and anthropologists.

Paul Stillwell: I would have thought you'd have a little advantage in having been a naval reservist and gotten some exposure, at least.

Captain Colbus: I had done some of the things that they taught. Being a naval reservist was most helpful in the actual on-board duty during your cruise in the summertime. A third-class midshipman then was really a third-class midshipman. He went down in the spaces and did what a boot was supposed to do. We had no air-conditioning. I'm not trying to sound like it was that tough, but you really lived the life of a novice sailor. Today I know that midshipmen come aboard and have to have separate compartments; we mingled. I remember that when we got to be first class, we got some officer privileges;

however, we rarely saw the wardroom.

Paul Stillwell: What ships did you spend these cruises in?

Captain Colbus: USS Burdo, APD-133.* I went to Europe in 1951 for my first cruise. I can't tell you how much fun that was and the characters who were there and some of the great names who were there at that time. We had a couple of characters who were midshipman officers.

Paul Stillwell: Did the reality of shipboard life live up to these expectations you'd created?

Captain Colbus: Yes, sir. The first ship I ever saw was this Burdo, and we're talking about a 318-foot, 1,800-ton DE, converted to an amphibious personnel carrier with four LCVPs on it.† The APDs launched the frogmen and did all those glamorous things. But you talk about rough-riding, top-heavy, light ships. We went to Norway and saw Northern Europe. I seemed to thrive in that rocking and rolling. I loved every minute of it.

Paul Stillwell: What kind of training did you have during that cruise?

Captain Colbus: I don't think that's changed that much. It was very dependent upon the ship and the personalities of the officers. We had a real hard-nosed exec in Burdo. He was a real old-timer.

One of the things I ought to mention is that many of the associations we had then were with seasoned World War II people: chiefs who'd enlisted in the mid-'30s and officers who fought their ships in the Atlantic. So we had an entirely different group in the '50s than you would think of today in the '80s. I'm talking about their backgrounds. Even the young officers, the young jaygees, had just come out of the Korean War.‡

---

* USS Burdo (APD-133) was initially designated DE-717. She was commissioned 2 June 1945 as a high-speed transport. She had a standard displacement of 1,450 tons, was 306 feet long, and 37 feet in the beam. Her top speed was 23.6 knots. She was armed with one 5-inch gun.
† LCVP—landing craft, vehicle and personnel.
‡ Jaygee—lieutenant (junior grade).

These chiefs had not quite 20 years in the Navy at that time, and it was a good starting point for us midshipmen. The old-timers went out and sat on the bitts on the forecastle after sundown. That was the only time they could take their hats off. It was just like in the movies, just exactly what you'd expect it to be. And that's why I enjoyed it so much.

Paul Stillwell: Did they treat midshipmen any differently from normal enlisted people?

Captain Colbus: Yes. As a matter of fact, I'll never forget on that ship there were twin brothers who were from my hometown. One was a boiler tender third class, and the other was a fireman. They picked on me unmercifully down in the fireroom. They knew I was going to be an officer, so they got their licks in when they could. I wasn't being sensitive about it, but they just bullied me because of the situation.

Paul Stillwell: The Navy of the World War II period was characterized as having a gulf between officer and enlisted. Did that still exist?

Captain Colbus: Oh, yes. Absolutely. I don't know what it was like before World War II, except what I heard, but there was a difference, and there was a definite line, even as midshipmen. You got in lines according to rank, and it was very, very cut and dried. With the privilege goes the obligation, which was preached all the time.

Paul Stillwell: Was there the kind of informal justice system that settled things at the division level rather than going up the chain of command?

Captain Colbus: Oh, absolutely, yes. During my midshipman days, and especially during my junior officer days, you'd be very embarrassed to have to take a problem to your senior. I learned this and preached this, and I hope I instilled it in some of my shipmates. When it gets up to the old man, it's serious. I guess I'm going back to my ensign days now. I'd be embarrassed to go in and see a department head who sure as hell didn't want to go tell the exec, "Here's a problem I can't handle." We handled things on our own level. Don't let your shipmate down. One hand for the ship, one hand for me. And we really worked together. Of course, this was a small ship I'm talking about. Yes, there was in-house justice. It wasn't nasty. It was very, very supportive.

Paul Stillwell: Was it fair?

Captain Colbus: Yes, it was fair. If you weren't pulling your weight, you heard about it. I had to work extra time because I was covering for you this morning while you were sleeping in. You wouldn't think of being late for watch, because that man was waiting for you, and every minute he had to wait was like an hour. We understood that and respected it. It was, I believe, very fair, and it built camaraderie.

Paul Stillwell: Was there great emphasis on smartness of uniforms?

Captain Colbus: Oh, absolutely, yes. Today I hear talk about these things. We just took that for granted. I should say there wasn't an emphasis on it; you just did it. And that's where I learned the term, "You're a rag bag." You'd never see anybody with any discrepancy at inspections, which we had every week. Quarters in the morning prepared us for Friday inspection, when you were inspected by your own. Saturday morning inspections were conducted with two watch sections. But the fellow who didn't meet the standards was put off to the side. He was hidden down in the compartment. You'd move people out. You never would see anybody who wasn't "ready for inspection." When the captain would walk through, it was admiration more than inspection.

Paul Stillwell: And the guy that got shoved to the side probably had a hard time getting his liberty card.

Captain Colbus: That's right. You had liberty cards, and that shipmate was given military instruction. He was "instructed" that he had disgraced the division, and that was that. Chiefs were really the backbone; they were all father figures. Every chief petty officer was an old-timer, gray-haired, with crow's feet around the eyes. You really looked up to those gents.

Paul Stillwell: Were they willing to teach somebody who was willing to learn?

Captain Colbus: Absolutely, absolutely. It's just as if you'd written about it in the book. It was a religion with them.

Paul Stillwell: What do you recall about liberty on that cruise?

Captain Colbus: Of course, it was three sections.[*] You were encouraged to go ashore. As I said, we had more money than the Naval Academy men did, which created some hard feelings, but not really. Liberty was there. We didn't do standbys. That was an unheard-of thing. You just did your turn, even if you met someone and were invited to someone's home. If it was your duty day, you didn't look for a standby. Another thing was that they'd have parties for midshipmen. You were anxious to go, in fact, delighted to go. It was a privilege. I think that's changed.

Paul Stillwell: What about a later cruise?

Captain Colbus: I went to South America in Missouri in 1953.[†]

Paul Stillwell: Draw a contrast between that and the ship you had been in previously as far as your own duties.

Captain Colbus: Thirty years later, you know, it doesn't appear to be that much different; it

---

[*] On a given day, one section would have the duty on board ship, and men in the other two sections could go ashore on liberty.
[†] USS Missouri (BB-63) was commissioned 11 June 1944. She had a full-load displacement of 57,600 tons. She was 887 feet long and 108 feet in the beam. Her top speed was 33 knots. In the mid-1950s she was armed with nine 16-inch guns, 20 5-inch guns, and 18 40-mm quad mounts. She remained in active service until decommissioned on 26 February 1955. She was best known as the site of the Japanese surrender in September 1945.

was just bigger. But then we learned about holystoning.* I know that was different. And I could really hide in Missouri. I used to sunbathe all the time. You could go up and sunbathe on one of the turrets, and no one could see you because it was so big. I used to sleep down in after steering. It was just tremendous back there. There was the noise factor. When I think of it today, I realize how dangerous it was. We'd go hide under a piece of rotating machinery. I was then a first-class midshipman. After I'd assign somebody a task, I'd go off and hide. They had those great engineering spaces.

Paul Stillwell: You had some kind of training forms to fill out, didn't you?

Captain Colbus: I don't remember it.

Paul Stillwell: How was the training provided?

Captain Colbus: On-the-job training. Later, as an ensign, you had a book, which was called a journal, that you had to fill out. I don't remember bringing any paperwork back, except I think they did fill out what they used to call a grease sheet about you.† It rated your conduct and military bearing; that was about it.

Paul Stillwell: Was there a contingent of officers along to provide leadership?

Captain Colbus: Oh, absolutely. We had a midshipman officer. I don't remember his name. Funny fellow. He wasn't a neat, squared-away, hero type; yet he was always on us for all the things that he did not represent. But you lived with that. Destroyers had one midshipman officer who was usually a lieutenant. We all started out from right here in Norfolk with this lieutenant from Purdue. He was assigned to that particular ship, which, of course, had midshipmen from many universities, as well as the Naval Academy.

Paul Stillwell: What about in the Missouri? Probably more senior there.

---

* Holy-stoning refers to the practice of cleaning a ship's wooden decks by scraping them with bricks pushed back and forth along the planks by means of wooden handles. It is a laborious operation.
† "Grease mark" is Naval Academy slang for an individual's grade in the area of aptitude for the service.

Captain Colbus: No, we still had lieutenants for our immediate advisers, but there was an entire contingent of them. Bigger, not much better, but easier. Maybe it was because I was a first class by then.

Paul Stillwell: Was there any glamour associated with serving in this famous ship?

Captain Colbus: Oh, yes. Everybody had their picture taken by the plaque that was right near the quarterdeck.[*] Our compartment was right near there also. Of course, people would come aboard when we'd be in port. That was a nice place to station yourself and explain to visiting guests and pretty girls about that plaque. I lived right there on duty days. That was very glamorous and a lot of fun. Rio de Janeiro was our big visit that year.[†]

Paul Stillwell: What were some of the other ports you hit?

Captain Colbus: We always went to Guantanamo Bay, and we visited Colon, Panama.[‡]

Paul Stillwell: Did you get involved in the firing of the guns?

Captain Colbus: Oh, yes. I was in the 16-inch battery. That duty was rotated. I went to a 5-inch mount, and when it was learned I'd done that in Burdo, I was privileged to serve in one of the 16-inch guns. I was scared to death! But it was easier than the 5-inch. It was a rumbling noise, you were in much cooler spaces, and it was much more spacious—a better deal all around.

Paul Stillwell: Were you in the turret yourself or down in the barbette?

---

[*] A plaque marking the spot of the September 1945 Japanese surrender was installed on the captain's veranda deck, starboard side of the Missouri's 01 level.
[†] For details on the Missouri's cruise that summer, see Paul Stillwell, Battleship Missouri: An Illustrated History (Annapolis: Naval Institute Press, 1996), pages 215-218.
[‡] Guantanamo Bay, on the south coast of Cuba, near the eastern end of the island, for many years provided a fleet anchorage and training area for U.S. Navy ships.

Captain Colbus: We were rotated through all of the stations.

Paul Stillwell: Including manhandling those projectiles?

Captain Colbus: Projectiles and great big bags of powder were hauled around mechanically with a manpower assist.

Paul Stillwell: Did you get to be in, say, the rammer spot that pushed the projectiles and the powder in?

Captain Colbus: No, I don't remember doing that.

We probably had a good eight weeks on that ship.* We got to know it pretty well. I remember one of the things that was, I guess, unique. That was when we went south. Of course, we crossed the equator, and everybody was indoctrinated into the realm of the deep.† We were now shellbacks. While we were in Rio de Janeiro, we were joined by a number of Naval Academy football players who were flown down, for some reason or other. They came aboard in July, joining us late. There was a big discussion about whether they would have to go through the ceremony going north, which nobody really wanted to do, since it was a lot of work. And they, of course, didn't want to go through it.

Paul Stillwell: Of course not.

Captain Colbus: But the young shellbacks such as myself said, "Oh, yes, they have to go through it." We did it a second time.

Paul Stillwell: When you were in school there in South Carolina, this was during the Korean War. Was there any feeling that you were slackers, that you weren't actively participating?

---
* The Missouri left Norfolk on 8 June 1953 and returned there on 4 August. The first equator crossing was on 19 June.
† In the Navy's traditional equator-crossing ceremonies, the novice pollywogs are initiated by the shellbacks who have crossed the line previously.

Captain Colbus: No. The only thing I can remember is just anxiety to get out. We wanted out of school. The rumors were flying all the time: "Boy, I understand they're going to shorten this. We're going to be commissioned as juniors. We're going out to do it." We were anxious to participate, plus we were anxious to get on a paying basis. We thought that was big stuff. None of us had ever been in a situation where we had money in our pockets. We wanted to (a) get to the war; (b) be ensigns; and (c) be salaried people who'd get out there and find out what it was all about. We really wanted to get out of school.

Paul Stillwell: I guess you in particular had a disadvantage, since you had to do one more year before you could enjoy those privileges.

Captain Colbus: Yes, I even talked about doubling up my last year. I was going to double up, but the professor of naval science and my father said, "Take another year. Take all the schooling you can get." That was the old-timers' way of doing it. So, yes, you're right. I wanted to get out, but I did the extra year.

Paul Stillwell: What did you study during that extra year you spent at Penn State?

Captain Colbus: Economics. I took my master's work up there, so that was very helpful.

Paul Stillwell: That's good, to get a master's in one year.

Captain Colbus: Yes.

Paul Stillwell: The midshipmen at the Naval Academy had a circumscribed social life because of all the regimentation there. How was it in the NROTC?

Captain Colbus: It was much more free. We had a very good social life. As I said before, you were really admired, and you were considered good students. I think there were 60,000 applications, and 2,700 were accepted. The community thought that you were probably something special, which gave us an edge. Plus, of course, I was in the South, where the military has always been a respected career. That surprised me too.

Of course, there was no drinking in South Carolina, except in private clubs. You could get beer and wine, but real bars didn't exist. However, if you were in the NROTC, you were allowed to join the UVA and the VFW and American Legion.[*] We had membership cards to all those places, so we thought it was pretty neat to take the girls drinking on a Sunday night and buy whiskey. That was an NROTC advantage.

Paul Stillwell: So you had to wonder whether they liked you for yourselves or for your membership cards.

Captain Colbus: Yes. I didn't think of that at the time. But the townspeople were very good to us too.

Paul Stillwell: I'm surprised they didn't have a little hostility, in that you were sort of carpetbaggers coming in from the North.

Captain Colbus: I think that again depended on the individual. Because I was just so glad to be there, I kept my mouth shut and didn't voice my opinions on what was going on between the North and the South. Of course, I was shocked to arrive down there and find that you'd go to a department store, where you'd see separate restrooms for colored and white. You'd see scuttlebutts, colored and white.[†] That shocked me, but I wasn't on a rampage to change anything. In fact, I was a great admirer of the Southern ways, other than these things that I wasn't used to. And I liked the food. I always raved about Southern cooking, so I was pretty much accepted. I was a good guy; I wasn't a damn Yankee; I was all right.

Paul Stillwell: You didn't protest the conditions.

Captain Colbus: Oh, no.

---

[*] VFW—Veterans of Foreign Wars. UVA—United Veterans Association.
[†] Scuttlebutt is a Navy slang term for a drinking fountain.

Paul Stillwell: Then you were commissioned in '54. Was there any special ceremony with that?

Captain Colbus: Yes. As a matter of fact, on the 18th of this month I wanted to go to Penn State, because Warren Rowlands, who was my classmate and closest friend, attended his son's commissioning at Penn State. I thought it would be great to go back, knowing it was going to be in the same environment, in the same hall.

Yes, we had the ceremony and put on the ensign bars. I had a new Buick coupe and went home to Altoona. On my way to Newport, Rhode Island, I swung by Wilkes-Barre to see my college girlfriend and ended up in Newport on the tenth of June, 1954. Again, picturesque, just as it's supposed to be. It was a beautiful June day in New England, with the rocky coast. Again, a whole new area to me. There was no bridge there then, so I took the ferry over, and that was an experience.

I was taught well at Penn State by Lieutenant John Swank, a very famous naval officer who was an aviator, black shoe, and everything.* He was our engineering professor. John Swank, who looked just like a movie star, claimed he got out of aviation because he was an ace. He'd wrecked three of our airplanes as an ensign or jaygee. Anyway, John Swank had told us, "When you go aboard, don't go lugging things. Go aboard smartly. The only thing in your left hand is your orders. If it's blues, gloves are all right, but you don't go carrying luggage. Go aboard smartly after 9:00 o'clock in the morning. Try to arrive about 2:00 in the afternoon."

Just as John had said, I parked my car, left everything in it, walked down, and got a boat at the landing. The ships were moored to buoys; we had no piers in Newport. I reported aboard just as one is supposed to, with orders in one hand, saluted with the other, and that was it.† So today when I see the fellows going down the pier with their tennis rackets and heavy bags and everything, I think, "Boy, they didn't have a John Swank."

---

* Lieutenant John A. Swank, USN. In the early days of naval aviation, the aviators wore brown shoes with their khaki uniforms and green uniforms. They thus acquired the nickname "brown shoes" to distinguish them from the traditional surface ship officers, who were known as "black shoes."
† The ship was the USS Albert T. Harris (DE-447), a John C. Butler-class destroyer escort commissioned 29 November 1944. She had a standard displacement of 1,350 tons, was 306 feet long, and 37 feet in the beam. Her design speed was 24 knots. She was armed with two 5-inch guns and three 21-inch torpedo tubes.

This was just one of the things we were told how to do. It's not written anywhere, just word of mouth.

Paul Stillwell: What was the advantage of 2:00 o'clock?

Captain Colbus: To report before yeomen were secured for the afternoon. They'd probably already completed their work. The officers weren't in the throes of mast or other things. Two o'clock was a good time to report aboard. The new man didn't get too involved. He didn't get on the next day's watch bill, because it had already been prepared. In other words, you had time to get your bearings and get organized.

I'll never forget my first day. I reported aboard, and the exec, John Grischy, took me up to see the skipper.* The skipper was Frank Hill.† He's retired now, living in Austin, Texas.‡ He was a very vivacious individual who was a very positive man and just a great, great individual. He sat me down and gave me a 15-minute introduction talk. By then it was quarter of 4:00. During our discussion he asked me how I got there.

"Well, sir, I drove up."

"Oh, you did?"

"Yes, sir."

"In a car?"

"Oh, yes, sir."

"Where is this car?"

"It's out on the pier."

"You've got a car?"

"Yes, sir."

"Gee, my wife and family went to Texas. I don't have a car. Want to go have a drink?"

"Yes, sir."

And, boy, that started the relationship. The captain and the new ensign went

---

* Lieutenant John S. Grischy, USN.
† Lieutenant Commander James Franklin Hill, USN, who was subsequently promoted to commander with a date of rank of 1 July 1954.
‡ Hill retired in January 1964 as a commander.

ashore, and we hit everything from the local on-base pubs to Fall River. We got back to the ship about 4:00 in the morning. I was just the chauffeur, but, boy, did I get an indoctrination into shipboard life.

We were there about a week until we got under way for Key West. This was a three-month tour, mid-summer in Key West, to service the sound school. We'd embark sonar students in the morning at 6:00 o'clock, let them work the gear, and bring them in port at 4:00. That was our assignment. There were four DEs out of this eight-ship squadron.[*] None of the families came to Key West, so here was a three-month tour with all these aggressive naval officers—working together and playing together. Key West was a very small area, so nobody got separated. It was really a close group and a heck of a good way to be indoctrinated into not only shipboard life but also the social life.

Paul Stillwell: Was it sort of the expected ethic for junior officers to live hard, work hard, and play hard?

Captain Colbus: Absolutely. It wasn't encouraged; it wasn't discouraged. We just did that. Weekends, of course, we didn't get under way. We moored to the pier in Key West, which was a big thing. At Newport we moored to a buoy, so we were dependent upon liberty boats and all the inconveniences of weather. So when you got to Key West, it was walk on and walk off.

The advantage of Key West was not only the social side of it but also the ship-handling program. You really got to know your ship. The currents at Key West are fantastic and provided tremendous ship-handling experiences. The captain very rarely handled the ship, so you really became a proficient ship handler. After you'd been in Key West, anywhere else was a piece of cake. I won't say it made a deep-water sailor out of you, but it sure made a good ship handler and coastal navigator out of you.

The captain's main objective was to get us new sailors qualified in the ship. That was accomplished by our standing behind the captain and listening to what he did. Or you'd stand behind the conning officer.[†] Let's say Ensign Benson is conning the ship.

---

[*] USS Albert T. Harris was in Escort Squadron 12.
[†] The individual with the conn—normally an officer—directs the ship's movements in course and speed.

You'd stand next to the captain, and when you thought it was time to put on left rudder, you'd actually touch him on his left elbow. You did all of the things that you thought you wanted to do by touching the captain. If you wanted to back on the port engine, you'd actually reach up and pull his arm back a little bit. And you were allowed this body contact to learn how to handle the ship. When you would react either ahead of the conning officer or better than the conning officer, it was your turn to do it yourself. Of course, you blew it right away, because you were so nervous on your first actual moor.

My first moor was in Key West, from which I'd gotten the ship under way that morning. We entered, and I conned up the channel. I thought I'd done everything well. I made the turn, and brought that ship right where it should be—I thought. I think the current was with me that day. The ship moved right over into place, and I was very proud. No crazy bells.* It wasn't letter perfect, but it was damn good. I was at that time dating Ginny Allen, who worked at the GE lab, and the lab office was right out at the pier.† Ginny was there waving at me, and I was so proud. That's when the captain told me, "That's a pretty good landing, Colbus, but we're at Pier Dog. We're supposed to be at Pier Baker.‡ I'll take it over there for you." It was a good landing for Pier Dog.

Paul Stillwell: What was your job on board ship?

Captain Colbus: I started off as the first lieutenant. Then, when the ship left Key West in September, I remained there and was a student at the sonar school. Upon return to the ship, I became the ASW officer and then fleeted up to be the gunnery officer.§ I also became the senior watch officer.

I have to tell you about Chief Walter J. Czajkowski. He was a chief boatswain's mate. If you would call Hollywood Central Casting and say, "Send me a chief boatswain's mate, World War II vintage," Chief Czajkowski would have appeared. He was 6 feet, 6 inches, overweight, big belly, Polish, Michigan, wore his hat at an angle, and talked very

---

* Each order to the engines is accompanied by a bell sound on the engine order telegraph. Thus, a "bell" is synonymous with an engine order. The fewer the number of bells in a given landing, the better.
† GE—General Electric, a long-time defense contractor.
‡ "Dog" and "Baker" represented letters in the phonetic alphabet of the time.
§ ASW—antisubmarine warfare. "Fleet up" is a Navy term that describes a move to a more responsible position in a given organization.

gruffly.

About my third day on board, after my great success as the captain's steaming buddy, the chief called me aside and said, "En-swine Colbus, here's what you do. You go into that cage in the morning. [Our office was an expanded metal cage in the officers' passageway. We didn't have offices; we had a little cubbyhole where we kept our books, administrative papers, and ordnance pubs.] And about 0740 you come out on the forecastle. You come up to me. I will salute you and tell you, 'All present and accounted for.' Now, I've already read the plan of the day, and I want you to have some words to say. I'll give them to you probably that morning or the night before. When you're ready to use your own words, you just let me know. But in the meantime, this is the way you operate. You listen to me and do what you're told, and you will be the best first lieutenant in the fleet."

I knew I couldn't say, "Thank you." I just said, "Very well, Chief Czajkowski." That's the way it was. Old Walter J. Czajkowski just led me that way.

What really broke the umbilical cord occurred in the 18th month. We were at sea, and it was the noon hour. I was having lunch when a messenger came to tell me, "We're picking up the whaleboat." The captain was on the bridge. I immediately left the wardroom, because I was to be present for all deck evolutions. Recovering the whaleboat was a complicated evolution. There were no gravity davits; they were Welin davits that had to be swung out, swung in, take two lines, marry them up at the forecastle. I won't say it was a difficult evolution, but it was intricate. The Navy sometimes killed people picking up boats. So I went up there to man my station. The chief boatswain's mate was already on station, and they'd started to pick up the boat.

I said, "Stop the evolution. Lower the boat to the water's edge." I called the chief aside and said, "Chief, you told me every time we recover the boat, we must pass rattail stoppers. I see you didn't do that. You are in a very, very dangerous situation here."

He looked at me and said, "Who the hell are you to tell me how to pick up a boat?"

I said, "You told me you never . . . " and I went on to repeat, "You're doing just what you told me never to do. That's unsafe, and I'm not going to allow it."

He looked at me, and he said, "Oh, my, I got me a first lieutenant." And from that day on, he and I were the best of friends; I just loved him. Later, as an exec, skipper, and commodore, I used to always tell the chiefs, "Go out there and get yourself some en-swine and make him a first lieutenant."

Paul Stillwell: How much Navy was there in Key West at that point?

Captain Colbus: There was a big presence there. That was the day when we had curfews and had to be off the streets by 0200. Key West was a wild place. This was after the Truman Administration had been down and put the place on the map because Truman had his winter White House down there.* There was a lot of press people. There was a lot of personages down there—well-known, famous people. The Navy was prevalent in Key West. However, it was tough on the Navy. You would have thought that we were in the minority down there. All you had to do was drive up the main street with your bright lights on, and you'd end up in jail. It was a very, very tense situation.

Paul Stillwell: Did that make it tough to be a division officer, because sailors will do things?

Captain Colbus: It certainly did. We always had problems at Key West. This is where you had to use your good judgment as to whether you were going to take the man to captain's mast or handle it yourself. You didn't want to cover up or hide things. If the man broke curfew, or if he was outside the gates at 0203, there was no way around it. He had to go to mast, because this was via the base commander. As I said, things were tough in Key West. Come out of the bar and stagger, which was not unusual, and you were in trouble if policemen were around. I had skirmishes myself with the Key West police—minor things, of course!

Paul Stillwell: What was the reason for this sort of attitude?

Captain Colbus: I wish I could explain it. It was just one of those things where the police and the sailor were at odds. As a matter of fact, before I got there, an admiral was sent

---

* Harry S. Truman served as President of the United States from 12 April 1945 to 20 January 1953.

down there to square things away, so to speak. Now, this is second- or third-hand, but I heard that he had told the city of Key West that if there wasn't more cooperation, he was going to put the entire city of Key West out of bounds, off limits. He would have the buses leave the naval station on Friday and take Navy personnel to Miami for liberty. Key West would not see any sailors. I think that must have improved things somewhat.

What had happened was that several months earlier there had been a big scandal in Key West. It was no secret that there had been a Navy Relief benefit show held at Boca Chica, and it got out of hand.* It was a fund-raising drive, where they did all kinds of games and things and sold chances; it was a carnival atmosphere. Well, they had some show girls from Miami. Those girls were not really USO girls; they were really . . .

Paul Stillwell: Professionals.

Captain Colbus: Professionals, thank you. I couldn't think of the word. These professionals got into a situation at about midnight. They were having what we used to call exhibitions, and they performed with some of the sailors in public. That blew the lid right off everything, and that's when the big investigations came down. Key West became a very, very tight place in which to live, go on liberty, or operate.

Paul Stillwell: Did the officers generally go on liberty in groups?

Captain Colbus: Oh, yes. There was one place in Key West that we all frequented. In fact, that's where I had my wedding reception, at the Sun and Sand Club. Anybody who was around Key West will remember that place. George Keyes and his wife operated this place called the Sun and Sand Club. It was just a little more than a lean-to on the beach, but a gorgeous beach, and that's where all our social activity happened. Officers were given a gratis membership. Locals paid, I think, $50.00 a year, and we had a lot of locals. It would be the country club of Key West. But, again, a very, very tropical setting and a lot of fun.

We'd go over there, for instance, as soon as we finished our Saturday morning ship

---

* Boca Chica Naval Air Station was on Boca Chica Key, five miles northeast of Key West.

routine. We would change into our swimsuits right there in the locker room, spend the day on the beach, go back to the ship to change into evening casual wear, and right to the Sun and Sand to have dinner. We'd be there from 10:00 o'clock Saturday morning till 4:00 o'clock Sunday morning. You spent your entire life over there.

The first time I went there, I was told, "This is where you should go." The skipper didn't go with me. I somehow or other went there by myself. I don't know why we were not in a group, but I went by myself, introduced myself, used the captain's name, and George Keyes, the owner, said, "Have a seat right there. Go in the bar. Meet the bartender, Bob, who is an ex-sonarman from the ship Peterson." I went in and met the bartender, who became my friend for the next ten years, I'd say.

It was a little bar with three stools. I was in one, and a fellow sat down next to me and started talking. He was very polite, very nice, overly solicitous, and it became obvious he was a homosexual. After five minutes of this, George Keyes came up, tapped him on the shoulder, and said, "I told you, one, don't come in here anymore; two, if you ever get in here, don't you bother these young Navy people. Out." The fellow left. It was Tennessee Williams.*

We had a lot of big names who came to Key West. Tallulah Bankhead was a big favorite on the beach.† Who else? Irma Goodbody, I remember, was a stripper from Philadelphia. It was just a fun place. And you ask any submariner, diesel boat sailor from that vintage, and they'll all remember the Sun and Sand. We called it—and that was pretty racy then—Sin and Sex. It was just all good fun, though.

Paul Stillwell: Did officers of that era have a tendency to talk shop when they were outside working hours?

Captain Colbus: No, no, not serious talk. Sea stories, fun things, but there wasn't a lot of technical discussion. Tactics didn't come into it. You told stories that everybody understood and related to. Where we really did talk shop was in the O-club in the late

---

* Williams was a noted American playwright. His works included The Glass Menagerie (1945), A Streetcar Named Desire (1947), and Cat on a Hot Tin Roof (1955).
† Tallulah Bankhead was a stage and screen actress.

afternoon.* We'd moor the ship late afternoon and muster at the Aero Palms, which was the local club. If you made a good landing, as I just talked about, your squadron mates, as well as your shipmates, would stand around and critique your landing, and vice versa. We did that before dinner. Then we went back to the ship for dinner about 1830, then over to Sun and Sand, where there wasn't too much shop talk.

Paul Stillwell: How well did you know the men in other ships and squadrons?

Captain Colbus: I'm glad you asked that. Extremely well. You knew your squadron mates as well as you knew your shipmates, and I think that's a fair statement. First of all, you moored in a nest. For the dinner hour we would exchange—not by design, not by the exec's ruling—ships for dinner. Perhaps I would have dinner tonight in Thaddeus Parker with my friend Charlie Fox, and then tomorrow night he'd come over and have dinner with me.† So you expected a full sitting, and those sittings would swap back and forth. In fact, I became so much a visitor on USS Tabberer, which was the flagship where my USC classmate Pat Reddick was stationed, that I actually had my name on the status board on the quarterdeck, showing whether or not I was aboard.‡

Paul Stillwell: Did you benefit at sea from this kind of association, in that you were more than likely to know what these people were going to do?

Captain Colbus: That's right. The skippers were very, very close. Everybody was close. For instance, we'd be out doing close-in maneuvers. We did torpedo attacks; we did sister-brother maneuvers in ASW when you had a 1,200-yard sonar and you'd be at 900 yards. You did everything according to what they called the Gitmo circle.§ If you were in one position relative to me, I'd turn to the right. If you were in another, I'd turn to the left. I'd go under your stern; I'd go around you. And that was done by design, and you trained to

---

* O-club—officers' club.
† Ensign Charles W. Fox, USN.
‡ The destroyer escort Tabberer (DE-418) had gained a measure of fame in December 1944 when she rescued 55 men from U.S. destroyers sunk in a typhoon off the Philippine Islands.
§ "Gitmo" is the nickname for Guantanamo Bay, Cuba, home of the fleet training group.

do this. Well, I'd hear my skipper say to me, "Who has the conn in Tabberer?"

I'd say, "Pat Reddick, sir."

"Oh, okay." He'd put his feet up and sit back and probably never look up from his book or some paperwork. That was fine. He knew those OODs as well as he knew his own OODs and put the same amount of faith or lack of trust.[*] So we knew each other very, very well. We knew what ships were "chicken of the sea," we knew which ships were aggressive, and all the skippers played it that way.

Speaking of Tabberer reminds me of a time when she and Albert T. Harris were conducting routine ops off Block Island with the submarine Diablo, which was homeported in New London. As USS Diablo came to the surface, she caught USS Tabberer and ripped about a 24-foot hole in her keel. USS Tabberer was flooding; she was in bad shape. USS Albert T. Harris took her under tow and got her back to Newport. Diablo had a bent mast and some damage to the conning tower; she returned to New London.

When we got Tabberer home and patched, she was towed by a fleet tug to Boston. USS Albert T. Harris was the escort ship. And the point of this story has to do with the camaraderie that existed not only within a ship but throughout the squadron. About halfway to Boston, Frank Hill, who knew the OOD at the time was my good friend Pat Reddick, sent him a message, stating: "It's the only time Reddick's been in station."[†]

Paul Stillwell: Nice little dig there.

Captain Colbus: Yes, but good-natured, of course.

Paul Stillwell: You've described the system whereby you learned to make landings. Was there a comparable system for formation steaming and ASW maneuvers?

Captain Colbus: Not those close maneuvers I just talked about where you'd be right there. You'd go on deck and you'd do it. You'd study, you'd be the JO, you'd be the phone talker, you'd be the tactical signal book decoder.[‡] You rotated through all these positions, and just

---

[*] OODs—officers of the deck.
[†] In or on station refers to the ship's assigned position in a formation.
[‡] JO—junior officer.

through osmosis you could pick it up very quickly because you did it all day. It was a four-hour watch, you had plenty of it, and it didn't take long to pick up not only the verbiage but the proper thing to do. When you displayed to the captain that you knew what was going on, he would let you conn. It would not be unusual to have an officer become a pretty seasoned OOD within six months of joining the ship. And I'm talking about close maneuvers, putting the rudder over hard, using the engines, not just out there steaming in station.

My favorite example was that I remember going to my first in-port watch in Newport the day after I reported. Here I was in uniform on the quarterdeck and wearing a .45. Petty Officer Lasiski, sonarman second class, came up to me and reported, "Mr. Colbus, Tabberer is coming up the channel with Item at the dip."[*] With all my preparation and schooling, I had no idea what "Item at the dip" meant. I didn't know if he was testing me or not. Of course, I learned that meant Tabberer wanted to come and moor alongside.

I didn't know that then, but I said, "Very well." Then I thought, "Oh, boy, what do I do now?" I wasn't going to ask Lasiski what that meant. I knew Item was a signal flag. I wasn't going to go look in the signal book, so I went into the wardroom to find the CDO, the command duty officer, who was Mr. Kurmin.[†] He was a jaygee, Korean vet. We called him "Mister Kurmin." I didn't call him "Bob." I knocked on his door. He was lying on his bunk with a book.

"Mr. Kurmin?"

"Yes?"

"Tabberer's coming up the channel with Item at the dip."

"Very well. I'll be out and help you moor the ship."

Ah, something about mooring the ship. He came on deck, and I watched him, and that's how you learned.

Within 12 months, Captain Hill was gone and our new skipper, Captain Sherwood, was aboard.[‡] One morning we were going to steam from the Newport anchorage up to

---

[*] "Item" was then the word for the letter "I" in the phonetic alphabet. The petty officer's report meant that the destroyer escort Tabberer was showing the yellow-and-black "I" signal flag on her halyard. At the dip meant it was partway down.
[†] Lieutenant (junior grade) Robert R. Kurmin, USNR.
[‡] Lieutenant Commander Charles Sherwood, USN.

Providence, Rhode Island. We were going there for a holiday season. Captain Sherwood came on board with his newspaper. I reported the ship ready for getting under way. The captain looked at me, still an ensign, and said, "Make it so." I got the ship under way, and I can remember going all the way to Providence. The navigator made recommendations, and the captain, who was sitting there, would nod to me and say, "Very well." I got the ship up there and put her alongside, just as it was supposed to be. And that was less than a year. We thought that was just great. And the skippers let you do it.

Paul Stillwell: That does a great deal for one's confidence.

Captain Colbus: It did that for everybody, yes. This skipper I just mentioned, Captain Sherwood, could be the subject of a book.

Paul Stillwell: Well, let's hear some of the things you might put in that book.

Captain Colbus: Chas Sherwood died three years ago. I had—what should I say?—the honor of representing the Navy at his funeral and presenting the flag to his widow. His wife is our best friend. We talk to her about three times a week. She lives 15 minutes from us. That's the kind of camaraderie we had. Everybody who was in that ship had the same relationship. We all are in touch with each other today.

When Captain Sherwood came aboard, he was 33 years old at the time, six feet two, looked just like Frank Sinatra—lanky, skinny, quiet.[*] Oh, he never raised his voice; you never heard that man raise his voice. He had the greatest amount of patience of any human being I've ever known. He was just a great image. Everybody admired and loved the skipper.

My second exec was Isaac Nelson Franklin, a good friend of mine.[†] He's a stockbroker now out in Dallas. I talk to Nelson a couple of times a year. But you talk about old school; he relished being known as a tough guy. Well, there was a balance there. People say if the skipper's nice, the exec is tough. Nelson was an excellent ship handler,

---
[*] Sherwood was born 30 September 1922.
[†] Franklin was then a lieutenant in the regular Navy.

brilliant tactician, and knew everything that there was to know about the Navy. He had come from cruisers, while Captain Sherwood had come from small ships. Captain Sherwood had been a minesweeper sailor, had commanded Albatross before that, and really was our leader. And he was the fellow who would lead us ashore.

We sit around and tell stories about Chas and some of his antics. He did drink. That man could drink Friday night, come back to the ship at 4:00 o'clock Saturday morning, be on the golf course at 6:00, play 18 holes, and be just as alert and energetic as everyone else. I didn't go with him, as someone had to stand Saturday morning inspections, but this is what they tell me. He had more stamina than anybody I've ever seen. As I say, a very quiet and effective naval officer who had patience and brilliance and who was just a natural leader.

Paul Stillwell: In what way did Franklin's tough nature manifest itself?

Captain Colbus: Everything that was done had a "Why?" "Why, Louis, why?" You had to answer everything to his "Why?" If you'd present him a piece of paper to be signed, he'd look at it and ask, "Why?" It was very difficult to answer. He was a great grammarian. Of course, we didn't know how to write in those days. Nelson taught us by being hard-nosed about it.

I'll give you an example of his tutelage. I was the mess caterer and treasurer. I sent the first class steward to the commissary to buy what we needed for a three-week at-sea period. We were getting under way at 1500. He went over after lunch and came back by taxi. Of course, I paid for the taxi out of the mess treasury. It cost $1.15 for a taxi from the commissary back to the ship. The steward took the taxi because he was afraid he was going to miss the ship. He didn't wait for the bus. The mess audits in those days were absolutely phenomenal. They were designed to give the JOs a bad time. A lot of it was done as training and in jest, but this was not. After I got through my mess audit with the audit board, I went in to get the exec to sign the statement before I went to the skipper. We must have spent an hour and a half talking about that $1.15: "Why?"

"Well, sir, he wanted to get back to the ship on time. I think that was a smart thing to do—spend $1.15 rather than miss ship. First class."

"Well, why didn't he leave earlier?"

"Well, he had to serve lunch."

"Well, why didn't he go this morning?" Everything was "Why? Why? Why?"

At one point I said, "I'll put in the $1.15."

"No, you don't get the point. Why? Why, Louis?"

Paul Stillwell: In those duels you'd have with the submarines, who seemed to have the relative advantage, the destroyer escorts or the submarines?

Captain Colbus: Well, the destroyer, because, first of all, they were out in an area off Key West. We're talking about the training evolutions.

Paul Stillwell: Right.

Captain Colbus: The sub would be in an area that was bounded. She would be on a course and speed with only, let's say, 30 degrees either side of the base course. She wasn't allowed more than a two-knot speed increase or decrease, because we wanted the sonarmen to have ping time. We didn't want the submarine to get away. So we would go over the submarine every time it was time to make an attack. After we got through with the basics, we'd go off to 1,000 yards and come in. As we'd cross over the sub, we'd throw over a green dye marker which would mark the place we had just simulated dropping depth charges. The sub would send up an air bubble so we could compare the two. We always had probably 90% of our—we called them slugs—slugs and the green dye in our favor. It was a training evolution for us.

Paul Stillwell: Was this active sonar?

Captain Colbus: Oh, yes.

Paul Stillwell: How capable were the sonars in that period?

Captain Colbus: Well, they were very capable at these close-in ranges, because we were talking, as I said, 1,000-1,200 yards. We had Hedgehogs, which had only about a maximum 300-yard range.* As you went in over the sub, you dropped the depth charges, and then K guns gave you a full pattern.† And you always had two ships to a submarine. That was one of the rules—two destroyers to one submarine.

Paul Stillwell: Was there any relationship between your shipboard work and the school there at Key West? I'm talking about the sonar school that you went to.

Captain Colbus: You conducted regular ship's routine. A ship would always come back to Newport in much better shape than when it left. I'm talking about appearance. I'm talking about cleanliness and smartness, because you could concentrate on those things. You had a very, very structured routine. You got under way at 0600, and you were moored that evening by 1700. You could plan your work. People didn't go on leave, because we were operating in Key West. How could you get the money to fly or take a train? There were very few personal cars. So it was a structured routine for the good group that was there. We played hard and worked hard, and the ship prospered in that environment.

Paul Stillwell: Did you have any training at Guantanamo in addition?

Captain Colbus: Not at that time. Later on, the ships would swing by Guantanamo. Another thing we did, though, was to steam the ship on weekends to Havana, Cuba. With some exceptions, a ship would go to Havana almost every weekend. A ship would get under way after the Friday session with the sonar school. A tug would meet the ship at the sea buoy, take the students back, and bring other passengers as riders. The ship would ring up 20 knots and in three hours be in Havana.

---

* Hedgehog, developed in World War II, was a British-designed spigot mortar that fired its weapons out ahead of the attacking ship. It was the first ASW weapon that could be fired while the surface ship remained in sonar contact with the target. Its name came from the collection of spigots in the launcher; they stuck up like porcupine quills.

† The K gun was used to fire depth charges off the side of a surface ship, instead of rolling them off the fantail.

Paul Stillwell: Please describe Havana at that period.

Captain Colbus: Our first trip over there was with Frank Hill. When we got over there, I called up Mike Rosik. He was a Puerto Rican who was married to a Cuban lady. Mike Rosik had gone to Pennsylvania State College with my father, and both of them graduated in the class of 1916. When Mike Rosik arrived at Penn State in 1912, he didn't speak English. My dad didn't have any money; in fact, he had to send home five bucks a month. You know, the old story about difficult school days. He and Mike became friendly. Mike came from a very wealthy Puerto Rican family, and I guess he paid my dad to help him with his English and do his homework. Both were studying engineering. I had met Mike when he'd attended a class reunion at State College. I was about 14 or 15 years old at the time.

I called Mike when we got to Havana. He was so glad to hear I was there. My dad had told him I'd probably be coming by since I was now in the Navy. He rolled out the limousine, picked us up, and took us to his club. He and his wife entertained the entire wardroom. They took us to the proper places in Havana. About 0100 they went home and told the chauffeur to take us anywhere we wanted to go, and that's how we learned Havana. We learned every hot spot, and we did every hot spot. We would, as I say, go over there at least twice during our three-month period with the ship in Key West. Then, if you wanted to go over on your own, you could always get off to find a ride. But we went as a group. Havana was better than Paris, better than anyplace I've ever been in my life. It was really the liberty spot of the world.

Paul Stillwell: How so? What made it better than Paris?

Captain Colbus: First of all, it was very inexpensive. Second of all, as I said, I knew it very well. We knew exactly what we were doing. We had our regular taxi drivers who would hook up with us. We had our regular bistros. I may as well talk about it, since I was a bachelor. It was not unusual to go to a house of ill repute for the clubby barroom atmosphere. You'd go in there, and they'd have card games, dancing, shows—anything hat was in the line of entertainment. Then, of course, there was the back room for the really wild shows, and there was the upstairs for the girls, the business end of it. And so I guess every ship had its favorite bar to go to. I guess the most famous club down there was one called the San Francisco Club. The San Francisco Club knew us and treated us right. You could have a swell time and party every night.

Also, of course, it was a beautiful city. By the way, Mike Rosik owned a big hotel. He had built the biggest hotel down there, the Nacional, and he had built a new one. I can't remember the name of that hotel on the outskirts, but we always had a suite there. So I was very well taken care of, and the ship was very well taken care of, making it exceptionally nice for us. We sure weren't strangers in Havana.

Paul Stillwell: It sounds like an exciting environment.

Captain Colbus: It was. We all had a good time.

In Key West you could go to Sloppy Joe's, right on the main street, and see Ernest Hemingway sitting in there.[*] In fact, one of my friends rented his home when he left and went to Cuba for his, I guess, final departure from Key West. I don't think he lived year round in Key West in '54, but he certainly did show up, and he had children who used to come there. So he was a figure, and people would go by to see him sitting there.

Paul Stillwell: You described your job as first lieutenant. As you moved up, what did you get involved in?

Captain Colbus: I became the ASW officer, as I said, and that was really a great job too. In those days we had an SQS-4 sonar. That was a great advance/upgrade from the QHB Able, which was really basic, so now we had a pretty sophisticated sonar.[†] The ship was very maneuverable. The sonar shack was up on the bridge, right next to the conning station in the pilothouse. We had Hedgehogs and depth charges.

What made it fun was that an individual did everything. You used a dime that you

---

[*] Ernest Hemingway (1899-1961) was an American journalist, novelist, and short-story writer. He was awarded the Nobel Prize in literature in 1954. One of his novels was The Old Man and the Sea (1952), about a Cuban fisherman.
[†] "Able" was the word for the letter "A" in the phonetic alphabet of the time.

put on what was called ASAP—the antisubmarine attack plotter. It was a CRT scope that showed where your sensor—your ping—was going.* When it picked up a contact, you'd have a little blip there, and that dime represented the distance at which you'd fire your Hedgehogs. You'd stand there with a dime, and when this blip met the dime that was laid next to the contact, you'd push the button and fire Hedgehogs. Then you started your stopwatch, which hung around your neck. I think it was 30 seconds later that you started firing depth charges, because by that time you'd drive right over the submarine. You had the conn. You used earphones to tell the OOD where to drive the ship, so you felt good about that and very powerful; that was your ship.

Paul Stillwell: Then you said you became the gunnery officer. How much armament did those ships have?

Captain Colbus: We had two 5-inch/38s, four 40-millimeters, and, if I recall correctly, six 20-millimeter guns. I'll tell you a story on that one. We had a commodore, Joseph Matthew McDowell, who was previously a submariner.† He was quite a guy and a lot of fun ashore. What I remember most about Commodore McDowell was that he enjoyed his comforts aboard ship. As I said, he was not originally a destroyer sailor.‡ After the war, he had commanded a captured Japanese submarine and brought it home, which gave him a lot of publicity and, I guess, a lot of notoriety when he was a submariner.§

We were out one day off Newport to do a gunnery exercise. Chas Sherwood was the skipper. We had a tractor aircraft towing the target sleeve. The target crossed over the ship. We didn't pick it up with the handlebar director. FT2 Koler couldn't see it; it was not a very good day for gunnery.** About the third pass, Chas Sherwood—who was a very patient man, as I said—looked up at me and said, "Louis, you think we ought to continue with this exercise?"

"Yes, sir, Captain. We've got our ammunition out." And I said, "Next round, I

---

* CRT—cathode ray tube.
† Commander Joseph M. McDowell, USN, served as Commander Escort Squadron 12 from July 1956 to August 1957.
‡ McDowell commanded the destroyer Taussig (DD-746) from 1951 to 1953.
§ McDowell commanded the former Japanese submarine I-400 from September 1945 to April 1946.
** FT2—Fire controlman second class.

want action, all stations." Well, this tow plane did the big circle, went out, and came in. I looked at the captain and said, "May I?"

He looked at me and said, "Commence firing." I gave them all the orders ahead of time, and the 5-inch went off. And all of a sudden we fired the 40-millimeters. I think we just fired the 20-millimeters. We didn't have that target anywhere near us. It was already out of range to port, and we were firing over to starboard. The exec had been a fire control officer on the cruiser Roanoke, and he was coming up just to kill me. Meanwhile, the commodore was down on the bridge, jumping up and down, saying that it was the best display of gunnery he'd ever seen. He just wanted the noise. He wanted to see and smell the smoke. The captain was down there smiling. So here was the exec, giving me all kinds of hell and damnation because I was wasting ammunition. And here was the commodore down on the bridge, just elated over the great show, and the captain was pleased with my gamesmanship. And I had to get the two together. That's how I served as gunnery officer.

When we would have these gunnery exercises, of course, we observed each other in those days. And I wouldn't say a naval officer would cheat, but we sure took care of each other. Everybody got 90s; everybody did very well. It was a club. It made it difficult to award the E for excellence at the end of the year, because everybody cooperated. Cooperation, graduation.

My first experience as an observer was with Chas Sherwood as skipper. He was aboard, and now I was the gunnery officer. I had just made jaygee. And his next-door neighbor was a famous destroyerman named Art Damon.* Art Damon lives in Newport today.† Again, he's the type of fellow about whom you could write a book. Art is a very close friend of mine, stops through here to visit with me when he's on his way to Florida. Back then he commanded the Fechteler, which was a destroyer and much more sophisticated in gunnery than our DE. But I was to go out as the chief observer for Art Damon's gunnery. He was not in our squadron, he was not our competitor, so all's fair in love and war.

This assignment had happened on a weekend. I'd gone by with my date to the

---

* Commander Arthur H. Damon, Jr., USN, became commanding officer of the USS Fechteler (DD-870) in February 1955.
† Damon retired as a captain in 1964.

captain's house, and Art Damon was there. He met me, and I guess he liked me. He said to the skipper, "Hey, can Louis go out Monday for three days while we do our gunnery exercises for the quarter?"

"I think so. Are you free to go?"

"Oh, yes, sir." So I showed up Monday morning at 0600, and the ship was getting under way at 0800. When I got aboard, they gave me the captain's in-port cabin. I got juice and toast; I mean, they treated me as if I were the admiral coming on board. We arrived on the range that afternoon about 1600. They got me up on the bridge, where I was given the captain's chair. They handed me a scoreboard on a clipboard, stopwatch, and coffee, then asked, "What do you need now?"

The first run that was made was for the 5-inch/38s. They had what are called premature bursts. It wasn't the ship's fault; it was the ammunition's fault. So they weren't TTBs, target-triggered bursts. They were premature, just a couple of hundred yards; I knew that. The skipper came over, put his arm around me, and asked, "How do you like that? First run, and look at all those TTBs. I counted four. How many did you count?"

"Four, Captain." And that was the way you ran it. You were intimidated by the captain. You weren't about to tell him, 'Those weren't target-triggered bursts; those were preemies."

Paul Stillwell: Especially after the way they were treating you.

Captain Colbus: Today you wouldn't do that. You'd stand up and let him know you knew better. Of course, they wouldn't do that in first place. It was another situation. I don't know if it was all that bad.

Paul Stillwell: Well, it certainly doesn't give an accurate reflection of your ability in readiness.

Captain Colbus: Well, we did a lot more. When it was time to do the job, we did it. That was gamesmanship, not cheating.

Paul Stillwell: How was your own ship's gunnery?

Captain Colbus: We were like everybody else; we had our good days and bad days. Crews were changing. It was constant training, constant training.

Paul Stillwell: Would it be fair to say those ships were better in ASW than AAW?*

Captain Colbus: Oh, absolutely. These were World War II ships that were built to convoy, expected to make one crossing, and that was success. Here it was ten years after the war; the Navy was still using them and using them well. Those ships served us well.

Paul Stillwell: How reliable were they mechanically?

Captain Colbus: They were very reliable. I'm sure people today with the 1,200-pound plants—and I've gone through all that growth—would say, "Oh, you guys just got under way with chewing gum and baling wire."† It probably was true, but it wasn't a dangerous situation. You didn't have 1,200 pounds of steam; you had a simpler plant. It was a two-boiler ship with two screws. You'd get under way and fix things as you went. The generators had old gravity governors on them—two lead balls and a screw. Anytime the lights would flicker on the ship, you'd see three chiefs and two first class petty officers come running out of nowhere in their bare feet. They'd go below, take a screwdriver to it, make an adjustment, and that was it. You'd just go on about your business.

Of course, today, with automation, that's not the way it is. You need to be an electronics tech, you need to be a sophisticated engineer. That was the way we did it, and it was successful. We'd steam the ship. I know we did things that weren't good engineering practices, but at the same time it wasn't a sophisticated ship; it was simple. And these were all old-time experienced sailors. It would be similar to the difference between taking your automobile to a diagnostic machine and getting it tuned or taking it to a mechanic who puts a nickel on the fender and works a screwdriver so the nickel doesn't

---
* AAW—antiair warfare.
† In the early 1960s, the U.S. Navy began equipping combatant ships with propulsion plants that generated steam pressures of 1,200 pounds per square inch. The standard before that had been 600 PSI.

jiggle anymore. We were that nickel on the fender.

Paul Stillwell: How comfortable a ship was it in which to live and serve?

Captain Colbus: In reflection, I don't know how any of us really stayed around. First of all, let's get back to my friend Mr. Franklin, the exec. If he heard this, he'd probably smile, because he knows it's done in respect. He made us wear blues on the bridge. Now, we're talking about a ship with a very low silhouette, not a big ship. I'd say the bridge was 25 feet above the water. Today's bridges are probably 40 feet. There was an awning over the open bridge.

Paul Stillwell: And a windscreen in front.

Captain Colbus: And a windscreen in front, and that was it. We did not have an enclosed bridge. This ship in the North Atlantic would be pitching, taking green water. You'd be standing there in a set of blues with a bridge coat, no foul weather gear, which, in reflection, was above and beyond. That was not smart. And I guess, even to this day, I wonder why Chas didn't just rule on that one. But that's the way we lived. You'd stand up there for a four-hour watch, come off soaking wet, and go down into your stateroom, which, by the way, was not watertight. They had portholes. That porthole and the doors permitted an inch, inch and a half of water to be sloshing around on the deck. Your uniform wouldn't dry out, and you'd be getting up at 0600, putting on that uniform. It was really miserable, cold, and damp. That's all I remember, cold and damp.

Paul Stillwell: What were the operations in the North Atlantic?

Captain Colbus: We practiced ASW. We escorted ships. We practiced convoying in the North Atlantic. You'd see ships coming back covered with ice. We knew how to deal with that. We had deicers out on deck, so you'd see people out there plugging in the steam line, deicing the ship for stabilization.*

---

* A ship's stability, the capacity to come back upright from a roll, is adversely affected by topside weight.

Paul Stillwell: I would think you'd not have too much of a problem, because those were pretty low-slung ships anyway.

Captain Colbus: Yes, they were. And, as I say, we lived in that environment and were very good at it. We didn't know any better.

Paul Stillwell: That was probably a saving grace.

Captain Colbus: You were a naval officer, and you didn't complain. You stood one in three, and I thought that was the way it was supposed to be. It wasn't bad.

Paul Stillwell: But you weren't ever allowed to say, "Why?" to the XO.

Captain Colbus: Oh, no. Absolutely not.

Paul Stillwell: What about liberty in Newport? What do you recall about that?

Captain Colbus: That was a great town, because, again, we were well received, well accepted, and dated all over the town. Everybody went ashore, and they had a couple of girls' schools up there. And the other thing that was very popular was to go to Fall River, New Bedford, and Providence. We had that whole area of Rhode Island and the corner of Massachusetts. In the summertime we'd go up to the Cape.

As I said, all of us didn't have an automobile, but those that did would share. There would be four of us in a car to go to Boston on a weekend. Also, New York was popular. We'd drive down there once in a while. You had every third weekend to yourself, Friday till Monday. Then one weekend you had the duty Friday till Saturday, which gave you Saturday and Sunday off. Then, of course, you had a duty weekend, which was Saturday till Monday. You had the weekend duty and day's duty on Saturday, and the weekend off. So those weekends were hallowed. But it wasn't any great strain to stay on the ship, be relieved at 8:00 o'clock in the morning, stand inspection for two duty sections, and then declare liberty for the off-coming duty section. That was routine. We liked it. We couldn't financially afford much more time off.

Paul Stillwell: Did naval officers have a social status in that time?

Captain Colbus: I think so. Again, especially in Newport. I had lots of local friends up there. The churches and synagogues were very, very open to us, and it was usual to attend services on Sunday. I, myself, went to the Touro Synagogue and was well received. That, of course, was the epitome of going to temple or synagogue in my group, because the Touro Synagogue, of course, is a famous, well-known historical landmark.

Paul Stillwell: Sort of like Mecca in another religion.

Captain Colbus: You're right. I had a seat right there in the front row. They were very, very glad to see Navy people, and they were very, very open. As I said, you had a lot of local friends up there. We go back today and visit people whom I know; their children and grandchildren are still there. It was and is a good area.

Paul Stillwell: Did you have any involvement with any of the schools in Newport—OCS, the war college?[*]

Captain Colbus: No, not really. I knew a lot of the people who were at the war college. If you'd go to lunch once a week at the club, which we liked to do as a wardroom, you'd see the people coming off the hill for lunch.[†] And, of course, the captain would call his friends over, and you'd meet people. The one character up there that I did get to know when I was

---

[*] OCS—Officer Candidate School.
[†] In Newport the Naval War College is at the top of a hill, and the officers' club is at the bottom.

an ensign—and it carried on through till I was a lieutenant commander—was Commodore Bates.* Do you know Commodore Bates? Admiral Bates?

Paul Stillwell: I know of him. He did some great studies on the war.

Captain Colbus: That's the gent. He also commanded a cruiser during World War II.† He was a known lecturer and a known personage there at the war college. I got to know him at lunch. The story that I tell of him is that I saw this commodore, one-star, broad-stripe officer at lunch, where he had a parking place that was for "Commodore Bates." In the evening, somebody had to go out and take that sign down and put up "Rear Admiral Bates." On active duty, he ranked as a commodore; as a retired officer, he was a rear admiral.

Paul Stillwell: A tombstone rank.‡

Captain Colbus: Yes. He was a bachelor, and I used to see him at breakfast when I was at the war college. I can say that we became great friends. He also would sit in a men's club across the street from the Redwood Library. You asked if we were accepted. The men's club was what you would imagine a men's club to be: the leather chair, well worn, and Admiral Bates would sit there. That's where I learned about this rank inversion, because one night I walked in there as a guest. I said, "Good evening, Commodore Bates. How are you, sir?"

And that's when I got a, "Come here, son. I want to tell you something." That's

---

* Commodore Richard W. Bates, USN, directed a number of analytical studies of World War II combat actions while on the staff of the Naval War College in the late 1940s. When he retired in 1949, he received a tombstone promotion to rear admiral on the basis of his wartime service. He then continued his studies as an officer recalled to active duty following retirement. See the Naval Institute oral history of Vice Admiral David C. Richardson, USN (Ret.)

† As a captain, Bates had been commanding officer of the heavy cruiser Minneapolis (CA-36) from July 1943 to May 1944.

‡ In the years after World War II, officers who had received combat decorations received a one-grade honorary promotion widely referred to as a "tombstone promotion." Although the individual still received the retired pay of his actual rank, he was authorized to assume the title of the higher grade. The practice ended in 1959.

when I was told, "At night I'm a rear admiral. You may call me 'Commodore' during the day."

Paul Stillwell: Also during that tour you mentioned that you had spent time at the sonar school. Could you describe that, please?

Captain Colbus: It was a brand-new brick building in Key West. The old-timers still referred to it as the sound school, but it was really the sonar school. I'd say it was very, very prestigious for a surface officer to go there, because we didn't have schooling then. You went aboard ship right out of NROTC and Naval Academy or OCS. We didn't have the schools that we have now. You did six or eight months, and then if they were good to you, you'd get to go to a specialty school. Well, since we were in Key West during my first three months in the Navy, the ship left me there for this eight-week school. The instructors were just tremendous, and you walked away from there a qualified ASW officer. Today you couldn't do that, because the sonars are so much more complicated, and it's such a different world. That really was fine for that time, and I wouldn't even try to make a comparison today.

Paul Stillwell: Why did you get picked for that school, rather than some of your shipmates?

Captain Colbus: Because that was the natural progression. They needed a first lieutenant when I was there. Bruce Wittmer was about to get out of the Navy.[*] I relieved him as first lieutenant. Bruce moved up to ASW. Bruce was a two-year NROTC contract. Bruce is a stockbroker in New York today. He and I had a house in Newport one summer. You had a regular flow that you looked to, because they knew that I was going to be there three years. The fellow who came on two days after me was going to be there three years. But because I was there two days ahead of him, I would end up being the senior watch officer.

Paul Stillwell: So it wasn't necessarily a reflection on quality or lack of it?

---

[*] Lieutenant (junior grade) Bruce H. Wittmer, USNR.

Captain Colbus: Not, not at all. You got it. You filled a number.

Paul Stillwell: Were these instructors in the school people who had had World War II experience?

Captain Colbus: No. These were relatively young fellows, Korean experience perhaps. I remember one fellow who was a graduate of Suwanee. He took great pride in his teaching abilities and worked very closely with the class. No, these were mostly three- to four-year lieutenants who taught at sonar school. Of course, when you'd get into technical things, such as working the stacks, you'd get the chief sonarman.[*] But they weren't World War II officers. Those were relatively young fellows, because sonar wasn't that prevalent. They didn't have that many sonarmen, and they certainly weren't specialized.

Paul Stillwell: Did they have simulations in the school?

Captain Colbus: We had stacks, and we had mockups that reflected the ship, but that was just to get you warmed up until you could actually get in the ship. Going out in the ship was the only way to train. That's why our ship was there.

Paul Stillwell: Was there a ship attached to the school, or did you just go back to your own ship?

Captain Colbus: Your being in the sonar school had nothing to do with working on your own ship. Now, chance may have it that you were there as a student when your ship was the school ship. That didn't happen with me. Every day I rode a different ship during our two weeks' underway time.

That's another good point I might make. You got to know the differences among ships. By the time you were at school, you knew the good ships from poor ships. I could tell the shaky skippers from the good skippers, just from the way they acted on the bridge.

---

[*] The assembled components of sonar gear are referred to as the sonar stack.

As a sailor goes aboard a ship and spends X number of months and years in the ship, that's all he knows. But that changes when you are exposed to a different ship every day. By then you've had enough of your own ship to know what the routine is supposed to be, and so very quickly you are able to judge. You'd think how lucky you were to be in Albert T. Harris.

Paul Stillwell: Was there a good deal of formality in those wardrooms?

Captain Colbus: Yes, there was.

Paul Stillwell: Did you dress for dinner?

Captain Colbus: No, not the way you're thinking. We didn't have short-sleeve shirts. They didn't come in till about '60. We wore long-sleeve shirts, and some ships required a tie. In port we wore ties. You didn't walk the ship unless you were in uniform. Dungarees were unheard of on the beach. To answer your question, there was quite a bit of formality for those small destroyers. Until I got to be a senior officer, I never had been in a ship that didn't say grace before meals. I've never been in a ship where everybody didn't stand at the wardroom table waiting for the skipper, except breakfast.

Paul Stillwell: Was this a non-sectarian grace?

Captain Colbus: Whatever you wanted it to be.

Paul Stillwell: It rotated?

Captain Colbus: Sure. We still do that. Pass the buck. That buck would come to you; therefore, you'd be the first to be served. I never knew what the big deal about that was, because we didn't start the meal until everybody was served, but the man who had the buck had the privilege of saying grace.

Paul Stillwell: I served in a ship where the captain was always served first, and he started eating right away.

Captain Colbus: When was this, in the '60s?

Paul Stillwell: Yes.

Captain Colbus: And today we still have the difference. When I had my squadron with 18 ships, I got to see them all. But in answer to your question, it was quite formal, even though they were small ships. It was done, I think, very well. We were very proud.

Another thing is that you'd always be proud to bring your guests on board. You were encouraged to do that, be it family, people whom you met in homeport, or away from homeport. The other thing was that wives would always come to the ship on their husbands' duty days. We all lived in the ship. I'd say out of the 15-16 officers, probably ten of them were married and six of us were bachelors. And of those ten, one of the married officers would have the duty, which meant that almost every meal in port would have a wife and maybe a child on board. We liked this. It was nice. After the meal they'd stay and see a movie or play bridge.

Paul Stillwell: You talked about getting to know all the ships pretty well. How did the official competitive standings jibe with your own informal evaluations?

Captain Colbus: I say to this day it was partly political. It was usually the ship the commodore rode, because he knew that best. The fair-haired lad got the E.[*] The commodore, even to this day, had 25 points that he would award in a 100-point decision. Those 25 points were based on smartness, timeliness, all the things that are very subjective. And that's fine; that's fair.

Paul Stillwell: Have we covered everything on your list for this ship?

---

[*] An "E," for excellence, is generally awarded to a ship or component of a ship as a result of top performance in competition with other ships during a given time period.

Captain Colbus: One other thing I might say about in-port duty. I had the duty one night and was about to sit down to dinner. Of course, I hadn't gone to the club, and I was waiting for my shipmates to come back from the club. The messenger came running in to announce, "Mr. Colbus, Admiral So-and-so is on the quarterdeck to see you."

"Oh, my goodness." I jumped up and went out to greet this gentleman standing there; to me he was an old man, probably about 50 years old—briefcase, distinguished looking, and well dressed in civilian clothes.

"Hi, I'm Admiral So-and-so. I just stopped by and thought we could have a chat."

"Yes, sir. Won't you come in the wardroom?" He wanted to know about my insurance program. Well, I think I was unusual then, because I enjoyed those people, and I would invite them to dinner. Pretty soon, they'd start telling us how it was. And these were tombstone admirals, as you used the word. I cultivated a pretty good group of insurance agents in Newport who were tombstone admirals; I heard lots of World War II sea stories. They don't have that anymore.

Paul Stillwell: No, they don't.

Captain Colbus: You asked if I had covered everything. We had a smart sea detail, and our sea detail signature was a Scotsman in kilts for formal enterings and departures of port. Scotty Maroon would parade in kilts and a bagpipe. Some of us liked it, some of us hated it, but that was our signature. Everybody on the East Coast knew USS <u>Albert T. Harris</u> as the one with the bagpiper.

We went to Nassau one time, and as we came into harbor Scotty was up there piping away.* We moored on one side of a pier, with a merchantman moored on the other side of the pier. It turned out it was a ship with a Scottish crew, and they invited us over. We went over, and the drinking was just horrendous. It was to the point where it was embarrassing, one bottle after another of Scottish whiskey. And finally one of us said, "We've got to head back to the ship."

"Why?"

---

* Nassau is a port on the northeast coast of Providence Island in the Bahamas group in the West Indies.

"Well, really, we are taking advantage. We can't return this kind of hospitality. We don't want to drink so much of your whiskey."

And the answer was, "Hoot, man, it's the cargo." It was a whole shipload of whiskey. We spent the entire weekend just partying with these Scotsmen.

That's when we were doing some experimental work down in the Bahamas. We were mooring in Nassau quite a bit. We went in one weekend when Princess Margaret came to town.* She arrived in HMS Britannia, and we went over and did the proper thing.† That's another thing we used to do. We'd see ships, cruise ships, Britannia. For any ship that caught our eye, we'd get out our calling cards, put on our service dress whites or blues, walk over, and present ourselves. We would "make a call." There were lots of good times doing that.

When we went and presented ourselves to Britannia, we were invited aboard, then schooled on how to meet and talk to Princess Margaret. Princess Margaret appeared, the dancing started, and all those rules went by the wayside. I was particularly told, I remember, "Don't speak to the princess. The princess will speak to you." By 3:00 o'clock in the morning, with shoes off and collars open, we were having a ball in Britannia. My skipper sent me back with a message that we would not be getting under way at 0800; we'd get the ship under way that afternoon at 1600 and just make a better SOA.‡ We delayed sailing for that one.

Paul Stillwell: Did you get to dance with her?

Captain Colbus: Oh, yes! We became big buddies.

Another weekend that we went to Nassau was when I went ashore with Captain Hill, who said, "Come on, you can share a room with me at the Fort Montague." And I did. I went with the skipper over to Fort Montague, where they were making at movie called Flame of the Islands.§ The paramedic with this movie company was a retired Navy

---

* Princess Margaret is the younger sister of Great Britain's Queen Elizabeth II.
† HMS Britannia was the British royal yacht.
‡ SOA—speed of advance.
§ Republic Pictures released the color film in 1955. An Internet plot summary describes it as, "Story of a cafe singer and the men who fall in love with her."

chief hospitalman. He saw us in uniform as we checked in. Somebody came around to our room and said, "If you officers would walk into the dining room this afternoon, be part of the extras, we'll buy you dinner tonight and invite you to our staff party after the shooting." We, of course, complied.

By 10:00 o'clock that evening, Yvonne de Carlo was our big buddy. She was the star of the movie. I don't remember all the names, but my wife would, because I've pointed out these different people in movies as they've appeared over the years.* Our star of the evening was Yvonne de Carlo. She became our good friend

Paul Stillwell: Please tell me more about Princess Margaret, your good buddy.

Captain Colbus: Let's see. Well, she was my good buddy; she was everybody's good buddy. I don't think I was her favorite; she didn't have any. She was very gracious.

Paul Stillwell: This was about the time of her fling with Peter Townsend.[†]

Captain Colbus: Was it? Maybe that's why she was in Britannia touring the Bahamas. "Princess Margaret's coming to town" was the Calypso song. But outside of the fact that it was a wonderful evening and very, very—I don't want to use the word romantic—what should I say? Exciting. I told you I joined the Navy to do all these things. Here I was in the flagship of the Queen of England. It was pretty good for a boy from a small town. Formality went away, but it was still very dignified and one of the great times we had.

Paul Stillwell: Did you ever compare notes with Royal Navy officers on professional topics?

Captain Colbus: Absolutely. When I later had command of the ship McCloy, I sailed with

---

* Among the actors were James Arness, Howard Duff, and Zachary Scott. Arness later became well known for playing the lead in the long-running television drama "Gunsmoke."
† On 31 October 1955, following a great deal of publicity in the royal romance, Princess Margaret announced that she would not marry Group Captain Peter Townsend, a British air attaché in Brussels. The principal objection from the Anglican Church—and a major factor in her decision—was the fact that Townsend had previously been married and divorced.

a NATO squadron, which was just a relatively new concept.* This was in 1967. It's now called Standing Naval Force Atlantic. That was the last year they called it Matchmaker. We had six ships, and just as I talked about my first squadron being close, that's how close we were. We each had something to contribute. There were a British ship, Dutch ship, two U.S. ships, a German ship, and then a Norwegian ship when we sailed in Northern Europe. Throughout the fjords we did a lot of good, hard partying, which leads to professional discussions, and, of course, we were swapping ships. We called it cross-pollinating. They still use that term.

Paul Stillwell: After you went for three years in <u>Albert T. Harris</u>, you then moved to a staff. How did that assignment come about?

Captain Colbus: You really want to hear that? I'll tell you how that happened. I mentioned Commodore McDowell. He would come aboard the ship and liked, as I said, the noise of gunfire. Through our shipboard and shore contacts, he and I became good friends. We went ashore on occasion or two. We got along socially as well as professionally. I did attend to him when he came aboard.

Paul Stillwell: In what way?

Captain Colbus: When he was on the bridge, I would defer to him, even though the captain was there. He liked to be talked to. After I would brief my captain, I would look to the commodore on the port side of the bridge and explain to him what was going on. I would make sure that he was briefed before gunnery exercises. The others didn't do that, because the rest of the ship and the rest of the squadron were pretty aloof with the commodore. But I figured I'd keep peace in the family, and I just did that. It was not, I don't think, unusual, since his staff was on board. I knew his staff very well. He just looked to me for a lot of things.

When it was time for his ops officer, who was a lieutenant commander, to leave on another assignment, he knew I was about to leave <u>Albert T. Harris</u> after three years. He

---

* NATO—North Atlantic Treaty Organization.

went to the skipper, without my knowing it, and went to BuPers and said, "I want Colbus as my ops officer." Well, when I found out about it, I was flattered. I was going to relieve a lieutenant commander and be ops officer for an eight-ship squadron going to the Mediterranean. That's how I got the job. He requested me, I was flattered, and I got it. And looking back on it, it was one of the rougher tours I ever had.

Paul Stillwell: In what ways?

Captain Colbus: Well, Commodore McDowell was a very difficult man to get along with. The commodore would sit over in his chair. As his ops officer, I used the radio headset, and I maneuvered the squadron, which I loved to do. On one training exercise we had 16 destroyers around the cruiser Des Moines. Admiral Daspit was the task group commander, and Captain Marsh Dornin was skipper of Des Moines.[*] We were en route to Canada to do some great exercises there. And, of course, my boss was the screen commander. We had destroyers and destroyer escorts.

One Sunday we were conducting highline for the chaplain.[†] I had it all laid out, and everything was going fine. McDowell looked over at me and said, "Lou, has Silversides changed with Sunshine?"

"But, Commodore—"

"Louis, I'm telling you, I want Silversides changed with Sunshine."

"But, Commodore—"

Now he was getting red in the face, and he told me a third time, and I said, "But, Commodore—"

In front of everybody he slapped his knee with his hand—which was his favorite maneuver—and yelled, "G-D it, I'm the commodore. You do as I say."

By then I'd had it. I picked up the handset and put out the proper signal. Then we got a call back from Sunshine, "I'm not capable, because I'm alongside doing a transfer

---

[*] Rear Admiral Lawrence R. Daspit, USN, served as Commander Cruiser Division Six from August 1956 to September 1957. Captain Marshall E. Dornin, USN, commanded the USS Des Moines (CA-134) from 31 August 1956 to 23 August 1957.
[†] The chaplain was transferred from one ship to another by highline in order to provide divine services for ships that did not have chaplains as part of the crew.

with the cruiser."

He looked at me and said, "You're disloyal. You put out a wrong signal. You've embarrassed me in front of the entire fleet." He stormed off the bridge and yelled at me, "Keep me advised." He went down and sulked in his cabin for the rest of the day, and I had a grand time.

Paul Stillwell: You can't win in a situation like that.

Captain Colbus: No. You learned to live with it. That was good training. As I said, it built character. Another thing, too, was he'd make me do wrong things. I mean, make me do wrong things. Here's another one. We maneuvered through search turns. One day we were at 500 yards. You can't do a search turn at 500 yards because of the danger involved.

Paul Stillwell: Was this in column?

Captain Colbus: No, line abreast. And the proper thing would have been to extend the distance 500 yards and execute the search turn. That was no big deal. Well, he said, "I want to see that search turn now."

"But, Commodore—"

"Now!" Of course, this was after the other incident. He never learned.

Well, I was saying, "But—" I used to get him when he was pleasant, and I'd say, "Commodore, I'll tell you three times when I think you're wrong. After the third time, I'll do it your way, of course." I went through my three "buts" and sent the signal. One ship came up and said, "This is an unsafe maneuver. Recommend all stop." He went bananas, and then I took the heat from him.

Then, when we'd get to port, I'd take the heat from all my shipmates who had been in the squadron with me before I became the ops officer: "You dummy, you should know better." What was I going to do? So I took a lot of heat not only from my boss but from all my shipmates who said the job was too big for me and that I didn't know what I was doing. Of course, some of the flagship guys said, "Well, he really tried, but he wasn't successful. He's putting out bum signals." It builds character.

Paul Stillwell: I would think it would have been pretty crowded putting a staff on top of an 18-man wardroom.

Captain Colbus: Well, it was.

Paul Stillwell: How big was the staff?

Captain Colbus: Four of us—myself, a comm officer, material officer, and the commodore.

Paul Stillwell: Not even a chief staff officer?

Captain Colbus: They called me the chief staff officer.

Paul Stillwell: How much did you have in the way of admin work?

Captain Colbus: Oh, a good deal.

Commodore McDowell was relieved in the summer of '57, so I was with him only about three or four months. The new commodore was Emmett Peyton Bonner, who later became Admiral Bonner.[*] This man was a genius. This man was in the same mold as Chas Sherwood, with the patience of Job. He was a soft-spoken southern gentleman who had everything in his head. He never had to pick up a book for anything. Emmett Peyton Bonner was just everything that a human being ought to be. He walked on water. It was so pleasant being with him. He came aboard and spent a year with us, moved the squadron from Newport to Key West, and then the squadron was disbanded in '58.

Paul Stillwell: Were you present at the disbandment?

---

[*] Commander Emmett P. Bonner, USN, served as Commander Escort Squadron 12 from July 1957 to July 1958.

Captain Colbus: Yes.

Paul Stillwell: What happened? Did all the ships get decommissioned or what?

Captain Colbus: They went to the reserve fleet. All of the ships in Escort Squadron 12 became Naval Reserve training ships—Galveston, New Orleans, New York—you name it. In 1961 the Berlin call-up activated every one of them, put them back into Escort Squadron 12.[*] That made USS John R. Perry, the ship in which I was then exec, the flagship for these ships that I'd ridden my first three years in the Navy. And that's another story.

Paul Stillwell: We'll get to that.

Captain Colbus: Okay. I'll tell you about the skippers in the Berlin call-up.

Paul Stillwell: When you were operating with the fleet, you mentioned the Des Moines and destroyers. Did you have the speed for that kind of operation, or did they slow down to your speed?

Captain Colbus: Well, those ships would go 24 knots—not often, but there was enough speed there. We were really in training in those days. As a matter of fact, on the midshipman training cruise, it took us up to the Canadian waters for a summer. We had the speed. Ships did 22 knots, and that was about it. In answer to your question, they probably adjusted everything. I wasn't in on that end of it.

Now, once in a while ships would have speed runs, and a detachment would steam on ahead and act as target ships. If memory serves me right, the cruiser would take off and run at 30 knots to go on out ahead and have tracking drills, which were not uncommon. Throughout my career, you'd always pick out a ship to go off, then come in, and that would

---

[*] On 25 July 1961 President John F. Kennedy, in an address to the nation, announced "a call to arms" because of the crisis that had developed in Berlin, Germany, over the late spring and early summer. The beefing up of armed forces included an increase in personnel numbers for the Army; recall to active duty of reservists; retention of Air Force planes; and an increase in the Navy's active fleet by one attack carrier, one ASW carrier, 26 amphibious warfare ships, 41 destroyers and destroyer escorts, and five destroyer pickets.

give your combat team practice.

Paul Stillwell: When you were in the DEs, did you operate with carriers at all?

Captain Colbus: Yes, we operated with the CVSs, not with the CVAs.[*] The <u>Wasp</u>, for instance, operated out of Quonset.[†] They'd send us the aircraft. As a matter of fact, that was the time when we would find a submarine, get control of the airplane, and we would vector the plane to the sub. They were really an adjunct of us.

Paul Stillwell: Were you formed into hunter-killer groups then?

Captain Colbus: Yes.

Paul Stillwell: How effective were they, in your estimation?

Captain Colbus: Very effective, but they didn't really come into their own until the '60s. Then I was in a destroyer and steamed with them. It was a whole new world.

Our experiences in the DEs were with convoys. Convoys were slow, and these ships were made to convoy. Anytime we would get ten ships together, we were going to convex.[‡]

Paul Stillwell: The idea there is that the submarines are going to come to you; you don't have to find them.

Captain Colbus: That's right.

Paul Stillwell: Did you work with nuclear submarines at all?

Captain Colbus: No. We saw them, but we really didn't work with them, because this was

---
[*] CVSs were antisubmarine warfare carriers; CVAs were attack carriers.
[†] Quonset Point, Rhode Island, was the site of a naval air station until the mid-1970s.
[‡] In this case "convex" is short for convoy exercise.

a diesel era down in Key West. The diesels were available, and the nukes were, I guess, too busy and too sophisticated and off doing other things.

Paul Stillwell: And probably too few.

Captain Colbus: And too few. I would say that we probably served as target for nukes when we used to run the pro-sub exercises out of New London.

Paul Stillwell: You've painted a word picture of Commodore McDowell. How about Bonner? Please flesh him out.

Captain Colbus: Okay. Commander Emmett Peyton Bonner: soft-spoken Georgia gentleman, married to a dynamic New York lady named Elizabeth, who is up in Washington, D.C. She was what you'd expect a New Yorker to be: very sophisticated, very talkative, and very much in the limelight, a very social gal. She was very good to the young people, enjoyed having them in their home, just as the Sherwoods did.

By the way, I didn't mention that back in the Albert T. Harris days, if I had a date on a Friday evening, it would be unusual if I didn't stop by the captain's to introduce this girl to my skipper and his wife. Everybody did that; it was family.

But getting back to Emmett Peyton Bonner, we all went to Key West. He had four children. He rented this big home in downtown Key West, and I had the cottage that was on the grounds but detached from the home. We were very, very close in that way.

In those days it was popular and very, very nice to go on what was called Exercise Springboard. We'd all go over to the Caribbean about February or March. The one time I went with Commodore Bonner, his wife went along and followed the ship from port to port, which made it very nice. All I can say about that man was that he was knowledgeable, soft-spoken, and very effective. He is one of my great heroes. In fact, I quote him all the time. His favorite expression was, "Louis, does it matter, and who cares?" And that is just so neat. People get so excited and lathered up over sometimes nothing. If his boss cared, he cared. If it mattered, it mattered to him. But he'd be sitting in his cabin on the ship and, looking around, would say, "What's doing?"

'Nothing. Everything under control, Commodore."

He always had a blunderbuss pistol. He'd sit there and cock that pistol and look through and pretend he was shooting. His concentration was on that pistol, and he'd say, "Well, let's go fishing." It would be 1000 in the morning, and we'd get a fishing boat, and away we'd go. He did no clock-watching.

I guess to best illustrate is to tell of our yeoman first class, who was to go on leave with his wife and two children in their Nash car. He came to me about 1000 one day when everything was quiet. Leave started at 1600. That wouldn't count as a day of leave, but that's when your leave started. As I said, this was 1000 when the yeoman came to me and said, "Is everything done? I'd like to start now."

"What?"

He said, "On leave." (Now, remember, I'm bringing with me the training of Isaac Nelson Franklin, who always asked, "Why?") He said, "I'd like to leave now.'

I said, "But your leave doesn't start till 1600."

He said, "Well, I have nothing to do, and I'd just as soon get started now and drive on up the Keys, and that will give me a leg up."

My training told me that if you wanted your leave to start at 1000, you should have put in for 1000 and be charged for it. So I said, "No." I told him all the reasons why he was not going to start leave. "Besides, what if you start on leave now and, God forbid, you have an accident up in the Keys. You're not on authorized leave, yet you're traveling, and it's my tail." I just told him all these things.

The commodore called me in. He shut the door and said, "I want to talk to you." He said, "Really, does it matter? Who cares?"

I said, "What if he has an accident?"

He said, "It would be the least of our worries if the guy's lying in a ditch somewhere dead with his wife and two kids. We're not going to worry about a couple of hours. If you can nicely get around it, I'd appreciate it if you'd let him go now, because he'll just sit there and stew till 1600."

Paul Stillwell: How did the commodore find out about this?

Captain Colbus: He heard it. I was sitting right outside his door.

I said, "Yes, sir. If that's the policy, I'd be glad to follow that." That's the kind of gent he was. Didn't embarrass me, gave me the way out, and I went out.

Paul Stillwell: He assumed the responsibility.

Captain Colbus: Yes. In effect, he said, "That's my problem. I'm the commodore. I'm in command here if there's any problem." That's one story.

Another story relates to our crossing to the Mediterranean with the commodore. Movement reports were very, very sacrosanct, as they still are. Well, I put out the movement reports, which were confidential. Of course, we didn't have on-line crypto in those days.* You went into the radio shack and typed everything up on this complicated machine. I'd sent out the movement reports, and everything was going fine. Well, a sailor in an engineering space of one ship was burned very severely by hot coffee. The entire squadron diverted, dropped the ship with the injured man off at the Azores, then turned and went back on track. I put out a movement report to advise about this diversion in accordance with page umpty-ump, paragraph so-and-so of ATP 16-1, and went to bed.† That morning about 0300 I was awakened and told, "Your movement report didn't fly."

"Oh, my goodness. What's the matter?"

"Well, you have a gig here that says you didn't do it right."

"Oh, oh, oh," and I felt nervous and upset because I let the commodore down.

Paul Stillwell: Who woke you up to tell you this?

Captain Colbus: One of the radiomen. We sat down in my stateroom to find my error. When you divert, you've got to do it. Somebody referred to paragraph umpty-ump, which says they need a message 24 hours in advance. I don't know how to do 24 hours in

---

* On-line crypto, which was introduced to the fleet in the 1960s, meant a message could be typed in plain language into a teletype at one end, went through the radio waves in garbled form, and was automatically decrypted onto a teletype at the receiving end. Previously, all encryption had to be done manually before transmission.
† ATP—Allied Tactical Publication.

advance when you have to divert. I worked up a very complicated message explaining all of this and said, "Well, let's go wake up the commodore." Remember, I still had the Commodore McDowell mentality: "You don't make mistakes, we're going to look bad, you'll make me look dumb." So I went in and woke up the commodore, who got up calmly.

"Commodore," I said, "I'm in the doghouse. I made a mistake, so the movement report center in San Juan tells me, but I can't figure it out, and I want to explain it to you. I hope that you see it my way. I don't want to get into a contest, but I'll explain it in this message."

He said, "What time is it?"

I said, "Four-twenty."

He said, "Where did it come from?"

I said, "The movement report center in San Juan."

He said, "Why don't we talk about it after breakfast?"

I said, "But they told me I made the wrong movement report. It's a slap on the hand."

He said, "Why don't we just talk about it in the morning when we're fresh after breakfast?"

I went back, and I wasn't comfortable. That morning after breakfast we sat around his desk, and I showed it to him. He said, "Oh, you're absolutely right. Tell you what, let's not even answer it."

I said, "Not answer it?"

He said, "Do they know where we are now?"

"Oh, yes, sir. That was just to correct that which I had done."

He said, "Does it matter, and who cares?"

I said, "Do you care?"

He said, "No, and I don't think it matters." And that was the end of that.

When we were coming back from this great cruise, we ended up in San Juan. This was months later. He said to me, "Hey, Louis, get the car. Let's go over to the movement report center. I'll show you something."

We went to the movement report center. We were getting the Cook's tour from a lieutenant commander communicator. There was a signalman first class present. The commodore said to this signalman, "Now, what would happen if I'd make a mistake in a movement report?"

"Oh, we would correct it?"

"Who would correct it?"

"Well, it depends on who's on watch."

He said, "Have you ever corrected a movement report?"

"Oh, yes, sir, I do it all the time."

"Who releases those messages?"

"I do."

"Very interesting. Just wondered." We got outside, and he said, "See? Some first class petty officer putting me on report. He can't harm me. Does it matter? Who cares?" I don't say he was flippant about it, and he certainly didn't look down his nose. He just had everything in perspective. I've never met anybody like that. Don't watch the clock, don't worry about that fellow running off the road, don't sweat the unnecessary.

Paul Stillwell: How was he in a tactical situation?

Captain Colbus: Oh, a genius, absolute genius. He did it all in his head. I won't say he had memorized the book, but he just knew everything that there was to know. He was also a weapons expert. He went on to do great things with BuWeps.[*] He also commanded the Seventh Fleet flagship, Oklahoma City.[†] He is famous for that. He took Oklahoma City up the Saigon River, spun her around, and never asked for a tug or a pilot. He was an expert ship handler, along with everything else. He was one of those people who was a genius, but not smug about it, certainly not casual about it. He just did his job.

Paul Stillwell: Projected an air of confidence, I take it.

Captain Colbus: Confidence but not cockiness, yes, that's exactly it. You now know

---

[*] From 1961 to 1963, as a captain, Bonner served as the Ship Launched Weapon Systems Officer in the Bureau of Naval Weapons.
[†] Captain Bonner was commanding officer of the guided missile cruiser Oklahoma City (CLG-5) in 1963-64.

Emmett Peyton Bonner.

Paul Stillwell: I take it he also would not make the kind of mistakes that McDowell made in issuing an order that couldn't be carried out.

Captain Colbus: No, no.

Paul Stillwell: What do you recall about the Med deployment during that tour of duty?

Captain Colbus: Yes, that was when we had the Lebanese crisis.[*] We got involved in that. My dad died, and the commodore again showed his true colors. He insisted I go home, even though we were very involved. Captain Bonner tried his utmost to get me ashore when I found out my father had died. He was most understanding and sympathetic. He couldn't do enough for me.

I just told him, "I've got a brother at home, and I've got aunts and uncles. I'm sure things will be as good as possible." He went out of his way to get me ashore, sent messages on ahead to make sure I was received in Athens and not just thrown in a pile. He made sure that I got back to the ship and just looked after me as a good leader would do. It wasn't just because it was I; he'd do that for anybody. But he didn't do it because he thought he should do it, and he didn't do it for anybody to know about it; he just did it. Very thoughtful.

During the Med cruise, the commodore introduced me to his classmate and roommate at the Naval Academy, Ned Beach, who commanded an oiler.[†] We were screening the oiler coming out of the Med when one of the ships in the screen, forward of the oiler, had a man overboard. Of course, all the proper signals went up, and Emmett and

---

[*] On 15 July 1958, at the request of Lebanese President Camille Chamoun, U.S. amphibious forces landed at Beirut to support Chamoun's government, which was threatened by both civil war and the prospect of foreign invasion. Two of the Sixth Fleet's three battalion landing teams went ashore within 24 hours. For details see Robert McClintock, "The American Landing in Lebanon," U.S. Naval Institute Proceedings, October 1962, pages 64-79.

[†] Captain Edward Latimer "Ned" Beach, USN, Naval Academy class of 1939, was commanding officer of the fleet oiler Salamonie (AO-26) from March 1957 to January 1958. He is well known as an author, having written a number of books, most notably the submarine novel Run Silent, Run Deep. For a profile of Beach, see Naval History, Summer 1988, pages 62-64.

I were on the bridge. Within minutes, the oiler's captain, Ned Beach, said, "I'm maneuvering to pick up the man." He took that big oiler, just moved everything the way he had to, and picked the man up out of the water. Normally, it's the destroyer picking up the man overboard from the oiler. Just being around and meeting Captain Beach and hearing these two gents, Ned Beach and Emmett Bonner, discussing things was a great experience.

Paul Stillwell: What are your impressions of Beach?

Captain Colbus: I've seen him since. I saw him at one of the Bonner marriages two years ago. Another genius out of that group, a man who whom you'd look up. Of course, I'd read so much about him. Rickover talks quite a bit about Captain Beach.[*] He is just another fine old-school gentleman.

Paul Stillwell: What was the squadron's participation in the Lebanon situation?

Captain Colbus: We conducted patrols off the coast. I remember it as a show of force. As I said, that's about the time I went home because of my father's death and came back within ten days. We were there, and it delayed our Sixth Fleet schedule.

Paul Stillwell: What do you recall about liberty during that period?

Captain Colbus: Well, there was one story about going ashore in Italy. This was before my dad died. We all went ashore in Naples as a closely knit squadron with this great man, Emmett Bonner, in command. On this occasion we had five of the seven skippers, myself, a few of the ops officers, and an exec or two. We mustered at the Grotto Romano, a nightclub situated on the side of the mountain overlooking Naples Harbor.

During the evening, at about 11:00 o'clock, Lucky Luciano, the owner and former U.S. gangster, appeared as the master of ceremonies. He approached the microphone, took

---

[*] Admiral Hyman G. Rickover, USN (Ret.), was considered the father of the nuclear Navy. He ran the Navy's nuclear-power program for many years. Rickover died in 1986, two years after this interview.

the spotlight, and was making a presentation in Italian. We all commented that it was time for the floorshow. Lucky then translated into English, saying, "It gives me great pleasure to introduce a man who's brought great pleasure to the world. It gives me pleasure to introduce Yul Brynner."[*] All of a sudden, the spotlight fell on me. I, of course, am as bald as Yul Brynner and did resemble him. I stood up, took some bows, sat down, and shrugged my shoulders. Everybody laughed. Well, it started—free champagne, free drinks, autographs!

About that time, a distinguished-looking gentleman came over and introduced himself as a United States general. He put his arm around me and said, "This young lady who is with me this evening is French. She met you five years ago in Paris and just wants to renew the acquaintance."

She started in French, and I interrupted her as best I could by saying, in my high school French, "Enchantee, permittez-moi presenter . . ." At that time, Tom Walsh stood up; he had just completed a tour as assistant naval attaché in France, was now the skipper of USS Tweedy (DE-522).[†] Tom took over, did all the niceties, and got me off the hook. I couldn't speak French well enough to converse with this young lady. The general and I became great friends. We were arm in arm, drinking too much, and having a grand time.

Somebody in the party asked, "What is he doing? Who is this guy pretending he's a general?"

I said, "Well, I'm pretending I'm Yul Brynner. Who am I to criticize? If it makes him happy, let's relax and enjoy the evening."

About 3:00 o'clock we broke up, and that was the end of that—so I thought. The next day the commodore had to attend a briefing of Operation Deepwater in the flagship Pocono; I properly saw him off at the quarterdeck. He got in his 26-foot motor whaleboat, and away he went. About 2:00 o'clock he came back with, "Ding-ding, ding-ding, CortRon 12 arriving." He came aboard and said, "I've got to talk to you." We went up to his cabin. He said, "Remember that general?"

"Yes, sir."

---

[*] Yul Brynner was a popular American movie actor of the period. His trademark was a completely bald head.
[†] Lieutenant Commander Thomas W. Walsh, USN.

"Well, he really was a general."* By the way, I had introduced the commodore as Dr. Bonner, because, as I said, he was a very professional-looking man, elegant, and with well-groomed hands. He looked like a surgeon.

While at this senior briefing of all the commodores in the Mediterranean in 1957, and all during lunch, this general kept looking across the table and said, "Commodore Bonner, don't I know you from somewhere?" Then, almost into dessert, the general shouted, "Hey, you're not Commodore Bonner. You're Dr. Bonner." And, oh, boy, I guess even my good friend Emmett had some quivers and felt guilty. The commodore just said, "The general wants to see you." I really knew my naval career was over.

I went over to see the general. I arrived at USS Pocono and was escorted in to see the general. He was seated at a great desk with flags on either side. I was scared and overwhelmed. He warmly shook my hand and said that my performance was the best act he'd ever seen. He admired my ability to carry off a great coup. All his party thought that I was really Yul Brynner. He stated that any time I wanted to join his service, the Marine Corps, I was welcome to do so, and he would be my sponsor. Is that the way I told it to you before the tape started?

Paul Stillwell: Well, there was more to it than that. Please go on.

Captain Colbus: When I was in BuPers in 1964 as a newlywed, I was walking down the passageway between BuPers and the Marine Corps headquarters one day, and I passed my general friend from the night at Grotto Romano. We both did a double take. "Yes, Yul. What are you doing in town?" I told him I was stationed in BuPers. "What are you doing in town?" I told him I was now married. "How about being my guest this Friday at the Marine Corps Eighth and I ceremony?"†

"Yes, sir, with pleasure!" He and I renewed our old friendship. We had a gala night at the Marine Corps retreat ceremony, and my new bride was impressed with my influential friends.

---

* The individual was Brigadier General Ralph K. Rottet, USMC, who served as Commanding General, Fourth Provisional Marine Air-Ground Task Force in the latter part of 1957.
† The Marine Corps barracks in Washington, D.C., is at the corner of Eighth and I streets, not far from the Washington Navy Yard. It is frequently the site of ceremonial presentations.

Then in 1965 I showed up in Norfolk, operating out of Newport in my ship, USS <u>Basilone</u>, as executive officer. We went as a wardroom to the officers' club one evening. A beautiful lady was coming out of the club as we were going in on a Saturday evening. I stopped her and asked if she would join our group to make a visiting ship's wardroom gathering a little more fun and festive on a Saturday night. She said she'd just stopped to get some cigarettes, but, yes, she'd join us, and she did. By 8:00 o'clock she called some of her girlfriends, who joined us. It turned into a great wardroom party. At evening's end, I said to Frank Bang, who was a young, good-looking, personable ensign on the ship, "Frank, why don't you invite these ladies to brunch tomorrow morning in the ship? Captain Stokes, is that all right?"

"Oh, yes, that's fine."

"Captain, may we borrow your car?"

"Sure."

"Frank, would you please collect these ladies in the morning?"

"Yes, XO, that'd be fine."

I said, "Now, ladies, where do you live so that we can call for you in the morning?"

Our original lady, who was the organizer and the hostess, said, "Oh, I'm right down the street here." She gave me the address.

"This is Admiral's Row. Dillingham, is it?"

"Yes."

"I don't recognize your name."

"Oh," she said, "that's my married name. I am now divorced. I kept my married name, because I have a three-year-old. I live at General Rottet's quarters. He's my father."[*]

I looked at Frank and said, "I'll call for the young lady. You don't have to." I thought it would be a fun thing. I would show up Sunday morning about 10:00 o'clock to get this young lady and surprise her father, my Naples general. Unfortunately, her dad had left for Washington that morning, so I missed seeing him. I just told her, "When your dad comes back, tell him Yul Brynner was here." And that's the end of the story.

---

[*] Rottet served from 1963 to 1966 as Deputy Commander, Fleet Marine Force Atlantic.

Paul Stillwell: You were talking earlier about having the Naval Academy graduates look down on the NROTC officers. Did you look down on the OCS officers?

Captain Colbus: No, I didn't. I was so glad to be there. Of course, OCS officers didn't go on cruises, so I didn't know OCS officers as midshipmen.

Aboard Albert T. Harris we had Lieutenant (j.g.) Bob Kurmin, OCS, and Lieutenant (j.g.) Jack Varney, OCS.[*] Jack Varney was my first department head and an absolute genius, a wonderful guy and fun loving. He was my gunnery officer. Jack moved over to ops officer, and then Tom Smithberger became the gunnery officer.[†] I was tutored and led and monitored by OCS jaygees on my first ship, so I didn't know there was a difference. They were fine officers.

Paul Stillwell: What was the general mix in, say, destroyer escorts in those years?

Captain Colbus: I don't remember that we had one Naval Academy graduate—not a one. The captain of Albert T. Harris was a World War II officer, as was the exec.

Paul Stillwell: When you were serving in one ship, you had a chance to observe how the commodore awarded the E on favoritism. How did it look when you were on the staff?

Captain Colbus: Pretty much the same. You've got to remember that I was a squadron commander 22 years later, so it's what you get to know and witness firsthand.

Paul Stillwell: How was the flagship chosen?

Captain Colbus: Well, I'd say it was a combination. The flagship of our squadron at the time was USS Tabberer (DE-418). Tabberer had had some modifications. There was a clip shack where 40-millimeter ammunition had been stowed at the very forward part of the superstructure. This ammunition space was rehabbed and made into the unit

---

[*] Lieutenant (junior grade) Robert R. Kurmin, USNR; Lieutenant (junior grade) Jack E. Varney, USNR.
[†] Lieutenant (junior grade) Thomas J. Smithberger, USN.

commander's stateroom, which was right next to the skipper's. There were two portholes and a couple of fans to keep things cool, and that was about it. Of course, they did the same thing years later in my ship, the 931 class.[*] Three-inch guns came off, and an ammunition ready service room up forward was converted into the unit commander's stateroom.

The captain in the DEs did not have a sea cabin; his in-port cabin and sea cabin were one and the same. When the commodore came aboard our ship, it was just for a daily ride. The skipper shared his cabin with the commodore and stayed on the bridge.

Paul Stillwell: The Tabberer had a built-in advantage.

Captain Colbus: Yes, sir. However, Albert T. Harris won the E in 1957, which was a surprise to the flagship.

Paul Stillwell: What can you say about the quality of the enlisted men in that era?

Captain Colbus: They were a hungry group. They were not the sailors I heard of from the old chiefs who saw boys joining in the '30s during the Depression.[†] However, my shipmates were a hungry group of hard-working men who were not very demanding, delighted to be at sea, stood one-in-three watches and were devoted to the ship. Many of them were uneducated. GED tests were extremely popular.[‡] I remember being the education officer, and it was not unusual to have to teach someone to read and write.

I had one Albert T. Harris shipmate whom I remember well: Teddy Schafer. He couldn't read, couldn't write, thought it was great to get a meal on a tin plate. The kid was really raised in the hills of West Virginia on, I guess, staples and had no clothes. He came into the Navy for a better life and was just delighted.

---

[*] This refers to Colbus's command of the destroyer Jonas Ingram, a member of the Forrest Sherman (DD-931) class.
[†] Following the crash of the New York Stock Exchange in late October 1929, the United States was plunged into the Great Depression, from which it did not recover until the nation geared up for World War II at the beginning of the 1940s. The Depression was marked by high unemployment and many business failures. Because jobs were scarce, the Navy could be quite selective and pick high-quality personnel to enlist.
[‡] The GED (general equivalency diploma) tests were a means of providing certification of high school-level education for those who had dropped out of school prior to graduation.

Gentleman Jim Sweet was a seaman on my ship; he was married and had three children. His family would sit on the pier and wait till liberty started so they could come on board and go onto the mess decks for the evening meal. They were delighted to be there, and we were, of course, delighted to have them. This shipmate couldn't make rate as a boatswain's mate. We finally transferred him to the gunnery division, and within a couple of months he was tuned up enough that he took the exam and became a petty officer third class. He'd been in the Navy 12 years! The fact that he was now a petty officer with prestige and an increase in pay provided a whole new life-style for that fellow.

You asked what type of people we had. Occasionally we'd get the wise guy. I don't say they were all sweethearts, but it was a work-hard, play-hard group. Today they would probably take my commission away for not being more keen to what they call alcoholism today. I had a chief quartermaster later on, in Basilone—when I was old enough to know better. He was the best quartermaster in the Navy, taught me everything I knew about navigation, as far as the practicality of it, and made me a hero as navigator. About once a quarter he'd come up to me, as the XO and navigator, and state, "Need about three days."

"Okay, Sam, I won't see you for three days," was my reply. He'd just go off to some hotel somewhere and get drunk for three days. Then he'd straighten out, come back to the ship, and be good for another two or three months. That was considered colorful; he was a good sailor, because he didn't do it on company time, didn't get in any trouble, was not a source of embarrassment, and kept at that distance.

Paul Stillwell: How did these men get by when they couldn't read or write? What about taking tests when they enlisted?

Captain Colbus: Some of these lads didn't take tests. I'd have to guess they met the quota for the recruiter. These lads just showed up. I don't know how they got in, but they did, and they ended up in the ship. And there was a place for these men! They really filled a need that we both had, and we were delighted to have them, because they were good sailors. They were never going to be career men, and they were never going to be master chiefs, but we took them aboard. This was home to them, and they became almost mascots of the ship. Maybe that was wrong to treat them that way. I'm not criticizing it; I'm just telling you how it was since you asked.

I've got to tell you about one sailor, though. He was a 17-year-old kid who came into the Navy. I was the first lieutenant in Albert T. Harris. It was 1956 when it all came to a head in the shipyard in Brooklyn.* The subject sailor was a Jewish boy from Bangor, Maine, and he looked to be about 13 or 14. I don't think he shaved; he was just a sweet-looking little kid. He came on board, had a tremendous education, based on all the schools he had attended, and turned out to be the biggest gangster in the ship. He ended up knifing one of our shipmates. He was just incorrigible, but he had this innocent face, and when you'd quiz him, the answer was, "Nuh-huh. I don't know." It was always as if it didn't happen: "I didn't do that. I bet you're wrong."

He was a real problem to the ship, to the point that even then we discussed getting him out of our Navy. He was incorrigible and untrainable. It turned out that he came from a very fine and influential family. One day while I was in the ship, we were going to process all this to let him go. I got a call from his aunt; she was in New York and wanted to come talk to me about her nephew, our problem child.

"Yes, I'd be glad to talk. Could you come to the ship?" She could come that afternoon, in the hot summer, in the Brooklyn shipyard. You just don't know how it is in Brooklyn in a ship that isn't air-conditioned. Her limousine drove up, the chauffeur opened the door, and up the brow came the aunt. Her plea was supported by written statements from all the schools he'd been to, that this was his last chance, and that if we couldn't do something for her nephew, whom the schools hadn't been able to do anything with, there was no other place to turn. She said, "Please keep him. Don't send him home."

So that will show you the mixture of different people we had. We had Teddy Schafer from the hills of West Virginia; he worked out just fine. And here was the Maine mate with the best prep schools in New England, a well-to-do family, and he couldn't hack it.

We had college graduates who were in the Navy at that time, because you could then enlist for two years. We had kiddie cruises which would meet your military obligation. A kiddie cruise meant that if you signed up before your 18th birthday, you

---

* This was the New York Naval Shipyard, which was later decommissioned in the 1960s.

were released from active duty just before your 21st birthday. We had the good ones, we had a few bad ones, educated ones, a couple of college graduates—it was a good mixture. We didn't have the technical people that the Navy has today. We didn't have that technical a ship. The fire controlman would learn on board. We had a Mark 1 Able computer that you wound up like a clock, and it clicked off range and bearing after you put in the variables.

Paul Stillwell: What happened to the incorrigible kid after his aunt showed up?

Captain Colbus: Oh, we finally discharged him and sent him home, and I'm sorry to say that we didn't have any more contact with him. He was a ship's character. That's another thing; ships did have characters. They were all known, just as in the family you have a cousin who's different. We had those boys in the ship.

Paul Stillwell: These mascot types that you talked about, did they just stick completely to manual labor as far as jobs?

Captain Colbus: As a rule, yes. The exception would be some fellow who would step out. All of a sudden, you'd be very proud of your leadership, because you'd turned a character into a 4.0 sailor. Of course, that's true even today. Point to someone who started out poorly and ends up extremely well, and you're proud of it. He's proud, you're proud, and everybody prospers. Everybody wants you to do well. It's good for us morally, professionally, and personally.

Paul Stillwell: By and large, were these sailors unmarried?

Captain Colbus: Yes. It was very unusual to have a young fellow married. And everybody lived in the ship.

Paul Stillwell: Officers and enlisted.

Captain Colbus: Unless you were married, you lived in the ship. As I said, one summer for about three weeks we rented a place in Newport, and that was so luxurious you couldn't believe it.

Paul Stillwell: Any more on the squadron staff tour?

Captain Colbus: On the squadron staff tour I was coming back from having been home after my dad died. I was sent to Naples, where I just missed the ship. I had a message at the receiving station from the commodore: "If you're looking for us, in three days we'll be in Palma." I got a plane ride to Palma, where I had never been before. I found myself up in the main square. Palma, of course, has always been very glamorous; today it would be called the jet set. Then it was just called posh.

I went into Tony's Bar, where I was sitting at 4:00 o'clock in the afternoon, knowing the ship would be in the next day. I had checked into the Europa Hotel. I was just sitting there in uniform, minding my own business. A very nice-looking lady was sitting in there also. She was older than I; if I was 25, she was 35. She was very nice and asked me about the ship. I told her, "It won't be in until tomorrow." Blah, blah, blah. We had a drink. All nice.

Paul Stillwell: Innocent.

Captain Colbus: Innocent. She said, "Would you care to come up to my villa?"

"Sure."

We went out. She had an electric car. I'll never forget it. We got in this car and went up to this gorgeous villa overlooking the entire bay. I knew I was in tall cotton. Her name was Pat, and she was an American. We talked. Some of her neighbors and friends came over. We had drinks. Who walked into the room? Errol Flynn![*] I knew who it was. I tried to be suave about it. It turned out that this was his wife. She had just befriended a sailor. So Errol Flynn heard that my dad had died and that I was waiting for the ship. He

---

[*] Flynn was a leading American movie actor in the 1940s, somewhat in decline by the late 1950s. He was known for his handsome profile and swashbuckling roles.

came over, shook my hand, and talked a while. He was living at the base of the mountain in his yacht, the Black Pearl. I thought that was glamorous.

The next day, my shipmates came off the ship as the ships arrived. I reported to the commodore, who asked, "How did everything go, Louis?"

"Fine. Everything's fine. Mother's fine, thank you." He knew my mother. We got to talking, and I said, "Now, to get into the lighter things, let's go up to Tony's Bar. I found a friend." That evening the entire squadron ended up at Pat's villa. Errol Flynn didn't show up that evening. My mates were a little disappointed in me. They thought that it was just a story. That was the squadron. That was our Med cruise. When we came back, as I said, the squadron was decommissioned, and the ships were dispersed.

Paul Stillwell: So you had to find a new place to serve. Your organization had gone up in smoke. How did you get to ComSoLant?[*]

Captain Colbus: Believe it or not, Nelson Franklin, my XO from Albert T. Harris, called me. He was the destroyer detailer in BuPers. And if I've said anything about him that was other than loving, kind, and admiring, I didn't mean it, because he and I are still big buddies. We were big buddies then. He called me and said, "I've got a real good job, and I think you'd fit the bill. How would you like to be aide to Jimmy Thach?"[†] Admiral Thach was then the commander of Task Group Alfa.[‡]

I said, "Oh, I'd like that very much." It turned out that that didn't come to fruition. I didn't even get interviewed. But about three weeks later he called me in Key West to say, "How about being aide to Admiral Ed Stephan, ComSoLant, as well as his communicator?"[§]

"Well, I'm not a communicator, but why not? Love to. I'm delighted." That's how that came about.

---

[*] ComSoLant—Commander South Atlantic Force.
[†] Rear Admiral John S. Thach, USN, was a noted naval aviation tactician of World War II. The oral history of Thach, who retired as a four-star admiral, is in the Naval Institute collection.
[‡] Task Group Alfa, which operated in the Atlantic, was a hunter-killer group for antisubmarine warfare.
[§] Rear Admiral Edward C. Stephan, USN, served as Commander U.S. South Atlantic Force from September 1958 to June 1960.

Paul Stillwell: Please tell me something about Stephan.

Captain Colbus: Another quality gentleman. He was the son of a Washington lawyer, therefore raised in the Washington environment. When I met him, he was chief of legislative liaison. I went to Washington, met Admiral Stephan, and he took me home, as well as under his wing. From that day until today, it's Luigi this, Luigi that.* He treated me as if I were his son. He's a great man, a submariner who had children my age.

This was June 1958, and the ComSoLant job was not available until December 1958. I had been detached from the squadron and was in Washington. Meanwhile, I was sent to Task Force 88, right there in Washington, to be the flag lieutenant to CTF 88, a brand-new rear admiral named Lloyd Montague Mustin, who is the father of our current-day Vice Admiral Hank Mustin.†

Paul Stillwell: What was the mission of Task Force 88?

Captain Colbus: Project Argus, which wasn't really revealed until years later. Project Argus involved a task group made up of USS Norton Sound; USS Tarawa, the old CVS; Warrington, a destroyer; the ship Chas Sherwood commanded years later, Bearss; and two DEs of the 1006 class.‡ I can't think of their names right offhand. We took that task force down to the Antarctic and tested the theory that when you popped these small—and I mean small—nuclear detonations at about 10,000 feet, which is, as I remember, the ionosphere, you would disrupt the magnetic forces. And it's true.

I wasn't technically inclined, but I was the flag sec who put out the op order and did all the things the flag sec and watch officer was required to do. That lasted about three months. We went from Washington to board the ship, which was moored in Quonset. We got under way in Tarawa on what everybody thought was a routine trip. Norton Sound

---

* Rear Admiral Stephan died in 1990, a few years after this interview.
† Vice Admiral Henry C. Mustin, USN, commanded the Second Fleet from September 1984 to September 1986.
‡ USS Dealey (DE-1006) was the lead ship of the first class of post-World War II destroyer escorts built by the U.S. Navy. She was commissioned 3 June 1954. She had a standard displacement of 1,280 tons, was 314 feet long, and 37 feet in the beam. Her design speed was 25 knots. She was armed with four 3-inch guns and Weapon A.

sailed out of Philadelphia; the skipper was Captain Arthur Gralla, who became a three-star admiral.*

Anyway, we all got under way and ended up in the South Atlantic, performing these tests. S2Fs flew off Tarawa to observe the phenomena, and I remember it was Norton Sound that did the actual firings of these missiles.† I have all the articles at home, because two years later it was all in Life magazine. I'd have to refresh my memory as to all the details, whether it was 10,000 feet or the ionosphere. We went down there and did that job. It was top secret then, big stuff. It really was big stuff. Of course, the political atmosphere at the time toward the testing of nuclear devices was very sensitive.

Paul Stillwell: This was also the Sputnik era, when there was concern about space.‡

Captain Colbus: Oh, yes. It was after Sputnik. Sputnik was the year my father died; I remember that. October '57 was Sputnik. Project Argus was a year later, in September '58.

Paul Stillwell: What was the finding in all this, and what was to be the military application?

Captain Colbus: I can't answer that. It might appear in that article that I have, but I was never privileged to know. We had a lot of technical people. This was out of the office that's now called DASA.

Paul Stillwell: Which Mustin later headed.§

Captain Colbus: That's right, but it wasn't called DASA then. Yes, Mustin headed it; that

---

* Captain Arthur R. Gralla, USN.
† Grumman S2F Tracker propeller-driven antisubmarine planes first entered fleet squadrons in early 1954.
‡ On 4 October 1957, the Soviet Union launched Sputnik I, the first artificial earth satellite. It caused great uproar in the United States, which had expected to be first in space.
§ In the early 1970s, as a vice admiral, Mustin served as Director, Defense Atomic Support Agency.

was his start in that business.

Paul Stillwell: Was there any precaution to prevent radiation hazard to people?

Captain Colbus: Yes. First of all, we weren't allowed topside when these things were being fired. As a matter of fact, I still fill out a form every two or three years from a medical facility as to my current health. They've kept tabs on it. As I said, it was very high, it was little, but it was still a nuclear detonation.

Paul Stillwell: Was it so high you couldn't see it go up?

Captain Colbus: No, you could see it go up. People in the planes wore goggles.

Paul Stillwell: What did it look like?

Captain Colbus: Daylight lightning, elongated lightning flashes.

Paul Stillwell: Was there any special security precaution on board the ship where they were stored?

Captain Colbus: I can't answer that, because it all emanated from Norton Sound.

Paul Stillwell: What sorts of things did you do personally?

Captain Colbus: Paperwork, watch standing once we were under way. But back in Washington it was to check with the technical people, make sure the op order was printed, carry the op order, carry all these administrative details between Washington and Newport on an airplane. I was armed with a pistol and the whole nine yards—big stuff. Admiral Mustin was also ComDesFlot 2. He was ComDesFlot 2 in Newport and CTF 88 in Washington. So I was the liaison and conducted the administrative details.

Paul Stillwell: Did this generate a lot of classified correspondence?

Captain Colbus: Absolutely. The op order, for instance, was top secret, yet I would review our work down there, get chapter umpty-ump, paragraph so-and-so straightened out. Then I would put it in my hot little hands, hold on to it, get in the plane, fly up to Newport, go to the flagship, work with the admiral on it during the next day, and then take it back to Washington. So, again, it wasn't anything unusual excerpt the classification and the type of operation it was.

Paul Stillwell: Did you have to get any special clearance because of this nuclear work?

Captain Colbus: I don't think so. If it happened, it happened before I got there. Many of the staff members that I worked with in CTF 88 were in the same situation I was, awaiting the commissioning and moving out of SoLant, but meanwhile I was in Washington working.

I would see Admiral Stephan and got to know him personally. He went to Trinidad in November, and I joined him in December. Captain Flash Dailey was here in Washington as the ops officer at the time.* The Daileys took me in as their own, so we did the Washington and Trinidad tours together.

Paul Stillwell: So it was mostly a matter of being available, it sounds like.

Captain Colbus: Oh, yes. Our chief of staff for CTF 88, who was to be the chief of chief of staff for ComSoLant, was a classmate of Admiral Mustin's by the name of William Joseph Dimitrijevic, Dimmy Dimitrijevic.† He's dead and gone now, poor fellow, killed in an automobile accident a year or two ago.

Paul Stillwell: What are your impressions of Admiral Mustin from that cruise?

---

* Captain Robertson Currie Dailey, USN.
† Dimitrijevic, who was then a captain, retired in that rank in 1962 and died in 1981.

Captain Colbus: Probably one of the smartest, toughest taskmasters I've ever been around. He was very determined, knew exactly what he wanted, gave some guidance, but you were just to carry out his direction. He was it, daring himself. Let me give you an example.

It was very difficult to stand a watch. I thought I was an experienced watch stander, having run the squadron under Emmett Bonner and under Commodore McDowell. By the way, Emmett was a student and protege of Admiral Mustin. They were very close friends. A message would come in that required a verbal reply. If you would say, "Per gra," you'd hear about it for the next two or three minutes.

Admiral Mustin was a stickler for everything. It wasn't the idea that he'd tell you, "Don't do that." He just assumed that you were an experienced officer, and you were stupid if you used "Per Gra." That was unprofessional; that was not the way we do it. The phrase is, "Permission granted." I one day referred to a tin can—boy, I thought I was going to lose my job. You don't refer to those gorgeous ships as "tin cans;" they're destroyers. We learned a lot from him, but everything was a knee-jerk experience. It was devastating. He'd get to you pretty good. He was a very meticulous man, very exact, who gave great attention to detail. Smart—oh, he was smart. He didn't miss a trick, knew everything that was going on around him, and, as I said, controlled everything that went on around him. Again, another type of individual.

Paul Stillwell: Would you put the label "brilliant" on him?

Captain Colbus: Oh, absolutely, as his son is.

Paul Stillwell: Did you have an appreciation for the technical things that were involved in this test?

Captain Colbus: Oh, yes. I couldn't give them the formulae and what have you, but I appreciated what was going on and the people who were working on it.

We had some very smart people. I'm talking about a Navy captain whose name I can't think of who was with us on that part of it. He knew all the physics of what was being done. He was under the gun, and I say that advisedly. He was under the gun just like the rest of us. In other words, he wouldn't tell the admiral what it was all about. He'd go in, and the admiral would tell him what it was all about, and he'd carry out the admiral's directions. He had the ability to do it, but the admiral knew what to do. Admiral Lloyd Mustin was a genius, a stickler, a perfectionist; that's for sure. When I say perfectionist, it was to the point that you couldn't get anything done.

Now we were out of Emmett Bonner's business of "Who cares?" Now we were into . . .

Paul Stillwell: Everything matters.

Captain Colbus: Everything matters. I mean, every "I" was dotted; every "T" was crossed. The admiral himself would take the most minor response to a routine message and completely change it and make it into a work of art. But he'd spend three to four hours doing this, rather than just letting someone else. As I grow older, I realize that we were bogged down in our own work, because everything had to be perfect, and everything had to reflect the admiral's wording and ideas.

Take fitness reports, for instance. He wasn't worried about timeliness and that aspect. He took every fitness report and wrote it himself. You might have given him the outline. If it just lasted as the outline, you were lucky. I was in SoLant calling him up there and saying, "Hey, what about the fitness report?" I'd keep reminding him by mail and by phone. He took his damn good old time, but, boy, every one was perfect. He wasn't going to worry about timeliness; he was worried about exactness. So for every fitness report that went out of his desk, he did it to perfection, and they were works of art, every piece of paper. You pick up any message that CTF 88 issued in that 1958 time frame, and you will read something that's prose, understood, clear, to the point, no excess verbiage. Everything was done by Admiral Mustin himself.

Paul Stillwell: So he didn't delegate.

Captain Colbus: No, he didn't.

Paul Stillwell: You've described him in the administrative sense. How was he operationally?

Captain Colbus: Oh, the same way. He knew exactly what he wanted. Emmett was the same, except Emmett did it in a very casual, smooth, I'd almost say a humble manner. "Why don't we . . . ?" was Emmett's style, where Admiral Mustin would tell you exactly what the signal was, exactly where the ship should be when the maneuver was over, and all you had to do was repeat what he told you. Yes, tactically he was as exact as he was administratively. He's a man of his time.

Paul Stillwell: Captain, we're talking about the period in 1958. You were then on the staff of Commander Task Force 88, and ComSoLant was just forming up. Had there been any predecessor organization that you could use as a model?

Captain Colbus: Yes. ComSoLant existed during World War II. Jonas Ingram was the commander, and that's a very dear name to me for a number of reasons.* Our 1958 ComSoLant was a continuation of the wartime command. Its mission was to unite African and South American navies into an effective force to protect our hemisphere in this underbelly. We know the shipping is all going to be in the North Atlantic. Is that what you mean by a model?

Paul Stillwell: I mean so that you didn't have to start from scratch? Could you go back and draw on some of this history, or was the situation that much different?

Captain Colbus: I think the situation was that much different. It was simple. First of all, ComSoLant had no permanent ships. All we had was an area. The staff consisted of about eight or ten officers at the most and 15 enlisted. We had all the support from right here in Norfolk. Admiral Jerauld Wright was CinCLant at the time; therefore, Admiral Stephan and Admiral Wright worked very closely on this, with much discussion, liaison, and

---

* Vice Admiral Jonas H. Ingram, USN, served in South America from February 1942 to November 1944. His billet had several titles along the way, including Commander South Atlantic Force and, later, Commander Fourth Fleet. The destroyer Jonas Ingram, which Colbus commanded, was named in his honor.

planning between ComSoLant and CinCLant.* We were given guidance. I'd say we were provided the framework: "This is what we want you to do." It was then liaison among the various commands. One was Commander Caribbean Sea Frontier, Rear Admiral Dan Gallery, who was located in San Juan, Puerto Rico.† ComSouth, which was the Army command in Panama, was also a player.

We worked with the Dutch Antilles naval officer over there and in Aruba and Curaçao. What we actually did was visit these area commanders with our main purpose for the first couple of years—and I would say it still is that way—to visit, show the flag, and create a working arrangement with all these South American and African colonial navies that were on station.

We would muster a task force that would leave the East Coast, transit to Trinidad, and embark us. We'd conduct a two-month transit of South America, then return to Trinidad, where we'd disembark. We would write our report with lessons learned. By then we knew the personages in South America. We had many friends and allies. We were creating a union. Then Admiral Stephan would travel to Norfolk and brief CinCLant himself, as well as the staff, on what we were doing and had accomplished.

Then we'd return to Trinidad and spend the next two or three months planning for the same type operation in Africa, where we'd visit both coasts. That would be a longer trip, more adventurous, and fascinating. We were really into an area that was untapped. I can tell you sea story after sea story about the incidents that happened over there.

Paul Stillwell: Please do.

Captain Colbus: I was trying to answer that question as to what we'd do. As far as coming up with any great war plans, it didn't happen the two years I was there. But we did establish communications checks, and we did write a standing op order. We knew upon whom we could depend, and we knew their capabilities. I'm talking about some of those

---

* Admiral Jerauld Wright, USN, served as Supreme Allied Commander Atlantic, Commander in Chief Atlantic Command, and Commander in Chief Atlantic Fleet from 12 April 1954 to 28 February 1960.
† Rear Admiral Daniel V. Gallery, Jr., USN, served as Commandant of the Tenth Naval District and Commander Caribbean Sea Frontier from 1956 to 1960. In addition, from mid-1957 he was Commandant Fifteenth Naval District and Commander Antilles Defense Command. His oral history is in the Naval Institute collection.

navies where they'd hot-wire electrical equipment on the ship. In the communications shack, for instance, rather than have a switch, there would be two hot wires. That's the kind of maintenance and operation we learned about, and we thought we were very successful in starting that group.

Our flagship for those cruises was usually a 931-class destroyer. The first deployment was to Africa aboard USS Bigelow. The next deployment was to South America aboard USS Jonas Ingram, which I commanded later. A third deployment was in Mullinnix. My last trip was in USS Macon.*

When we went to South America, everybody remembered ComSoLant as Jonas Ingram, and now we were in his shadow, so to speak. I can remember South American ladies, probably 50-ish, rolling their eyes and cooing, "Oh, Admiral Ingram. Ooh, when Admiral Ingram came to town . . ." He was loved down there. I never met him, of course; he was dead and gone by my time.† He was CinCLant after being ComSoLant. If you look at his picture, he is a Santa Claus without the red suit and the beard. I've never seen a picture or a painting that he didn't have a twinkle and the red cheeks. He was just the most pleasant-looking gent. I feel that I know him. I heard these stories. He was a man who loved life. His son William was his aide, which I learned later on.‡ William is in Atlanta, Georgia. I corresponded with him when I was commanding officer of Jonas Ingram. Admiral Ingram was a great man to follow.

Admiral Stephan was a very soft-spoken, low-key officer who went to South America and Africa and knew the right things to say and do. He was a polished diplomat, having been the chief of the Navy's Office of Legislative Affairs, so he knew the right things to say at the right time. He was smooth as silk and sincere as all get-out. Neither of us spoke Spanish, which I thought would be a detriment, but we understood perfectly. By the time I left there, I could listen to the Spanish and understand what they were saying. That was our modus operandi.

---

* USS Macon (CA-132) was a Baltimore-class heavy cruiser commissioned 26 August 1945. The other ships mentioned in the paragraph were Forrest Sherman-class destroyers.
† Admiral Ingram died 10 September 1952.
‡ William T. Ingram II graduated from the Naval Academy in the class of 1938. He resigned from the regular Navy in 1947 and eventually retired as a captain in the Naval Reserve.

The ships in our task force would embark us, with their destroyer squadron commander in company. He'd operate from one of the other destroyers. We operated from the 931-class ship in the group. We also had a shore detachment made up of P2Vs, which started out at Brunswick and went all the way south.[*] Vice Admiral Barney Rapp, now retired, was then the commander of one of those VP squadrons, and I got to know him then.[†] He is now in the area, and we get together to talk about these great deployments. This includes Captain Flash Dailey, now retired, who was my boss; he was the operations officer for ComSoLant.

Paul Stillwell: Where did the name "Unitas" come from?[‡]

Captain Colbus: I can't answer that. I could guess.

Paul Stillwell: I thought it was an acronym.

Captain Colbus: No, I think it was "United" something or other. To my knowledge, it's not an acronym. It just came about.

Paul Stillwell: Do you remember any particular operations with the South American navies?

Captain Colbus: No, not particularly, because we were dealing with basic training. We're talking about tactics that I said we did in Key West. We were good because we'd work together. We were a task group of ships that worked together and knew each other. We visited each country, and the first thing we'd do after mooring the ships was to engage in social amenities. The protocol was very, very heavy, as you can well imagine. They wanted to start off properly, and that was how they did it: socialize to get us on the right

---

[*] P2V Neptunes were Navy long-range patrol planes based at Naval Air Station Brunswick, Maine.
[†] Vice Admiral William T. Rapp, USN (Ret.), was a commander when he commanded Patrol Squadron Ten, 1958-60.
[‡] This is the name for exercises involving ships from the U.S. Navy and various Latin American navies. They operate together in the waters off South America.

foot. At these social gatherings you would meet your counterpart, where you'd really establish a rapport.

After about two days of this, maybe three for liberty's sake, we'd get under way with these ships and start from ground zero. It was basic maneuvering—just exactly what you'd expect a brand-new group of ships to do. Then we'd bring the submarine in so that we could conduct more basic training evolutions. On the average, we'd do that about five days. At the end of the five days, the learning curve was up, and we were doing well. It was then over, because we had to transit to the next port or the next country.

We wouldn't see them until the following year. We'd visit and operate five days and see them next year. But we did know the people and whether we could count on them in time of mobilization. We changed publications. We made things compatible among the navies. We now had the doctrine so that we wouldn't be learning the ground rules when we returned. We had the ground rules; it was just getting operational ties together.

Paul Stillwell: How much of it was symbolic? How much of it was substantive?

Captain Colbus: Let me think about it. Well, things such as turning OTC, officer in tactical command, over to your fellow South Americans was symbolic, of course, because they weren't that versed in commanding a task force of ships.

Paul Stillwell: The whole thing was in a large sense symbolic, just to say, "We're your friend, and we can count on you to be our friend."

Captain Colbus: True. I was thinking of symbolic and substantive in an operational mode. In fact, to emphasize what you just said about being symbolic, sometimes the flagship wouldn't get under way. The other destroyers would get under way with the destroyer squadron commander as the task group commander. We'd stay ashore to go to Parliament and to state lunches. Of course, I'd stay with the admiral as his aide.

In answer to your question, we did at times separate the symbolism from, as you said, substantive items. The ships did get under way and conduct training. Whether we stayed with the beach group or went with the ships depended upon the at-sea exercises versus the protocol in the city. We would always carry a USIA representative.[*] We also carried a State Department rep. As I said, Admiral Stephan was very astute in international relations. He had been born and reared in Washington, was the son of a lawyer, and had experience in legislative affairs. When he went somewhere, he knew exactly what the situation was; he was a keen, personable, even-tempered gentleman.

Paul Stillwell: That's undoubtedly why he was picked for the job.

Captain Colbus: It was obvious.

Paul Stillwell: You said you didn't have a communications background coming into this. Did you acquire one?

Captain Colbus: To a point, yes. I had a very fine chief radioman, and our communications weren't that complicated. I knew my squadron communications; I knew what circuits to use; I knew the administrative details; I knew what had to be filed and what didn't have to be filed. As far as communications, we were doing just the simple things. The main thing we did as ComSoLant was, as I said, use some antennas that were already in place, crank them around, and physically move them in order to beam them to Africa. Every Thursday at 2300 our time we conducted tests to see if we could establish communications. That was symbolic, but it was there.

In 1959 it was announced that (a) President Eisenhower would go to South America on a goodwill mission and (b) ComSoLant would be the operational commander responsible for planning and execution of this visit from the support side.[†] We, of course, were the kingpins down there, so it was our visit. USS Macon was the flagship. This was toward the end of my tour.

My communications abilities and capabilities were just outnumbered, and I screamed for help. Messages were fast and furious. I was spending 20 hours a day just preparing, translating, and transcribing messages. Plus the fact that Macon would need to

---

[*] USIA—United States Information Agency.
[†] Dwight D. Eisenhower served as President of the United States from 20 January 1953 to 20 January 1961.

be equipped with all the material and all the comm gear that would permit the President to patch into the ship from anywhere he was located and talk to the White House. So they sent us, all of a sudden, warrant officers from the White House staff. Trinidad was a beehive of activity. We finally did get the flagship, USS Macon.

With the flagship came the Navy Band and a very sad story. The band arrived by plane because they couldn't spend all their time riding the flagship. The landing area was at Piarco Airport, 27 miles from the naval station. If you ever saw 40 or 50 prima donnas, we got them. That's typical with musicians. I certainly don't say that to be critical, because they were a fine crew. The bandmaster was Commander Bender. By act of Congress he was made a commander, because we didn't have a billet in the Navy for a commander musician. The billet was for a lieutenant commander. This is an indication of his importance and influence.

I was in charge of arrangements, as you'd expect the flag lieutenant to be. He and I got wound around the axle the very first day, because he didn't like his stateroom. I had to go to our ops officer, who was a captain, and ask him to relinquish his stateroom just to keep peace in the family and let me put Bender in there. Well, we got that straightened out. It was just one problem after another. When the airplane landed at Piarco, they had 27,000 pounds of gear. That included uniforms, timpani, you name it. I had three trucks there.

Someone with the band said, "Unh-unh, can't be put in the trucks."

"Why?"

"Because they're open."

"What does that have to do with it?"

"What if it rains?"

"It doesn't rain in Trinidad."

"It rains between 1200 and 1400."

"It's now 1600. It won't rain."

"Unh-unh, can't lose that stuff. What if some dirt falls on it?"

That was, I guess, our first crossing of swords. Where do you get covered trucks in Trinidad to haul 27,000 pounds? Nothing is impossible, but we would have had to wait weeks until we got some down from Puerto Rico. Somehow we got over that. Then we had room assignment problems. Then we had parties and protocol, so we were off to a rocky start.

I was very anxious to go with this band, because one of the band members was Dick Harl.[*] He was a musician first class, a trumpeter. He and I grew up in Altoona, Pennsylvania. Dick Harl's father had the local appliance store. He and his dad were concert-variety trumpeters. I was a violinist. Dick was about two years ahead of me in school and perhaps a year or so older. I was just delighted to see him.

I was then in pretty good with the Navy Band. They were going to fly in an R6D that was already positioned at Trinidad and follow the President to tone up for the visit.[†] I wanted to go with them. The admiral told me, "Louis, you've worked hard for two years. You're on your way to line school. Let the flag sec take this one. Bob Brown doesn't get to do any of these things. You get all the glamour."[‡]

"Well, he's the flag sec. I'm the flag lieutenant."

I talked to Admiral Ed about this at great length, and he finally said, "No, I appreciate your loyalty, but you get on your way. We're going to let Bob take this one."

"It's because you won't trust me around the President."

"No."

I said, "I met him up at Penn State one time. I know his brother Milton."[§] I said all the other persuasive things I could muster. I wanted some of this glamour. I liked that.

"Can't go."

That's when the Navy Band crashed at Rio de Janeiro.[**] Nearly everyone died, including Bob Brown, who took my place. It was chilling at the time. He was a young lieutenant—30, 32 years old—five kids, a brand-new baby and a beautiful wife named

---

[*] Musician First Class Richard D. Harl, USN.
[†] The R6D Liftmaster was a four-engine propeller-driven transport built by Douglas as the military counterpart to the DC-6 civilian passenger plane. The Navy designation after 1962 matched that of the Air Force, C-118.
[‡] Lieutenant Robert S. Brown, USN.
[§] Dr. Milton Eisenhower had a distinguished career as an educator.
[**] President Eisenhower's three-day tour of Brazil was marred on 25 February 1960 by the crash of a Navy R6D transport that collided with a Brazilian airliner near Sugar Loaf Mountain in Rio. The R6D had flown in from Argentina with 25 members of the Navy Band and an ASW team that had been assisting the Argentine Navy. Of the 38 on board the Navy plane, only three survived. All 26 on the Brazilian plane were killed.

Doris back in Trinidad. I was a bachelor. This was the most trying time of my naval career. Dick Harl was killed. Bob Brown was killed.

Every time the Navy Band traveled, the chief musician/administrator would provide those insurance policy forms that you get in the airport. He didn't do it on this flight. Because he had done it on previous trips, it was considered by the families of those poor dead-and-gone musicians that it was the Navy's responsibility. There is still litigation about the accident. You hear about it up in BuPers if you go to the right office.

Admiral Stephan got some bad press in Washington about two years later. The Navy Band—including those who weren't on the plane plus new members—appeared to play at the wedding of Admiral Stephan's daughter, out of courtesy to the admiral. It was a very warm feeling that had been established between the admiral and the band. The press came out and gave us some bad coverage on that, saying that Admiral Stephan had—in order to improve his image—insisted that the Navy Band come to South America. Then, after the plane crash, he was going to use the band at his daughter's wedding—that kind of nastiness.

As to the Navy Band coming to Trinidad, the last thing we needed, with all our aggravation, were 30-some prima donnas to come down and board the flagship. Of course, once there, they were great shipmates and did a great job while they were there. But it was a very sad time, of course, and then I went on my way.

Paul Stillwell: So they never got to meet the President during all this?

Captain Colbus: No.

Paul Stillwell: What are your impressions of spending some time in the Macon after all your time in DEs?

Captain Colbus: It was another world. The skipper, Reuben Whitaker, went on to make flag.* I didn't get to know him. I was too busy, really, to run around doing the social

---

* Captain Reuben T. Whitaker, USN, commanded the heavy cruiser Macon (CA-132) from 2 November 1959 to 17 December 1960.

things. And I did not sail with the ship. The ship sailed with my relief, who was relieved four months later. It was decided Bob Brown would coordinate the band. What we were going to do was to have my relief come aboard and be my shadow. By the time we'd be halfway through the cruise, I'd fly back and then go on to Monterey. But the admiral said, "This young man has taken hold. Bob Brown knows the flag lieutenant duties. He'll do them." That's how it happened.

Paul Stillwell: Had you already gone by the time the band was killed?

Captain Colbus: Yes. I was en route to Monterey and read about it in the paper.

Paul Stillwell: I presume you might have been kept on longer had it happened a little sooner, because there was a void after Brown was killed.

Captain Colbus: A lot of things would have happened differently.

Paul Stillwell: You said you had some sea stories to tell about the African cruises.

Captain Colbus: Oh, the African cruises! First of all, nobody believed it, but I talked about my family in Johannesburg and Durban. Everybody thought I was kidding again. When we arrived in South Africa, there were my cousins, who had migrated there. They'd been to visit Altoona. The father had been mayor of Johannesburg. When we went up to Pretoria, he came over and met us. When we arrived in Durban, his children were there on the pier. One is a dentist; one has a citrus fruit farm.

It was very good and a nice assignment. We began the trip on the West Coast, of course, and came all the way around. Cape Town was fantastic. We didn't worry about the politics and apartheid; we all went ashore. And each group went its own way. The black sailors would be out on the pier directing working parties, doing their work, standing watches. We didn't separate the crew. And, of course, people in South Africa were just amazed that a black petty officer could supervise white enlisted. So in that manner I think we did a lot of good.

Paul Stillwell: What about the blacks going on liberty? How were they received?

Captain Colbus: Well, that was the next part. They were segregated. Each group would go their own separate ways. Filipinos would go with their community, and the whites would go in their group. Each group was met by the Rolls-Royce crowd. Each group was taken to their particular community, and that community represented the whole social and economic spectrum. There were the very wealthy blacks, along with the middle class and the poor people. You had the wealthy—I guess they call them coloreds, that would be browns, but colored included the Filipinos and Orientals. Each group had a social structure all of their own. And, of course, the Caucasians would go off in another group, in this case. And I'm willing to say that you could ask any one of those groups how they liked it, and they loved it. They were always anxious to return.

Paul Stillwell: So that the black Americans did not get exposed to apartheid, really.

Captain Colbus: Well, I think so.

Paul Stillwell: But they didn't face hostility, because they were taking a place that had already been separated out.

Captain Colbus: They went to the black community, which was a cross-representation of everything that you could want. As I said, you'd have some of them going off in a Rolls-Royce with the black leaders in town. And most of them did that, because they were very respected, coming from the States, being petty officers, and being leaders among a mixed group. And, of course, the blacks who went ashore were just amazed to see all these wealthy, prosperous, influential people in the black community, with whom they mated up. The Filipinos did the same.

Paul Stillwell: What was your role in Africa, as compared with South America?

Captain Colbus: I'd say it was completely different, because in each area you had to adjust to a new social climate. I mentioned that during the first few days you'd learn the area, establish rapport. For instance, when we started out, let's say, in Senegal, Scotland Yard would host us. That was just like being back in Trinidad. Then, as we moved down the coast, we'd get into the Ivory Coast.

We'd have President Tubman on board.[*] Then we were in Liberia, where the entirely black community operated that country without European influence. Other African nations were discussing independence. This was just the beginning of Africa as we know it today. Back then it was colonial British, with few independent nations. Then we'd visit South Africa, which is today as it was then, with some change.[†]

We then went to Mozambique, into Portuguese Africa. That was the difficult area. The Portuguese were great city builders, as seen in Rio de Janeiro, Lisbon, and Lourenço Marques. They were probably the toughest and roughest taskmasters that we'd observed. As we saw it, they were absolutely cruel to the locals. As an example, natives would line up for miles just to walk aboard the ship and use a telephone, be it a sound-powered phone or be it a dial phone. Just amazing. And I'm talking about people who probably walked 30 miles from the inland portion of Africa.

We'd be there to receive them, and I got great pleasure out of watching these people and talking to them. They didn't speak English, but we'd somehow communicate. One day I saw a person, maybe 200 yards from the ship, get out of line to see how the line was doing. A Portuguese policeman—a Caucasian—took his nightstick and clubbed that poor African until he couldn't get up. They were tough as nails with those people. We saw that wherever we went; the Portuguese, I thought, were cruel.

South Africa was something else. The natives did very well. We'd see all of them in sharp uniforms during the day. We'd visit the military reservation where there would be a black African contingent. Then we'd go to a European's home for evening drinks and dinner. As we'd be going back to the ship at perhaps 2330, we'd see those same soldiers

---

[*] William V. Tubman served as President of Liberia from 1944 until his death in 1971.
[†] Conditions in The Republic of South Africa changed dramatically subsequent to this 1984 interview. In 1990 the government lifted its ban on the black African National Congress party. In February 1991, President F. W. de Klerk announced the end of all apartheid laws that directed racial segregation. In 1994 Nelson Mandela of the ANC became South Africa's President.

out around a bonfire with leather thongs and native dress—back to their native state. We'd say, "Those aren't the people I saw today."

"Oh, yes, they are."

You could almost understand why they kept these people organized. They would just switch from one civilization to another.

Paul Stillwell: Did you go into Kenya at all?

Captain Colbus: No.

Paul Stillwell: That was a time of considerable unrest in the Belgian Congo. Did you go there?

Captain Colbus: The ships didn't go there. We flew up to the Belgian Congo. You could call it R&R.[*] The military attachés had aircraft assigned to them. We'd become, of course, friendly with the military attaché. In Cape Town the admiral and myself and two of the other staff men took off on a private and personal trip. We didn't officially tell anybody. We just borrowed the R3D, the "Gooney Bird," and flew to the Belgian Congo. We went to Brazzaville and visited there. I hesitate. We may have gone there officially, but I remember one time going to Victoria Falls. That was a so-called boondoggle. We just went there. We went to Brazzaville, perhaps, on official business. We did go up the Banana River into the Congo. That was interesting. We steamed the ship as far as we could and then boarded a minesweeper that was stationed there and went up a little farther.

Paul Stillwell: Was there any time at all when you felt concern for your personal safety?

Captain Colbus: Never. Not once.

I've got to tell you about a fueling stop we made in a bay that had black oil and was associated with a rubber plantation. I'm referring to the bay just north of Lourenço Marques; it's a beautiful, big bay. We were in Jonas Ingram and had to wait until the tide

---

[*] R&R—rest and recreation.

was set for us. We crossed the bar, went in, and used a tractor for the forward mooring line and a tree stump for the after line; that's how we moored the ship.

This was a primitive port where we were going to take fuel. This was a fueling depot operated by an American and a few Englishmen; this was in conjunction with a rubber plantation. I remember the American coming aboard and asking if anybody wanted to go inland and visit the plantation. I said, "I'll go." I was the only one who accepted his invitation. The admiral wanted to sleep. He'd had enough of this. He had to rest up for Dar-es-Salaam; he'd just left Lourenço Marques.

I went off with this fellow in a Jeep. We must have traveled 20 miles to this rubber plantation. The work force consisted of pygmies. Pygmies were the population and the workers. I'd never seen pygmies. I remember those Tarzan movies, and this reminded me of that. I was in tropical white uniform—shorts and high socks. We finally came to a clearing, and there was what you'd call, I guess, a mud adobe-type one-story building, a pretty big place.

"This is our local tavern. Let's go in and have something." It was now dusk—7:00, 7:30. We went in this native jungle bar. I know my memory serves me right that I saw—I didn't count them—about a dozen of the most gorgeous women I have ever seen in my life; they were Caucasians. I was a bachelor and thought, "This is it." I had really arrived. I knew about colonial Africa with the Brits and the French and the Portuguese, which was a lot of fun, with a lot of pretty gals. There was always someone to dance with, date, and see the area.

Now here I was with 12 gorgeous women in the middle of the jungle! However, they wouldn't even speak to me. My host finally told me what the situation was. These were 12 prostitutes who had come there for a six-month period. All nationalities were represented by these Europeans. The pygmies earned $1.00 a day for working in the rubber plantation, and the reason for working was that when they amassed $100.00 for 100 days, they would be able to come here and have one of these Caucasian women. These women were there for a six-month stint with no overhead. They would return home wealthy women. Damnedest thing I'd ever seen in my life. I just sat there, fascinated. These pygmies would come and go. I guess some of them came back with a second 100 days' pay.

Paul Stillwell: That's a lot of work in order to get one night of pleasure.

Captain Colbus: It was a real education.

Paul Stillwell: These names that you've been reeling off sound very exotic. This was the sort of thing you had been looking for when you were in Altoona.

Captain Colbus: An answer to my prayer. And then when we completed the deployment in Dar-es-Salaam on our first trip, the staff didn't have time to return on the ship. They flew from Dar-es-Salaam, Tanganyika, to Nairobi, Kenya, to Rome, Paris, London, Washington, and finally, Trinidad. That took five days. It occurred to me that someone had to stay with the flagship since our enlisted staff, gear, and admiral's barge would remain on board, bound for Trinidad. I approached the admiral and asked, "Admiral, do you really need me on this trip?"

"What trip?"

"Rome, Paris, London, Washington."

"Well, sure I need you."

I said, "How about the enlisted staff on here?" All of a sudden I was magnanimous. I was concerned about the enlisted staff. I said, "How about the barge? We've got the barge on here. I recommend that I ride the ship back to Trinidad."

"You're going to skip Rome, Paris?"

"I think I really should." I haven't given you the gloomy side of being on that staff. Every commander and every captain used me as his aide. That was why—when I got to be a senior officer, and especially chief of staff to three different admirals—I was so protective of the flag lieutenant. I ensured that nobody "spoke" to the flag lieutenant. He was the admiral's flag lieutenant and aide. If I ever observed anybody junior to me go near the flag lieutenant, I'd grab him. Anyway, everybody used me for his personal needs: "Hey, Louis, by the way, . . ." "Since you're handling the admiral's bag, why don't you take mine?" "Pay the bill, and we'll settle later."

"Oh, sure, Commander." What was I going to say? Maybe I was too humble. I would not say no to a commander. The chief of staff had me do all his personal work, even to the point that I charged everything on my credit card. In those days I was the only one who owned an American Express card. I'd get back to Trinidad and have a $6,000 bill. That was unheard of then. I was a big man with American Express. But I got it just for this job. When we'd get back to Trinidad, everybody would settle up with me after they settled their travel claims.

The chief of staff would say, "Let's see. How much do I owe you?"

"You owe me $1,242.62, chief of staff."

"Well, here's some of my money from Tanganyika," and he'd give me all this change, as well as various monies from all the countries visited. It was an accounting nightmare. Well, I got tired of that.

I thought, "I'll beat the system this time." So I talked the admiral into it by saying, "You don't really need me."

"No, I don't need a wet nurse."

So I rode the ship to Trinidad and repeated every one of those ports going back. It took me 30 days to get back to Trinidad, with nothing to do. Nothing to do. I sat up in the admiral's cabin in Jonas Ingram, learned to play bridge with the USIA rep, the ship's doctor, the skipper of the ship, Bob Adrian, and myself.[*] What a time that was. And my shore leave in every port was unrestricted. Overnights were the norm. The admiral's cabin and stewards were mine.

I also met a lovely lady in Cape Town, Felicity Scott. When I returned there, I had no duties and spent three days in Cape Town. Oh, here's one that got into my later married life. One night in Cape Town I attended one of these great parties at somebody's mansion. About 2:00 o'clock in the morning the hostess said, "Would anybody like to go out to the veldt?"

My hand went right up, with a couple of other hands. She got out a four-wheel-drive Rover, and off we went to the veldt. I thought they had a lodge in the veldt; no, we went to another mansion. The hostess led us in, clapped four times, and servants came out

---

[*] Commander Robert N. Adrian, USN, commanded the USS Jonas Ingram from 1 August 1959 to 22 July 1961.

from everywhere. While we were having breakfast, they explained to us that they used ostrich eggs. They showed me this one ostrich egg, and for me they put a pinhole in this egg, drained it, and gave me the egg.

Well, I had everybody autograph it, and it went with me on the rest of this cruise. This big ostrich egg was autographed by all these gals whom I met in Pretoria, or wherever we were: "Hey, sign my ostrich egg." That was, as I said, '58. When I married in December 1961, I still had that ostrich egg. That's about all I had. I carried that ostrich egg with me until 1970. It was in a drawer with my shirts. Every so often, I'd get it out, and my wife Jody would say, "I wish you'd get rid of that ostrich egg. Grow up. Those girls are past."

"No, I like my ostrich egg."

Then Jody came home one day, all excited. She had been down to Garfinckel's department store, or somewhere fancy in Washington. "Guess what's the rage? Ostrich eggs pasted on a wooden base." And they were selling for $125.00. "Let's pull out the ostrich egg. It's a great conversation piece. It's a work of art." Guess what? I couldn't find the ostrich egg, and to this day I don't know what happened to it.

But I did get to the veldt. We went on safaris, flew all over Africa, went up, as I said, to Victoria Falls. What a life! I'll tell you, I could have paid thousands and thousands of dollars and not had an experience like that.

We had one of the first Polaroid Land cameras. That camera was a big hit. Everywhere we went with the admiral, we'd take that camera. I'd take a picture and give it to them on the spot. Everyone thought that was great. You couldn't do that in Northern Africa, because they thought that you were taking a part of their life. They thought we'd taken some of their spirit away. But in the part of Africa we were visiting, it was very, very popular. That was a big conversation piece.

Paul Stillwell: What can you say about Admiral Stephan as a diplomat in these situations?

Captain Colbus: He was the smoothest, finest, most elegant gentleman you've ever seen or met. He just knew how to do everything right. For instance, they would send limousines to pick us up. By then I was used to riding in a Rolls-Royce; no more Chevrolets! When they'd bring a Rolls Royce down, they'd come to me and get flags—a U.S. flag and a two-star admiral's flag. They put these on the fenders, and away we'd go. This was the procedure for visiting VIPs.

One day they sent an official escort. So here came the sirens, the cars—again, like the movies—and we were whisking through town at 40 miles an hour, pushing everybody out of the way. The admiral stopped the whole thing and said, "Take down those flags. Poor impression." He was very sensitive about something like that. He said, "Any time you can low-key this, let's do it. I want to go in style, but if they insist on this speed and this kind of notoriety, this kind of spotlight, get the flags out of there." Just little things like that. He was very, very warm, always dignified, and with a twinkle in his eye. The admiral was always most considerate of his staff. He always insisted, "You're an aide, you're a dignified naval officer. You don't hold my coat, you don't need to do those things." Of course, he was a great operator. He'd had a lot of submarine wartime experience, of course, and wore the Navy Cross.

His wife Peg, who didn't travel with us, I would say is probably the most beautiful and refined lady I have ever met in my life. She just portrayed elegance and class and didn't even work at it. Her favorite expression, when we'd have a problem, such as the party's to begin in five minutes and the electricity has just gone out, was, "Fire, fire in the paint locker." She could imitate a deck boatswain's mate to a T. As I said, they were just the perfect couple.

He told me one day about making flag. He said, "It just happens. You wake up one morning, and you're a flag officer. You don't know how it happened. At first you're just so startled by it, you can't react. Then, by the time you get used to it, it's just another job."

Paul Stillwell: Not everybody looks at it that way.

Captain Colbus: No. And he had that reputation, as a very warm-hearted individual, very close to his family.

Paul Stillwell: Did he work through interpreters in these ports?

Captain Colbus: Absolutely, which at times became a problem. Our chief of staff in ComSoLant, as I mentioned, was Dimmy Dimitrijevic, who had been Admiral Mustin's chief of staff in Task Force 88. He was a very well-read man with a photographic mind; he never forgot anything. He considered himself a linguist since he spoke Spanish, French, and a couple of other languages. He would always put himself in the middle as the interpreter. However, he wasn't a professional interpreter. He was fine, I guess, at a cocktail party, but when it came to sitting down at the table or press conferences, you'd have to get Dimmy out of there. But yes, to answer your question.

Of course, as I said, in Lourenço Marques we would embark the USIA representative or a consular agent for the next port—in this case, Dar-es-Salaam. So by the time we'd get there, we'd be briefed on the political situation, certainly what to do, who to know, what have you. It was very well orchestrated, and Admiral Stephan insisted on that. He was very good at getting the State Department to cooperate with us.

I've had plenty of experience since then dealing with the State Department during my own ship visits. When we conducted a visit, we always had the local State Department representative available, from the ambassador on down. I've never seen any group work as neatly and as smoothly and as capably as they did, because Admiral Stephan knew the right string to pull, knew where to go back in Washington, and bring them aboard; it was effective.

Paul Stillwell: Was intelligence-gathering any part of what you did?

Captain Colbus: Absolutely. In fact, on the one trip we had an Army major who was an intelligence expert for Africa. We even one time carried the Under Secretary of State for African Affairs. He didn't ride the ship very well; he was green all the time. He was a heavy in the State Department and came from Washington to ride with us. He became a great friend of ours and a strong supporter of ComSoLant. He was our PAO back in Washington.[*]

---

[*] PAO—public affairs officer.

Paul Stillwell: What types of things were they trying to learn—mostly political?

Captain Colbus: Very much so, because the entire area was in a state of unrest. Everybody was looking for independence. The Portuguese were the only ones who were holding their colonial line. Everybody else was just pulling out and leaving the country as is, and the Africans weren't ready to do their own governing. They didn't have the knowledge, they didn't have the experience, they didn't have the education. The smart, capable people who could have led the country were studying in Europe and either hadn't come home yet or stayed in Europe, so you really didn't have the proper people who could smoothly take over.

The Brits were ready to pull out at the drop of a hat, since it was no longer lucrative to stay there. France had too many problems of their own. So, in answer to your question, the political unrest was phenomenal. You never really knew who was doing what to whom. For instance, we'd return the following year and have to begin again. You couldn't count on what you learned last year. In fact, it would be better if you'd wipe it out and start anew.

Paul Stillwell: Maybe so.

Captain Colbus: Sure.

Paul Stillwell: What about South America? Was it essentially the same?

Captain Colbus: No, it wasn't so bad, comparatively speaking. South America was easier to deal with. You knew what the factions were down there. Now, you may have revolutions. In fact, we had a revolution when we were in Venezuela.[*] I'll never forget that. We went to Caracas, which is right up the mountain from the port of La Guaira, about 20 miles. Caracas is one of the great cities of the world.

---

[*] Venezuela experienced a series of political upheavals that began in January 1958 and continued throughout the year. The result was that the previous ten-year dictatorship ended, and the country held free elections in December 1958.

The admiral and I were living in Circulo Militaire, the elegant and opulent BOQ.* It cost about $2.00 a night. This was built, in those days, at a cost of $14 million to the country of Venezuela, and it catered to the military and the power sources. Across the street were the flagos. These were the shacks made out of tarpaper, packing boxes, anything that they could get, and if anybody was lucky enough to steal an electric wire, they had a light bulb. We're talking about an entire hillside, a city. They called it Diablo. So here was opulence among the poorest living conditions I've ever seen.

There was a minor revolution, and we got stuck in Circulo Militaire. You could hear bullets pinging. They had the guards all around. We were safe, but we could still see mortar holes and bullet holes in the next two days when we went out. To show you Admiral Stephan's composure, here we were in the middle of this minor revolution. We couldn't get to the ships, the ships couldn't get to us. Our favorite word down there was "regular." We'd go to these fabulous places, be treated so well that you couldn't believe it, and the admiral would look at me and say, "Regular."

I'd say, "Yes, sir, just like Altoona—regular." It's regular, nothing special.

We didn't speak Spanish, but every morning he'd get up, and when we'd meet it would be, "Buenos dias, Almirante."

"Buenos dias, Luigi."

"Que pasa, Almirante?"

Or "Que pasa, Luigi?" And the answer would always be, "Nada," because that's all we knew to say. During the revolution we were looking out the window and observing the street fighting. He looked at me and said, "Buenos dias."

"Buenos dias, Almirante."

He said, "Que pasa?"

"Nada." He just was a marvelous man—a mentor, a teacher, and a profound friend.

We did the same thing in Africa. We stopped at a place I've just revisited in '82 in the Mauritius Islands on the east coast. We were treated to two nights at the governor's mansion in Port Louis. We awakened one morning. We were surrounded by mosquito net in a room, I guess, 18 feet high. There was an Indian (from India) standing there in full dress. The servant pulled the net aside and gave me hot tea. As I stepped out, there was a

---

* BOQ—bachelor officers' quarters.

bath already drawn. I couldn't move without somebody being there. The admiral came in, looked around, and said, "Just like in Altoona, isn't it, Louis?"

"Oh, yes, sir."

He said, "I wonder what they're doing back there."

"Same old thing."

"Right. Have some breakfast." What a great time and experience.

Paul Stillwell: Were you trying to collect military intelligence?

Captain Colbus: Sure. The sizes of the piers, capacity of the piers, all the things you'd expect to see in a port directory, which we didn't have, so we were really trail blazing. Nothing that secretive. In fact, this Army major that we carried with us, Keith—I can't remember his last name—came back and said, "Well, I went ashore in uniform, and I met the local yokel who's an intelligence officer here. He said, 'What can we exchange openly? I've got brochures. I'll tell you anything I can, and you ask me. I'll ask you, and you tell me anything you can.'"

"What's the size of that ship?"

"Four hundred eighteen feet long."

"Great." It just went on and on like that, so they knew what we were doing. And we wanted descriptions of the local people, which was one of the assignments. Upon return to the ship, we'd compare notes: "I met So-and-so. Well, he's a lieutenant, but I bet you in five years he'll be one of their leaders. Write him up." So every bit of information that we could put down, we did, and we just had scads and scads of it. Then the smart people back home would catalogue it.

Paul Stillwell: Did you have any ties with the CIA at all?

Captain Colbus: Not to my knowledge.

Paul Stillwell: The Cuban revolution came during this period.* Did that make any changes for you?

Captain Colbus: Not for us, no.

Paul Stillwell: You weren't trying to reach out to Cuba anyway.

Captain Colbus: No, but I told you about my Cuban ties. We were one of the last ships to visit there when I was in Escort Squadron 12. That all happened in '58. I remember going to Cuba and visiting Phil Klepak, who was the assistant naval attaché.†

Paul Stillwell: Just to finish up that tour with ComSoLant, maybe you could describe Trinidad as you've described Key West and some of the other places.

Captain Colbus: In Trinidad, we all lived at Macaribe. That was the naval station. We had a big complex out there. During the war that was the amphibious aircraft base. There were ship sinkings right there in Gulf of Paria, which is the body of water between Trinidad and South America.

It's only about 30 miles across—this beautiful island of Trinidad. Again, the caste system. You had the British colonials who were there, and they did very well. All of them were in business. The police force leadership was made up of the British colonials. Being in a British colonial police force was like being in the military. People had rank, and it was very prestigious. An individual was not a policeman; he was an administrator of justice.

Then they had a group of what they called "mixed crowd." I'm talking about mixed backgrounds: some Oriental blood, some Negro blood. They were socially in with everybody else. You had some prominent black people down there who joined this social set of Americans from the base, British colonials who were in business, and the police.

---

* In 1956 Cuban revolutionary Fidel Castro began a guerrilla campaign against the regime of dictator Fulgencio Batista, who had been in power since a revolt in the early 1930s. On 1 January 1959 Batista fled into exile, and Castro seized power. Castro became Prime Minister of Cuba on 16 February 1959.
† Commander Philip H. Klepak, USN.

The mixed blood crowd consisted of some very wealthy Orientals, some Spanish people, and black people.

The blacks were divided then into three groups. The black man who was a native Trinidadian called himself a BeeWee, a British West Indian. He was a laborer from the cane fields and was really what you'd expect to see in a local Trinidadian. Then you had the educated and well-to-do black Trinidadians. They wanted nothing to do with this mixed social crowd because they wanted independence.

They were led by a man named Eric Williams, who was a dictator, a bigot. Talk about a racist, this guy was perfect. He's been written up. He was going to form a coalition of all the Caribbean islands and get rid of the whites. He hated the United States. He was going to take Macaripe and the naval station back because that would be their political headquarters, where they wanted to build their government buildings. Trinidad/Tobago had a governor and a governor general. The governor was black, and the governor general was a Brit. So that was the make-up.

As you'd expect in a climate like that, there was a lot of servants, a lot of good living, a lot of money, many elegant parties, a country club that you just couldn't touch. We stayed out on our base, because we didn't live in town. Everything was on the base. They—"they" being the prominent group—loved to come out to the base, be it to watch the movies, to play bingo, to go to this gorgeous beach. It was a very, very nice time. I was, as I used to claim, the only white bachelor on the island, and if you had an niece, cousin, child, and she was single and on that island, you'd fix me up with her.

I had taken my Buick to Trinidad. That was a big thing in Trinidad: a U.S. car with power brakes and windows. It was a nifty car. Of course, down there they had Jaguars and Rolls, which were common, yet a U.S. car outshone them all. My Buick was licensed to go into Port-of-Spain, 20 miles from the base. That license cost me $700.00! Membership was $11.00 a year to the country club, so I took advantage of that. Therefore, I mingled with the locals since I had wheels and membership. I mean, it was one great life.

Those people were very, very concerned about the future, because this Eric Williams came into great power, and he finally did get us out and he finally did politically take over down there. I haven't kept up with it, except that Trinidad has become independent as Trinidad and Tobago now.*

Paul Stillwell: Why was that the base for ComSoLant?

Captain Colbus: The Panama Canal was close by, and we, at the time, were desirous of keeping a presence there. We needed it, and I'm sure there were some other less obvious reasons. As you know, ComSoLant has gone back to Puerto Rico. They're at Roosevelt Roads now.

Having said all those great things about my friend Admiral Stephan, who now is living the winters in Florida and summers in Silver Spring, he and Admiral Dan Gallery, who was an institution of his own and stationed in Puerto Rico, for some reason or other, were not big admiral buddies.†

As a matter of fact, when we'd use Admiral Gallery's ComCarib Sea Frontier's Convair, we shared it. That was an R4Y. It was Admiral Gallery's, but we could have it any time we wanted it, since both admirals worked for CinCLantFlt. That plane would come down to Trinidad, pick us up, go up to San Juan to refuel, and pick up Admiral Gallery. Admiral Stephan would sit on one side, Admiral Gallery on the other, and they might not speak the whole time en route Washington, which I could never understand.

I knew about Admiral Dan Gallery and his Pandemoniacs, which was a famous steel band. He was deaf; that was one thing. But he and I became buddies. I liked him very much. I saw him as another great character. He and I would sit in the plane and talk at great length. If I'd go up to San Juan by myself on a milk run or go to a conference of communicators, as we did occasionally, I'd stop by and visit with Admiral Dan. He looked like a cigar-store Indian, somber-looking fellow. He could scare you when he stared at you. He was nearly 60 then. As long as you yelled at him, he was your buddy. He'd hear you. I think that was Ed Stephan's problem. He was soft-spoken and never got through to

---

* Trinidad and Tobago achieved independence on 31 August 1962. On 1 August 1976 the country cut its ties with Britain and became a republic, though it did remain in the British Commonwealth.
† Stephan retired as a rear admiral in 1963 and was then recalled to active duty to serve until 31 March 1964. He died at Silver Spring, Maryland, on 5 September 1990 at the age of 83. Rear Admiral Daniel V. Gallery, Jr., USN, who was born 10 July 1901, served as Commander Caribbean Sea Frontier, 1957-60.

Gallery.

Admiral Dan V. Gallery—did you ever read his books?

Paul Stillwell: Sure.

Captain Colbus: What a character. I just thought getting to sit with him on an airplane for two hours was an education.

Paul Stillwell: We have his oral history, and it's a delightful thing.

Captain Colbus: They just don't make them like that anymore, do they?

Paul Stillwell: Not so many.

You were detached from the mainstream of the U.S. Navy on these cruises, away from the normal umbilical. How did you get logistic support and communications support?

Captain Colbus: Well, the fuel stops were port stops. Cars, food, material, etc., were locally purchased, rented, or provided. How we made those distances between ports in the time allotted amazes me. Anyway, we depended upon the shore support as we went along. We didn't have many material problems, as I recall. The ships were relatively new. The DE-1006 class had only been around since the early 1950s, and the DD-931s were new. For the 931s, many of these deployments were maiden voyages. We were also showing these ships off to the South Americans. I remember going out in Mullinnix, my first really demonstration of that ship. The skipper's here in town, I see him occasionally.

Paul Stillwell: Clyde Anderson?*

Captain Colbus: Yes. Do you know him?

---

* Commander Clyde B. Anderson, USN, was the first commanding officer when the USS Mullinnix (DD-944) was commissioned 7 March 1958.

Paul Stillwell: I've interviewed him.*

Captain Colbus: When we took those ships to sea, we'd never seen powerful ships like that.† I claim they're the most powerful ships we built. Now, we hadn't had the DDG-2 class yet.‡ The 931 would ring up flank speed, and the ship would accelerate like an Oldsmobile 88 and take off. When you put the rudder over, the turn was fast and sharp. We'd embark CNOs and admirals and generals and just show off that ship at every port.

We'd also run them hard. We'd go port to port at 33 knots, so you knew we were using fuel like crazy. But we always went port to port and refueled. We didn't even use non-U.S. oilers when we got to South America or Africa. Our crossing of the South Atlantic was a challenge in operational logistics. We went from Trinidad to Dakar in French Equatorial Africa. Then we'd make these short port hops. Freetown was a stop in South Africa. Then from Freetown to the mouth of the Banana River might have been an overnight steam, and we'd ring up 33 knots because we had to be there the next day. Of course, we'd consume all the fuel, then top off at the next port; we never worried about that.

Paul Stillwell: Were you buying your food ashore too?

Captain Colbus: Yes.

Paul Stillwell: How about communications? No problem?

Captain Colbus: No, because what communications we conducted weren't immediate. When we'd get into a lull, we'd get into a situation attributed to sunspot or whatever. We just used the best times of the day to communicate and get our traffic back to the States.

---

* Prior to his destroyer command, Anderson was operations officer of the USS New Jersey (BB-62). He shared his recollections of that ship for Paul Stillwell's book Battleship New Jersey: An Illustrated History (Annapolis: Naval Institute Press, 1986).
† Ships of the Forrest Sherman class had shaft horsepower of 71,500 each and full-load displacement of 4,916 tons—a ratio of 14.5:1 and a maximum speed of nearly 35 knots.
‡ USS Charles F. Adams (DDG-2), first of her class, was commissioned 10 September 1960. Ships of the class had shaft horsepower of about 71,000 each and full-load displacement of 4,526 tons—a ratio of 15.7:1 and a maximum speed of around 34 knots.

No, we didn't as I recall it, have any communications difficulties, because there was no great requirement for the speed or security associated with our naval communications.

Paul Stillwell: Well, winding up that tour, you went from the ComSoLant staff to Monterey. Was that something you had applied for?

Captain Colbus: No, it was just time in my career to go to school. I swung up through Pennsylvania, where I bought a new car, having sold my Buick down in Trinidad. I left Altoona in my new Chrysler Imperial and drove cross-country to Monterey.

Paul Stillwell: What was your curriculum there? How did you choose that?

Captain Colbus: Line school. You didn't choose it. This was a bone-up for people who had not been to sea, and the only thing that I really had to bone up on and had never studied was electronics. The class was made up mainly of aviators. I was one of the few black shoes out there who really didn't need the course because I'd been navigating, I'd been gunnery officer; they didn't teach me any more in engineering than I had learned in NROTC. You really had an NROTC course repeated; that's exactly what it was.

Paul Stillwell: Were they trying to tell you something?

Captain Colbus: No, I don't think so. I'd had enough education that I figured I didn't need to go to postgraduate school. That was for engineers. I had no background in engineering, no math, so what else was there? That was ten months of lascivious living. That was 1960. I lived on the beach right next to the Frank Lloyd Wright house that was featured in the movie Summer Place, which was filmed right there.* So, there again, I'm in this glamorous area. That's what I joined the Navy for. Ladies all over the place.

San Francisco was at its height then as far as—we didn't talk Haight-Ashbury, we talked North Shore.† The Coexistence Bagel Shop. Beatniks were everywhere. That was

---

* Frank Lloyd Wright was a noted American architect.
† The Haight-Ashbury section of San Francisco became notorious in the late 1960s as a center of the hippies—the drug scene, counter culture, and anti-Vietnam War movement.

the thing. I brought my brother out there as a young college boy and took him to San Francisco; he just didn't believe it. It was Hollywood central casting: "Send me the beatniks." And then they'd come down to Carmel. Of course, Carmel has never been a slouch area.

Paul Stillwell: You're right.

Captain Colbus: Here I was in this gorgeous cottage/guest house, next to this famous mansion built by Frank Lloyd Wright, looking down at the beach, and every weekend all the folks would be on the beach. I'd go down to the beach, meet the folks, use my place as their headquarters and for changing, partying—you name it. I thought the glamour and fast living were all over when I left Africa and South America. But this was fantastic. That was for ten months. Again, lots of bachelor buddies out there, and we just had a really great time.

Except for this electronics course, the only other subject I had trouble with was meteorology. It was similar to learning navigation. All of a sudden, one day it came to me, "Oh, now I understand what he's talking about—the weather." We also studied physics, which was new to me. But in answer to your question, it was more a social time for me than anything else. I met a lot of people.

Every time I went to a school—ASW school, line school, war college, and the Idaho Falls engineering school—I established friendships that still are meaningful. And the cross-fertilization or pollination, whatever you call it, was really worth more than anything else you acquired. You met other people, other naval officers from other communities. You met naval officers from your own community, and you saw fellows who weren't shipmates and got an entirely different view. You learned that they're not all like they were in Albert T. Harris. All of a sudden, everybody wasn't a true blue, 4.0, great shipmate. There might be an odd guy in the crowd.

That was a rude awakening for me, because I thought everybody in my Navy was perfect. I had never run into anything but warmth and camaraderie. In my experience all the competition had been friendly. Now, all of a sudden, this associate competes because he has to be number one in the class in order to graduate, and you saw this. That was a shocker to me.

Paul Stillwell: Some of these officers came out of the Naval Academy, where they'd been brought up that way, so it was no problem.

Captain Colbus: A few got into a school environment and they turned into absolute lechers. We also had a lot of foreigners enrolled, and that was interesting. We got to know a lot of the people from other navies—junior officers, of course; we were all junior. And Monterey and Carmel were ideal. I was there from February till December.

Paul Stillwell: How would you evaluate the instructors in the courses you took?

Captain Colbus: Everywhere from excellent to indifferent. Some of them were out there strictly for the rest. Some of them were bitter, because back then instructor duty at the line school was not considered top drawer. For instance, if you had a commander teaching you engineering, he was lucky to be a commander and unhappy as hell that he didn't have a destroyer.

Paul Stillwell: And would it be fair to say that they were unlikely to become captains?

Captain Colbus: Yes. Many of them were on their twilight tours. At the same time, many of them just enjoyed life and were very, very pleasant about the whole thing. It was a pretty wide range.

Paul Stillwell: Were most or all of the instructors naval officers, as opposed to civilians?

Captain Colbus: We had, as I recall, two civilians. One, who taught psychology, was a young fellow, 28 years old, who was very dynamic, Mr. Deither Brumbaker or Brumbach. He was a breath of fresh air and had a great, great admiration for naval officers. He really was impressed with people in the Navy, and told us what great psychologists we were, so it was a good "love" affair. He told us how great we were; we loved it because we hadn't been told that by the rest of the staff. And he was a very, very good teacher.

In fact, the most helpful course I was exposed to out there was called personal finance. It taught me subjects that were most helpful on a day-to-day basis. An example: the Contingency Option Act. What is that? Those were the days when you had to elect in your 18th year—not your 19th year, your 18th year—whether you wanted to become a player in the insurance program that allowed your retirement to go on. We call it SBP today.

Paul Stillwell: Survivor Benefit Plan.[*]

Captain Colbus: Yes. The Contingency Option Act had four variations to it. Anyway, you learned all these details. It was interesting. The one thing I carried away that did me well in my next ship was this knowledge on the COA—that you had to commit in your 18th year. The first thing I did as the exec aboard my next ship, USS John R. Perry, was to muster the senior people. This was on the mess deck—a lot of first class, all the chiefs, one or two officers, including one mustang who had maybe 15 years in.[†] I asked for a show of hands and said, "How many of you realize that your retirement dies when you do?"

"Oh, no, no, you're wrong, XO, you're wrong."

Everybody thought his pension just went on after he died. The next thing I told them was, "And you have to elect in your 18th year; you must make a decision." All of a sudden, the senior people found out that here was somebody who not only knew but who was interested. As I say, that course did me more good in my next tours than, I guess, anything else, because as I said, the other material I'd already had in NROTC. So that was a worthwhile experience just for that one bit of knowledge. I didn't realize how fouled up people's financial lives were. Being a bachelor, all I did was keep gas in the car and buy some beer now and then.

---

[*] Essentially this plan permits an about-to-be-retired service member to opt for a reduced annuity in retirement, in which case the member's spouse will receive an annuity after the death of the service member.
[†] "Mustang" is Navy slang for a former enlisted man who has risen through the ranks to become an officer.

Paul Stillwell: Did the psychology course help you as a better leader?

Captain Colbus: I don't think so. I read today, and all the things I hear about leadership were instilled in us at home through religious training and by our senior officers. When we went aboard ship—I'm talking about all of us—we were so delighted to start earning a salary, so pleased to be there. And we realized that we were given advantages and opportunities that required commitments. These commitments included 15 to 30 people who looked to you for leadership guidance. We practiced "Follow me." What a thrill that was. We took it seriously. We worked diligently at our duties as division officers. Our seniors were true role models who worked and played with us. We just did it. Today they preach about it. I don't understand that.

All four of the division officers in <u>Albert T. Harris</u> walked aboard the ship as ensigns within a week of each other. When I look back today, I can say that every one of us was a natural leader and division officer who just took to it and worked, learned, and associated with our shipmates. We met in staterooms, working on courses, explaining and discussing subjects with shipmates—chastising them and walking about the decks with them. We all just did that.

We didn't have too many technical distractions. We didn't know computer printouts, and that's what the young fellows have told me about today's Navy. I say, "Why don't you fellows just get out there? It thrills me when I see you walking around, leaning over, looking into some sailor's chipping hammer as he fixes his goggles."

"It's not our job today. Our job today is to make sure all this stuff runs properly." They're so tied up to the technical end of it.

Paul Stillwell: Did you have mustangs in that course at the General Line School in 1960?

Captain Colbus: Boy, did we. Do you want to hear about Charlie McComis?

Paul Stillwell: Sure.

Captain Colbus: Charlie McComis was a mustang.[*] If I was 29, Charlie was close to 40.[†] I was driving a new Chrysler Imperial, a beautiful car. He rode up in a Cadillac. He was a lieutenant, older than I, senior to me. Well, I'd been a lieutenant two years. Then Charlie McComis suddenly showed up with an Oldsmobile station wagon. Hmm. Charlie McComis had an airplane. Charlie McComis lived out at Pebble Beach. Well, he and I became friends. He had a wife and two little children, and I think he had a grown kid or two.

Charlie told about entering the Navy in 1941. This was now 1960. Charlie McComis had been around a lot. He said when he was waiting to come into the Navy on a quota system back in the Depression days, he was hanging around the gas station. He would wipe somebody's window for a tip, anything to get some pocket change. One of his customers would give him a nickel when he wiped the windshield. This fellow was always dressed in a suit and driving a Buick car. He said to Charlie, "And when you get in the Navy, son, and you have extra money, you send it to me so I can look after it."

And Charlie took the man up on it, even though he was making only $21.00 in those days.[‡] He worked as a mess cook for the chiefs, so they gave him an extra $5.00 a month. And Charlie would send $20.00 home, or he'd send $15.00 home. During the war, he became a chief petty officer. He was an aviation storekeeper, I believe. He told me he was in his carrier for three years and never went ashore. He knew the ropes as a young chief petty officer. I don't think I can get him in trouble telling this story. He was running floating crap games, perhaps sending thousands home now. He was sending serious money back to his buddy, the banker. He got out in 1946 and went back to his hometown. He wanted to buy a new Ford car, which cost, he said, about $1,500. He went down to see his "banker." He walked in and said, "I want $1,800."

"Well, you have to wait two days."

"What do you mean, I have to wait two days?"

"Oh, because I have to sell your stocks."

"What stocks?"

---

[*] Lieutenant Charles W. McComis, USN.
[†] McComis was born 11 September 1923.
[‡] In the early 1940s the monthly base pay was $21.00 for an apprentice seaman, $36.00 for a seaman second class, and $54.00 for a seaman first class.

"Stocks I've been buying."

"Where's my money? You're a banker."

"No, no, I'm not a banker; I'm a stockbroker." So all those years, Charlie had been putting his money into stocks, and I don't have to tell you how they had grown in that period. So that was the big mustang in our class; he was an extremely wealthy man. He bought the plane to fly his family to Disneyland. Yes, we did have mustangs.

Paul Stillwell: How would you characterize them as a group? Were they eager to learn or just coasting along?

Captain Colbus: They were very aggressive and eager to learn—more so than I. As I said, I was sort of resting on my laurels as an accomplished but inexperienced naval officer among that group. Of course, the aviators had come to me and asked me all these surface questions.

Dick Donnelly ended up being the number-one man in the class.[*] He's a commodore today, serving up in Washington.[†] Dick had the same background that I did, yet he was very driven. He was one of those students who'd go home at night and do his homework. I'd go out and chase girls and drink whiskey. He ended up number one, a 4.0 record, while he was in line school.

Paul Stillwell: Were the aviators very conscientious about trying to make up for shortcomings in their backgrounds?

Captain Colbus: No. When they would work hard and compete, it was as fighter pilots or whatever their community was. It was to keep up: "No one's going to catch me with my pants down." "Louis, if you make an 85, I sure can do that. I don't care about surpassing you, but I'm going to keep up with you." And they did.

---

[*] Lieutenant Richard F. Donnelly, USN.
[†] For a few years in the mid-1980s, including the time of this interview, the one-star rank in the Navy and Coast Guard was known as commodore. It was subsequently changed to rear admiral (lower half), the title now in use.

On the other hand, they didn't want to do too well, because if they were seen as taking to this stuff, they were going to end up in a "boat." That's where I learned my first lesson in the carrier Navy. Aviators don't want to be in a carrier as part of ship's company! Black shoes don't want to be in a carrier because it's too big, and one can't show off as he could in a destroyer. My question was, "Who's manning the carriers?" I could never figure that out until I got aboard a carrier. Aviators wanted to fly on and fly off, but they didn't want to serve as part of the ship's crew.

Paul Stillwell: But they wanted to be COs, though, eventually, didn't they?

Captain Colbus: Yes, but I guess they weren't thinking of that at a young age. They were just good aviators. The aviators excelled, of course, in meteorology. They excelled in engineering, strangely enough, though it's not strange when you analyze it. I found that to be true when I was a captain going to school with aviators at Idaho Falls. They would think in systems. To them it was a system. And most of them had engineering backgrounds. When a fellow got into flight training, he probably had an engineering background, maybe mechanical or electrical. So he did well in engineering, and he did well in electronics. And they did well in meteorology since they were so weather-conscious.

Paul Stillwell: The aviators say they don't have too much problem making a transition to ships because it's relative motion, and they've known that in the air. Did you see that aspect?

Captain Colbus: Yes. I saw that back in <u>Albert T. Harris</u>. At the end of my three years, an officer named Bill Myers reported aboard. He was a former aviator who had lived through a midair collision at 1,500 feet; he was a very serious man. He had a sense of humor, but he was more serious than the rest of us. When he'd tell why he transitioned into destroyers from aviation and gave up his wings, he talked about this midair collision. After lying in the hospital for six months in traction, he said, "I had some very serious thoughts. I just lost my incentive to fly." Damn right he did.

Anyway, he came on board as the ops officer. This was his first ship. It took him three weeks to relieve me as the senior watch officer. I was to teach him everything I knew. When signals came over the radio to maneuver the squadron, he'd very quickly translate them mentally into relative motion. He knew he wanted to be over there, and he'd point and say, "I want to be over there about 4,000 yards. How do I get there?"

"Oh, you say, 'Right standard rudder.'" All he needed was the terminology. He could see that relative motion. We were doing 18 knots, and he was used to 200 knots. The same thing happened at line school. The aviators understand systems, they understand speed, and they are very quick to react.

Now that I'm older and wiser, I think the fighter pilots probably have the quickest minds of anybody I've ever been around, with due respect to my attack pilot friends. They're very keen. I'm talking about their wit, their response. They're never at a loss for a quick, sharp, succinct answer. That's because they're in that environment, plus they're very competitive.

Paul Stillwell: I wonder if it's the environment that produces the individuals or if there's a natural selection that picks this kind of person to be a fighter pilot.

Captain Colbus: I think it's A. I think it's just that they develop that discipline in that environment.

Paul Stillwell: How was the social life when you were at line school?

Captain Colbus: It was just tremendous. This was where you got to know all your associates very well, because now we were living in a civilian community. The BOQ rooms were few and far between. We'd never before received an allowance to live ashore. All of us went to live in Carmel. Now this separated the men from the boys, so to speak. The sailors were interested in the good life—the serious R&R from Friday till Sunday--were living in Carmel. Money was no object; their motto was, "A few cents more--go first class!" I spent over $2,000 more than I made in those ten months. That was serious money in 1960.*

      Happy hour with these aviators on a Friday night in downtown Carmel would start out with four of us bachelor students. Pretty soon six good-looking schoolteachers would join us. Carmel was populated with schoolteachers. We'd end up with 12, 14 people partying all night. The bill would come, and it would be $85.00 split four ways. Well, when you made only $400.00 a month, you can see how our funds had to be stretched. We lived very, very well out there, played hard, and didn't have that much studying to do.

Paul Stillwell: You talked about the cross-pollination. Was that valuable for you getting exposed to aviators and so forth?

Captain Colbus: I think so. If you were a career man, you were going to meet and work with these fellows, as I did later on in my career—on staffs, at war college, and work with them at sea. In my case, I went aboard carriers, and there they were.

Paul Stillwell: Were there submariners in this also?

Captain Colbus: No, I don't remember one submariner. If there were, they were running silent and deep. They have their own pipeline, their own training. I don't mean to take away from them; they don't need outsiders to train them. They do very well on their own.

Paul Stillwell: On balance, would you say that this tour made you a better naval officer?

Captain Colbus: Any exposure to others will help, be it in school or seminars. It convinced me that I was in the right profession. Where else could you get paid to live in Carmel, California, where everybody thought it was smart to go to happy hours and have a different girlfriend every night of the week? It was very good for a young fellow.

---

* As a lieutenant with six years' longevity, Colbus received the following monthly: basic pay, $440.00; basic allowance for subsistence, $47.88; basic allowance for quarters, $85.50. The monthly total was $573.38, and the annual total was $6,880.56.

Louis Colbus, Interview #1 (8/30/84) – Page 116

Paul Stillwell: Then you went to the John R. Perry. Please tell me about that tour.

Captain Colbus: John R. Perry was a new ship.* I went aboard as exec, and my first skipper was a great man named G. G. Ely Kirk—George Griswold Ely Kirk.† He was right out of the book, right out of Winds of War.‡ He was colorful, glamorous, extremely capable, one hell of a leader, loved good times, and was an elegant gentleman, liked the good life, and knew how to run that ship. He gave the ship to me and just let me do everything I wanted. Once in a while, he would take a round turn just to let me know he was the skipper.§ It was a very, very fine tour.

I relieved in Key West. The next day we were going from Key West directly to Charleston to dry-dock the ship. The purpose was to update the sonar dome. It would require about two to three weeks of dry-docking in Charleston. Well, I talked about this new car I had, which was a gorgeous Imperial that I had now brought to Key West. I'd had a good time at line school for ten months, and that was all over. It was time to go to work and earn my living as the exec of a destroyer. I was going to be all business and give up the wild living. In fact, I decided to leave the car in Key West and not even take it to Charleston.

By the way, when I got my orders as exec, Captain Flash Dailey gave me a book entitled Tragedy at Honda, which was about the navigation disaster in 1923.** Well, I read that book, and, boy, I'll tell you, I was not cocky about navigating a ship. I'd done it but never as the navigator. So I was cautious and rightfully so, meticulous to the point where I was an old lady. Plus I had this new image—no boozing, no chasing. I was the exec.

Paul Stillwell: You were going to be Mr. Serious now.

---

* USS John R. Perry (DE-1034) was a Claud Jones-class destroyer escort commissioned 5 May 1959. She had a standard displacement of 1,314 tons, was 312 feet long, and 38 feet in the beam. Her design speed was 21.5 knots. She was armed with two 3-inch guns and six 21-inch torpedo tubes.
† Lieutenant Commander Kirk commanded USS John R. Perry from 21 September 1960 to 30 May 1962.
‡ Herman Wouk, Winds of War (Boston: Little, Brown, 1971). This is a massive novel that depicts the events leading up to World War II through a series of fictitious characters.
§ In nautical phraseology, taking a round turn means putting two loops of line over a bitt or bollard, thus restraining the ship at the other end of the line. In a figurative sense, it means restraining unwanted behavior.
** Charles A. Lockwood and Hans Christian Adamson, Tragedy at Honda (Philadelphia: Chilton, 1960).

Captain Colbus: Exactly. This is really about Ely Kirk. We departed Key West for Charleston with Ely as CO and me as XO. Our quartermaster was a petty officer first class, QM1 George Chovan from Cleveland. What a 4.0 shipmate he was. True, old-timey sailor who was probably the best navigator I've ever seen. I remember his hands; he had hands like a bear. He himself was a big man, but he used those hands with great skill and delicacy. He could make the most cautious erasure on a chart and pen-and-ink a buoy on there. You'd have thought an artist did it. He was just great. He taught me how to navigate, including the tricks of the trade: "Yes, you may turn the sextant upside down when you shoot the stars at night."

"I never knew you could do that."

"It's all right if you know what you're doing."

Well, we arrived at the mouth of the Cooper River in Charleston. Ely Kirk had been there before with my predecessor. He rang up 22 knots and steamed up that river. I was lost! I couldn't lay down fixes that fast. I don't think Magellan could lay down fixes in the Cooper River at 22 knots. I said to him, "I'm not fixing this ship."

"Why not, XO?"

I said, "We're going too fast. I recommend we slow to ten knots."

He said, "You don't understand the current in this river."

Silence.

I said, "I'm not fixing the ship at any intervals. It's been six minutes now. We don't have a thing. I'm worried."

He said, "Don't worry about it. I know this river. I'm going to proceed."

So I turned to the junior quartermaster who was keeping the log, and, in front of the captain, I said, "Log that."

Paul Stillwell: I presume you had no pilot on board.

Captain Colbus: Oh, no.

Well, I thought he was going to throw me off the bridge right then, and that was the end of my exec's tour. However, I wasn't going to be part of this grounding. That's a treacherous river. Well, we proceeded, and he never did slow down. I was just standing there, doing my best, watching buoys go by. Of course, then we had ranges. Once we got on a range, I felt more comfortable, but it wasn't good. We moored the ship. By the way, on the way up there, we created such a wake that we rocked a few of the local yachts, caused a few complaints, and we were criticized for ship speeding. Yes, we got a speeding ticket. The skipper was going to be chastised, and I have to tell you who bailed him out.

The officer who was then the chief of staff for Commander Destroyer Flotilla Six, was Gene La Rocque, who's now famous up there in Washington.[*] Gene La Rocque was probably the best friend a sailor ever had. He would do anything for us destroyer men. We thought very, very highly of him during that tour. If you were a visitor in Charleston, you got the best treatment.

We arrived in time for cocktail hour. (That was Kirk's modus operandi.) The captain didn't fire me. He put his head in my door and asked, "XO, going to the club?"

"No, sir, I have work to do." I was setting up files, doing all this administrative stuff. This was probably my fourth or fifth day on board. No car.

He said, "Okay," and he left.

Next day, of course, we had arrival conferences and all the business it takes to get the ship organized. I learned everything that's supposed to be learned during that cycle.

By the way, the fellow I relieved took me to the XO's stateroom, which I was about to take over from him. He opened the medicine cabinet and said, "I'll just leave all this."

"What is it?"

"Tranquilizers, Pepto-Bismol." I learned that he'd get up from the luncheon table, go in his room and throw up, he'd be so upset.

Ely Kirk's predecessor would sit at the wardroom table and hold court: "All right, what about so and so?" He held his meetings while having meals. That's when I learned, rather emphasized my learning, that you never discuss anything businesslike at a meal, because you may embarrass someone. Ely wasn't like that, but this XO was still recoiling from the previous skipper, Tiny Atkinson.[†] Anyway, I don't take medicines. Why I

---

[*] Captain Gene R. La Rocque, USN, served as chief of staff to Commander Destroyer Flotilla Six in 1961-62. In May 1962 the command was redesignated Cruiser-Destroyer Flotilla Six. He subsequently retired as a rear admiral in 1972 and became the head of the Center for Defense Information in Washington, D.C. The organization is noted for having views different from those of the Defense Department.
[†] Lieutenant Commander Wilton L. Atkinson, USN, commanded USS John R. Perry from the ship's commissioning on 5 May 1959 to 21 September 1960.

mention this is that the next day I was really getting into this thing. I found there was a lot to do on this ship, and I was now the exec. I found out that things weren't as sweet as they should be, and I had some projects to do.

Second day. Skipper came by and said, "XO, you going ashore?"

"No, sir, I have some things to do."

He said, "I'm inviting you to cocktail hour."

"That's very nice, Captain, but look at me. I walked the ship today, and I've got to get all this stuff done so I'm ready for tomorrow."

He said, "I'll send a car back for you later on."

I said, "No, no thank you, sir. Don't care to." That was the second night.

The third night was a Friday. He told me, "I don't care what you have to do. If you can't go steaming with me, you're not my exec. There's more to this than just this on-board relationship. I want to see you on the beach."

"Yes, sir."

"I'll send a car back for you at 7:00 o'clock."

"Yes, sir." I got dressed and at 7:00 o'clock, he sent the ship's car back for me. I hit the beach with him, and that was it! Goodbye, Charlie! He and I went several places, and we ended up down at Francis Marion Hotel that Friday night. I think we left there at 4:00 in the morning. We didn't know how to get back since we had ditched the Navy car. We had a ball. This man was my big buddy now. Ely would walk into a place, take it over, and wipe it up. He is one of the most charismatic men I've ever known.

Saturday, I got up, held quarters, and took care of the ship's business. I asked, "Captain, how often are we going to do this?"

He said, "Every night."

I said, "We need wheels." I went out to a used-car lot on Mendel Rivers Road and bought a 1952 Chrysler. I came back, and Ely Kirk and I tore up Charleston for the next three weeks. We became very, very good, close friends. That whole wardroom was a good wardroom. Here I was again in an environment where those guys could just work all day long. They had that ship looking like a yacht. There wasn't a ship around that was as good-looking and squared away as USS John R. Perry. People were happy because they were proud of the ship.

I introduced things such as playing musical tapes. This was when sonar was coming into its own and we had big tape recorders. I would play "Reveille" on a tape recorder for everybody. Ely would have guests at night for formal sit-down dinners. He turned the signal bridge into a dance floor, and we'd have a Navy band come on board to play dance music while we had dinner under the stars. What a time. And that's what I did with Ely Kirk.

Paul Stillwell: So you lasted about a week as Mr. Serious.

Captain Colbus: No, not even that long—four or five days. We arrived in Charleston on a Tuesday, and by Friday I was with the boys. That was a great crowd. We really had a good ship and a good time.

When we took the ship to Gitmo, Robert Edward Brady, who now lives in Arnold, Maryland, relieved Ely.[*] He's in the state comptroller's office. He was completely opposite: quiet, serious, with the deepest disguised sense of humor of anybody I've ever known. Bob was fantastic! He came aboard, didn't turn things around, but gave it a much more relaxed atmosphere.

With Ely we were always pushing to do something, as I said. On the weekend I always had some kind of a starlight dance on the flag bridge or was sending the steward out to buy a case of some stuff that was effervescent and you thought you were drinking champagne, only it was non-alcoholic. Then with Bob Brady, it was all business. He wasn't that interested in raising hell and terrorizing the natives. We did a lot of steaming with the ship and Captain Brady.

Paul Stillwell: Is there anything memorable about the yard period that you can relate?

Captain Colbus: Yes. Admiral Charlie Weakley came down in his flagship, the tender Yosemite.[†] His aide was a good friend of mine named Jim Thearle, who's here in town

---

[*] Brady, then a lieutenant commander, commanded USS John R. Perry from 30 May 1962 to 21 April 1964.
[†] Rear Admiral Charles E. Weakley, USN, commanded Destroyer Force Atlantic Fleet from 21 January 1960 to 14 October 1961.

now, a Navy captain about to retire.* Thearle and had I worked for Admiral Lloyd Montague Mustin in the late '50s. Thearle was the aide, I was the flag sec. Thearle was a roommate of Mustin's son Hank at the Naval Academy.† He and I had become friends on Mustin's staff, and now he was the flag lieutenant for Admiral Charlie Weakley. They were there in Charleston to do inspections.

Getting to know the admiral was a great experience. He had more charisma in a quiet way than anybody I've ever been around. The man was absolutely the epitome of a gentleman who really cared for those around him. Whether you were a lieutenant or a fellow flag officer, you were treated the same. He was very involved with you when talking to you.

About every morning the flagship was in Charleston, I'd go over and have breakfast or lunch on board. He had a doctor on the staff, Captain Joy, who was gray-haired and distinguished.‡ He was called the "Silver Fox," and he was something special. The staff came to town, and that was a memorable week for many reasons, social and professional. One learned a lot by being around these senior officers because they would critique everything at the end of the day. I was privileged to sit in at their mess at least once a day and hear what was going on—not business but I guess you'd call it gossip. That was a memorable situation. And I got to know Admiral Weakley, which I consider a highlight of my career.

Paul Stillwell: He was Mr. ASW.

Captain Colbus: Oh, absolutely. He smoked a cigarette using a cigarette holder, the same as FDR.§ But it wasn't an affectation for the admiral; it was natural. He was, as I said, a very, very fine gentleman.

---

* Lieutenant William James Thearle, USN.
† Henry C. Mustin graduated from the Naval Academy in the class of 1955; he eventually retired from active duty in 1988 as a vice admiral.
‡ Captain Ernest H. Joy, MC, USN.
§ FDR—President Franklin D. Roosevelt.

Paul Stillwell: Do you have any examples of this subtle sense of humor of Brady, your second skipper?

Captain Colbus: Yes, but things that I can't say. I recall things that he said in front of his wife and mine, but I don't think the remarks would look right in print. He was serious-looking, which only added to his sense of humor. As a matter of fact, when I went on to the war college years later and he was CruDesLant's ASW officer, he came down to the school to speak. By then people at the school knew me and when they met him and found out I had been his exec, somebody said, "How did you get along with that guy? What a heavy."

I answered, "No, no, no, no. You missed the whole thing."

He was an outstanding ship handler. John R. Perry was a single-screw ship, but Bob Brady could do anything with it. I hope I haven't used this term too much, but he was probably the most competent naval officer I've been around. He was a destroyer man's destroyer man. I'll give you an example of this great skipper. He was mooring the ship one day and showing us how to do it. I was standing beside him, and he was doing everything perfectly. A pretty heavy wind was blowing there in Key West. He was doing all the right things. Everybody was tense and alert, and the skipper was as cool as a cucumber.

He looked upon the pier on mooring. Of course, Key West in the summertime produced some scantily dressed ladies. There was a dependent on the pier, and she had less than short shorts on. It was very obvious that she was going to catch somebody's eye. The captain finally gave his last bell, looked down at her, looked at me, and smacked his lips. And that was the end of that. He never made a remark, but he acknowledged that there was that good-looking lady in short shorts on the pier. Other people didn't see that. He only did that in my earshot. That's the type of sense of humor he had. His wife Helen was very outgoing. Their son is a lieutenant in the Navy today.

Bob Brady relieved Ely Kirk down in Gitmo. Let me give you an idea of how we operated down there. Ely Kirk, as I've indicated, was a very social man and a Navy politician extraordinaire. When we got arrived at Gitmo, we found out that the training officer, which was a big job, was Captain Art Damon. You remember he was the skipper of <u>Fechteler</u> when I went aboard as an ensign to observe gunfire drills. He and I had gone to Boston together, partied together, and got in trouble together.

I've got to tell you that, back in <u>Albert T. Harris</u> days, I went by my skipper's house one night to say, "Captain, I'm going to Boston. I have a date at Boston University, so I'll see you on the ship Monday."

As I was leaving, Art Damon, who lived next door to my skipper in Newport, came running out and yelled, "Hey, Louis, where you going?"

"I'm going to Boston, Captain."

"May I ride along?"

"Oh, sure."

He said, "Give me two minutes." So he ran in, came out with a little suitcase, threw it in the car, and we were on our way up to Boston, an ensign and a commander. When we got to Boston, Damon said, "Where are you staying?"

"I'm staying at this hotel. I've got a room."

"I'll stay with you."

"Great."

"Now what are you doing?"

"I'm going out to pick up . . ."

He said, "I'll go with you." He didn't have anything to do, so he became my shadow.

Well, we went out, and I got my girlfriend, who's since married and now lives in Belmont, Massachusetts. I picked her up from the dorm, and Art went along with us, so there were the three of us. We went steaming, visited all the college places, and had a hell of a good time. We did that Friday night, Saturday night, and drove home Sunday.

As we arrived at Art's house and I let him out, his wife Mary came out and read me the riot act as to how I led him astray and that I was just another no-good naval officer. So here was Ensign Colbus with Commander Damon, and I said, "He's a grown man. Talk to your husband. Don't talk to me about it." I finally got out of there. I didn't care for her any more than she cared for me. That was in 1955.

We are now in Gitmo in 1962. Captain Damon and his wife Mary were down there. I was reading the roster, and I said, "Oh, there's Captain Damon, the training officer."

"Do you know him, Louis?" asked Captain Kirk.

"Oh, yes, I know him real well."

"How do you know him?"

"First ship." And that was all I said. Well, we went to the arrival conference, and old Art came over and grabbed me by the shoulders. He hugged me and said, "Hey, Louis."

"Hey, Captain, nice to see you."

"This is great. We'll have to get together."

"Yes, sir."

We left there, and the captain was mad as hell. He said, "Why didn't you ask him down to the ship?"

"Yes, sir."

"In fact, tonight we'll just go call on him. You go calling."

"No, sir, we're not going near his house."

"Why do you say that?" And I told him quickly what I've just told you.

"Oh, I don't believe you. You don't know the guy."

"Okay, let's just drop it. I'm not going near his wife. I mean, she was really angry with me."

By the way, they'd been divorced two times and remarried. He's not married to Mary today, and I tell this in front of him and his new wife, whom I know very well.

Anyway, to drag this story out, I invited him down to the ship for lunch. He came aboard, and everything went fine. We were still not going to his house. I kept saying, "No, Captain. No, Captain."

I guess we'd been there about a week when we had a casualty to our engineering plant. We could get under way, but we couldn't do engineering drills. This happened on a Sunday. They told the skipper we were not going to be able to meet our engineering schedule.

"Okay." The skipper then instructed me: "Here's what I want you to do, XO. Go up to the fleet training center and switch everything because we can do our gunnery this week. Let's just flip-flop. Next week we'll do the engineering when we have everything back on the line. That pneumatic clutch won't allow us to do casualty drills."

"Yes, sir, Captain." So I went up, put the arm on some lieutenant up there, scheduled it, and flip-flopped everything. I then went to the beach, walked up to Ely Kirk, and reported, "Captain, mission completed."

"Good, XO. Sit down, let me buy you a beer."

"Thank you." Well, I was sitting there having a beer in my uniform. Then across the beach came Art Damon, in shorts and very red-faced. He came over, grabbed me physically, and read the riot act to me: "Who the hell do you think you are, coming down to Gitmo, some snot-nose lieutenant, just because you know me and are taking advantage of my name. How can you go down there and change everything in my training schedule? How about other ships? You're selfish."

Then he turned on Ely and took off on him: "And you probably sent him to do it because he wouldn't do it unless you blessed it. You guys come down here, and you're the guy who says you can do this course in five weeks; you'll be lucky to be out of here in eight weeks." And this was in front of everybody. Art Damon then turned around and stormed off.

I said, "See?"

"Yeah, oh, well."

I said, "And it's worse when his wife's around."

About the third or fourth week, Bob Brady showed up. The change of command was going to take place, so Bob Brady would finish the training. As true as I tell you, on Friday night our ship's officers went up to the club: the PCO, the CO, myself, and the rest of the wardroom. We were quietly sitting there.

Across the room were Art and his wife Mary. She spotted me, came over and glared at me, and started in, "Well, I hear you got up out of the gutter and did the marriage bit. I heard you got married." She then read the riot act to me in front of everybody. I thought, "Oh, boy, I don't need this." She told me what a lousy person I was, that I was a poor leader, that I didn't deserve to wear a uniform, and she pitied the entire wardroom that had to live with me. She then walked away.

Poor Bob Brady was new to all of this and said, "What happened?"

And I said to Kirk, "See?"

"Man, I guess I know now why you didn't want to go calling on those people."

Well, somehow or other there was a pact, and we got together. We bought them some drinks and they came over, and before you know it, Ely Kirk had both of them eating out of his hand, as only he could do. Next we went to their home. We got in the car, and that was a scene to behold. We went there about 60 miles an hour, and the Damons were arguing.

Well, by the time we got to the house, it was so bad that this new skipper—this quiet, reserved Bob Brady—just didn't know how he got into this crossfire. During the argument that occurred at the house after we left the club, all of a sudden Art turned on Bob Brady, the new skipper, and said, "I know your type. You came from the bureau, didn't you?"

"Yes, sir, Captain."

"Well, you sons of guns sit up there and you wait until you see a nice new ship like this one. You get a fine exec like this who's going to keep you out of trouble, and you just come down here and live off this guy. You're a leech!" He picked on Bob Brady for being a BuPers guy who happened to get a good ship. We ended up walking home that night. But that was the flavor of Gitmo at the time.

Paul Stillwell: So did you get your people trained?

Captain Colbus: Yes, sir. When it was all over, Art came out, he himself rode the ship for our ORI, gave us an up-check, and made sure that we were kosher.*

Paul Stillwell: There is one question I meant to ask earlier. We know this long pipeline training they have now at PCO and PXO school. Was there anything like that then?

---

* ORI—operational readiness inspection.

Captain Colbus: No, absolutely not. This was, as I said, '62 when Bob Brady came aboard. I'd just married.* Ely Kirk and his wife were my witnesses. No, you did your tours, on-the-job training and then came to the ship. I think you might have passed through the force headquarters and gotten some briefings, but no schools.

Paul Stillwell: Any more memories of Captain La Rocque during that period?

Captain Colbus: No.

Paul Stillwell: Any professional reputation he had among destroyer men then?

Captain Colbus: Yes, that which I said. He was looked up to and did a fine job and was a good chief of staff. He kept you out of trouble, and you never heard from the admiral, Red Ailes, whose son Bob is an admiral today.†

Paul Stillwell: With this great social life you've been describing, how did you manage to get married?

Captain Colbus: Well, since you asked, all I had to do in John R. Perry was say, "We have to do such-and-such. Do it well, and I'll work the skipper over and get a stop in Fort Lauderdale." "Where the Boys Are" was the popular theme then. We'd visit Fort Lauderdale quite often. We'd be on station monitoring the Polaris test shoots.‡ This would occur off Bermuda, where we would spend about two weeks. Then we would visit Fort Lauderdale, gas up, and return to station for another three weeks.

As a bachelor, I had the funds to get a hotel room, which we made into what we called the admin. I didn't stay there; I'd always go back to the ship, but we'd use the hotel room as our headquarters. On this particular visit, Ely and I were in the cocktail lounge,

---
* The wedding was on 1 December 1961.
† Rear Admiral John W. Ailes III, USN; the son is Rear Admiral Robert H. Ailes, USN.
‡ The first version of the Polaris missile, the A-1, was 28 feet long, 4« feet in diameter, and weighed about 30,000 pounds. It had a range of 1,200 nautical miles. The missile entered fleet service in 1960 in the ballistic missile submarine George Washington (SSBN-598).

having a grand time. He'd been out golfing, and I was in the bar at the Jolly Roger with two ladies I'd met on the beach. These were two girls I'll never forget. They were dancing instructresses from Cincinnati, just what you'd expect two Arthur Murray dance instructresses to be: good-looking and outgoing. We were there wining and dining them.

A group that was on a nightclub tour arrived at the lounge. One of the ladies who walked in was a genuine knockout, about 5 feet, 6 inches, dark hair, beautiful big eyes—an extremely busty gal with a tiny waist. She was wearing a very fashionable dress that was open all the way down the back. This beauty was with an older woman. (I later learned that she was about 40 and an Army widow.) I called the waiter over. I asked him to take these women my card and drinks.

Then I went over myself to meet these two ladies and get to know them. The good-looking one would have nothing to do with me. (She later told me I was obnoxious and fresh.) She wouldn't even talk. I said, "By the way, I have a beautiful ship down here, if you girls would care to see the ship."

The older woman said, "I have two teenage daughters who would love to see your ship."

"Give me a call. Here I am."

Next day, I got the call, missed the call, called again. She'd like to see the ship. I said, "Tell you what. Have you wheels?"

"Yes."

"Why don't you come by here, and we'll go down and see the ship at 5:00 o'clock this afternoon." This was a Saturday. At 5:00 o'clock, up rolls this beautiful four-door Buick Electra. No children, just these two women again. And the good-looking girl was driving. She was loaded with diamonds, and I recognized a very good sweater trimmed with a mink collar. I immediately figured this lady was married. She was just here to see the ship. We went down to the ship. This beauty still hadn't spoken to me yet; the older lady was doing all the talking. We toured the ship, and then I said, "Would you ladies care to go back to the hotel and have a drink?" They agreed.

Back at the hotel, we sat down, and Ely came in from playing golf. "Captain, please come over and meet my friends."

"Nice to meet you."

"This is my commanding officer." I said, "Won't you join us?"

He said, "Well, I don't know. I'll probably get stuck with the old one." Well, that didn't go over too well, but we partied the rest of the night.

I told these ladies, "Come to Key West, or I'll visit with you again."

The next thing I knew, I had the beauty's name and number, and she said, "If you care to come back, fine."

"I'll tell you what," I said. "Next weekend I'm in Key West, I'll drive up here and visit with you."

"Fine."

Back in our homeport of Key West, I called up and asked, "May I come up on Saturday morning?"

"Sure, come on up." Saturday morning I was ready to go and called her home. No answer, no answer, no answer. I didn't know what to do. I was stood up. But I remembered her girlfriend's number and called her. She said, "She's here. She's a very, very bad, migraine headache sufferer. She came over last night in great pain, but come up anyway; she'll probably be all right."

I went up to Fort Lauderdale and started dating this girl. She'd visit Key West, loved the skipper and his family, and sort of tolerated me. She became part of our wardroom social life, and six months later we were married in Key West.*

Paul Stillwell: She evidently warmed up.

Captain Colbus: No, not really. She still shakes her head in the negative. "How did I get into this mess?" Great gal.

Paul Stillwell: I presume you went on some sort of deployment after that shakedown?

Captain Colbus: No, that's when we shifted homeport. We had a three-month overhaul in Norfolk, plus the Berlin Crisis activated my old Squadron 12. This shift was one of the reasons I'd gotten married. Everybody in the ship said, "He had to." Then when there was

---

* The bride's maiden name was Jody Rierson.

no child, they said, "She had a miscarriage." Oh, they were so mean to me. However, they were glad to see me get married and get off the ship. We moved to Norfolk because we were going through a shipyard overhaul.

Paul Stillwell: Was this another overhaul?

Captain Colbus: No, no, this *was* the overhaul.

Paul Stillwell: What was the thing in Charleston?

Captain Colbus: That was just a three-weeker to groom the sonar dome. Now we were in Norfolk, which was followed by the Gitmo story I just told you when we ran into Art Damon. Ely brought the ship to Norfolk for two reasons. One, we were going to get a three-month overhaul with a change of homeport. Then, when we completed the overhaul, we were going to be the flagship for the rejuvenation of Escort Squadron 12. They were activating the reserve ships, and by the time we finished the overhaul, we were the flagship for the ten reserve ships.

I was just a month married when we came up here. We had a collision as we left San Juan, on the way to Norfolk. Ely was so glamorous and adventurous that, rather than going directly from Key West to Norfolk, as everybody thought we'd do, he submitted a request that stated, "This ship's in perfect shape, and I hate to take it directly to the shipyard. I want to go on a Caribbean cruise for three weeks on the way up to Norfolk." And we did. We went to Barbados, we went to San Juan. Coming out of San Juan, we had a collision with a merchant.

Paul Stillwell: What were the circumstances on that?

Captain Colbus: You enter San Juan on a southerly course, 181 degrees true. To get on that 181 course and come in through the heavy breakers, you've got to start, according to sailing directions, about two miles out. You come in and you come in fast, and then you have to make a quick left turn, which we knew how to do and which we did. We moored in San Juan and had a good time. My new wife flew over.

Before we got under way again, we embarked a professional Navy photographer to make a travelogue of this cruise. This was one of the great things that Ely wanted to do. When we were in San Juan, Ely talked to a fellow named Skeeter Gardes, commodore of an amphibious squadron.[*] He was aboard the brand-new ship Francis Marion, which had a helicopter aboard. This was big stuff. My skipper got Commodore Gardes to lend us his helicopter with our photographer embarked to film this grand exit of USS John R. Perry. Well, we came around the corner and started to exit on a northerly heading, 001, with a range behind us. The ship answered beautifully. I was navigating and went forward to take a bearing on a castle ashore.[†] Sitting right off the castle, parallel to the beach, was this tremendous merchantman bobbing up and down with these heavy breakers. At his waterline, forward of amidships, was a pilot boat. He did not show the pilot flag. I took this all in and said, "Captain, that merchie is in trouble."

The captain agreed, "He sure is. He shouldn't be there. He's going to get washed up. He's going to broach. Something's going to happen to that ship." All of a sudden, the ship shot ahead. The pilot boat got in front of it, and we could see all this. Our photographer was in the helicopter and was cranking away.

One of our bridge team observed, "I think that guy's going to try to enter the harbor."

"No, he's got to go out to get lined up to get in the harbor." What happened was that the pilot boat was leading the merchant through good water. As he came around to come into the entrance, we were already committed. The captain asked, "How much room do I have?"

"You have no room to starboard. There is some room to port."

"Okay." He said, "I'm going to have to pass him."

I said, "He's coming in, and he's on your right hand."

The captain said, "Let's make it a starboard-to-starboard passage, because I've got more room on the port side."

---

[*] Captain Alfred W. Gardes, Jr., USN.
[†] Morro Castle, begun in 1539 and completed late in the 18th century, is a stone fort that lies on a bluff at the entrance to San Juan Harbor.

"Yes, sir." We sounded two whistles, which means, "I am altering my course to port."

The merchant answered, "We're all set."

"How far over can we get?"

"Well, we are over pretty far," I said. "No more! No more! That's it. We're left of the range now." The merchant never did make his turn. As he crossed our bow, the two bows scraped and backed off. He had a big gash, and we lost the port anchor. It wasn't that serious, but it was a collision. We turned around and came back to San Juan.

There were tears in the captain's eyes. "Why me? We should have never gone on this cruise."

"Well, Captain, it wasn't your fault." So we had a long green table there for the next two days.[*] That was our collision. He was exonerated, but at the same time he was heavily criticized for proposing a maneuver contrary to the rules of the road.

Paul Stillwell: I think that's where the General Prudential Rule comes in, doesn't it, that under certain circumstances you can do something different from the norm.

Captain Colbus: He proposed it. It was agreed to. But it didn't come out that way. As I said, he wasn't relieved, but he did get a letter that he finally had rescinded from the record. He was criticized for proposing a maneuver contrary to good seamanship, normal seamanship. The word "seamanship" was in there. It didn't read well. And the big Norwegian skipper stated at the long green table, "Ya, ya, I tried. My ship not turn fast enough." As I said, we were already committed. So that was our collision.

Paul Stillwell: It's extremely rare that you'd get a film of a collision.

Captain Colbus: That's right. It was and is probably the only collision in the history of the Navy that was filmed. You could see the whole thing. We, of course, produced that film.

---

[*] "Long green table" is a slang term for a Navy investigation in the wake of a mishap. By tradition it is conducted at a table covered by a green tablecloth.

Paul Stillwell: Was that shown in evidence?

Captain Colbus: Yes. My turn at the long green tables was like this: "Are you the exec?"

"Yes, sir."

"Navigator?"

"Yes, sir."

"Are you a party to the part?"

"What's that mean?" asked the skipper, who was sitting right there. "Let me tell you that the XO was giving me his utmost support; he told me everything I needed to know. The decision to come left, the decision to move over, the decision to propose starboard to starboard. Mine. I'm the commanding officer. No, he's not a party to the part."

How many skippers in today's world would do that? I don't know. I don't say they wouldn't, but that's the real test. He could have sat there and kept quiet. He again proved himself.

Paul Stillwell: What do you remember about the Polaris tests and your role in those?

Captain Colbus: Boring. We never got to really do that much. We were there really to cover for the submarine. He was submerged, of course. We would see the missile come out, but that was it. It was just a station ship, communications, relay to the submarine. I can't say that it was professionally rewarding.

Paul Stillwell: What was accomplished in that three-month yard period?

Captain Colbus: They overhauled the engines. Task lights were installed on the ship. Other modifications brought the ship up to date. The big thing we had going was that if something had no use, get rid of it. That's what made that ship immaculate. For instance, on bulkheads, if there was a little gismachi there and it had no use, cut it off. Even a three-year-old ship picks up things. When we left there, that ship was slick, it was easily maintained, and you'd never find a rust mark on that ship. That's when I learned about waxing the deck. We'd painted it enough. Put some wax on it. Beautiful ship. The captain called it his yacht, and he drove it like a yacht.

We came out of the shipyard as the flagship for CortRon 12, Commodore Latham, because we did have a unit commander's stateroom. We all went to Gitmo after that.

Now, let's talk about these reserve ships that were recalled: <u>Tabberer</u>, <u>Albert T. Harris</u>, <u>Thaddeus Parker</u>, <u>Hughes</u>. All these older ships were World War II DEs, sent to the reserve fleet in '58, now reactivated in '61 into the active Navy with reserves aboard. <u>Hughes</u>, for instance, had a skipper who was a teller in a bank, while the quartermaster third class was the president of the bank. Now, that's an exaggeration, but that's the type of environment. And the best group of men. We had to work hard to keep up with these reserves. Their exec's job was a piece of cake. He came on deck every morning and made the assignments. He was talking to mature, successful men who were in the reserves and delighted to serve again, and they just did what they had to do and did a hell of a job. They were tough competition.

USS <u>Darby</u> was one of the ships. I think <u>Darby</u>'s skipper was the vice president of Schenley's distillery in Baltimore. He was probably an $80,000-a-year man, which was big money in '61. While in Gitmo, he overexpended his budget; his ship was in trouble financially. He had spent more money than the ship was allotted. So ComDesLant sent some kind of a team down from Newport to chastise this skipper, straighten him out, and get him back on a good financial footing. I wasn't there; this is secondhand. He just looked at them and said, "I don't have time for this review. I don't have time for your tutelage. How much did I overexpend? I'll write you a check. If that doesn't do it, just kick me off. I'll go back to my job in Baltimore and give up playing sailor."

The skipper of <u>Albert T. Harris</u> was a Greek fellow from New York City; his name every so often appears on the TV credits. I can't remember his name. He, too, was as bald as Yul Brynner. He was a four-striper on this 318-foot DE that I had served in when we had a lieutenant commander as skipper. He was a very glamorous, colorful bachelor. When we were in Norfolk, he rode around in a big, gorgeous Buick Electra convertible. In Gitmo he was kingpin.

His ship steamed from Gitmo to Montego Bay, Jamaica, for weekends. Somehow or other, his sailors went into a hotel there and tore up a bar, which made a big stink back in Gitmo: "We can't have that. You did $4,000 worth of damage. What are you going to do about it?"

The skipper said, "I'm getting on one of our planes. I'm going back to Montego, and I'll pay them." He went there, presented the hotel with $5,000, and said, "I don't want to hear any more about it. You call Gitmo and tell them everything's settled. Are you happy?"

"Oh, yes, we're happy." That was the end of the Montego Bay hotel incident.

Speaking of the planes, they were all S2Fs from Floyd Bennett Field.* The ASW aviator reserves were called up and ordered to Gitmo as a result of the Berlin Crisis. All of them were 6 feet, 2 inches, all of them were commanders, all of them were New York Irish detectives, and if you ever wanted to see a crowd of steamers, these were the ones. They were out of one of those books. They were all good-looking, all fun-loving, and all serious pilots. Of course, coming out of New York, there wasn't a thing that they didn't know or couldn't do. They operated in the big time in Montego Bay, because they had the milk run. Every day they had two planes over there, liberty, stores, you name it. We had a hell of a group in Gitmo for working up deals with our reserve ships and reserve aircrews.

Paul Stillwell: What did these ships accomplish once they got trained?

Captain Colbus: They steamed very well, they could shoot, and they could operate. They provided a presence and made up in enthusiasm anything they lacked elsewhere. These ships had been allowed to go down while they were in the reserve fleet because they weren't used. This reserve squadron developed a very, very capable group of ships that could have escorted very well. They were all armed, all ready to go, and in good shape. They not only looked good, but everything worked.

Paul Stillwell: What kind of operations did you get involved in?

---

* Grumman S2F Tracker propeller-driven antisubmarine planes first entered fleet squadrons in early 1954. In 1962 the Tracker was redesignated S-2. Floyd Bennett Field was the name of the New York Naval Air Station.

Captain Colbus: Task force ASW, squadron tactics, surveillance, and operating as a unit, By the time we departed Gitmo and came back to Norfolk, we were a good group and could steam with the best of them.

Paul Stillwell: Did you deploy at all?

Captain Colbus: No. I left John R. Perry on February 14, 1963, and it was all winding down. Everybody was going back to their old ways. So I had about 18 months of it.

Paul Stillwell: Did you get involved in the Cuban Missile Crisis at all?[*]

Captain Colbus: Oh, yes. Oh, all the way. I remember that very well—Monday, October 22nd of '62. My mother had taken ill by then. My wife and I drove up to Altoona, Pennsylvania, from Key West on routine leave. We arrived on a Saturday. By Monday we heard on the radio what was going on. I was beside myself and called down to Key West. I learned that, yes, the ships had deployed. We jumped in the car and drove right through to Key West.

By the time I got back, which was Tuesday evening, the ships were at sea. The only way I could get aboard John R. Perry was when she came in to fuel, which might be never, because this was a diesel ship and drove forever. But on Wednesday afternoon, the ship returned, having sailed Monday, and picked me up. I don't know what else we picked up, because we sure didn't need fuel. All the ships floundered. Nobody knew where they were going, nobody knew what to do. I guess by Friday we were organized, but still no communications. You just got under way. By Friday, I think it was, we had the blockade organized.[*]

---

[*] In mid-October 1962, U.S. reconnaissance plane photographed a Soviet nuclear missile site in Cuba and the presence of Soviet bombers. On 22 October President John F. Kennedy went on national television to announce a naval quarantine of Cuba, to be implemented on 24 October. On 28 October Premier Nikita Khrushchev of the Soviet Union notified President Kennedy that he was ordering the withdrawal of Soviet bombers and missiles from Cuba.

Paul Stillwell: What did you do in the meantime? Who was giving orders?

Captain Colbus: Nobody. We were talking to each other, but we had no direction. There was no plan, so to speak. I believe this was all spur of the moment. Who'd known about a Cuban blockade? At least I didn't know anything about any war plans. So I'd say by Thursday—Friday at the latest—we finally had our assignment. We steamed to Miami, went up and down the coast, observed shipping lanes, viewed other ships, and talked to people. We went back and ended up, I'm going to say by the first weekend, off Havana, patrolling. We were between Key West and Havana, patrolling, watching the "Komar" boats coming out of Havana.[†] We could monitor it just as if we were in one of these electronic war games that we have today.

We'd see a "Komar" boat start to come out of Havana, and in no time we'd see jet action on the north side; the jets would come out of Key West. And that's what we did. Of course, we were now getting press, we were now getting intelligence, we knew about the missiles, we knew about the ships that were actually doing the intercepting.

Then USS Joseph P. Kennedy, with Nicholas Mikhalevsky in command, went down there and did her thing, if you remember that.[‡] We weren't involved with that. That was on the other side of the island. Joseph P. Kennedy went over there and sent a boarding officer bedecked in sword, medals, and choker whites to do his trick on that Soviet ship. And that I can remember as being a major breakthrough. Now we were really in the blockade business. And what we did was just that—took pictures, intercepted ships, and asked, "What is your destination?" Of course, we were right there in all that Florida Strait traffic, so we had a lot of activity.

---

[*] For details, see Forrest Johns, "The Cuban Missile Crisis Quarantine," Naval History, Spring 1992, pages 12-18.
[†] "Komar" was the NATO-assigned name for a class of Soviet-built guided missile patrol boats. Each was 88 feet long, displaced 80 tons, had a top speed of 30 knots, and was armed with launchers for two SS-N-2 surface-to-surface missiles.
[‡] On 26 October 1962 the destroyers Joseph P. Kennedy, Jr. (DD-850) and John R. Pierce (DD-753) halted and boarded the Soviet-chartered, Lebanese-flag freighter Marucla. After the Americans inspected her cargo, she was permitted to continue to Havana, Cuba. The commanding officer was Commander Nicholas Mikhalevsky, USN.

Paul Stillwell: Did you think this was going to be the big one?

Captain Colbus: No, not really. I don't know if it was because I was uninformed, naive, or what. I won't say it became routine, but it became a modus operandi. That's what we did. I had more excitement in Jonas Ingram in 1972—when there was no missile crisis and there was no blockade—than I had in 1962. Around Cuba in '72 we actually had the boats come out and come alongside. We'd see the Cuban sailors face to face. We'd break out guns and be ready to go. That was sudden; that was unannounced.

But getting back to this blockade, there was a lot of interesting aspects. After a while it became known that we would come into port every six days or so. While we were fueling in Key West, if we behaved ourselves, the commodore, who was sitting on the beach controlling all this, would call the captain's wife, who would call the exec's wife. That would start the chain. The wives could come down to see us and spend an hour or two with us. The first time this happened, we were steaming up the channel, and the commodore saw the ship. He called the captain's wife, who called my wife, and so on. Within half an hour, we were moored at Key West. As they started to bring the fueling hoses on board, the wives arrived. "How's everything?"

"Fine."

"How are the children?"

"Everything's good." Nice visit, ship's topped off, we've been there two hours.

"Bye, girls." Back out, and we were gone out for another six days. Well, we did this two or three times. One day we were steaming up the channel for our fueling stop. We didn't even have the first line over, and the communications officer's wife appeared on the pier with a few of the other young wives. In about half an hour or so, the rest of the wives arrived. Our wives had tried to call the younger ones, but they were already down at the pier.

The same thing happened the next time we came in, and the captain got a call. After he called on the commodore, he came back and said, "Got a job for you, XO."

"Yes, sir."

"I want you to get the communications officer's wife up here and tell her she has to get rid of that Halicrafter." The comm officer had told his wife that any time she wanted to find out what was going on, she could tune her Halicrafter radio to short wave, such-and-such a channel, and listen for our call sign. When she heard that call sign requesting permission to port, she would have time to get down to the pier and meet the ship. It was just one of those nasty things. Little things became very irritating.

Rumors were abundant all the time. When was this operation going to end? There was no answer. Were we going to be home for Thanksgiving? Well, we weren't. Just before Christmas we had a wind-down. When we came in, it was for a visit by President Kennedy to Key West and the ships. When he walked aboard USS Sarsfield, he got his hand full of paint, because they'd just painted the port side of the ship. (We all gun-decked a quick paint job.) He was a good sport about that.

When the Cuban Crisis first occurred, women left Key West because they were afraid it was going to be bombed. They just jumped in their cars and took off. One woman forgot her child in Sigsbee Park, which was the Navy housing area.* I didn't see that, but that was the story. My wife said she knew that happened in the neighborhood. The woman took off, got up the keys, and then asked, "Where's the baby?" Then she turned around and went to retrieve her child.

And, of course, the build-up was tremendous. The Army moved in, aviation moved in, and Key West was on the map.

Paul Stillwell: After you got up to this big readiness peak, then how did the blockade itself go?

Captain Colbus: We did our job, as I said, until it became an every-day occurrence. We knew how to hail ships. We were filing reports; we tracked everything; we passed merchant ships over to the next Navy ship on station. We challenged every ship that went through the Florida Straits. It was just a matter of ship count.

I know we were home in Key West for Christmas. I couldn't go to Altoona to see my mother at Christmas, because we were still on call. She died on the first of the year, and we went home for her funeral. That was January '63. By February we were back to

---

* It was named for Captain Charles D. Sigsbee, USN, who was commanding officer of the battleship Maine when she exploded at Havana, Cuba, on 15 February 1898. A number of Maine crew members killed in the blast were buried in Key West.

normal routine, planning on whatever we had to do. It was a trying time because it was indefinite; we learned a lot.

Paul Stillwell: Under whose opcon were you after things got organized?*

Captain Colbus: ComNavBase Key West, Admiral R. Y. McElroy.† He was running the show down there, and it was some show! He was in charge of the forces, as you would expect. We had heard wild stories of what went on in his headquarters, which had been a nice, easy, sleepy command. All of a sudden—bingo.

Paul Stillwell: After your tour as exec, you went to BuPers. You had managed to escape Washington duty up to then. How did that tour come about?

Captain Colbus: It was time to go to Washington, and I just didn't know any better. I was told that was my next assignment. When you got a set of orders, you just went. No fuss, no muss, no crybaby.

We left Key West on February 14, Valentine's Day, 1963. We took a nice long auto trip, just Jody and myself. We'd only been married about a year and looked forward to Washington. We visited with Frank Hill, my former skipper in Albert T. Harris, who was a Washington sailor by this time. We bought a house.

I was assigned to Pers-A31, plans and policy. I was there from February '63 to July '64, when I went on to the war college.

Paul Stillwell: Did this job deal with manpower levels?

Captain Colbus: Exactly—manpower plans and policy. Again, I felt very lucky, because this was the greatest job one could have. I wrote the billets while others in BuPers filled them with the bodies. I had a lot of attention. People would come to me, for instance, to upgrade a billet for a yeoman third class to a first class, and they'd provide the justification.

---

* Opcon—operational control.
† Rear Admiral Rhodam Yarrott McElroy, Jr., USN.

That was routine business. The glamorous part of it was that I had such interesting activities as the presidential yacht Honey Fitz right there in Washington; the Eisenhower farm in Gettysburg; the White House mess; all the naval districts; cats and dogs; shore billets, and the Navy Band.[*]

Paul Stillwell: What did you have to do in connection with the presidential yacht and the farm at Gettysburg?

Captain Colbus: I was strictly a recorder and keeper of the billets. I really didn't have the power to change, but if the Honey Fitz yacht needed, let's say, a boatswain's mate first class instead of a second, or needed another engineer, it was my job to write the billet, as such. I had to keep all the numbers straight and make sure I didn't exceed the Navy's end strength.[†]

Stewards for living quarters were one of my activities. After the President was assassinated and Jackie decided to keep her steward, who was a chief petty officer, over in Georgetown, it was my job to see that that happened.[‡] Well, you didn't do much about it. You just let that thing lie fallow, even though you never balanced out in your computer run when it came time to balance billets against bodies. For instance, I think the number was 560 stewards for quarters. Well, Jackie had one of them that wasn't authorized. Now there were 559, which meant we were missing one. But as long as you could explain those things, you were in pretty good shape.

Paul Stillwell: Was this just enlisted personnel you handled?

Captain Colbus: No, I had the officer billets, too, for those particular commands.

Paul Stillwell: No seagoing.

---

[*] "Honey Fitz" was the nickname of John F. Kennedy's maternal grandfather, John Fitzgerald. After he left office as President on 20 January 1961, Dwight D. Eisenhower and his wife Mamie moved to a farm near the Civil War battlefield at Gettysburg, Pennsylvania.
[†] End strength is the number of personnel for which Congress appropriated money in a given budget year.
[‡] John F. Kennedy served as President of the United States from 20 January 1960 until he was assassinated on 22 November 1963. His widow Jacqueline later remarried in 1968.

Captain Colbus: No, no seagoing commands. I did have BuPers itself, OpNav, and all the other Washington activities. This was how and why I got to know all these areas and commands very, very well. I thought it was just heaven that I could, on a particular day, take a ride to the Gun Factory, walk aboard <u>Honey Fitz</u>, and see if there was anything I could do for the billets.[*] It really should have been the detailers, but I had the time and inclination to do it. I went to the White House mess on occasion: "How's it doing over here? Where are all these billets I've been writing?"

Paul Stillwell: Why the Gettysburg thing? Eisenhower certainly wasn't a Navy man.

Captain Colbus: I think that was just something that we inherited. We had two billets for seamen at the Eisenhower farm in Gettysburg. Since I was a Penn Stater, I always watched for Penn State graduates and would tip off the detailer as to who was graduating and who might come into the Navy from Penn State. Since they were probably Penn State aggies, we'd send them down on the farm to fill the billets.

Paul Stillwell: What did they do?

Captain Colbus: Whatever you do on a farm. I guess they worked and advised, in that they were probably very well educated agricultural students who somehow ended up in the Navy and through that great process would end up at the farm.

My favorite place, though, was the Naval Home.[†] I wrote the billets for the Naval Home, which was in Philadelphia then. Admiral Gentleman Jim Holloway was the governor of the home.[‡] I had to go up there one time to look the activity over.

They had a very, very difficult situation up there, and they needed a storekeeper first class. The duties and the justification for having a storekeeper first class were to be (a) on independent duty; (b) operate the canteen, which would include dispensing beer; and

---

[*] The yacht was moored at the Washington Navy Yard in southeast Washington, D.C. For many years the yard was the site of the Naval Gun Factory.
[†] The Naval Home is a long-established retirement haven for elderly former naval personnel.
[‡] Admiral James L. Holloway, Jr., USN (Ret.).

(c) show a movie every night. The reason that they wanted to do that was these gents in the Naval Home had nothing to occupy their time in the evenings. Of course, they were free to come and go as they pleased. They'd go out on the town and drink too much beer in the local pubs. Then the people running the Naval Home would have to go out and collect these old-timers at 11:00 or 12:00 at night.

You should have met some of these boys; they were really the old-time sailors. Some of them had served in sailing ships. They'd teach you the sailing rigs as you talked to them. These were men in their 70s who still would pull a liberty in Philadelphia and have a good time. The idea for having a storekeeper first class was to provide a better atmosphere in the Naval Home so the old men wouldn't go out on the streets. They could do their drinking and carousing right there at the Naval Home. Great group.

Paul Stillwell: Did it work?

Captain Colbus: I can't answer that, because I left about two months after that, but you can just bet that Admiral Holloway got his desired billet,

Paul Stillwell: Did you have any encounters with Admiral Holloway yourself?

Captain Colbus: Oh, sure. I went in to see him. If I didn't please him, he would go right to Admiral Smedberg, who was our boss at the time.[*] Meeting with him was a real experience, and, of course, I explained to him that I had come into the NROTC as a Holloway student, which I understand was a follow-on to the V-12 program.[†] That put me in solid with the good admiral, who was a great man to talk to. He was very understanding and certainly devoted to the Naval Home.

---

[*] Vice Admiral William R. Smedberg III, USN, served as Chief of the Bureau of Naval Personnel from 12 February 1960 to 11 February 1964. His oral history is in the Naval Institute collection.
[†] In 1946, the Holloway Plan was enacted to establish a Naval ROTC program that would pay for the college education of individuals and grant regular, rather than reserve, commissions upon graduation. It was named for then-Rear Admiral Holloway, who had much to do with its development. Holloway wrote two articles about the program for the U.S. Naval Institute Proceedings. See "The Holloway Plan—A Summary View and Commentary," November 1947, pages 1293-1303, and "A Gentlemen's Agreement," September 1980, pages 71-77.

Paul Stillwell: And he had the background, since he'd been the Chief of Naval Personnel himself.[*]

Captain Colbus: That's right. And he did a grand job and knew exactly what string to pull when it was time to get something done.

I also used to travel with the BuPers inspector general to look into these billets, be it shore patrol, naval stations, whatever. Our inspector general was Captain Stone. His assistant was a man named Commander Al Carlson, who's been retired for 15 years, still works in BuPers. Captain Stone was an artist. In fact, he has done some paintings right around Washington in some of the government buildings on commission. He's a well-known artist from Annapolis. I'd participate in these inspector general trips and look over the billet structure, how they were being filled, and what the people were being used for.

One of the trips we made was to Charleston, the home port of USS Bainbridge, which was brand-new at the time.[†] By that time, I thought I had some experience by which to judge a destroyer. You remember, I'd come from the DE Navy, associated closely with the destroyer Navy, and now all of a sudden I was visiting a DLGN. We went aboard USS Bainbridge, got to talk to Captain Peet, then we were turned over to the ship's company and shown the ship.[‡] They were very gracious about all this.

First of all, I guess I was mesmerized by the size of the ship. I guess I also felt intimidated because I thought as a destroyer man, I should be able to do anything around a destroyer. I remember telling Al Carlson, "Al, I feel uncomfortable here."

He said, "Why's that Louis?"

I said, "I couldn't get this ship under way. I wouldn't know where to begin." So that made me feel uncomfortable. Here I was on a destroyer, supposedly a destroyer sailor,

---

[*] As a vice admiral, Holloway served as Chief of the Bureau of Naval Personnel from 2 February 1953 to 31 January 1958.

[†] USS Bainbridge (DLGN-25), a nuclear-powered frigate, was the only ship of her class. She was commissioned 6 October 1962. She had a standard displacement of 7,600 tons, was 565 feet long, 58 feet in the beam, and had a maximum draft of 29 feet. Her top speed was 30-plus knots. She was armed with two twin launchers for Terrier missiles, two 3-inch guns, ASROC, and six torpedo tubes. She was redesignated a cruiser, CGN-25, in 1975.

[‡] The first commanding officer of the Bainbridge was Captain Raymond E. Peet, USN. For a pictorial on the new ship, including Captain Peet's comments, see U.S. Naval Institute Proceedings, July 1963, pages 88-103. The oral history of Peet, who retired as a vice admiral, is in the Naval Institute collection.

and I wouldn't know how to get that ship under way. What do you say to a nuclear power plant? What do you say to a ship this big?

We went to luncheon in the wardroom after our morning session. If memory serves me right, I sat next to the reactors officer, a young lieutenant commander who was talking about the engineering plant. He said, "Of course, after lunch, I know you gentlemen would like to see the plant in Bainbridge." And I very jokingly said, "I don't know if I can go down there or not, because I understand that stuff down there makes your hair fall out, and I'll end up with no hair." Of course, I was as bald as a cue ball by then.

He looked at me very seriously and gave me a 15-minute dissertation on the whys and wherefores, and that was really an old wives' tale, and the nuclear plant would not affect me with my bald head. Then, of course, I went on to say something about childbearing, because I had no children. He also played down that risk. He never did pick up on the fact that I was joshing, pulling his leg. I sort of felt this fellow didn't have much of a sense of humor.

I guess that's when I formed my opinion of nukes. I admired their seriousness, but also it bothered me that they had absolutely zero sense of humor. They didn't pick up on any of the things we were making light of. And, of course, we went on a tour of the plant. It was very educational, it was very, very professionally rewarding and all these things, but I worried about that young lieutenant commander. He never did pick up that which we were saying.

Paul Stillwell: Do you have any impressions of Captain Peet himself?

Captain Colbus: Oh, yes, sir. We went up to his cabin, and, of course, I was about the fourth or fifth gent in line to shake his hand. We listened to him, and I was very impressed. A powerful man, an impressive man, and I would have certainly been more than delighted to have served for him, with him, and what have you. I never did really get to know Captain Peet. This was just a 15-minute meeting in his cabin. He was gracious and impressive.

Paul Stillwell: Was he less stiff than the junior officers?

Captain Colbus: Oh, yes, absolutely. Sure. Captain Peet was what I'd expect a skipper of a destroyer to be. He was lighthearted about some things and he just had the right attitude about our being there. He was a very gracious gent.

Another interesting area for which we wrote billets was the movie exchange up in Brooklyn. There was a commander up there who ran the movie exchange. He had an adjunct in Los Angeles that looked in on those things and kept the movie world straight when it came to buying films and distributing them to the United States Navy. I got a little piece of that and had a little bit of knowledge of how the movie distribution buying system worked.

By the way, it required that at least once a month I'd go into the BuPers auditorium on a Thursday afternoon at 2:00 and review the latest movie from Hollywood to see if it was fit for us to buy and send to the fleet. I remember only one that was controversial enough to get every flag officer in Washington to attend. We didn't have enough room to show it there in the BuPers office, so it was shown in a downtown theater. That was Seven Days in May.* I was in the back row. I didn't even have a vote on that one.

Paul Stillwell: What was the vote?

Captain Colbus: Positive. We got that movie.

Paul Stillwell: What do you recall of Admiral Smedberg, the bureau chief?

Captain Colbus: Not too much. I would see him, of course. I was down the hall from him. My boss's boss was Rear Admiral Charlie Duncan, whom I can still see walking into our office.† He was a very, very personable gent, quiet, low-key, and effective. If he wanted something, he just told you about it.

---

* Seven Days in May, a political thriller released by Warner Brothers in 1964, starred Burt Lancaster, Kirk Douglas, Frederic March, and Ava Gardner. In the scenario, the Chairman of the Joint Chiefs of Staff tried unsuccessfully to unseat the President because of his stance on a disarmament treaty. It was a topical story during the Cold War atmosphere of the early 1960s.
† Rear Admiral Charles K. Duncan, who later served as Chief of Naval Personnel, 1968-70. The oral history of Duncan, who retired as a four-star admiral, is in the Naval Institute collection.

Admiral Duncan, as Pers-A, was the gent who really held all these quarters stewards' billets close at hand. I was his reporter, so he and I had a lot of interface. I guess what I remember most about him was that he would not push a buzzer and say "Come on down." He'd walk into my office, which was made up of about ten of us sitting around desks in the lineup—bullpen fashion. He always seemed to jingle the change in his pocket. He'd walk over, sort of park himself at my desk, and talk over the steward situation at NAS Olathe, Kansas, for instance.* He'd talk about it, tell me what he wanted to do, say "I know you'll take care of it, Louis," and walk out.

Paul Stillwell: Admiral Holloway was a much more formal individual; I can't imagine him taking that approach.

Captain Colbus: No, no, no. Different situation. But, as I say, I knew him as the civilian governor of the home and a fine gent to do business with.

I remember one Saturday going in to Admiral Smedberg's office. His aide was a lieutenant commander named Jim Linder, who went on to be an admiral and is here in town.† I see him all the time. Then-Lieutenant Commander Linder asked me one day if I was going to be around on Saturday. I said, yes, I had to come in and do some paperwork. Then he asked, "Would you mind sitting in the chief's office, because I don't want to come in Saturday?"

"Fine. I'll stand by for you, realizing you can't pay me back." So I went in and sat at the desk, and I watched a parade of admirals going in and out. That was an education! They all went in and sat around and they were discussing admiral detailing. They did not shut the door, so I could not help but hear, and I got a run-down on many of the flag officers in the United States Navy. I heard comments such as that one fellow couldn't have a particular job because he was too difficult, too hard to get along with. Another admiral couldn't be ordered here because he really wasn't that much up to speed. I heard all these very personal things about admirals that I thought my tender ears shouldn't hear, but it

---

* NAS—naval air station.
† Lieutenant Commander James B. Linder, USN.

taught me that admirals have a pecking order among themselves, just the same as the rest of us did when it came to getting jobs.

Paul Stillwell: I've read some articles about that, and it's amazing how well the Chief of Naval Personnel knows all these people.[*]

Captain Colbus: I think he used the word "stupid;" one fellow was called stupid. I guess among admirals, he was considered not so brilliant as the rest of the admirals, therefore they couldn't send him. One fellow was too harsh, one fellow was too soft. So Admiral Smedberg and the boys discussed each fellow very, very personally. It wasn't from a sheet of paper, as I could hear them talking.

Paul Stillwell: Did they find anybody who was right for the job?

Captain Colbus: I'm sure they did. I was impressed, I guess is the word, with the fact that (a) they knew that kind of information and (b) they would talk that way about an admiral.

Paul Stillwell: I've gotten the impression also that in addition to whether the characteristics matched with the job, there was also the importance of timing. So-and-so, who might be good for that job, wasn't available now.

Captain Colbus: I never heard that come up. I think these were all the contenders. I guess at this late date they had eight contenders for three or four important jobs there in the Washington area. Then Admiral Smedberg was relieved by Admiral B. J. Semmes.[†]

That's the year that they asked me to be the judge of the Miss BuPers Beauty Contest. I went down to get the Chief of WAVES, which was what we called them then.[‡]

---

[*] See, for example, Robert M. Ancell, "The Path to Four Stars," U.S. Naval Institute Proceedings, January 1981, pages 46-51.
[†] Vice Admiral Benedict J. Semmes, Jr., USN, served as Chief of Naval Personnel from 1 April 1964 to 31 March 1968. His oral history is in the Naval Institute collection.
[‡] WAVES—Women accepted for Voluntary Emergency Service. The term originated in World War II and was in use until the 1970s, when women became more and more integrated into the service as a whole.

That was probably the most sweet, squared away, wonderful woman I've ever met, Captain Viola B. Sanders. She agreed to be on the selection committee, and I got the Chief of Chaplains to serve on my committee.* We needed and got the necessary dignity. So here I was, a lieutenant, rounding up all these heavies to be on my team to select Miss BuPers. It was a beauty contest, and I really enjoyed that. It ended up that we went to the Sheraton Hotel, and Hardin and Weaver were the final judges.

Paul Stillwell: They're still on the radio there in Washington.

Captain Colbus: Still going strong. I can't get near Washington that I don't listen to them on the radio.

We couldn't get B. J. Semmes really interested in the contest. I don't know if it was because he didn't want to or because his staff wouldn't go in and really round him up, but Admiral Semmes never really got enthused or involved in our beauty contest. So I had to depend on the Chief of Chaplains, Chief of the WAVES, Captain Viola B., myself, and a couple of others who enjoyed the better things in life. A lot of fun.

Paul Stillwell: Did you get close enough to make a comparison of the personalities and so forth between Smedberg and Semmes?

Captain Colbus: No, not really, except for those two experiences that I just discussed. Admiral Smedberg, I thought, was much more outgoing, much warmer. Admiral Semmes was very aloof and, I guess you'd say, if he was interested, he didn't show as much interest in things—not just beauty contests—as did Admiral Smedberg. Admiral Smedberg was more dynamic.

Paul Stillwell: He's such an enthusiastic person.

Captain Colbus: Yes, that's the word.

---

* Rear Admiral Joseph Floyd Dreith, CHC, USN, served as the Navy's Chief of Chaplains from July 1963 to June 1965.

Paul Stillwell: Contagious enthusiasm.

Captain Colbus: And it rubbed off on his son, Admiral Bill Smedberg, whom I've been privileged to know when he was the OP-96 guy, and when he was down here as ComDesRon 10.* Yes, he's a fine man too.

Paul Stillwell: The label of plans and policy, did that fit at Admiral Duncan's level?

Captain Colbus: Yes, he was, as I said, Pers-A, head of plans and policy. Those were long-range plans, those were the billets I just talked about. On the other side of the passageway were the sea billets, headed up by a famous naval officer, Captain Maylon T. Scott, who had the fleet side.

Paul Stillwell: It sounds as if your job was much more short-range than plans would suggest.

Captain Colbus: I think you're right. I was the keeper of the books and balanced things out. But they had promotion plans, which were in Pers-A. I was in A31. I think A32 was the fleet side of that. There were a lot of divisions in there. You're absolutely right. Mine was the day-to-day work, not plans, and I guess not even policy. It was head counting--billet counting, I should say. By the way, that was later merged and moved over into OpNav in OP-01.† I think I'm correct in saying it's now back in the BuPers, NMPC side.‡ So that shifts back and forth. Quality and quantity. We were quantity, B was quality.

Paul Stillwell: Did you find it professionally satisfying as well as fun?

---

* William R. Smedberg IV graduated from the Naval Academy in the class of 1951 and eventually retired as a rear admiral in 1982.
† OP-01 is the Deputy Chief of Naval Operations (Manpower, Personnel, and Training), a title that has varied slightly over the years. It has been held concurrently by the Chief of Naval Personnel.
‡ For a time in the 1970s and 1980s, the title Bureau of Naval Personnel was temporarily not in use. Some of the BuPers functions were carried out by an organization called the Naval Military Personnel Command.

Captain Colbus: Oh, yes. It was, as I said, a real education, in that I wasn't just stuck at my desk. I got to travel all over Washington. I got to see not just the Honey Fitz and the glamour parts and the recruiting stations, I also learned that—what's the word? I also learned that you lie. We would hide billets. We would hide billets over at the Naval Station Anacostia, so if Admiral Duncan would call me and say, "How many billets for end-strength count do we have? How many billets do we have at Anacostia, NAS?" Or Naval Station Washington, whatever the case might be.

I'd say, "Seven hundred forty-two. That includes the 42 billets that we're keeping in reserve to move somewhere else." He'd understand that.

Sometimes a staff member would call me from some congressional office and ask how many billets were at the same activity. The answer to him, "Six hundred twenty-four." We had to be very, very versatile in what numbers were provided. I learned there if you lie, you get tripped up, because it was very difficult to remember who was doing what to whom, and what number I gave him yesterday.

Paul Stillwell: What was the purpose of this double counting?

Captain Colbus: Oh, the purpose was Washington strength. Don't hold me to these numbers, but I think we were allowed to have 3,400 Navy types in the Washington area. When we got to that 3,400, perhaps there was a special project to which we wanted to add 15 more officers. Well, they couldn't be assigned to Washington activities because we'd have been over our Washington strength. Therefore, I would write those billets—as they called it—and then their orders would read to, let's say, Naval Recruiting Washington, which didn't come under this ceiling. It was really quite difficult to keep a daily muster.

I'm sure that when musters were taken, as we did aboard ship, you could have 12 officers in your office, let's say, in OpNav somewhere, and five of them were assigned to Naval Recruiting, Washington, D.C., even though they were working in OpNav. You still had the fitness report responsibility, but you didn't have them in the daily muster. If anybody ever tabulated all the numbers, we'd probably have had—I'm guessing—4,000 instead of 3,400. These billets were just "buried" all over the Washington area.

Now that I look back on it, did it matter? Who cares? I don't know. Did anybody ever tabulate all these numbers? I don't know. But I was a lieutenant and told to keep these numbers straight; don't give them away. I gave them a, "Yes, sir," and away we went. Washington was a tough place to keep tabs on billets for the Washington activities.

Paul Stillwell: Did it ever come up that Washington was an awfully expensive place for an enlisted person to live?

Captain Colbus: Oh, it came up all the time. Of course, you didn't have variable housing allowance, which came along later. Yes. And we tried to do the best we could. We had housing over at Anacostia, as I remember, which was premium housing. We had quarters K, which was right next to the BuPers complex.[*] It is all now either parking or highway. When the young people came there as unmarrieds, of course, they went in the barracks. That's what they wanted to do. Very few times would they want to move out onto the civilian economy.

Paul Stillwell: How was it for a married lieutenant living here?

Captain Colbus: I thought it was just great. We bought our first house, bought a new Lincoln automobile there. We were living, I thought, high on the hog. I guess I didn't know any better. Of course, I'd just been married a year, year and a half. We'd bought this house. Unfortunately, my mother had died, so I took the money from my family home and used it to buy the house. When I married, I married a gal who already had all her furniture, so personally speaking, it was easy for me. I wasn't one of those just-starting-out guys.

Paul Stillwell: This was a time when Captain Zumwalt was the EA to Nitze, and he was concerned about getting better pay for enlisted people.[†] Did you see the impact of that at your level?

---

[*] The BuPers complex was in the Arlington Annex, a multi-wing building adjacent to the Arlington National Cemetery.
[†] Captain Elmo R. Zumwalt, Jr., USN, who later served as CNO, was executive assistant to Paul H. Nitze, Secretary of the Navy from 1963 to 1967.

Captain Colbus: Not then. They didn't really take hold, I would guess, until the late '60s. Then I saw an appreciable amount of increase in salary. Now all of a sudden the salary really was comparable to anything we could have seen in the non-Navy world.

Paul Stillwell: There's a perception among people not at BuPers that those who are in BuPers rig things in their favor for upcoming assignments and for their friends and so forth. Is there truth to that?

Captain Colbus: No, there's no truth to that. It is true, however, that people from BuPers get the best assignments. And I think that only makes sense, if you stop to think of it. Now, I eliminate myself, because I was not in the BuPers inner circle. That's in the Pers-B side, where they get the records and where they see who are the comers, who are the sleepers. That's also where they do the fleet assigning to these great, desirable billets we just talked about. What happens—and, if you think about it, it's very obvious—BuPers is in the personnel business, so it would be pretty stupid not to pick the best people to come to work for them in the Pers-B area. So I think the fact that they're in the personnel world, they have the pick of the entire United States Navy, they pick the best people. Then these best people do very well in BuPers. Isn't it just natural they'd go on to bigger and better assignments?

Paul Stillwell: If you follow the presumption that they get the best people.

Captain Colbus: I think that's a good assumption.

Paul Stillwell: If you got there, then you must have been one of the best.

Captain Colbus: No, sir. I said I was in Pers-A. That doesn't count. It was the Pers-B crowd, really, the detailers who did very well, and rightly so.

Captain Colbus: I liked Washington, I found it exciting, and it certainly was rewarding. During the rest of my naval career, I used those things that I learned in BuPers that I just talked about. The fact that I'd been there in that billet writing, I think, helped me a lot, in looking back and understanding and realizing you just couldn't do some things. I knew the mechanics on how to do it if I wanted to change something.

Paul Stillwell: What might be an example of that?

Captain Colbus: Well, you get out into the fleet and all of a sudden you're on a destroyer that has, let's say, a 48 radar.* A 48 radar takes certain technicians with certain designators, certain NECs, certain key numbers that show their schooling, to get them in the ship.† Well, what should happen doesn't just happen. Just because you have the equipment doesn't mean you're going to get the technician to go with it. Somebody has to think of that; somebody has to crank that into the system. Somebody at, let's say, the force level has to earmark every ship that has a 48 radar and put in a request to change a billet: "We want to do away with such and such. Our compensation is this, and we want that for every ship in the following categories." So if all of a sudden you ended up with equipment and you didn't have the people, don't get angry. You know what to do and whom to see.

Paul Stillwell: How much a part did computers play in your work there at BuPers?

Captain Colbus: We did have computers, and that was called Pers-M. These sheets and forms that I tell you about required changes, of course. To make a change, we utilized a computer-like form that would be fed into the machine. Every six weeks it produced a machine run that gave you your balance. So the computer did come into play then but away from our individual desks—no remotes, no desk consoles.

Paul Stillwell: Were you concerned about matching actual numbers of people in each rating with the number of billets at that rating?

---

* The SPS-48 search radar has been used by a variety of U.S. warships, including carriers, cruisers, and destroyers.
† NEC—Navy enlisted classification code.

Captain Colbus: Not the people, no. We may not have those people. That wasn't part of my business. All I knew was that the overall end strength reflected X number of petty officers, X number of firemen, X number of seamen, and my activities were allotted so many of these. It was just keep everything in balance.

Paul Stillwell: And each one would be broken down even further, so many chief boatswain's mates, etc.

Captain Colbus: Exactly. And then, of course, the man sitting at the head of our division saw that the entire shore establishment represented our proper share. The fleet side did the same, and when it all came together, there were 432 chief boatswain's mates in the United States Navy, this many in the shore establishment, this many in the sea side and match them up.

Paul Stillwell: Anything else about that tour that's worth recording?

Captain Colbus: Yes, there's one more thing we've got to talk about. That was the first year that I ever attended—and it might have been the first year it ever occurred—the Destroyer Ball out at Bethesda. You're asking what more was keen or what should I remember; that was a renewal of friendships. I'd been in the Navy only nine years at this point, but everybody I'd ever met, anybody I ever knew, was going to go through Washington. You either knew him from his duty there or you'd bumped into him as he passed through the halls of BuPers looking for his next assignment. In November of the first year I was there, we attended the Navy Destroyer Ball. That was something else. I mean, it still is, of course, but it's not called Destroyer Ball now; it's called something less impressive.

Paul Stillwell: Surface Warfare.

Captain Colbus: Something like that. Anyway, I'm being parochial now. The Destroyer Ball attracted Admiral Arleigh Burke, the CNO, anybody who was somebody in the destroyer world.* Everybody would be there, and you'd run into them. I went there, as I said, newly married. I was proud to introduce my wife to everybody I saw, and I can proudly say that everybody I saw was just delighted to see me. I'm talking about young fellows, I'm talking about skippers, I'm talking about squadron skippers, men who weren't my skippers, <u>ad infinitum</u>. This was the first time my wife ever saw me drunk. We walked out of there, but I couldn't walk straight. The reason for this was that everybody you saw, you had to have a drink with. If you ever wanted to see the epitome of camaraderie, fraternity, the destroyer ball of 1963 had to be it.

Paul Stillwell: Anything else?

Captain Colbus: I would say it was a very professional tour of duty, in that you were doing something brand-new, you were learning it, you were working at it, and we didn't have that 5:00 o'clock, "Let's all get together." While I mentioned that you knew everybody and all your associations were renewed, some lived in Bethesda while you lived in Fairfax, so there wasn't a lot of getting together. People were house poor and delighted just to get home.

We did work late hours; I remember that. In our group it was 6:00, 6:30. In the detailing world, they'd be there from 6:00 in the morning until 8:00 at night. People over in OpNav, I know, worked even more wild hours because they were in early to do the briefings and there late at night to do whatever else had to be done.

Paul Stillwell: You went from there to the Naval War College. Was that something you requested?

Captain Colbus: No, not at all. In fact, I thought I'd been fired. I'd only been in BuPers 14 months, had bought a house, liked my job, loved the people with whom I was working.

---

* Admiral Arleigh A. Burke, USN (Ret.), had served as Chief of Naval Operations from 17 August 1955 to 1 August 1961. His oral history is in the Naval Institute collection. Burke had a notable record in destroyers in World War II.

Then, I was told in April, having reported there the previous June, "You're going to the war college," which would give me 12 to 15 months; it ended up being 14 months. I just didn't believe it. Why are they getting rid of me? I was told that it was a good deal since I was still a lieutenant. I was told that to go to the war college was great, prestigious, and all those things. So I packed my bags, and Jody and I moved to Newport in the summer of '64.

Paul Stillwell: Do you have a feeling for why you were moved early?

Captain Colbus: No, no idea. A funny thing happened as far as my relief went. As part of my job, I wrote the BuPers billets, so I wrote for the Pers-A3 crowd. Pers-A3121, which was my code number, was a lieutenant, surface, 1100—we didn't say 1110 then—and I was, of course, to be relieved by a surface lieutenant 1100.[*] And that's all that was stated. Then, of course, on the Pers-B side, they'd put in quality requirement.

We had a detailer over there with whom I worked closely. He put the bodies in all these Washington billets, and his name was Whitey Weidner, a submariner. He was a commander, bachelor, gourmet cook, now married to Whitey Hunt's sister.[†] He detailed my relief, who walked in about two weeks before I left. He was about six feet tall, about my age, and it was like looking in the mirror. The guy had a shaved head, he was from Providence, Rhode Island, he had just married, as I had done when I came there, he was Jewish, I was Jewish. He was absolutely a clone. I went over to see Whitey and I said, "You did this."

And to this day he says, "No, it just happened that way." But I'm telling you, he was my twin.

Paul Stillwell: Was it unusual for a lieutenant to be ordered to the Naval War College?

Captain Colbus: I think that was the first year that might have happened, but there were about four of us who did it.

---

[*] The officer designator 1100 was for an unrestricted line officer who was not a naval aviator. The designator 1110, surface warfare officer, was established in the 1970s.
[†] Lieutenant Herman Lamar Hunt, USN.

Paul Stillwell: I would think that was a feather in your cap.

Captain Colbus: I guess it was. I didn't think so at the time because I'm not much of a student. In fact, just to say that everything isn't sweetness and light and roses, I guess my most disappointing tour was the war college. I didn't enjoy those ten months there.

Paul Stillwell: Why not?

Captain Colbus: Well, I didn't like the environment. It wasn't that stringent, really, at the time. It was before our friend Admiral Stansfield Turner got there.* Our president was Admiral Melson, and his deputy was Admiral Nuessle, which is another story.†

That was when I really found out about the competition among the ranks. We had the "spring butts;" that's where I learned that term. This occurred when the auditorium was filled with the students in the command and staff course, which I was in, lieutenant commanders and commanders; the senior course, with the commanders and captains; and the Naval Command Course, which were the foreign officers. All these officers gathered in the auditorium to hear four-star Admiral So-and-so discuss whatever, or three-star General So-and-so discuss whatever. These were very, very interesting, high-level discussions. And at the end it'd always be, "And now are there any questions?"

We had what we called the spring butts. There would always be some officer who had to make a high-visibility run, jump up, raise his hand, and tell the admiral or the general or the senator, "That was a very interesting speech." Well, damn right it was interesting. And then he'd go on to pontificate how much he knew about the subject in two sentences, which would be closed with a brilliant question. Those were the spring butts. It was near lunchtime, and those of us who didn't have springs in their butts were sitting there, antsy, ready to go to lunch.

---

* Vice Admiral Stansfield Turner, USN, served as president of the Naval War College from 30 June 1972 to 9 August 1974. He instituted a much more rigorous curriculum than the one in place when he arrived.
† Vice Admiral Charles L. Melson, USN, served as president of the Naval War College from 31 July 1964 to 25 January 1966. Rear Admiral Francis E. Nuessle, USN, was deputy and later acting president.

As I said, it was a very, very competitive group, competitive to the point that one man was accused of cheating, even though to this day I'm sure he wasn't. He was accused of cheating, which we didn't do. There were no really big incidents. It was just a nice pace, really. Many of us took the George Washington University night school course. As I said, I was busy.

We had no children up to then, and Jody became pregnant while we were there. Because of complications, she had to stay in bed almost nine months of the ten months I was at war college. Our son Jonathan was born there in April 1965.

The war college was over in May. It was a good tour. We bought a house up there, as many of us did, hoping we'd stay. The highlight, of course, was what they called the gaieties—not varieties—gaieties. This was at the end of the school year. All of us got together and put on skits in which we'd take jabs and jives at the staff. We call it a roast today. That was a lot of fun. Admiral Nuessle was referred to as Admiral Hershey, and with due respect, I don't think to this day he recognized that he was the subject of the roast.[*]

Paul Stillwell: What kinds of things did you study?

Captain Colbus: International law, tactical formations, international affairs. Operational planning was really the meat of the course, and that was certainly worthwhile. I learned a lot, including how to write papers. Being a college graduate with graduate school experience, as I talked about earlier, should have provided me an analytical background. The war college was really the place where I learned how to write staff papers or how to write studies, how to catalogue, how to write bibliographies. That was probably the highlight of it for me. It was all worthwhile because nobody had ever really taught us or exposed us to planning procedures.

I told you I was the ops officer for CortRon 12. We wrote op orders, controlled 18 ships, and steamed all over the North Atlantic and Mediterranean. I always wrote the op orders based on what I'd seen in previous op orders. I guess you'd call it boilerplate, in that we just changed dates, names, and places. At the war college you really sat down and

---

[*] Despite the different spelling, his name was pronounced the same as the Nestle candy bar.

pulled it apart. Now, you just didn't do it by rote; you understood what you were doing. So it was well worthwhile and necessary.

Paul Stillwell: Did you find anything tactically useful, or was it more strategic type studies?

Captain Colbus: More strategic, as I remember. And as I say, more the nuts and bolts of how to do things on a staff level.

Paul Stillwell: Did you get into war gaming at all?

Captain Colbus: We did war gaming, yes. Our son was born during the week of our major war gaming. I was playing the logistics commander up in the North Sea. I guess if I'd paid more attention, it would have paid off in later duty stations, but I was more interested every day in getting over to the hospital and seeing the newborn baby. We had one fellow in my group who was so eager and such a spring butt that every time you'd go to do something, he'd grab the pencil and paper out of your hand, grab the pub and do it; he was a one-man band. We all sort of, to be gentlemen, sat back and let him do it. That was our big war game.

Paul Stillwell: Have you noticed whether the spring butts have prospered since then?

Captain Colbus: We had a very, very distinguished class. Many of them today are flag officers. I can't think of one of the flag officers who was a spring butt, now that you ask me. I'll have to answer no. All good guys. They were anxious to get to lunch too.

Paul Stillwell: You're probably familiar with the current, fancy, sophisticated electronic war games. How was it during that time, 20 years ago?

Captain Colbus: It was leading up to that. It wasn't as sophisticated as it is today. I've been up there in the past two years to play war games with the battle group staffs. For those times, it was very, very well received, highly respected, and certainly well-run, because many of the officers who would graduate from the war college would go to the war gaming section. We had a good interface there. In fact, we probably did better, prospered more, and enjoyed that more than we did some of the other academic things.

Paul Stillwell: What kinds of things did you write papers on?

Captain Colbus: Jody typed them. I ought to call her, she could tell me. What did we write papers on? I'm trying to remember just one. Based on all those things we talked about in the South Atlantic, I remember writing about the defense of the South Atlantic in the big war; that was one paper. We did do a lot of work in international law, because that was something new to all of us, especially law of the sea. As I sit here and go over some of these subjects, it really was a worthwhile year, and even though I said at the beginning it wasn't my best year, I did walk away with probably more than I reckoned.

Paul Stillwell: It sounds as if it did a lot more for you than the PG School.

Captain Colbus: Oh, no doubt about it. But that wasn't the PG School; that was the line school. The line school was, as I said, a repeat of NROTC. War college was much, much better. I just didn't enjoy ten months of it.

Paul Stillwell: You were on a staff before you went there, and then you were on staffs after. How would you compare your staff capability as a result of that war college experience?

Captain Colbus: Oh, much advanced, but you've got to remember when you talk about staff on an escort squadron, with due respect, it was on a lower echelon; we wrote on a daily support basis, just keeping things together, no long-range planning. We made sure that eight ships showed up at such-and-such a place. When you talk about that type of staff work, that was just day-to-day, very reasonable, fun things.

When you get to the big staff and even the big staff that I talk about is the carrier group, we had a plans officer who was writing the plan or at least knew the plans. And, of course, we got into NATO when I was on my first major staff, and that really wasn't that big a staff. On Carrier Group Six, I was the plans officer, and the staff itself was the NATO carrier striking force. Then you really relied on a lot of this. It also gave you the ability to know where to go and where to look things up. For that portion it was invaluable. I guess what it really boiled down to was that I didn't like wearing civilian clothes, going to school every day just as if I were back in college, plus the spring butts who showed up.

Paul Stillwell: What do you remember about the city of Newport?

Captain Colbus: I liked it very much. My wife, of course, is from the South. It was too cold, too damp, too this and too that. But we really had a very good time there, made lots and lots of friends. I can remember the fog rolling in. What's the expression, "Don't like the weather? Wait, it's going to change in the next few minutes." But I enjoyed my tour there. Newport, of course, is an ideal area and we liked it.

Paul Stillwell: Did you get to the jazz festival and that sort of thing?

Captain Colbus: I'd done that before. I don't think we did that while I was in war college. Did they have a jazz festival in '64 and '65? I don't think so.

Paul Stillwell: I was in Newport for those two summers when I was going through OCS. I remember hearing about both the jazz festival and what they called a folk festival.

Captain Colbus: You're right. Because when I went there in '71 to go to prospective commanding officer school for two weeks, to teach me how to be a CO, after having been one, they had a jazz festival/folk festival. See, that all pales by the fact that when I was there during my Albert T. Harris days, we had the real jazz festival. They really first started it in the '50s, and it was sponsored by a well-known tobacco family who vacationed in Newport. It was the Lorillard family who was active and popular. They were the ones who started the festivals, which then turned into an annual affair.

Paul Stillwell: Did you get kind of wistful during that year, looking out at the harbor and seeing destroyers?

Captain Colbus: Oh, yes, I was anxious to get going, get back to sea, do something. My desire, my wish was to get a destroyer out of Newport. We'd bought a home there, we liked it, and all these things. My son was born there. I was lucky enough to get a destroyer out of Newport.

Paul Stillwell: Let's move on to that tour.

Captain Colbus: USS Basilone (DD-824).[*] I met the ship the week of the Fourth of July in 1965 in New York City. The skipper was Don Bayly.[†] We sailed together for only three weeks. Then, a new skipper came on board; he was my man. He had been an instructor at the NCC, the foreign officers' course at the war college. When I got orders to Basilone, I found out that Commander Bob Stokes was going to be the skipper.[‡] I knew him because he didn't live that far from me. I'd see him in school, and when I went up to see him, I said, 'Guess what? Going to be your exec, Bob.' He was delighted, I was delighted. We planned all the things we were going to do when we became shipmates. Within three weeks after I took over as exec, he came aboard as the skipper, and we went from there.

Paul Stillwell: When had you been promoted?

---

[*] USS Basilone (DDE-824) was a Gearing-class destroyer modified for the ASW role prior to being commissioned 26 July 1945. She had a standard displacement of 2,425 tons, was 391 feet long, and 41 feet in the beam. Her design speed was 35 knots. She was armed with four 5-inch guns, four 3-inch guns, and five 21-inch torpedo tubes. In the early 1960s ASROC replaced Weapon Alfa as the principal ASW weapon. The ship was reclassified DD-824 on 30 June 1962.
[†] Commander Donald C. Bayly, USN.
[‡] Commander Robert Edward Lee Stokes, Jr., USN.

Captain Colbus: I had been selected for lieutenant commander by the time I left BuPers and went to the war college as a lieutenant commander.

Paul Stillwell: Was there any PXO school at that point?[*]

Captain Colbus: No school—just go do it. Since I'd already been an exec, this was easier. When I was exec of a DE, I was a lieutenant, the ops officer was a lieutenant who was maybe a page junior to me and probably the same year group. He knew as much as I did and was as experienced, but I was the exec and he had to be made to know it. You walk aboard a destroyer, you're a lieutenant commander, you're a seasoned guy, everybody else is a lieutenant, you're just automatically exec. You didn't have to prove yourself. It was great.

That was a very, very interesting tour. We started out operating around Newport in Basilone, which was a famous ship, by the way. It was a post-World War II destroyer, commissioned in '49 right here in Norfolk. She went hard aground in '58 off Fort Story, where she was aground for two days. They had a drink out at the fort called "Basilone on the Rocks." When she finally was free and was being towed back to the piers to determine what was going to be done, the extent of the damage and what have you, the skipper, who, I guess, knew it was all over, sent out a famous message from Basilone to everyone in the chain of command, "Under way, under tow, ready to join the fleet." That was not considered funny, they tell me, but we thought it was in the aftermath.

I've talked about Captain Bob Brady. His brother Frank was in the ship at the time of the grounding, so I got a lot of good dope from that. So Basilone was a well-known, famous ship, named for a Marine, Manila John Basilone.[†] At the war college we had Marine guards, of course, for security. When they heard I was going to USS Basilone,

---

[*] PXO—prospective executive officer.
[†] Gunnery Sergeant John Basilone was awarded the Medal of Honor for heroism on Guadalcanal on 24-25 October 1942. He was later killed in action on Iwo Jima on 19 February 1945 and awarded a posthumous Navy Cross.

they fussed over me because of my association with the name Basilone. I had to attend the Marine Ball on November 10.*

Paul Stillwell: He also had some relatives involved in the ship.

Captain Colbus: Yes, we talked about that at lunch last time. When I took over as exec in New York from Chuck Davidson, I asked Chuck about the Basilone family.†

I'd known there was a theater out in San Diego named for John Basilone. I knew there was a Basilone bridge on the New Jersey Turnpike, so where were the Basilones? Well, the Basilones are a tough family in Raritan, New Jersey. Chuck said to me, "I wanted to bring them down to the ship." The ship, by the way, had been FRAMed the year before in the Philadelphia Naval Shipyard and was recommissioned.‡ It was during this overhaul that Basilone received ASROC.§ It was quite a ceremony, and Chuck Davidson was now explaining to me why he didn't invite the Basilones to the commissioning. He couldn't get in touch with them, many reasons, but mainly because they were connected with unusual activities in Raritan. I let it go at that.

Within three weeks after the ship was back in Newport, I got in touch with Anthony Basilone in Raritan, New Jersey. He was delighted to have heard from me, wondered about the ship, was concerned, and I told him, "The ship is yours. You come visit us. We'll bring the ship to you at our first opportunity, be it New York, be it Earle, New Jersey, for loading of ammo." Within a week, I heard from Tony Basilone to ask if he could come up and visit with us. The answer was, "Absolutely." He showed at the piers about 11:00 o'clock up on a Sunday morning. He was there with three of his brothers, and I think there was a sister or a cousin.

The party came aboard ship, toured, and were delighted with what they saw. They became fast friends of the ship and, I like to say, fast friends of mine personally. We then

---

* Each year the Marine Corps holds a birthday ball to celebrate the anniversary of its founding on 10 November 1775.
† Lieutenant Commander Charles H. Davidson, USN.
‡ FRAM—an acronym for the fleet rehabilitation and modernization program. Under this program many U.S. destroyer-type ships of the 1950s and 1960s were substantially modernized by extensive rebuilding that incorporated later technology than that available at the time of original construction.
§ ASROC—antisubmarine rocket. It entered the fleet in the early 1960s in new-construction ships and in FRAM I destroyer conversions.

went by my home, and I introduced them to Jody and my son Jonathan. They raved over the new baby. They were very warm and friendly people, and back they went to New Jersey. When I called the ship's officers together on Monday at quarters, I told them, "If you know of any Basilone sailors going to New Jersey, let me know so they might be able to take our best wishes and regards to Raritan."

Within a week, three of our young sailors were on their way down there. One lived in Trenton, which meant they had to go through Raritan. The Trenton sailor was taking two of his buddies with him. I asked, "Would you mind, on your way down, stopping at Raritan and stop in at Tony's Bar?" I think that was the name of it. They said they would.

That was the end of that until Monday, when these fellows showed up at my stateroom door. They looked like death warmed over. Yes, they'd stopped. No, they never got to Trenton, because the minute they walked in there with Basilone nametags on their shoulders, they were the object of great affection and attention. The car was taken from them, it was washed, it was polished, it was gassed up, it was greased, everything. And they were taken from one bar to the other, and I guess from one house of ill repute to the other. There wasn't anything that they didn't do or they didn't get while they were in Raritan, New Jersey, and pretty soon the word was around the ship. If you were a Basilone sailor, make sure you stop in Raritan.

Paul Stillwell: Did the family subsequently visit the ship again?

Captain Colbus: No, I don't ever remember seeing them again. We didn't take the ship to New York or to Earle as I'd hoped we would. Just never worked out that way.

Paul Stillwell: What sort of operations was the ship involved in then?

Captain Colbus: Well, from the time I went aboard, as I say, the weekend of the Fourth of July, till the sixth January, 1966, we did ASW ops, we did Gemini recovery ops.[*] This involved going out and getting in a line of ships across the ocean to recover the Gemini

---

[*] As the U.S. space program progressed in the 1960s, it went from the initial one-man Mercury capsule to the larger Gemini version, which had two astronauts sitting side by side.

capsule. We worked with the carrier Wasp. That was all local ops until it was time to go to Vietnam in January 1966. We were the second East Coast squadron to deploy.

On a January morning, eight destroyers got under way, with Commodore Bob Guy riding Davis.* Davis was commanded by Bob Hilton, who later was my squadron commander down in Mayport when I was skipper of Jonas Ingram.† We had known by November that we were going to Vietnam. November and December were intensive months of readying the ship for wartime deployment.

Air-conditioning units were placed in all the compartments, spare parts were loaded, and all the things you would imagine you'd have to do to a ship to make it ready. The main thing that was probably the most impressive, difficult, and important was the influx of people. If we had normally, let's say, 190 to 210 personnel on board, all of a sudden we became 270. By the time we left in January, anybody who was going to be there only till June left the ship, because we didn't want to have to send him back from the Far East. We therefore had all these new people, and it was a complete training evolution.

The first squadron to leave Newport for Vietnam had its problems: collisions and all kinds of devastating things that happened to them between Newport and Hawaii.‡ Most of their problems occurred before they got to the Panama Canal, which I believe included in the Panama Canal one grounding in the lakes. Well, we profited from their problems. Commodore Guy put us in a 2,000-yard column, and away we went. We did nothing but train and integrate all these new sailors. We taught them port and starboard, taught them how to put the wheel over, taught them all these basics. By the time we got to the Philippines, which was a 40-day transit, we were in good shape. People knew what they were doing, in that we'd had underway replenishments, GQs by the dozens, and every training evolution.§ We were a shaken-down ship and ready to go. The rest of the tour over there was performed by a very, very experienced, enthusiastic crew, and that made deployment very easy.

---

* Captain Robert S. Guy, USN, Commander Destroyer Squadron 12.
† Commander Robert P. Hilton, USN.
‡ The initial destroyer deployment from the Atlantic Fleet began on 29 September 1965. The eight ships included six from the Newport-based Destroyer Squadron 24, commanded by Captain Carl A. Sander, USN, and two from Norfolk squadrons. The Newport ships got back to their homeport on 28 April 1966.
§ GQ—general quarters.

Paul Stillwell: Why did you have so many more people than you'd had for local ops?

Captain Colbus: Because it was realized that operating the ship as a three-section, Condition III watch required those numbers. That's what was ship called for, so make it look like the complement, make it look like it was supposed to, because now it's no longer going out for two or three weeks. People get tired. Even in the Med, you'd go for ten days and moor or anchor for three or four, which gave a break. We didn't see that in the Vietnam environment. Because it was going to be intensive, we had to have the people. After we got over there, that was very true. We were on the gun line 18 to 20 hours, which meant you needed very, very competent, fully manned gun crews.

Paul Stillwell: Had you had any specific shore bombardment training on the way over?

Captain Colbus: Yes, we had to qualify before we went over.

Paul Stillwell: Where did you get the experience, since ASW had really been the ship's role before then?

Captain Colbus: Well, the ships either made a run down to Culebra, down in the Roosey Roads area, or we'd run up to Bloodsworth Island in the Chesapeake and get qualified in gunfire support.* We don't use Bloodsworth today.

Paul Stillwell: Did you get any help from the fleet training group in this kind of thing?

Captain Colbus: Everybody was turned on. It made it easy. Here are all the sailors. Now what do you do? All you had to do was say what you needed. We just filled the ship with spare parts. In fact, we did so well in supplying our ship and overloading it that the skipper was called in and asked what he was going to do with all these over expenditures. The answer was, "Getting ready to go to Vietnam." And that was just the magic word.

---

* Culebra is a small island near Puerto Rico that was used by the Navy for many years as a shore bombardment target. Roosevelt Roads is the site of a U.S. naval station in Puerto Rico.

Then as it proved, once we got over there, we were practically the supply ship for the entire squadron.

We had as chief engineer Larry Blumberg, who is now the ops officer in Charleston for Cruiser-Destroyer Group Two.[*] You'd enter his spaces, and there were spares I couldn't even identify hanging from the bulkhead because they couldn't store them all. The ship was a floating warehouse, and it proved to be very prudent, even though I'm sure we cheated other ships; we were ready.

Paul Stillwell: Well, they could come to you to get the things they needed.

Captain Colbus: That's exactly what they did.

Paul Stillwell: Did this good relationship you had developed with the CO continue?

Captain Colbus: Oh, absolutely. Bob Stokes was a very difficult taskmaster. With him it was black and white, no gray. He was a very principled man. In fact, he was principled to the point that you sometimes wondered if it was sincere, and, of course, it proved to be so.

One of the things that my wife appreciated so much was his absolute ruling that in <u>Basilone</u> you could not take the Lord's name in vain. Now, I won't say he didn't curse, but his cursing was cursing, not swearing. He'd use a nasty word now and then, but he never took the Lord's name in vain. Anybody on there who did that was in big trouble. So after an indoctrination period, everything worked out just fine; everybody was squared away and knew and understood the captain.

He was a very religious man, very devoted to his wife and three girls. Not that we weren't, but he was especially so, and I think he had a very frustrating time over there in that deployment. A lot of that, I guess, you could attribute to me, because when we'd go to places such as Kaohsiung, Taiwan, which is just a marvelous liberty port, we'd go to town Saturday evening, have dinner, and just have a ball. All the crew would muster at a place called Nancy's Harbor Bar, and that would go on till the wee hours—just good, clean fun.

---

[*] Lieutenant Lawrence B. Blumberg, USN.

Then Sunday morning he'd get up, and I think he was disappointed in himself, in that he'd been out too late and probably had more to drink than he thought was the right amount, because he was a man of moderation. Besides that, his "girls" weren't around to go to church. So he'd start on me, "XO, I want to see you right away." He could find more things wrong on the ship on a Sunday morning than the law would allow. Sunday was a bad time in port, but then by the afternoon he'd calmed down, and we'd straighten things out. He was a man who seven days a week wanted the ship to look like it should look at its best. We wouldn't even talk about excuses. There was no reason that that ship on a Sunday morning at 9:00 o'clock couldn't be ready for inspection with everything spic and span.

Paul Stillwell: What kind of material condition was she in?

Captain Colbus: As good as any ship you've ever seen, again due to the fact that she had only been out of FRAM two years by then and that he was a very, very tough taskmaster and an excellent shipkeeper; he had high standards. He wrote 3x5 cards. You might have seen me reaching for some of mine. I learned that from Bob Stokes. As he would walk about the ship, he would actually write down what he saw and didn't particularly like, and then leave the cards for me on my desk. For instance, he would tell me about rust spot that was at the 6:00 o'clock position on a porthole that was on the port side, forward of the wardroom. I would go out there, and, sure enough, there'd be a rust spot. So I'd have somebody up there and correct it. That's how he ran the ship. It was immaculate. He just did nothing but ping all the time on that ship.

Paul Stillwell: Was he concerned to that same degree about operational things?

Captain Colbus: Absolutely. We were, I'd say, the only ship in the Atlantic and maybe even the Pacific that had a fully operational DASH.

Paul Stillwell: Drone antisubmarine helicopter.

Captain Colbus: Drone antisubmarine helicopter. We had two of them, and we were probably the only ship that had those two helicopters flying as a routine item. His rule was, "Any time this ship is beyond ten miles of land in a clear environment for flying, and it's 0800 after quarters, I want to see my DASH in the air." And he just harped on that until it became a standard. In the morning, immediately after quarters, the boatswain's mates of the watch piped flight quarters, and off would go the DASH. We could fly our DASH anywhere. We had some very, very good operating time. We would send it over the horizon and bring it back. He was very proud of that. So that was just one thing.

He was an excellent ship handler and a very bold naval officer who really believed in accountability. Everything on that ship was his. If it didn't work, you either corrected it or you got rid of it. And so when you ask how was he operationally and technically, as sound as anybody could be. Not popular. What I liked about him most was, you always knew where you stood with him. He had absolutely no qualm about calling in somebody, sitting him down, looking him right in the eye, and saying, "You're not cutting the mustard. This is not a threat. This is not a promise, but let's not wait till fitness report. I'm not too happy." It wasn't an ultimatum; it was just where you stood. And people appreciated that.

Paul Stillwell: Did the DASHes serve any useful purpose?

Captain Colbus: We used them to transfer material at sea. That trip I just talked about en route to Vietnam, we used it to transfer material. We could take it off and turn control over to another ship, and they could land it on that ship. It could drop torpedoes for us, which it did, when necessary. So as far as our interest and satisfaction, both were there.

Paul Stillwell: I've gathered overall that the program was not a success.

Captain Colbus: No, it wasn't, because I think people expected it to do more than it was designed to do. It was designed to deliver a weapon. We did more than that. It was a new system, and people said, "I can't send it up because if I lose it I'm in big trouble." Each DASH had a unit cost of $150,000 or $175,000, which doesn't sound like much today. It's my contention that the people didn't use the DASH because they were afraid of it. Therefore, it died by the people's own prediction, which I think is also true of ASROC.

ASROC was never used as it should have been, and you can't blame the ship's skipper too much for that. What I'm saying is that you got to fire, if you were average, two ASROCs per year. Those shots were competitive. You weren't just firing them for fun. You should have had some practice, but most ships didn't. Now you're down to two firings. Well, you'd have the target submarine out there, and as the submarine would come in, you'd get set up. You weren't going to shoot that ASROC as you would have in a real situation. In wartime, the minute you had it within range and you had any idea you had a submarine, wham, you'd fire that weapon at, say, 9,000 yards. You would get a weapon in the water because you had a threat.

But when you were doing it competitively with a friendly submarine and it was all simulation, people said, "Let's wait. Let's get set up here. Let's find out what the range rate is. Let's do all these things. I want a perfect solution. I want a hit. I want 100%." You'd wait until the target was in at 2,200 yards, and all of a sudden, ASROC is not all those things it should be. We made it a short-range weapon, which was not what it was supposed to be. I got to see this later when I was in the DX program and the FFG-7 program.* People said ships didn't really need ASROC because it's a short-range weapon. Why did they say that? Well, look how it was utilized. We killed DASH because it didn't work. We had the helicopter replace it, so that's better.

Paul Stillwell: Please describe some of those 18- and 20-hour days on the gun line.

Captain Colbus: Got in very, very close and did a lot of waiting to respond to calls for fire from the Marines. The most hectic part in South Vietnam, down in IV Corps, was the very marshy terrain.* It was extremely difficult to navigate, and besides hazarding the ship, it was very difficult to lay your guns, since there was nothing to fix on. You'd wait and wait till it was time to shoot, and you might not shoot those 18 hours, but you were sitting there

---

* These were destroyer and frigate development programs in the late 1960s and early 1970s, discussed later in the oral history.

waiting to go, and you were steaming very slowly. You had to watch the currents, because you'd run into eddies that would all of a sudden grab the ship. You weren't but a few yards off shoal water.

Captain Stokes said there was one reason why we were there, and that was to provide gunfire support; therefore, he didn't want to hear about going aground. He wanted to get in as close as possible, and if it wasn't comfortable, that was my problem. At the same time, I was not to hazard the ship. We didn't want to ground it, because then we were really ineffective. I don't want to say he wasn't cautious, and I don't want to say he wasn't concerned about going aground, but his main interest and main concern were to do his job. He'd take the ship in very close, closer than anybody else—not for the bravado of it, but just because that's where we belonged. As I said, he was a very principled individual.

Paul Stillwell: The closer you got to the shore, the farther your guns can reach inland.

Captain Colbus: Very true.

Paul Stillwell: Did you wind up doing much troop support?

Captain Colbus: Yes, we did that quite a bit; in fact, all the time. I forget what the exact statistics were, but we expended around 5,000 rounds of 5-inch while we were there.

Paul Stillwell: Did you have air spotters?

Captain Colbus: We did, yes; we also had ground spotters. We'd bring the spotters to the ship so that we could get to know them.

Paul Stillwell: How good were you at putting an initial salvo on target?

---

* South Vietnam was divided into four corps tactical zones. The southernmost was IV Corps, with headquarters at Can Tho. It was responsible for operations in the Mekong Delta. It ran from Dong Tam on the Gulf of Tonkin around to the Cambodian border in the Gulf of Thailand.

Captain Colbus: We were very good, we really were. That was because we had an experienced and enthusiastic crew, combined with Bob Stokes's leadership and his demand for perfection.

Paul Stillwell: Did you ever get any of the troops out to the ship?

Captain Colbus: Oh, yes.

Paul Stillwell: I would think that would build morale on both sides.

Captain Colbus: In fact, any time we'd be anywhere that we'd see small craft or Swift boats, we'd invite them on board.* We'd slow the ship, just keep way on, and bring the boats alongside. We brought the crews on board to visit, shower, mess, replenish, or whatever. To them we were a big, fancy ship. They'd take their showers, have a good meal in the wardroom, and visit the ship's store. Yes, we hosted those folks when we could get them alongside.

Paul Stillwell: How long a period, generally, would you spend at sea at a time off Vietnam?

Captain Colbus: I'd say an average of 30 days.

Paul Stillwell: Was there an oiler, say, making the circuit every few days?

Captain Colbus: All the time. It was just a round robin. You would finish gunfire support, and as you'd steam away, you'd rendezvous with an oiler or an ammo ship or a stores ship on the horizon. You'd take off, chase that ship just as you'd chase the Good Humor man around the corner. Ten minutes before getting alongside, you'd call the crew away, and

---

* The Mark I PCF (patrol craft fast), also known as the Swift boat, was built by Sewart Seacraft of Berwick, Louisiana, adapted from the design of Gulf of Mexico oil rig boats. The PCF was 50 feet long, 13 1/2 feet in the beam, and drew 5 feet. It was armed with three .50-caliber machine guns, one 81-millimeter mortar, and had a top speed of 25 knots.

they'd be on station in no time. There weren't these half-hour preparations. Everybody was wartime mode. As I said, same crew, seven months there, constantly alongside, so we could call away the detail as required. We learned that we could take our time and straggle up there, and as long as we had ten minutes' notice, that worked out perfectly. We didn't need a half hour to ease up there to station. I'm sure all of the ships did that.

Paul Stillwell: How demanding was this on you physically in terms of hours a day?

Captain Colbus: We all put the time in. We had a very good arrangement in Basilone, because one of the things that he used to say to me was, "A well-rested exec is better than a tired skipper." So if I wasn't navigating and things weren't that pressing, he would insist I go down and nap, be it afternoon, whatever. Then, after I'd had three or four hours' sleep, I'd come up, and he'd go in and lie down. So we really spelled each other on the bridge.

Paul Stillwell: You must have developed a pretty good duty section navigating team to keep you off the shoal water.

Captain Colbus: We had a quartermaster first class by the name of William English, who was very, very good. The only problem was, he didn't like the skipper and he wouldn't talk to the captain. I was never forceful enough, clever enough, leader enough to get him to break down. Don't get me wrong. He would answer the captain. If the captain said, "Good morning," he would answer. But what I'm saying is that he wouldn't come out, go to the captain, and say, "I think we're being set down by the current. I recommend [such-and-such]." So any time we were in a tough situation, I had to be up there just to talk to the captain, because, as I say, English had some kind of a disconnect.

Paul Stillwell: Did you work with the carriers at all?

Captain Colbus: Yes. Our carrier was Ticonderoga.* We were always with Tico.

---

* USS Ticonderoga (CVA-14) was an Essex-class aircraft carrier, originally commissioned in 1944. Her WestPac period ran from 25 October 1965 to 7 May 1966. Her Air Wing 5 at the time included F-8s, A-4s, A-1s, A-3s, RF-8s, E-1s, and UH-2s.

Paul Stillwell: What do you remember about those operations?

Captain Colbus: Exciting fast lane, and made it easy to ship people over.* Those were the days when I had lines waiting outside my stateroom door. When I'd come off the bridge to do administrative things, everyone was in line waiting to reenlist. We'd be on one side of the oiler, the carrier would be on the other side of the oiler, both of us doing our unreps. While the carrier was unrepping, of course, she was launching and recovering. You'd see a plane coming back with half the tail shot off; you'd see the bullet holes; you'd see that these planes weren't just up doing cyclic ops; they were in over the beach, and somebody shot at then. Boy, that just pumped my shipmates full of sunshine. They were really doing it; they were in the war zone. Little things such as free mail—boy, we're in a war zone, hazardous duty—hey, we're going to get fired on, and tax-free salary up to $500.00 a month. These activities had my shipmates shipping over left, right, and center.

Paul Stillwell: Running in the wake of a fast-moving carrier calls for an entirely different set of skills from shore bombardment, where you were moving slowly up and down the beach. How did you make the adjustment?

Captain Colbus: An all-purpose destroyer must do all those things, and we did. I'm just not being swashbuckling there. When we were behind the carrier, we had the ops team on station. They were doing the tracking and the necessary operational things. We also had the forecastle crew standing by in case we had to act as rescue destroyer, which we did on a couple of occasions. We had to go in and pick up remains. I don't remember picking up live pilots, but on occasion I can remember going in to find what we could of wreckage, of planes that didn't make it back. So now, instead of the boatswain's mates being out rigging for unrep, they'd be grappling for wreckage debris or standing by and staying in the wake of that carrier.

Paul Stillwell: Did you have swimmers trained to go in the water and pull people out?

---

* "Ship over" is a Navy slang term for reenlisting.

Captain Colbus: Yes.

Paul Stillwell: Any specific incidents in working with the carrier that you recall?

Captain Colbus: The carrier Tico experienced a catapult problem that really made her a less than fully operational carrier. At some point, the decision was made to take that carrier back to Subic for a three-day fix on that catapult.* We made a speed run of 25 knots from Yankee Station all the way back to Subic, with Basilone as escort.† We just ran that ship hard; I think it was 25 knots for 24 hours. We arrived at Subic at 2200, and the carrier moored to a pier. By then it was 2330. Captain Miller, skipper of the carrier, exercised his authority prior to getting there.‡ The entire base, including the exchange and clubs, was open for Tico and Basilone.

Paul Stillwell: What do you recall of liberty at Subic?

Captain Colbus: Wild, woolly stuff right out of a book when it came to visiting the officers' club with the aviators. They released all their tensions, did all the crazy things that you read about and hear about, and we just joined in with them. I had some friends stationed there. It was a nice respite.

Paul Stillwell: Did you do any sightseeing at all in the Philippines?

Captain Colbus: We went to Olongapo every chance we had.§ That was as far as I got. That was all I could handle. Olongapo, I say, is one of the great cities of the world. I don't

---

* Subic Bay in the Philippines provided an enormous amount of logistic support to Seventh Fleet ships during the Vietnam War.
† During the initial stages of involvement in the Vietnam War, the U.S. Navy maintained aircraft carriers on two stations based on Civil War designations—Yankee Station off North Vietnam and Dixie Station off South Vietnam. The latter, which began on 16 May 1965, was dropped 15 months later once airfields were available ashore in South Vietnam.
‡ Captain Ward Miller, USN.
§ Olongapo, the town right outside the U.S. naval base at Subic Bay in the Philippines, was noted for its raunchiness during the Vietnam War period and later.

say that facetiously. Before a man dies he ought to see Rio de Janeiro, the most gorgeous city in the world, sure as hell ought to go visit Las Vegas, because that's unreal. If he hasn't seen Olongapo, he's missed something. May not want to go back, but got to visit Olongapo. Have you been there?

Paul Stillwell: I've been and have no desire to go back.

Captain Colbus: Then you know what I mean. You ought to see it, it's unreal. Twenty-four hours a day, it's like the midway at the circus—great place.

One of the great things on that deployment happened while we were en route. We stopped in Hawaii, where I went to see a shipmate of mine from John R. Perry days; by this time his ship was USS Philip. I went to visit him, and he took me home to see his wife and family. We decided to go out that evening. So here were my friend, his wife, myself, and, I'd say, the skipper and maybe six or eight of the wardroom.

Well, we went to Don Ho's, just as all tourists do in Hawaii.* While we were sitting there, a fellow came over to our table and shook hands. It was a man who'd gone to high school with me, and now he was a druggist here in Hawaii. Well, isn't this great? My goodness. Then we bumped into somebody else whom I'd known, and I just thought that was great, and we shook hands. This was somebody, let's say, with whom I'd gone to sonar school. This happened on a couple of occasions. I'd just danced with Karleen, my friend's wife, and I was taking her back to our table. This fellow whom I recognized heralded and smiled at me. I stopped to talk to him, saying, "Hey, how you doing?"

"Fine. How are you?"

"Good to see you."

"Nice to see you." And just small talk, no meaningful conversation whatsoever because I couldn't even think of his name or where I'd met him to I could introduce him to Karleen. Finally we concluded our dance-floor patter, "Good seeing you."

"Great."

I went to our table, sat down, and was asked, "Do you know him?"

"Sure."

---

* Don Ho, a popular Hawaiian singer, had a nightclub in Honolulu.

"From where?"

"Damned if I know."

"Don't you know who that was?"

I said, "I guess it must have been somebody I went to war college with—no, it wasn't war college, because that was just last year. Sonar School? No, he's too old for that; he's older than I am." My friends then told me it was Richard Boone, the actor who played Paladin in "Have Gun Will Travel."[*] I knew I knew him, and that was the laugh of the whole cruise: "Louis knows everybody!" But in this case I really didn't.

We steamed out with Ticonderoga and ended up in Hong Kong for a big visit. This was big time. While we were in Hong Kong, Ticonderoga's crew took over the ballroom of the Hong Kong Hilton. As their gun ship, we were invited along. We attended that party. We circulated. We knew some of the sailors from the carrier, they knew we were destroyer sailors, and we all had a grand time.

Standing over in the corner was this very distinguished looking man: silver hair, maybe 55 or 60. He had to be an admiral or an ambassador. I recognized him, so I went up and started talking to him.

"Yes, sir, how are you?"

"Fine, thank you." He said, "You don't remember where it was?"

"No, sir."

And he played cat and mouse with me. I was getting very uncomfortable. "Well," he finally said, "Nobody remembers me. I play these bit parts. I'm out here making the movie Sand Pebbles.[†] I always play the preacher."

"Right." His name was Larry Gates. You don't know him, I don't know him, but if he comes on television, we all say, "There he is."

"Oh, yes, I've seen him." He and I continued our conversation. I said, "We're in port aboard Basilone. We're anchored right out there. Would you like to come to lunch?" He and the some of the crew members from the movie came out to the ship the next day.

---

[*] "Have Gun Will Travel" was a popular television Western series that aired from 1957 to 1963. He had served in the Navy during World War II.

[†] The Sand Pebbles, released by 20th Century Fox in 1966, was the story of a fictitious U.S. Navy gunboat, USS San Pablo, operating on the rivers of revolution-torn China in 1926. Steve McQueen starred as a machinist's mate in the crew; Larry Gates played a character named Jameson.

We got to know that crowd and palled around with them on a couple of occasions.

Paul Stillwell: I have much happier memories of Hong Kong than Olongapo.

Captain Colbus: Each has its place in a sailor's life. It was very popular then for the sailors to go over and order automobiles, in that there was a big saving, and we had money. This was the first time we had pocket money. The bachelors, especially, had cash because we were drawing hazardous duty pay for Vietnam. It was only $65.00 a month, but that was $65.00 we never had before. We certainly weren't spending any, because we were at sea; also, your first $500.00 a month were tax-free. We were buying automobiles.

One gunner's mate second class came back one day and came up to me to get the automobile paperwork signed, because this was part of my routine: Get the exec to sign this, saying that you're authorized and you're reliable, good boy type thing. He said, "And the man who's over there with whatever company that's ordering these automobiles and delivering them when we get home said that he wants to talk to you because you and he served for the same skipper." He was in USS Bearss during the Cuban Crisis with Chas Sherwood, and Chas Sherwood had told many stories about his days in Albert T. Harris. He said, "He'll come by here at 1800 to take you for drinks and dinner, and please bring the skipper and anybody else."

So I rounded up about four of us, including the skipper. We were standing on the quarterdeck at 1800. Here came a craft that was modeled after a Chinese junk, looked like a Chinese junk, but it was a completely appointed oceangoing yacht. There was a crew of three in uniform, with the uniform being those rigs that the sea chanteys wear—the old-timey striped shirts. Anyway, three crew members in uniform, beautiful cabins, head with a bidet—that kind of luxury on this yacht.

The topside consisted of lounging cushions and he had about half a dozen of the best-looking Eurasian women you could imagine. Also a few white Russians. Again Hollywood, playboy motif. We cruised around in that yacht, went and had dinner with him, and he just couldn't get over the fact that he'd gotten out of the Navy and was doing his merchandising there in Hong Kong. Of course, we took them back to the ship for coffee at midnight and just had a grand time. He had to show off his yacht and show off his beautiful Hong Kong women.

Paul Stillwell: It seems to me that getting as far north as Kaohsiung was sort of off the beaten track.

Captain Colbus: We went there more than we went anywhere else. That was a favorite spot, again, not only for the liberty, but because the tender was there. We'd come off the gun line, go out into Yankee Station, and then take off to the east for Kaohsiung, passing Pratas reef, on which USS Knox went aground.* That story was still fresh in everybody's mind when we arrived.

Paul Stillwell: Why didn't you use Subic so much?

Captain Colbus: That was much farther, and it was also a matter, I think, of distributing the wealth.

Paul Stillwell: Did you get to Japan at all?

Captain Colbus: No, we didn't get to Japan, and we felt bad about that. Then, of course, we came back through the Suez Canal, which gave us a round-the-world deployment. This included the Malacca Straits; a stop in Penang, Malaysia; Cochin, India; into the Arabian Sea, through the Suez; visits in Athens, Barcelona, and on home.

Paul Stillwell: I guess you didn't beat the closing of the Suez by too many months. That was in June of '67.

---

* The destroyer Frank Knox (DDR-742) ran aground on Pratas Reef in the South China Sea on 18 July 1965. She was finally refloated on 23 August after five weeks of intensive salvage efforts.

Captain Colbus: That's right, we sure didn't. We departed Newport in January 1966. We transited the Suez in September, made the Mediterranean port calls, and arrived in Newport in October 1966.

Paul Stillwell: You were gone the better part of the year.

Captain Colbus: Yes, sir.

Paul Stillwell: Did you have some kind of familygram set up, some way of staying in touch with the families?

Captain Colbus: Other than what you just mentioned, familygrams, letters, audio tapes. Videotapes didn't come till the '70s. People accepted the separation; they didn't expect it, they accepted it.

Paul Stillwell: What was the chain of command out there? You worked for CTG 70.8?*

Captain Colbus: Yes, we did.

Paul Stillwell: So he would allocate who was going to do gun line at a certain time and who was going to be with a carrier?

Captain Colbus: We had a number of bosses, as I recall. We worked not only for the surface commander out there and also ran with the carrier in Yankee Station. You then shifted your control, your tactical command, and became an entity in the cardiv world out there.

Paul Stillwell: CTF 77.†

---

* Commander Task Group 70.8 was the operational title for Commander Cruiser-Destroyer Group Seventh Fleet.
† Task Force 77 is the fast carrier striking force of the U.S. Seventh Fleet.

Captain Colbus: Yes, exactly.

Paul Stillwell: Did you have a bunch of tired guys by the time you got home?

Captain Colbus: No, we weren't that tired. As I say, people became used to a routine. I don't say that we thrived on it, but—like anything else—we adjusted to our routine, which was about three or four hours of sleep a night. It's the old story of a sailor: he can sleep anywhere and anytime. We grabbed sleep when we could. We weren't one of those ships that said, "Well, it's working hours now. You can't lie down." No, no. Sleep when you can; work when you have to. They were an enthusiastic group. We didn't tire them out.

Paul Stillwell: Always before you had been one of the boys. Now the junior officers worked for you instead of your being at the same level with them. Did that give you a problem?

Captain Colbus: We never had a problem with that. That was always a nice thing. It was just like with the captain, go ashore with the captain and we were one of the boys, we were a group. When you got aboard ship, there was no problem. In fact, that is one of the beauties of Navy life: work together, play together, and no one forgets who is who. One of the sayings I picked up says it all: "In an organization that has rank in its structure, the junior, if he is a gentleman, never forgets it. The senior, if he is a gentleman, never thinks of it."

Paul Stillwell: Did you have a good set of OODs?

Captain Colbus: Like anything else, I think we had a mixture. We were using chiefs. A chief could qualify, cut the mustard, and the captain trusted him. He could be a fleet OOD under way. So, in general, yes we had good OODs, again through practice. We were at sea enough, and everybody got his turn. There were ones who were outstanding, and there were ones who were mediocre, and I can say, under Bob Stokes, you didn't have many that were less than excellent

Paul Stillwell: Did you get involved in any situations where you were receiving gunfire from the beach?

Captain Colbus: Yes, we did. On a number of occasions, we'd go in close enough for counter-fire. It wasn't heavy fire; it was always light stuff. But that brings up a point that will show you what kind of a sailor Bob Stokes is. We had at that time what was called a Helena sister hook—Helena for the cruiser, sister hook for the piece of hardware that attaches in this case, the jack to the jackstaff.[*] When hoisted, it closed up to the truck, and there was no gap. Before this Helena hook that we'd learned about, we'd always have perhaps an inch and a half between the top of the jack and the flat truck on the staff. That's not nautical. A squared-away ship has it closed up. Closed up means just that—not slack, not dipped. Well, this sister hook allowed the jack to be flush, and there would be no question about it.

One Sunday we were going up the river right there near Vung Tau. It's at the end of a peninsula, with a lot of shipping in there. We had to go into a cove. The area was very narrow, difficult, and a lot of ships at anchor. We went in there and decided it was proper to anchor. We usually didn't anchor; we kept the ship moving. But it was easier and best all around. We anchored the ship on a Sunday morning, ready for call for fire. We could pick up the anchor and steam on short notice. We didn't think we could shoot from an anchored position. We'd never done that before, just because it wasn't safe. Anyway, be that as it may, we dropped the anchor. We were close enough to the beach that we could see Vietnamese on either side. Old Bob Stokes called me over and said, "XO, I want you to put that Helena hook on the jack."

"Yes, sir. I did."

"That isn't any Helena hook. Look at it. I can see there's a big gap."

"Well, Captain, sir, I won't say it's a big gap. There's more gap than I would expect, but it's a great improvement."

"Well, you're wrong. I don't think your signalman put on this Helena."

---

[*] The union jack is a small flag that amounts to a portion of a U.S. national flag—the part with white stars on a blue background. It is typically flown from a jackstaff on the bow of a Navy ship when she is moored or anchored.

"Oh, yes, sir."

"Did you inspect it?"

"No, sir."

"How do you know?"

"They told me it was accomplished."

"I think they're pulling your leg."

"No, sir, they don't pull my leg."

"Want to ask them?"

"No, sir, I don't want to ask them. They told me that's it."

"You do down there and you inspect it. I want you to see."

"Now, sir?"

"Now." I put on a bulletproof vest, a flak jacket, and a helmet. I opened the bridge doors, and the minute I went onto the forecastle, there was small arms fire. So I wondered what the hell I was doing there on Sunday morning checking the damn jack. I should have been on the bridge where I belonged, inside the ship. Not that I was frightened; I just thought this was dumb. I was embarrassed. The crew knew why I was out there. Well, I inspected the jack. It went up maybe another half inch closer. I reported back to the Bob Stokes, "Captain, that is a <u>Helena</u> hook."

"Well, I'm disappointed."

"Yes, sir." And that was that. Tough guy.

The captain came out of the sea cabin one morning on the 0400 to 0800 watch, and the OOD was over on the side of the bridge, nice and calm. We weren't in restricted waters; we were just steaming, waiting for an oiler or something. The OOD was on the starboard wing, sitting on the gunwale. Sitting. The captain called me in a fury, "Get up here and relieve the OOD. I don't want to see him on the bridge anymore." He threw him off the bridge. It took me about three weeks to get that OOD back up on the bridge. You don't sit down when you're the ODD. Stand up there as you're supposed to. No second chance, no warning. The OOD was wrong. We ran the ship like that. I will admit that we had a good ship.

A very sad thing occurred on the way home from that deployment, while we were between Barcelona and Newport. As we were making our crossing, the selection list for captain came out. Captain Stokes did not get selected. He was a non-select. He didn't make it the second time, but did the third time.

Paul Stillwell: That's unheard of, isn't it? I thought two strikes was out.

Captain Colbus: Normally, but he hung in there. He made it by going to Washington and working in OP-06.[*] That's a long story about whom he had to see. Why did he fail selection? He was told it was because he had no Washington duty. He was then ordered to Washington duty. I went to Washington again myself in '68, after commanding my own destroyer escort. I socialized with Bob Stokes, who was a very disappointed man. All the great things he did in that ship and all his accomplishments, he had to come to Washington to get selected. He said, "This ain't my Navy." After that, his heart wasn't in it. What a disappointment. He did everything a sailor had to do at sea but twice failed selection, with the second time being still in Basilone. He was selected after going to Washington, where he played around with pieces of paper in OP-06 and served two captains. He later went out to Great Lakes as a captain, served as the admin officer, and then retired.[†]

Paul Stillwell: From the way you've described him as a skipper, he should have been a captain.

Captain Colbus: Should have been an admiral.

Paul Stillwell: What happened after your ship got to Newport? Did you have a stand-down rest period?

Captain Colbus: Yes, 30 days. That was in October of '66. I remember because Jody's dad died, and we went down to Winston-Salem for a few days. Then back to Newport, where

---

[*] OP-06 was the Deputy Chief of Naval Operations (Plans and Policy).
[†] Stokes was promoted to captain with a date of rank of 1 August 1968; he retired in February 1973.

we operated the ship locally. I was called and told, "You're getting command of McCloy." I left the ship in December and went to McCloy.*

Paul Stillwell: That's unusual to go right from an XO tour to CO, isn't it?

Captain Colbus: No, that was the routine then.

Paul Stillwell: I see.

Captain Colbus: XO of a destroyer, CO of a DE.

Paul Stillwell: I would have thought there would have been a shore duty in between.

Captain Colbus: I guess there could have been, but it wasn't in this case.

Paul Stillwell: Where was she home-ported?

Captain Colbus: Newport. I just moved across the pier. I relieved a friend by the name of Paul Treagy.† The exec was Terry Siple, who was a story in his own.‡ Terry Siple came into the Navy in 1954 from Meadville, Pennsylvania. He went aboard ship and within three years had become a personnelman first class. He was exceptionally hard-working, nose to the grindstone, absolutely brilliant, and a very forward-thinking person. He was selected and sent to OCS, where he was commissioned in 1960. His first assignment as an ensign was USS Joseph P. Kennedy, and he just had this tremendous rise to power; everybody raved about him. I was fortunate enough to have him as exec.

---

* USS McCloy (DE-1038) was a Bronstein-class destroyer escort commissioned 21 October 1963. She had a standard displacement of 1,792 tons, was 372 feet long, and 41 feet in the beam. Her design speed was 26 knots. She was armed with three 3-inch guns and two torpedo tubes, and ASROC.
† Lieutenant Commander Paul E. Treagy, Jr., USN.
‡ Lieutenant Terrence E. Siple, USN.

He went on to do bigger and better things too. He was the commissioning skipper of the destroyer escort Ainsworth.* In all fairness, he became too big for his britches and didn't want to listen to anybody. Now, that wasn't when he was with me. I'm talking about later on. He told everybody how the Navy ought to be run, would write letters to whomever. After 20 years he said the Navy was too far behind, he was too fast for it, which was true, and he retired.† In McCloy in 1967 he told me I needed to have a more liberal approach to marijuana, because it was going to be the thing of the future.

I said, "Get out of here. Get out of my cabin. What are you talking about? Nobody should even think like that."

He answered, "You watch. Someday we'll understand this problem, and we may not accept it in the Navy, but we'll be more tolerant of it."

In those days, if you even heard of such a thing, that was terrible. But he was already preaching that we ought to be more liberal. As I say, a very, very smart man. While I greatly respected him, I was always amazed—maybe shocked—at how liberal Terry was.

Paul Stillwell: How did he do as exec?

Captain Colbus: Four point oh; he just did everything. It was an interesting ship because I relieved a man who was a one-man show—a brilliant, very, very enthusiastic and exceptionally aggressive man, who had enormous amounts of energy. Paul Treagy just did everything himself. When I walked on board, I thought the exec should be running it, as I ran Basilone, and turned it over to him. He appreciated the opportunity to excel. I stayed out of his business.

Oh, I'll tell you one thing that made him great. After our deployment as the flagship for the NATO squadron, we returned home and entered the Boston Naval Shipyard. We were converting our sonar from the SQS-26, which was the most recent, large, big, powerful sonar in the world, to an SQS-26-AXR. That changed some of the equipments, modularized some of the components, and just made it a better sonar. It took

---

* Siple was a lieutenant commander when he and his crew put USS Ainsworth (DE-1090) into commission at the Norfolk Naval Shipyard on 31 March 1973.
† Siple retired as a commander in April 1975.

a six-month period in the shipyard to do accomplish this. As we steamed to Boston, Terry's cry was, "I want to start PACE in McCloy."* This was college courses on board ship.

I told him, "Can't do it, not on here, Terry. It's too small a ship. That's fine for the cruiser Boston, that might be fine for a tender, but not on a destroyer." I was not against it; I just said it wouldn't work. He harped on me and pinged on me until I said, "Well, you can look into it."

He went to Harvard, got a very, very prestigious group lined up, and said, "We want to do PACE on a small combatant, where it's never been done, but we'll do it." This Harvard group came to the ship to look into the possibility.

We had a luncheon for these Harvard hoi polloi people, and after the luncheon we were sitting around while Terry was describing how he would make PACE work aboard McCloy. They were finally convinced. I was not, as I said, against it, but I wasn't that convinced. One of the visitors said, "Well, we'll come back next Tuesday and talk to the people."

Terry's answer was, "Tuesday isn't a good day because of the 18 people who are interested, three are in fire-fighting school." And he gave a complete resume, roster, of what those 18 people would do, indicating we'd end up with six of them.

"How about Wednesday?"

He went through the same thing. He knew. I looked at him and said, "Terry, I know it's going to work better here than in a big ship." He just had that thing down pat.

They said, "You're right."

I said, "As commanding officer, I was hesitant about this. I didn't think it would work for many reasons, but after hearing the exec, such control, such attention to detail, it'll work just fine." We all agreed, and that was the marriage. We were the first small combatant to have a PACE organization on board, and it was all due to Terry Siple.

Paul Stillwell: Was this done both at sea and in port?

---

* PACE—Program for Afloat College Education.

Captain Colbus: Well, at that time, just in port. But it was so successful, we, of course, carried it to sea.

Paul Stillwell: How many instructors were involved?

Captain Colbus: Three. We had a history instructor, an English instructor, and a math instructor.

Paul Stillwell: Was Siple able to communicate his enthusiasm to the sailors to get them involved?

Captain Colbus: Yes, his enthusiasm was very low key. It was more by example.

He's divorced now and remarried, so I can tell the story. We went up to Norway, where we transited the fjords. We had a ball. We were flagship for the StaNavForLant Dutch commodore, Frantz "Happy" Visé.* One day we were getting under way from a Norwegian port. I had been to a party with Terry the night before at one of the local gathering spots. The underway time was 8:30. I came out on the bridge at 8:10, and the ops officer reported the ship was ready to get under way.

"Where's the exec?"

"Not aboard, sir."

"What do you mean, he's not aboard?"

"Exec is not aboard."

"Ah-oh. Where is he?"

"Nobody knows."

Well, I got under way at 8:30. I was worried. Was he lying in the gutter somewhere? How was I going to handle this? I'd better break out the manual and start doing XO's work again. I had to do it myself, because I didn't have an exec. Well, as the ship was backing away—and the commodore was surprised that I didn't wait and go look for Terry—somebody yelled, "There's the exec, getting out of a cab on the pier!" There he

---

* StaNavForLant—Standing Naval Force Atlantic.

was, decked out in an ascot with a blue blazer; he was a very elegant dresser and a really spiffy guy. I was thrilled! I stopped the ship and began to return to the pier.

The commodore said, "Louis, why don't you use the tug that's standing by?"

"Oh, right, Commodore." I was so excited and relieved I wasn't thinking. Anyway, we got the tug to pick up the exec and deliver him to the fantail.

I got the ship under way and turned it over to the OOD. That was, as I say, 8:30 or so. By 10:00 the exec still wasn't on the bridge, so I buzzed his room. He answered, "Yes, sir?"

I said, "Terry, are you going to get up and navigate the ship or do I have to do that too?"

"I'll be right up, sir." He came up and came over to me. I didn't say a word. He looked at me sheepishly and said, "Want me to navigate?"

"Yes, of course."

I went below and had lunch; Terry came to the wardroom and had lunch. We were now out into the blue water, and things were going well. It must have been 1600 when I went in my cabin to do something. The exec was still on the bridge. I called him, "XO, let me talk to you."

He came in and he said, "Yes, sir."

I said, "What happened this morning? I'm not going to do a thing about it. It's really beyond me. You, in front of this entire crew, embarrassed yourself, embarrassed me, embarrassed everybody. But you've got so much gravy going for you, you're going to have to live with it. Now, what you can do is handle it when you have a sailor come aboard, miss his ship, or is late. You've got to handle it yourself. Don't come crying to me. Live with your sin."

"Have you read my letter?"

"No, what letter?"

"I put it in your incoming box."

"Terry, I don't have time for incoming boxes when we're busy getting under way and doing these exercises. I'll read it later, though."

He said, "You mean what you just told me isn't based on the letter I gave you?"

I said, "No, I haven't seen your letter." He said maybe he ought to take it back. I said, "No, I'll read it."

So after dinner I got it out, and it was beautifully written: "Dear Skipper, We've been friends, etc., etc., etc. I don't expect any leeway based on friendship. I know what you have to do. Not only is my naval career now down the tubes, I'm sure my family life is, because my wife, of course, will wonder why I've been relieved of my duties and sent back." The next line said, "How about the farm? I'm a big boy; I know what has to be done. Your job is not easy." He was just that kind of a guy. Outstanding man. The Navy lost a good sailor when he retired early.

Paul Stillwell: We must certainly hear about the your role as the ship's Jewish lay leader.

Captain Colbus: Oh, that's written up in your magazine. In McCloy I had a running gun battle with Fred Brink, the force chaplain.[*] At a moment of levity I wrote a letter to Chaplain Brink in Newport. I forget how it got published, but it was in April of '76, right before I went to Idaho Falls.[†]

I jokingly wrote this letter when the ship was deployed above the Arctic Circle. It began, "From: Jewish lay leader aboard USS McCloy to Force Chaplain via Commanding Officer, USS McCloy. It has come to my attention that the Jewish holiday of Passover is up and coming, at which time it is appropriate for all Jewish people to eat unleavened bread."

Paragraph Two: "It's also appropriate at the seder to have wine with the meal."

Three: "In that I don't know of any Jewish Eskimos, it is requested that you provide this command with the appropriate food stuffs and allow wine to be served at the seder meal. Signed, Louis Colbus, Jewish lay leader."

First endorsement from commanding officer: "This lay leader is the most outstanding lay leader in the ship. He has 100% attendance at all services." I was one of only two Jewish persons in the ship; the other was the ops officer, Roy Himmelfarb. The

---

[*] Captain Frederick W. Brink, CHC, USN.
[†] "The Jewish Lay Leader and I . . . ," U.S. Naval Institute Proceedings, April 1976, pages 66-67. The words in the oral history represent a paraphrase of the letter reprinted in the magazine.

endorsement then went on to praise the great work of the Jewish lay leader, concluding, "Signed, Louis Colbus, Commanding Officer."

I got a letter back from Fred Brink that said, "Granted. You didn't date your memo, you dummy." Something like those words. He just had a good time with it. Fred did provide us with the matzos and the canned kosher chicken, which, by the way, was awful, also a bottle of sacramental wine. We all sat around the wardroom table, including the Dutch commodore, and had wine with the seder meal. I explained what was happening, and we had us a Passover dinner.

Paul Stillwell: What do you remember of the multinational ops you were involved in in that ship?

Captain Colbus: We started out by joining the NATO squadron down in Bermuda, with lots of ship problems with McCloy. This was her first deployment. That is a story in itself, but we pretty much straightened out. The commodore had to be convinced that the ship was seaworthy machinery-wise to cross the ocean. I had to convince the folks back in Newport that we were capable of making the crossing. USS Zellers (DD-777) was along with this squadron because McCloy had never deployed, did have a lot of design problems, mainly in making of feed water and potable water. It just wasn't a sure thing, but we got that put to bed.

As we were crossing between Bermuda and the Azores, Limburg, which was the Dutch ship in which the commodore was embarked, broke its back and became very, very tender. Any time the sea pounded, it had to stop, so it couldn't really keep up with the squadron. We then became the squadron flagship. Though we were the smallest ship, we did have a unit commander's cabin, so we brought these Europeans aboard. The only U.S. officer on that staff was a fellow named Holman.

When they got aboard McCloy, the European squadron staff was in an entirely different environment. This was a U.S. ship, where there was no wardroom 24 hours a day. What made that wardroom in the Dutch ship or the British ship so conducive to gathering was that it served booze. I don't mean that they sat around drinking all the time, but it was just different. What we traded on, of course, were excellent meals, which were very, very plentiful, and movies every night like clockwork. We had a movie each evening at 8:00 o'clock, which their ships didn't have. So we indoctrinated these European officers in the ways of the U.S. Navy, and they just stayed with us the entire time.

As I mentioned, the commodore was a Dutchman named Frantz Visé. His nickname was "Hap," because he was always happy, I guess. He was a very fine man. We did Northern Europe, port to port. Of course, each port had a uniqueness, each port had a sea story to go with it. That's what really makes it so much fun. It isn't so much the activity at the time; it's going to sea the next day and rehashing all the details, and maybe even embellishing some of them. It makes a great time.

Paul Stillwell: In retrospect now of nearly 20 years, what are some of those stories?

Captain Colbus: Let's see. I guess my favorite story is about one of the ships in the squadron, HMS Berwick. It was a Royal Navy ship, commanded by a Royal Navy commander named Dickie Fitch.[*] Dickie Fitch was 40; I was 35, 36. Dickie Fitch was the elegant Brit, tall, stately, good-looking, and—unless you got to know him—you might even say pompous. He was always dressed properly, always the epitome of the naval officer, an excellent ship handler and all the things that you'd expect a great Navy man to be. He was a true bachelor, having never been married. He and I went ashore quite a bit and would take the commodore with us.

Jody, my wife, was following the ship. She had her married sister with us, and many times the five of us would go out: Dickie Fitch, kindly escorting my wife's sister, a married gal with three kids, Jody and myself, and the commodore—a good group. We went to visit Lisbon after Jody and her sister had returned home. While we were in Lisbon, we went aboard a French ship. The French ship was not in the NATO squadron, of course. She was just there, and we went aboard as invited guests. While we were in this ship, I looked across the wardroom and saw the most gorgeous blonde lady I'd ever seen.

Well, I went right over to her and tried to start a conversation. She did not speak English. My high school French was not doing me any good whatsoever, so I called

---

[*] Commander Richard G. A. Fitch, RN.

Dickie Fitch over: "Dickie, I'd like you to meet Kathleen. Kathleen, my friend, Dick Fitch." Of course, he broke right into French. The two of them were doing all the talking. I found a young lady who was, I later learned, the Duchess of Albuquerque, a true Portuguese duchess. She spoke English, and we teamed up, because after we left the ship, we were all going to dinner at a very famous fort in Lisbon; it was a state dinner. When I say state, I mean just that.

Anyway, Dickie Fitch and this good-looking blonde, whose father was the local French banker there in Lisbon, palled around that evening and the next day. We left Lisbon and went on about our business. That was April of '67. In February of '69, I was invited to their wedding in France. I didn't make it. We've been great friends ever since. He married Kathleen, and every time we're together, we rehash this same story. Of course, today she is an English-speaking lovely lady, living in the British countryside.

Dickie was just promoted to three stars as the Royal Navy's ASW Force Afloat.* Dickie Fitch commanded the ship Hermes and came here to Norfolk in Hermes a couple of years ago with his wife. So that was one of the fun stories—the climax of the whole cruise.

Paul Stillwell: Speaking of language, how did the squadrons communicate with each other?

Captain Colbus: Very well and, of course, in English.

Paul Stillwell: Was it a prerequisite that the foreign crews had to speak English?

Captain Colbus: All the NATO pubs, all the NATO signaling, all the voice communications, of course, are in English.

Paul Stillwell: How would you compare that multinational operation with the one you had known off South America?

---

* His official title was Commander Third Flotilla, first as a rear admiral and later as a vice admiral.

Captain Colbus: Another ball game. That was, you might say, a sandlot game that we'd pick up as we'd go along. Here we are in NATO now, with proper procedures, we were testing the NATO infrastructure. We had a Dutch commodore who was really taking us through the paces. Everybody was politically attuned to look good but not to embarrass anybody—that kind of thing. It was probably the best workout you could ever get.

By the time we got to Europe, those ships were steaming as a fast, fast group. Where squadrons normally steamed around at 10 to 20 knots, that crowd would go up to 25 knots and do maneuvers in very smart formations, coming and going. Everything was smartly done; we made a good impression. We were selling NATO to Europe. I was selling the SQS-26 sonar to the Brits, and it just went on and on. Everybody was selling something, and everybody was looking good. The associations that were made in that squadron still stick today. Most of those Europeans have attained flag rank. You go over there today, and you find them in leading positions.

Paul Stillwell: You described how these NATO ships got working so well together. How would they do vis-a-vis a U.S. squadron's ability in that same period?

Captain Colbus: Well, they were far ahead of any squadron I'd operated with. They were better because they were together. They entered port and left port as a unit. So for six months, they worked as a unit. Now, on occasion, as I said, the Dutch ship dropped out, and another ship came in. Berwick left at one time, and another British ship came in. So, with those few exceptions, everybody knew everybody in the squadron.

You knew to stay away from So-and-So because he was shy. You knew that that ship didn't turn as rapidly as this ship. Again, it was just close associations. Even our U.S. destroyer squadron, which got under way and went to Vietnam together, went to various assignments after the first 30- to 40-day transit. We all got under way and went to our various jobs. But the NATO squadron steamed together, moored together, screened together, played together!

Paul Stillwell: What did you screen? Did you operate with some high-value target?

Captain Colbus: Oh, yes, any time we could pick up any high-value target, we did. For instance, the Brits would send out unrep ships. We'd screen them and do our thing with them. Not then, but now, of course, StaNavForLant joins the battle group that's in the North Sea when they are exercising. If they're in the Med, they join up and they become part of the active battle group.

Paul Stillwell: Did you get submarine services to test how good you were in ASW?

Captain Colbus: We sure did. Especially around Great Britain, we had a lot of submarine services. Our port calls were fabulous; the crews, from the old-timers to the brand-new 17-year-olds, got on fabulously, and it was nothing but outstanding.

Paul Stillwell: Then did you come back to the States after that?

Captain Colbus: We did. We had a ten-day maintenance period in Newport, which turned out to be just outstanding, because now we were in our homeport, where we entertained these folks. We were entertained when we were in their homeport. For instance, we were in Rotterdam at Easter season, and the skipper of the Dutch ship, as well as the commodore, just entertained us royally and showed us everything. When we went to Plymouth, the Brits took over.

In any of these places we visited, typically we had a reception the first night in port. That was the way to go: invite all the people, get to know them. We'd have as many as four days in port, then under way for an operational period. Shipboard receptions were never in the U.S. ship because we didn't serve booze. We would provide the food, and we'd just outdo ourselves. The Europeans weren't as—I guess the word is—wasteful as we are. They still had that wartime rationing concept, where we just go at it. And we carried our load that way. However, after the on-board reception, we'd go out on the town. It wouldn't be unusual at this time or even later to come back to the U.S. ship for coffee and light breakfast.

Paul Stillwell: How did you spend the time back in Newport after you returned from that cruise?

Captain Colbus: For one thing, Jody and I took the commodore to New York for two days. We toured all around and showed him a great, relaxed time. By the way, he moved off the ship and moved in our house with us and became one of us. There was no fuss, no muss, no formal meals, just "Hap, you got it. Here's your room. If you want a car, drive that." He just became one of the family. When it was time to go to the store to buy Jonathan's formula, he would go along.

Paul Stillwell: That's going beyond the required international cooperation.

Captain Colbus: He loved it. He was a real family man. He just wanted to see what it was like, and he got ten days of living in a U.S. house. The neighbors knew him. It was very, very comfortable for all of us. He was a very appreciative, wonderful, fine man. He took a great shine to Jody. We have heard from him since then. He's retired now—Hap Visé.

I'm trying to think what else happened on that deployment. Operationally, as I said, without going into the details, McCloy had many problems, which we took one at a time. By the time we came home, that ship was a fleet steamer.

We went to a shipyard right outside of Bergen, Norway. The purpose of the visit was to make voyage repairs and to test the NATO infrastructure. When we went in to Haakynsvern shipyard, we had a wish list. My wish list had everything from three cruise boxes for chief petty officers that were leaving to an aluminum OOD weather station on the quarterdeck, and a wooden ladder from the quarterdeck up to the flight deck. Most of these were things the ship needed. Now, we didn't need a wooden ladder, of course, but I requested spiffy stuff, status stuff.

The shipyard was great in the woodworking world. They came into the wardroom and made us a wooden magazine rack. When we left the Haakynsvern shipyard after ten days, they had accomplished more work than we could have had in six weeks in a U.S. shipyard. They retubed the evaporators. They just did everything, plus all this artisan work. Again, it was to test infrastructure. What could they do? What couldn't they do electronically? My supply officer and the squadron materiel officer would check very carefully with ComCruDesLant as to how this would all be paid for. Well, it was all going to be paid for through NATO channels. And this went on and on. Well, by the time I got back, I was in big trouble because I'd spent $40,000—which is a drop in the bucket, as you know—on such things as, "Why do you need three cruise boxes?"

"Because those chiefs served well, and they worked their butts off, and they were going to leave in style. They would have gotten cruise boxes in the States. We didn't visit the tender."

"Too much money—$300.00 apiece."

"Why do you need a wooden ladder?"

"Neat, looks good, sharp ship."

"Why the weather deck OOD station?"

"Because of morale. Talk about shipping over sailors, if I can provide them shelter in inclement weather, up on my quarterdeck, which the ship hasn't had, I'm going to do it."

"But this is baseboard heating that you plug in."

"Damn right. First class." On and on and on. Oh, I was in big trouble with the supply people, I was in big trouble with the material people. They said I spent money foolishly. I said, "No, not foolishly. I didn't think I was going to have to pay for it because it was coming out of NATO infrastructure funds."

"There is no free lunch."

"I know, but we were testing NATO infrastructures." Well, anyway, at $40,000, it was a bargain. If I'd have known that, I'd have still spent it. That isn't the way you work it.

The other problem I had was while we were in Hamburg. We spilled about 500 gallons of fuel oil. The German barge was pumping, we had phones rigged, we used hand signals. When our tanks were at 94%, we talked and signaled the barge to cease pumping. The man in the barge never stopped, and out spilled black oil. Well, that wasn't as catastrophic as it is today, but it still wasn't good. The next morning we had everything cleaned up and even went around and asked ships if we did any damage: "May we clean your sides?" No, the spill was contained and cleaned up, nobody was concerned, and we departed.

The local U.S. Navy representative in Hamburg was an intelligence type who had never been to sea. He sent out a message to report, "By the way, it's been three days since USS McCloy left port. However, if I get any claims for this oil they spilled, what shall I do with them?"

Well, the next question was, "CO, McCloy, what oil?"

"Oh, yes, we spilled oil."

"Why didn't you report it?"

"Had nothing to report. Spilled it, cleaned it up, left in good shape."

"Well, that isn't the way you do it. Investigate it." Well, that's hard to do at sea, after the fact. I did investigate the spill and sent the report to ComCruDesLant.

The third problem we had was a ship's store shortage. That was definitely our fault. We were short; it wasn't malicious. We reported it properly to the supply people, and we just made that up. There was a proper procedure for doing that, and we followed it. It wasn't catastrophic, but it wasn't within the limits. We knew we had to report it, and we did.

Well, by the time we returned from this deployment, which was successful, we just thought we were great. The ship was operating well, the sailors were proud, and the commodore was happy. One Sunday I got a call from my commodore, O. K. Hallam.[*] He said, "Why don't you stop over and see me? I really didn't want to bother you with this, but I've got to do something about it." He said he'd had this thing for the past two days. It was a letter signed by the ComCruDesLant chief of staff to me, to find out what's going on in McCloy: "You had three problems: oil spill, overexpended your maintenance funds, and a shortage in your ship's store."

"Well, Commodore, there's nothing wrong with McCloy. You know each story." My U.S. commodore composed a letter, which he worked up with me. That's what we did the rest of the Sunday afternoon. Keith Hallam delivered that letter to the chief of staff at CruDesLant on Tuesday. I was under the gun. And I can tell you why the fellow in Hamburg put out that message. He was nasty because we had a face-off in which he asked me if I'd provide three stewards for a party, and McCloy would pay for this reception.

---

[*] Captain Orval K. Hallam, USN, Commander Escort Squadron Ten.

"Sure, glad to." We sent the stewards over to his quarters. I happened to walk over about 3:00 o'clock to check on the preparations for the reception. My shipmates were there washing windows and doing housekeeping up in his private quarters, which were above the consulate.

I said, "No, no, no. They're here for tonight's reception. They're not here to clean your quarters. That's not part of the deal."

Another thing that upset him came when he gave me a guest list for this party. He forgot to add McCloy's 18 officers and the six wives who were following the ship. He said, "Oh, it'll just be you and the exec."

"No. We're paying for it, so all our officers will attend." He didn't want the ship's officers there.

Back in Newport, I got a call one day to come over to ComCruDesLant. There was the lawyer. By the way, the lawyer did not like my investigation. The fact that oil was spilled was now irrelevant. The fact that I messed up on the investigation and that it wasn't letter perfect made him other than happy. He was a captain, I was a lieutenant commander, but I was a commanding officer. I said to him, "Well, Captain, why don't you come down and get my ship under way? I'm sure that between the pier and the Dumplings, you'll be aground. So I don't think it's fair for me to ask you to conn my ship. I don't think it's really fair for you to ask me to make investigations after the fact that are letter perfect." Boy, he didn't like that.

Paul Stillwell: I bet he didn't.

Captain Colbus: So the lawyer was angry at me, the supply officer was angry at me, and the material officer was angry at me. They were all in collusion, I think. Admiral Clyde Van Arsdall called me one day with the commodore, brought the chief of staff in, and said, "I have reviewed all this that you've sent in to me. I've read the letter that complains about Louie. It sounds to me that Louie is just a good sailor out at sea trying to do a good job. I want this whole thing put to bed. Any objections to that, chief of staff?"[*]

"No, sir, Admiral."

---

[*] Rear Admiral Clyde J. Van Arsdall, Jr., USN, Commander Cruiser-Destroyer Force Atlantic Fleet.

"Commodore, how do you feel?"

"That's a fine solution, Admiral."

That was it with Clyde Van Arsdall. The "attaboys" overcame the "ah, hecks." That was sort of my deployment in a nutshell.

Interview Number 2 with Captain Louis Colbus, U.S. Navy (Retired)

Place: Captain Colbus's office at Sonalysts, Virginia Beach, Virginia

Date: Friday, 31 August 1984

Interviewer: Paul Stillwell

Paul Stillwell: Captain, last night when we finished up, you were talking about your command tour in the USS McCloy. One of the conceptions of ship command is that this is an area where a man can be king in his own province. Did you enjoy that kind of a feeling in McCloy?

Captain Colbus: Absolutely. It was total fulfillment, absolutely total fulfillment. Again, I was blessed with a very, very outstanding crew. I don't say that just because it's the thing to do. First of all, you've got to remember that this was a new ship with a new operational concept. It was the first operational SQS-26 ship in the fleet. I was a lieutenant commander, and I think somebody with wisdom up in Washington must have said, "Let's shore up this inexperienced, young lieutenant commander and make it easy for him." Somebody was making that ship look good.

You have never seen a more talented wardroom in your life. In fact, I used to say I wondered if maybe we had too much talent in McCloy. I was only worried about the ship, but I think in the wisdom of the Navy, they should have spread some of that around. Also, chiefs' quarters was an outstanding group of young chief petty officers, all of them eager. We didn't know what problems were because they solved them. And when it got down to the crew, we'd changed from the commissioning crew, which naturally was a hand-picked, so to speak, group, but we still had a carry-over from that commissioning crew. So from the exec, whom we've discussed as being outstanding, down to the new seaman, McCloy was blessed with outstanding people.

Let me give you one example of what kind of outstanding shipmates I had. The ship came out of the Boston six-month retrofit, when we upgraded from the SQS-26 to the

SQS-26 AXR. That was a single-screw ship. I learned single-screw ship handling aboard John R. Perry, under the tutelage of Bob Brady and Ely Kirk.

I knew a little bit about single-screw ships. What made this ship different was it had this bulbous dome on it. When the dome was filled with water, which it had to be to be operational, it was, I think, ten tons. It was as if the ship were holding an onion on the bow. Since we're talking about that, it made McCloy a very, very rough-riding ship because that tremendous dome would hold the ship down when it wanted to rise with the sea. Then, when it was time to go down, it would cushion the ship, so the ship was very, very rigid. It just would shake and chatter very heavily, more so than any ship I'd ever ridden.

The ship was bigger than a World War II destroyer and had the same horsepower as the Dealey-class DEs that were built in the '50s. But, anyway, it was a very strange ship to get the feel. Once you had the feel, it responded very well. It answered the rudder exceptionally well, since it had a great big barn-door rudder. The only thing was the ship was underpowered with this Dealey plant of 20,000 horsepower. We're going to talk about that. But, as far as handling the ship, we got pretty good at it, because, as I said, it was very responsive.

The psychological effect of that dome being up there was inhibiting. You were told, "Don't get the dome near a pier." With most ships, you drive right in, get the bow in, and then spin the stern in. With McCloy you could come in and at the last 100 feet or so from the dome, with the bow pointed in to the pier, put the rudder over, just add a few turns, which is contrary to most ship handling, and the bow would swing away from the pier. The ship would swing as if a tug were on it. We were pretty good at it.

We went to sea on our sea trials. We were backing the ship into a slip in Boston, and we were doing very well. People were amazed with this single-screw ship, 380 feet, backing itself, using its own engines, and we did. We got the ship placed very nicely. The pier master called up to say how great it was, what a good job. Everybody had his chest out, very proud. Then he said, "If you could move back another 30 feet, you'd be perfect."

We rang up a back one-third bell and were so busy strutting and being proud, that, guess what? I forgot the back one-third bell was on. The ship started moving as it should. About that time, the lee helmsman, who was a seaman, called out, "The engine's backing one-third, sir." All of a sudden, I realized, and I immediately went ahead with a standard bell to check the movement of the ship. If that young man hadn't done that to remind me, we'd have backed that ship just fresh out of the yard into a barge that was behind us. That kid saved the ship. Well, we made a big fuss over him immediately, rewarded him on the bridge, because he saved the ship; he really did. That's the kind of response we had in that ship.

You never told the forecastle what to do with lines, because the chief boatswain's mate knew exactly what to do. He knew what you wanted to do. The engineers didn't need me chiding them. They answered bells very well. It was a great team effort, which I inherited from my predecessor, and I'm sure he got it from his predecessor. But, anyway, that's the way it worked. Good ship.

Paul Stillwell: Bronstein and McCloy were the only two ships in that class. Does that indicate that wasn't such a terrific class of ship, that it wasn't worth producing in greater numbers?

Captain Colbus: No, I think it was a transition where we went from the Dealeys; as I mentioned, we had the Dealey plant with a larger hull. The hull design, of course, was carried over into the 1052 class, which was produced and today is, I think, one of our most supportive ships.[*] That ship was built as an ocean escort. Today it runs with a carrier and performs all kinds of destroyer roles. So the Bronstein class was an interim that wasn't produced in quantity. I think there was a 1039 somewhere in one of the foreign navies.[†] McCloy wasn't a ship that could run; it was truly an escort ship, and we advanced into the 1040 class from there.[‡]

---

[*] USS Knox (DE-1052) went into commission on 12 April 1969 as the lead ship of a class of 46 single-screw ocean escorts. They were reclassified from destroyer escorts to frigates in 1975.
[†] DE-1039 became Almirante Pereira da Silva in the Portuguese Navy.
[‡] USS Garcia (DE-1040) went into commission on 21 December 1964 as the lead ship of a class of ten single-screw ocean escorts. They were reclassified from destroyer escorts to frigates in 1975.

Paul Stillwell: Did McCloy have any design deficiencies or bugs in it as a result of being an interim ship?

Captain Colbus: Yes. Well, first of all, when I took command of the ship, it was a wardroom joke, which I didn't think was very funny, that the ship would go to sea for two or three days, have a casualty to the distilling plant, and return to port. I think, being fair to everybody, the ship probably had only ever been at sea a maximum of five days, and something would happen and the ship would have to come home. It was considered shakedown. Well, now in retrospect, there were design deficiencies, but I think everything that happened to the ship, even the routine maintenance problems, were attributed to "design deficiencies." When I got the ship under way for deployment, I decided we were going to go out there and make it work. Well, being determined and making it so are two different things. However, everyone was committed.

Let me tell you what it was really all about. First of all, I said it was an SQS-26 ship. A true 26 had a steam generator that supplied all the power to this great sonar, the biggest sonar in the world. The steam generator looked like a big old diesel engine down there in the engine room. It took a lot of steam. That was an unusual user of steam in that particular situation.

The ship had two distilling plants, which were new. We weren't that familiar with them and found that they gave us lots and lots of problems. So there were two factors that affected water consumption in the ship. One was the consumption by the steam generator; secondly, these new plants were not really up to capacity. If they had worked at their full capacity, we probably had enough water to go. The third thing was that the ship's exhaust system for condensate drained into smaller piping. As I recall, we had probably 6-inch and 5-inch drains going into the final stage, which was a 4-inch drain.

When the ship operated at a fast speed, let's say, 22 knots and then suddenly slowed to 12 or 10, whatever the case may be, a lot of back pressure was created. The condensers wouldn't take it, so all this condensate would go out the stack as steam, so we were losing water. Now, we were not making enough water because of the distilling plant. We were using a lot of water because of this gigantic steam generator, and we were not economically recovering the condensate. It was a losing situation. We were always short of water.

Now, we were running those distilling plants at maximum capacity all the time, trying to stay even, so we had breakdowns because the plant was overloaded. It was a bad situation. Everybody knew it, everybody acknowledged it, and they were going to do something about it at the first opportunity.

Well, we wrote the letters, we did all the right things and documented it. I'll never forget how the engineer, of course, had all the technical details. We filled out all the technical portions of this letter, and I can remember the last sentence, which was mine, an operational phrase, and that was, "In a ship that is two years old, the pride of the destroyer force, with the biggest, most sophisticated modern sonar in the world, when fog sets in and the captain has to sit on the bridge and debate if he can spare the steam to blow the fog whistle, we're really in bad shape." And that was a true statement. If you added the fog whistle, which uses steam right out the stack, of course, and did it every three minutes or two minutes, you were in bad shape.

With those conditions, we went on this six-month deployment, with everybody betting that the ship probably wouldn't make it. Well, we got to San Juan, where we operated with this Matchmaker squadron, which was to become StaNavForLant, Standing Naval Force Atlantic. We had all the problems that were predicted, frequently went alongside the tender, always trying to get these evaporators fixed. At the end of the two-week period, we were confident that we could do it, and with much coaching and really pleading not only with CruDesLant but with the NATO squadron commander, we did take the ship all the way to the Azores. By the time we got to the Azores, the problem wasn't water, it was fuel, because that was a long, long haul for this short-legged ship.

When we arrived in European waters, things started picking up. People were very proud of the fact that they could do it and they did make it, and I like to say by the time we came home we were a fleet steamer. So that was the design deficiency that was referred to. Of course, we went into the Boston Naval Shipyard after the deployment, and they corrected all those things when they did the retrofit on the sonar. By the time the ship came out of Boston shipyard in March of 1968, she was in good shape, went to Gitmo, where the ship was just on the climb. I was relieved in May of '68 in Gitmo, and the ship went on to do bigger and better things. She's around today and doing well.*

Paul Stillwell: What happened as far as the distilling capacity? Was that increased?

Captain Colbus: Yes, it was increased. They improved on those evaporators, having learned through experience. This wasn't a solo shell system, it had like a grate in there with holes in it that allowed the water to fall through and that's what cleansed the water, so to speak. They improved on that. The baskets were fixed so that they didn't leak. I think, in fact, the entire baskets were changed to a better metal, and that exhaust system was corrected by using bigger valves. She now would take the steam and turn it into condensate, back into fresh and feed, and we were in good shape.

Paul Stillwell: When you had this marginal system, how did you compensate in order to make a deployment?

Captain Colbus: By being very careful, by everybody being aware that the ship had a water problem, even when it was operating at maximum capacity. As I say, sailors can do anything, and we did.

Here's another thing that made it unusual. The evaporators were in the fireroom; that was not a design deficiency but a design peculiarity. Evaporators are always in the engine room, so engine room personnel can work on them. Since we had them in the fireroom, it was a question as to who should maintain the evaporators. If it's the enginemen, they don't like to go down into the fireroom. But if you give it to the people who are in the fireroom, the BTs, they don't really understand or have experience with evaporators, so that was a union problem, which, again, we whipped.†

---

* McCloy, by then designated FF-1038, was decommissioned 13 December 1990 and stricken from the Naval Vessel Register on 4 October 1991. The ship was transferred to Mexico on 1 October 1993; she now serves as Nicolas Bravo (E-40).
† BT is the abbreviation for the enlisted rating of boilerman.

Paul Stillwell: Did the evaporator situation pose any hardships for the crew in terms of fresh water use?

Captain Colbus: When I came aboard McCloy, that was prior to this deployment. I came aboard on the 23rd of December 1966, and we began this deployment on the 12th of January 1967. The crew was used to and actually lived with water problems based on the things we've discussed before. So they were used to water hours, and they were very good about this. Once we got under way and were steaming at sea, they certainly pitched in. The crew not only did their best to help correct the problem, but the entire crew cooperated by not wasting water. So it was a crew effort to save water, it was an engineer effort to make water, and the two did come together. As far as being a hardship on the crew, yes, it was.

Paul Stillwell: You almost had a real potential problem, didn't you, in terms of low feed water?

Captain Colbus: That was the most important thing, and everybody realized that. I made a statement, which was probably brash, that if I got to where I had to burn salt water in those boilers just to get us back, I'd do it! We were not returning to port at the first sign of an evaporator problem. So having 60% of feed water capacity was bad; at 50%, I was sweating it; and, of course, as I said before, when you get down to 20%, this was a disastrous situation. Everybody felt it. One of the things that I inherited when I came aboard the ship was a status board on the bridge that showed the percentage of feed water, and we watched it like a hawk. Everybody on the ship was conscious of feed water. So when you say, was it a hardship on the crew, yes, it was, but the crew had lived with this so long that it became part of their daily living.

I guess the great breakthrough came when we were in Europe. This was all past now, and we had done great things with the ship. The tender Acadia had squared us away or at least helped us. Let's talk about late spring of '67 when we were over on this deployment. One day I made, again, a brash statement, "Let's knock off keeping the feed water percentages on the status board on the bridge. We'll let them do that down there in the engineering plant." That meant that we had really gained some confidence in the plant, in the making of water, in the usage of water, even though we had not taken care of any of these design problems. However, we had overcome the design problems and the heavy usage by the steam generator for the sonar, and lived with it.

Paul Stillwell: What was the lowest the percentage of feed water got while you were in command?

Captain Colbus: As I recall, the lowest was 17%. We were in the Caribbean on this so-called shakedown cruise, working up the ship with the NATO squadron, Matchmaker, and we were having some evaporator problems in conjunction with some other associated design problems. We were losing more feed water than we were making. Fresh water was not even discussed. We were losing out to the point that, I think, let's say, 60%. We now were keeping a running dialogue, half-hourly, as to what the percentage of feed water was.

Well, at this particular time, we'd been to San Juan alongside Hernandez Yunca pier, where Acadia, the tender, was moored, so I knew it was in there. We were having evaporator problems, and our 60% red line was now exceeded, and she started dropping. I'd say within a 12-, 15-hour period, we were down to 20%, and I said to the crew, "No, we're not going into port. We'll correct it. Our alternative, if we don't correct it, we'll go alongside Mississinewa tomorrow morning, and Mississinewa will give us feed water. But in the meantime, we're going to stick it out here, and we're going to correct our problem."*

We didn't correct the problem, so my ace in the hole was Mississinewa. We went alongside Mississinewa first light, Saturday morning. She told us she had feed for us, but we discovered she didn't have the capability of transferring feed water to us; I can't remember the reason. It was due to pumping or hose connections. It was a technical problem. I was in big trouble now, and I knew that. However, we were still only, let's say, 40 miles from San Juan.

So, upon completion of fueling the ship, we made a run for San Juan, moored alongside Acadia, took on feed water, secured the plant, did what had to be done. I think we were under way the next day, Sunday, late afternoon. But in answer to your question,

---

* USS Mississinewa (AO-144) was a fleet oiler.

we were down to at least 17%, which would shake the soul of anybody who's been to sea in a situation like that. And I think I, in a brash statement, had said, "We'll burn salt water when it's time," which, of course, would destroy the boiler. We didn't have to do that, and the second alternative was, we went to port and corrected our 17% feed water problem.

Paul Stillwell: One of your fellow destroyer skippers at that time was Ted Kosmela, who had USS John King.* What do you recall about the example his ship set for yours?

Captain Colbus: We were in Gitmo in the spring, and I'm going to say it was April of 1968. We had completed a good day's work with the fleet training group in Gitmo. We came in, I remember mooring the ship port side to, which was the easier of the two landings with a single-screw ship, and I was critiquing the landing to my officers. We were proud of what we'd done, the boys were doing very, very well. I was talking about the landing, what was good, what could have been better. We had everything laid out on a chart up on the bridge.

When we looked to starboard, and there, going by us at probably two-thirds speed, was USS John King. As we saw the ship, everybody on board appeared to be manning the rail, but they really weren't. They were at quarters, but every single solitary sailor was-at quarters, topside, with a white T-shirt two sizes too small, which made it look very, very sharp, no sagging T-shirts. Every sailor with a pressed pair of dungarees, every sailor with a polished belt buckle and shined shoes. That was what you saw as John King flashed by.

All of a sudden, she backed down, and the ship slid over starboard side to the pier across from us. I suddenly had to stop what I was doing. I said, "Boys, that's what we have to do. That's the way a destroyer is supposed to look and be handled." Well, they took that aboard. I walked off the ship, walked around the pier, and went aboard John King. By then, of course, the ship was moored the lines were doubled up.

I walked up to the bridge, and there was Ted Kosmela, critiquing the landing. I walked over to him and told him who I was. I said that my reason for being there was to pay my respects, to tell him he was my watermark now, that I had to get up to that which he had just done. Of course, he was a very proud sailor, proud of that ship, and he was

---

* Commander Walter T. Kosmela, USN.

pleased. The ship was just absolutely immaculate, not a mark anywhere. He was a destroyerman; he was a ship keeper. And the rest of the tour down there in Gitmo we watched John King. She just did everything. He was a driver; he expected everybody to work as hard as he did.

Our later encounter was when both of us were together in OpNav. I was already in OpNav, because in May of '68, I was relieved in McCloy while the ship was in Gitmo. I went on to Washington, where I became a member of the OP-03D, new construction destroyer program, DX/DXG/DXGN, which today is the DD-963 and the Virginia-class cruiser.* By that fall, Ted Kosmela showed up as one of the other officers working for Admiral Weschler.† We were office mates, so to speak. When I met him, he, of course, remembered me from our Gitmo days, and we started a very, very close and personal relationship.

Paul Stillwell: Having had that kind of an example from Commander Kosmela, and having had the example that your own CO, Commander Stokes, imparted to you, did you then build on this in trying to get your ship in very spic and span order?

Captain Colbus: Yes, I sure did. That was just a matter of pride. It's instilled in you, and that's the way we were raised. We talked about people who were ship keepers. There are all kinds of phrases that we used. I later carried it with me as I became a squadron commander, and I guess it was sort of a joke. I don't know if they took it seriously or not. They teased me about it. Whether behind my back it was serious or frivolous, I don't know, but I emphasized such things as waterlines.

One day when I had my squadron, one of my destroyer skippers brought me over a pipe that was painted. He gave it to me and said, "Is this a good enough waterline?" Ha, ha. We used to look at a ship and we'd start at the mast, and we'd come down, look at the ship's bell, up in the bridge area. If it was shiny and if the ship was shipshape and there

---

* DX/DXG/DXGN refers to the experimental phases of the program that included gun-armed (DX), guided missile-armed (DXG), and nuclear-powered guided-missile (DXGN) versions of the ship. For an excellent overall study of the entire program, see Michael C. Potter, Electronic Greyhounds: The Spruance-Class Destroyers (Annapolis: Naval Institute Press, 1995).
† Rear Admiral Thomas R. Weschler, USN. The oral history of Weschler, who retired as a vice admiral, is in the Naval Institute collection.

were no Irish pennants and no obvious rust, and you go down to where the waterline was razor sharp, you'd get around to the fantail and the fantail had no rust runs, the old man was a ship keeper. I can't tell you what they used to say about ships that had rust runs, but I learned it from Chief Boatswain's Mate Walter J. Czajkowski when I was an ensign. These things made our ships, I think, very sharp, and that was a matter of pride.

Paul Stillwell: Did you ever get any feedback from how your crew thought about this insistence on ship keeping?

Captain Colbus: Yes. They loved it, they really did. They thrived on it. Aboard John R. Perry we had the tape playing of "Reveille" and "Stars-and Stripes Forever" in the morning and all the appropriate bugle calls we had on tape, just as you do in a cruiser or a battleship. They became very prideful of this. It was a mark of distinction. If you remember, I told you about the bagpipes aboard Albert T. Harris. People would say, "Oh, the bagpipes again." They'd moan about it and groan about it, complain about it. Yet that was inside the ship. Outside the ship, they were very proud of that. We're different. We're unique. We have something that makes us better. That also permeated the ships that had the music, had the squared-away appearance that, in this case, was Ted Kosmela's ship. I think that made sailors doubly proud, they worked hard to do it, but there was a reward.

Paul Stillwell: As you said, after you wrapped up your assignment in command of McCloy you then went back to the Washington world. Could you please describe the experience of working with Admiral Weschler?

Captain Colbus: Yes. Admiral Weschler, of course, was Mr. DX at the time. I came into the program in July of 1968 and became a member of this eight- to ten-man team; I can't remember the exact numbers. Our deputy was a very famous destroyer sailor named Larry Caney.* He was highly regarded, loved by all, and a truly devoted, hard-working officer who made everything happen. With Admiral Weschler's enthusiasm, devotion, and many,

---

* Captain Lawrence D. Caney, USN.

many attributes, plus Larry Caney's hard work and dedication, we charged off on this DD-963 program.

My job was ASW officer, which included LAMPS, which was then a name only; ship control, not ship command and control, just ship control (everything from the bridge to the steering in the after conning station); and communications. We had some tremendous people on that staff. Ted Kosmela joined us, if I remember correctly, in the fall of '68. I joined the summer of '68. Already in place was a very, very outstanding, impressive, fun-loving, perfect naval officer named John Beecher, who later, during that tour, became an engineering duty officer only, and is today the FFG-7 project manager.[*] So with that kind of environment, the destroyer world was just charging ahead.

Paul Stillwell: Beecher had been a destroyer man up to that point.

Captain Colbus: Yes. He'd been exec of Cochrane, was about to get command of a destroyer, and, I'm sure, with great tearing of heart and gnashing of teeth, he changed his designator. He went on to contribute to the Navy, as you well know, probably more so than had he stayed a line officer and commanded a couple of ships. But, anyway, John Beecher is one of the all-time greats.

Admiral Weschler, I might say, was a very, very difficult man to work for. When I say difficult, we've talked about Admiral Lloyd Montague Mustin. Admiral Weschler was probably as difficult but much more congenial. I don't mean that to take away from Admiral Mustin, but let's go on. Admiral Tom Weschler was 24 hours a day. The only thing he knew was Navy.

When he went to a dinner party, it was to find out what was going on in the Washington scene. He would come back at 7:00 o'clock the next morning and hit you with things that he had learned at that party by talking to, let's say, Admiral Jerry Miller, who was OP-705B, about the wonderful world of LAMPS.[†] Well, you were working with some

---

[*] Commander John D. Beecher, USN. Later, when he was a captain, Beecher described the program's development. See his professional note, "FFG-7: The Concept and Design," U.S. Naval Institute Proceedings, March 1978, pages 148-150.
[†] Rear Admiral Gerald E. Miller, USN, served as Assistant Deputy Chief of Naval Operations (Air), 1969-70. The oral history of Miller, who retired as a vice admiral, is in the Naval Institute collection.

commander who was getting all this secondhand. So until it would cross the line from the OP-05 arena into the OP-03 arena, I'd be always behind the power curve.

That was Admiral Weschler's modus operandi. He was always ten steps ahead of everybody, except John Beecher. He could call down and ask John Beecher at 11:35 for a paper on such-and-such, because he had to go to the Congress the next day to defend the DX program. As true as I sit here, John Beecher, between 11:35 and 12:10 would have that paper not only written, but had Jeannie, our secretary, type it, and deliver it to Weschler at 12:12. We were in the basement of the Pentagon, and Admiral Weschler was up in the fourth deck. John Beecher--and I hope I'm not getting anybody in trouble--would then be at a three-martini lunch by 12:25. He just was superb, brilliant, ahead of Weschler, and he was the only one in the office who could do so. There were other fine people working in the office, and I won't go into all of them.

Paul Stillwell: What do you remember about the interface between your organization and NavShips?[*]

Captain Colbus: It was very close. As a matter of fact, Admiral Weschler wore, I'm going to say, three hats. He had his OP-03D hat, which gave him the operational side of the CNO. He wore what they called the Mat-09X hat, which was at ChiefNavMat.[†] He'd go over to ChiefNavMat and be Mat-09X, which put him at the top of the pile in the material world.

We started out at Main Navy, and then were the first tenants at the National Center in Crystal City.[‡] He wore one hat as part of NavShips. So he had three hats: OpNav, NavMat, and NavShips. He had staffs in each area. The 09X hat was really just a hat. I

---

[*] NavShips—Naval Ship Systems Command, which was the successor organization to the old Bureau of Ships.
[†] ChiefNavMat—Chief of Naval Material.
[‡] Main Navy was the popular name for the old Navy Department building was at 17th Street and Constitution Avenue in Washington, D.C. The building remained in use from World War I until the early 1970s, when President Richard Nixon directed that it be demolished. Crystal City is the name for a large modern office complex in Arlington, Virginia, not far south of the Pentagon.

don't think we actually had anybody physically sitting in the NavMat side of the house, but we did have a large staff, comparatively speaking, in the NavShips arena.

Paul Stillwell: What was the purpose of having this thing so fragmented?

Captain Colbus: It gave him the latitude to move from one community to the other. He could, I guess the word is dictate the requirements that he wanted in this ship. He wanted it to go 30 knots plus, he wanted it to have extended long legs, he wanted it to be able to do all these things. In his OpNav hat, it was for him to say what that would be. Then he could go across the river and go over to NavShips and say to his staff over there, "How are we going to meet these OpNav requirements? No, we don't want to do nuclear power. A steam plant is not it. Yes, let's look at this gas turbine world." He did, of course, and we ended up with the gas turbine.

Paul Stillwell: Why was nuclear power ruled out?

Captain Colbus: I wasn't privy to why it was ruled out. This all started in 1966 with Admiral Peet, who was the program manager before Admiral Weschler.[*] Nuclear power, in my opinion, was too big and too costly.

The gas turbine, even though it had not been used in the United States Navy, was certainly the way to go. We always referred to the Danish Navy, which had a ship by the name of Peder Skram that was gas-powered.[†] One of the gas turbine prototypes that we looked to was Admiral Callaghan, which was a merchant ship.[‡] So yes, there were gas turbines on the high seas.

---

[*] Vice Admiral Peet's Naval Institute oral history covers the reasons for his departure from the DX/DXG program.
[†] The Danish frigate Peder Skram had an engineering plant known as CODAG, combined diesel and gas turbine.
[‡] Admiral William M. Callaghan was designed and constructed specifically for charter by the Navy's Military Sea Transportation Service. In fact, the ship's name honored the first commander of MSTS, which was established in 1949. Admiral William M. Callaghan, which went into service on 19 December 1967, was the first all-gas-turbine ship constructed for the U.S. Navy.

The Canadians of course, were six to eight months ahead of us in the DDH 280 program.* By the way, we worked very closely with them. So in answer to your question, I guess nuclear power was too tough. It was a Rickover arena that we didn't get into, and I have no reason to say that other than that which I think—that the gas turbine was the way to go.†

Paul Stillwell: Wasn't, though, the nuclear-powered Virginia class part of what you were doing in this overall umbrella?

Captain Colbus: Yes, and that was nuclear power from the word go. That was in Captain Dick Fay's hands, and he ran the DXGN program as a separate project.‡ And this ship, of course, was very costly. We knew that from the beginning, not only costly in initial procurement costs, but we looked at the 20-year life-cycle cost. When you consider training a nuclear-powered sailor to operate that ship versus a gas turbine sailor, you had a great, great delta there.

Paul Stillwell: One of my impressions from interviewing Admiral Weschler is his splendid command presence. You know that this man is in charge. What was your impression?

Captain Colbus: That's it. You have stated anything that I might have to say. The only thing that I could say that I'm especially proud of, and I guess it's a vain thing, was, many times Admiral Weschler and I on the telephone were mistaken for each other by his own secretary Mildred. I was proud of that. When we went somewhere, even though I was a completely shaved head guy, he had closely cropped haircut and a couple of years older than I.§ We didn't use the word "clone" then, but I was called "Tom Weschler, Jr." I followed around in his wake. He didn't have an aide, but I guess if he did on these trips, I was it. And I enjoyed that image: Tom Weschler's boy.

---

* Canada built four helicopter-equipped destroyers of the DDH 280 class. The first was the Iroquois, which began construction in January 1969 and went into service in July 1972.
† Vice Admiral Hyman G. Rickover, USN (Ret.), ran the Navy's nuclear-power program for many years.
‡ Captain Richard C. Fay, USN, an engineering duty officer.
§ Weschler was born in 1917, Colbus in 1931.

Paul Stillwell: Please describe some of your own particular contributions and accomplishments in that program.

Captain Colbus: First thing, let's talk about the trips we used to make. Joining them in 1968, we had six shipbuilders who were vying for the contract. Within months that I was there, it boiled down to three contenders. One was Bath Iron Works in Bath, Maine, but their main corporate efforts emanated from Gibbs & Cox in New York City, at the foot of Wall Street. Gibbs & Cox was as prestigious in the design world as Bath was in the shipbuilding world. We would go to Gibbs & Cox on the ninth floor of this great building, right next to the New York Athletic Club. That's where we did the program review every eight weeks. We also would go to General Dynamics in Quincy, Mass., and do a design review. And we would also go to Litton Industries out in Culver City, California, to do a design review.*

They were each paid different amounts, but each contractor got $9 million to do a complete shipboard study as to how to meet these requirements that were issued by NavShips, as asked for in the requirements area by OpNav. So OpNav to NavShips to the contractor. And they were paid these monies so that at the end of the design phase, the Navy could take in all the designs, because we owned them and we could combine them as we saw fit. As memory serves me, that's exactly what happened.

There were some features of the Bath ship that were incorporated into the Litton design. The Litton design, of course, had the three after decks. That was not a Bath feature, but there were features of the Bath ship that we brought to Litton. So this was all ongoing.

Paul Stillwell: Was it completely ethical to do that?

Captain Colbus: I learned, yes. That's why they were paid. It wasn't just, "Go out and design us a ship and tell us about it." It was, "We'll pay you to go out and design a ship, and we will take your design and look at it and tell you, (a) who the winner is, and (b) how

---

* For the perspective of a member of Litton's team, see J. W. Devanney III, "The DX Competition," U.S. Naval Institute Proceedings, August 1975, pages 18-29.

we're going to use your design." So we got their ideas. Yes, that's perfectly ethical. Apparently so, because it was done that way.

Let me give you a story that might give you the flavor of how the design background was. Let's put it this way. First we went to Quincy to look over the design there. We were met and greeted and spent, let's say, two days there reviewing that which they had done. That lasted for only a while, because pretty soon they dropped out.

Then we landed at the airport in New York, checked into our hotel, and went to downtown New York, as I said, at the foot of Wall Street next to the New York Athletic Club. We went up to the tenth floor of the Gibbs & Cox ship design office. We were greeted there, where we were going to be presented with their efforts. A sweet little old lady—about 70 years old, I'll never forget her—came around at, say, 9:00 o'clock in the morning on that first day of the design review. She came up to each of us and said—and I use my own self as the indicator—"Commander Colbus, what are you going to have for luncheon today?"

"Well, ma'am, I would like a cheese sandwich and whatever."

She said, "Would you like milk with that?"

"Oh, yes, ma'am."

"That will be an extra 15 cents, so the total is $1.15." And I gave her $1.15, which gave me the working lunch up on the tenth floor. The only thing modern in that building was they did have air-conditioning. But they still had the green eye shades and the old-timey ship designers. It was just a very good feeling. If you want tradition and you want experience, go to Gibbs & Cox and Bath, ergo, the little old lady with the tennis shoes, the $1.15 luncheon.

Paul Stillwell: I've been to Bath. It still has some of that image.

Captain Colbus: Hey, that was great. We were home. We understood that. We finished up our work there and went back to Washington for two or three days to finish out the week.

Then Sunday evening or Monday morning we'd take off for Litton. I certainly don't mean this as a blast at Litton, but I think it portrays the difference in environment, ambience, whatever. We stepped off the plane in Los Angeles, and we were met by representatives of Litton. At that time, 1969, miniskirts were in vogue. Some good-looking 30-year-old honey would come up to me and say, "Hey, Commander, where are we going for lunch today? Will you be available?" And yes, I was. She would organize a lunch at the neatest place in Culver City, and all these good-looking secretaries would show up to provide color. It was a real Hollywood production.

They had all these great, modern ideas, and all of a sudden you turned your entire thinking around: "Hey, that's a great idea. Yes, we ought to see that on a destroyer. We've never had it that way before." As I said, three decks—one deck for replenishment, one deck for helicopter replenishment/underway replenishment, and one deck to do that which had to be done on the fantail. Hey, that's a good idea. I know we didn't envision that ourselves, and I do attribute that to Litton.

Paul Stillwell: How did General Dynamics fit between these two extremes?

Captain Colbus: Nondescript. I didn't say anything about General Dynamics. It didn't leave an impression with me; they were there, and a short time after I came aboard, they fell out. It was a Bath-Litton race, as I remember it.

Paul Stillwell: What was your contribution to the overall process?

Captain Colbus: Well, it was a non-contribution. Toward the end, we were down at the finals. We were given the reviews, we were given all the books, all the plans, all the diagrams, and all the RFPs—everything.* We had, I'm going to say, a four-week time frame in which to go over all this and come up with that which we liked, that which we didn't like, and comments, criticisms.

As I said before, I was into the ship control, which included the bridge and the signal bridge. I had never served in a ship that gave you the proper visibility when you were on the signal bridge. You were always running, looking, trying to see aft. As I read through this presentation by Litton, as I looked at the pictures, I suddenly saw a ship that

---

* RFPs—requests for proposals.

had a signal shack, with signal flags, that gave you a true 360-degree arc for visibility. Man, this was great. I gave that a big up-check, and I wrote about that and called all my fellow destroyer sailors' attention to this: "Isn't this wonderful? What a plus this is." And it was. That was one of my contributions. It was one of the things that I spotted that I really wanted in a destroyer of the future.

Then I got my orders to Jacksonville and to take command of <u>Jonas Ingram</u>. I hadn't been aboard <u>Jonas Ingram</u> three weeks when I got a call from Larry Caney, the chief of staff, who said, "Louis, I thought you said that the signal shack was . . . " as I just described.

"Yes, sir, Captain. It certainly is."

"Let me tell you something. It isn't that way at all." And he read to me that which he saw it as.

I said, "I don't know how that happened. I looked at it, my fellow destroyer sailors looked at it." I forget the captain who was in charge of this construction, but he looked at it. Our contribution of this big up-check was fine when it was described in a brochure, and it was fine when it was shown on a picture. But when it got to be hard lettering of the contract, it didn't appear that way and fell out. That was a big lesson.

You asked me what my contribution was. That was my contribution, which became a non-contribution and they had to do some renegotiating. I guess Captain Caney was upset with me because I hadn't presented it the way it actually was in the contract. The point is that what we as sailors saw and what came out as the lawyers and the controllers and the people who do contracting presented were entirely different. I learned a lot from that lesson.

Paul Stillwell: What would cause that kind of a disconnect?

Captain Colbus: Verbiage—our unfamiliarity with contracts, unfamiliarity with what you'd put down in writing. I guess it's like buying a house. I know what I want, I sure can describe it nicely, and we all agree to that which I want, but if it isn't in the contract that I signed on the dotted line, I guess I don't get it. That's what happened. I think that was probably unusual and stuck in my mind after all these years.

On the other hand, we looked at the entire ship and saw things that we were just wild about. There were criticisms that the ship doesn't have this, it doesn't have that. You've got to remember the ship was conceived in 1966. It was contracted for in the 1969 to 1970 time frame, and it was delivered starting in 1975.* What weaponry can you put into a ship over that kind of a time frame? What do you want? Do you want to put an ASROC in it? Do you want to put in the 5-inch gun that we knew at the time? We did that. However, what was built into that ship were space and weight margins—space and weight. We all acknowledged those words, but I don't think people really understood or appreciated those words.

Let's look at a 2,200-ton destroyer that came out of World War II. By the time that ship was FRAMed, I think I'm correct in saying that she was a 3,200- to 3,400-ton ship, top-heavy and no longer a 35-knot ship. What I'm saying is that ship grew like topsy, but it was still a very, very fine ship. Nobody's here to knock the 2,200-ton ship. Well, the 963s are going to be around for as long, if not longer, but if the onset of that ship, people such as Tom Weschler and, I'm sure, Admiral Peet, were smart enough to say, "Build the ship so that it has a growth capability. Don't tie it to today's weaponry. The ship will be here, but by the time it's delivered, the weaponry is going to surpass it; therefore, give it a growth potential."

I used to think of the ship as being like a model. You can just reach in there and take out an entire section and put in a new section, true of both the 963 and the Virginia class. And I remember that Admiral Weschler used to talk about that ship as he would talk about the new family, the brand-new young man and his wife who marry and build a house. They don't want to build the house for four children because they can't afford it at that time. They build the house for what they can see at that particular time, but they are keen enough and brilliant enough to build into that house a growth potential so they can add on to it. As we did with the 2,200-ton destroyer, we are going to do with the 963. I think probably 25, 30 years from now, people will still be-talking about what a great ship it is and how easy it is to convert to the state-of-the-art weaponry today.

---

* USS Spruance (DD-963), lead ship of the class, was commissioned 20 September 1975.

Paul Stillwell: The ship has a huge bridge and has a place for the OOD to sit down. I've always wondered why they would do that, since God meant for OODs to stand up. How did you as a destroyerman view that bridge?

Captain Colbus: My question would be, "Oh, God didn't mean for the destroyerman to stand up?" You didn't stand enough watches, because destroyermen used to sneak a seat in the captain's chair on mid-watches. I never saw that, of course.

We had to be forward thinking, as I tried to give my example of Litton. They were forward thinking. The aviator controls everything from the seat, and we got that aviation concept into our destroyer thinking. We also wanted to reduce the personnel on that ship. That was another way to do it. If the OOD wasn't sitting there doing everything, at least the helmsman was able to sit there and control engines, control rudder, and do all the things that you know of. We had a bridge so designed aboard McCandless.[*] We had that experiment on the bridge.

Of course, they still haven't adapted fully to this aviator concept of the cockpit instead of the conn. How did I adapt to it? I think that I adapted to it very well, because the guidance from Admiral Weschler was, "You've got to be forward-thinking." He used to tell us, "If Rip van Winkle awakened from his 20-year sleep, what's he going to see in the year—add 20 to 1968 to '70 time frame?" So we did that. We even talked about ships coming into port and instead of getting lined up on buoys, they'd steam in as they do in the aviation community: guide in on lights buried in the water, and you'd have a runway, so to speak. "You've got to think about it. Don't be stuck to the past. We have the time and we have the ability, and we certainly have the engineers." That's one of the things that Litton had. They had the aviation community out there on the West Coast pretty well sewed up, so we were forward-thinking, and we thought that was great.

Paul Stillwell: Did you get into the idea of the facility that Litton was building down in Pascagoula to construct these ships?[†]

---

[*] USS McCandless (DE-1084) was commissioned 18 March 1972.
[†] The shipyard that built the Spruance-class ships is in Pascagoula, Mississippi. Previously Ingalls Shipbuilding, it was acquired by Litton and modernized to use modular construction techniques.

Captain Colbus: Not personally, but I knew this was part of the program. I knew that this was a weight factor in contracting. I can't honestly say that I was into that, other than during the design reviews, Litton's people would show this facility up on a chart and they would speak to the chart, and this is what's happening, and this is the concept. We thought that was great, but, again, I really talked more and thought more and concentrated more on the ship itself.

Paul Stillwell: Did you have any misgivings on all of the class being given to one shipbuilder?

Captain Colbus: No, not at all, because I had lived in ships that were not very similar even though they were of the same class. My favorite example was in the laundry. Every damn laundry on every destroyer was different. They had been built by so-and-so Green, built by so-and-so whatever, and we had problems when it came time to repair one of those laundries. And, believe me, laundries are very important on ships. Sailors are clean, and the laundry is the keystone of that cleanliness. We always lived with a laundry problem, machinery problem. Now we were going to have 30 ships that have the same laundries that will be supported logistically in a proper manner. That was great.

Paul Stillwell: Was there any thought given in your shop to building up a training pipeline for a substantially different type of ship?

Captain Colbus: Oh, yes, absolutely. That was part of it. We called it a turn-key operation. This was the first time we talked about integrated ship logistics. This was the first time we talked about life-cycle costs. The program had a shore-based facility in Pascagoula that the first ship would utilize. That particular facility would be actual hardware that would be used in, let's say, ship five and six, and this was all laid out very nicely in a line diagram.

Each crew would go down there, sit in that ship—today we call it a land-based test site—and they would get their entire training and they would get their entire knowledge of the ship by actually sitting in what might be called a mock-up. It was actual ship hardware that was being used by the people going aboard the ship, which not only trained the sailor but it also would shake down that particular equipment. That was a great idea.

Paul Stillwell: Do you have any other examples of Admiral Weschler's foresight and forward thinking on this program?

Captain Colbus: Yes. Admiral Weschler one day said to me, "As my communications officer, I want you to go out, and I want you to miniaturize the communications that are on our ships. Why do we have to have these great big powerhouses of gear when I know aboard airplanes they communicate very nicely, very easily, by using small drawers? Why wouldn't we put that for saving of space and weight on our ships?"

"Yes, sir, Admiral." I suddenly became interested and talked to all my aviator friends about what they do in an airplane. Well, they talked about AN/ARCs and they talked about things that sounded right to me. I also got some smart destroyer-type communicators to talk to me. All of a sudden, we found out that instead of putting in the great big cumbersome equipment—the URTs and the XYZs and the ABCs that took up entire compartments in the after end of the ship, let's do what the aviators do. We'll use AN/ARCs, and we'll be able to dial in frequencies and all these great things. That became a project of mine with everybody cheering and saying, "Yes, that's the way to go."

Now, I'm not an electronics engineer, I'm certainly not a professional communicator, but I did get these people on my side, and we were carrying out Admiral Weschler's direction. Everybody was charging down pretty well until it came to the ship design people.

Well, they explained to me, "This is all fine and dandy, and yes, these are pieces of gear that exist, but we'd have to marinize them to bring them aboard ship."

I asked, "What do you mean by marinize?"

"Well, we're going to have to test them, we're going to have to put them under the conditions that they would actually have in environmental conditions at sea."

I said, "Now these are pieces of gear that are already in airplanes, A-6s, whatever."[*]

---

[*] The A-6 Intruder was an all-weather carrier-based bomber that served in the fleet from the 1960s to the 1990s.

"Yes, but you've got to remember, we've got to . . ."

"Give me an example."

"We've got to give it a shock test."

"What's that mean?"

"Well, we've got to take it in the case that it now utilizes and drop it eight feet and see if it breaks."

"Whoa, whoa, whoa. If it's in an A-6 and if I am correct, that particular piece of gear that we're talking about that you say has to be marinized, already comes aboard a carrier. That's a controlled crash; that's much more stringent than an eight-foot drop test."

"I know, but . . ." And then, all of a sudden, NavShips was balking. As I remember it, the thing just sort of died down, and we never got this program because it was too hard to overcome the resistance, I would say, that we met in the shipbuilding and in the electronics community.

Paul Stillwell: Did you encounter any other disappointments like that?

Captain Colbus: Yes. Admiral Weschler was very, very keen on saving manpower wherever he could. For example, we were going to read the satellites for navigation, and those readings would go into a computer program that would allow us to save one man. He wouldn't have to physically go up and take the readings and then go down and physically crank them into the program. It was all input. Well, when it came down to final contracting, the ship was costly. We had exceeded cost, so we had to start making cuts. All of a sudden, we weren't talking about the 20-year life-cycle cost that saved a man. We were talking about—and I think this is a true figure—$80,000 more per ship, and we were talking 30 ships. That's a decent size amount of money.

It's almost as if you go down to buy your automobile and you know if you buy radial tires for $400.00, you're going to drive them for 40,000 miles. Buy regular tires for a 20,000-mile run, you're going to pay $200.00. You've got to do it because you don't have the extra $200.00, even though you get an extra 20,000 miles out of the tires. That's what we got down to. It's great, it's true, but the cost of the ship is too much. So automation, life cycle costs, savings, in my opinion, became secondary when it came to what's the cost of the ship going to be in fiscal 172, 173, whatever. I thought that was disappointing.

Paul Stillwell: What concerns about habitability for the crew were cranked into that design?

Captain Colbus: That was a big item. Habitability was a top-notch priority, number one item, and such things as ease of maintenance, also big, though not habitability, were directly related. We were going to have a reduced number of people on board; therefore, they couldn't be out chipping and sanding and painting. Inside bulkheads, for instance, were made of some laminated plastic. We had interior bulkheads that were going to be laminated which (a) required no painting, and (b) required only wipedowns. I was on the habitability team, and remembered my time in McCloy. I was asked by my commodore, "Why do you spend so much money on consumables?"

Well, my consumables were such things as Phos-it. This was a chemical that was applied on the sides of the ship. Because we only had 11 people on the deck force in McCloy, I knew what it was to save personnel. You could put this Phos-it on with a roller. It did cost $55.00 for a 55-gallon drum, which was big dough in those days, but you'd arrive in port and apply this Phos-it. The sailors would sit on the piers for ten minutes and then come along with a hose and wash it off. There went all the grit and any rust runs that happened to be there. It didn't prevent future rust runs, but it got rid of this stuff.

We also were using such things in McCloy as something I used to call Easy-Off. To see a sailor standing around with rubber gloves and some kind of steel wool, cleaning an oven, really wasn't practical when you could chemically clean it in half the time with less effort. We carried that into the 963. We had these laminated bulkheads that would go on, and then all you had to do was come along with that spray stuff I used at home and on my automobile.

Paul Stillwell: Fantastik?

Captain Colbus: Fantastik, yes, but that wasn't the product I used as a generic name. It was just going to be to wipe this stuff down. This was all bought and everybody cheered, and we could show what labor-saving material this was. Heads were going to be modular, just as today's household is. You buy a plastic unit and you set it in to your bathroom. It's all rounded, and you don't have the corners that get the mildew. That was the way the ship was going to be designed and built.

Then, of course, I went off to war in Jonas Ingram. When I walked aboard the Spruance, down in Pascagoula in 1975 as an OpTEvFor rep in the Ship Evaluation Division, I guess if I'd have been a female, I'd have cried.[*] All these things we talked about really didn't show up. Some parts of the ship, yes, but heads that I just talked about, modular construction, ease of cleaning, no. We had the old heads with the stainless steel. While nice, it was going to take maintenance that we had not counted upon. So, there again, there was a gap between what we proposed for 20-year life-cycle costs and what actually came out. The ship still is gorgeous. I don't mean to take away from it. I was just looking for idealism, perfection, whatever.

Paul Stillwell: The United States Navy has four guided-missile AAW versions of that ship.[†]

Captain Colbus: You mean the DXG, which went away because we couldn't afford it.

Paul Stillwell: That sort of answers my question. In more detail, why did we not get more of the Kidd class and fewer of the Spruance version?

Captain Colbus: Money, money, money. We designed the ship, it was a cruiser, so to speak, superstructure, with the missile systems, and 963 hull, and that's what exactly, of course, the Kidd class is.[‡] It's the DXG. It's fulfillment. Admiral Weschler knew that's

---

[*] OpTEvFor—Operational Test and Evaluation Force.
[†] AAW—antiair warfare.
[‡] Four ships of the DXG variant were ordered for delivery to Iran. After that country's government fell to the Ayatollah Ruhollah Khomeini in 1979, the ships were completed for the U.S. Navy. The USS Kidd (DDG-993) and her three sisters went into commission in 1981 and 1982.

what we could have. By the way, you can, by design, take a 963, the Spruance herself, take it into a shipyard, and within a certain time frame, go up there and lift out the 5-inch/54 gun mount and put in something else. You've got all the electric and hydraulic power right there. You could put the missile system on the forecastle of that ship and make it look just like a Kidd-class ship. As we were told, as memory serves me, the 963 Spruance could be made to look just like a Kidd-class DDG if we had the bucks to do it and the need to convert.*

Paul Stillwell: One criticism of the Spruance class is the boxy, top-heavy appearance, that it's not as esthetically pleasing as destroyers of old had been. Was that a consideration in the design?

Captain Colbus: I think it was because if we didn't talk about it, we certainly looked at the artist's conception of how the ship would be. We had some very distinguished destroyermen there. I'm talking about senior people such as Weschler, Larry Caney, ad infinitum. They looked at the ship as it should look, but because the gas turbine area had to be as it was, I think they accepted that.

As an example, let's look at the DD-931 class. I don't think there's a more gorgeous ship ever been built than a true 931, Mullinnix being the last 931 class we had that was not converted. When we converted the 931-class ships to the ASW model, which included Jonas Ingram, my ship, we put a deckhouse on the after part to house the ASROC. I don't care what anybody says, that destroyed the true destroyer lines of that ship. Two years ago, when both ships were in commission, if you put Jonas Ingram alongside Mullinnix, Mullinnix would steal all the awards for grace, beauty, and what have you. But which ship was the more effective, the more modern? Which had the more punch? The conversion.

Paul Stillwell: And the one that really bastardized the appearance was the DDG conversion in that class, the Parsons and the John Paul Jones.

---

* Because of Navy down-sizing and because they were equipped with pre-Aegis technology, the Kidd and her three sisters had relatively short service careers in the U.S. Navy. The four ships were decommissioned in 1998-1999.

Captain Colbus: West Coast ships. I had friends who commanded them, but I never really was running in task groups with those ships.

Paul Stillwell: During this period also, there was a possibility that you might have gone to serve in Vietnam. Would you cover that, please?

Captain Colbus: Yes. During my time in OpNav, I was called and told that I was earmarked as a Vietnam sailor who was needed over there. This was, I'm going to say, about September or October of 1969. I'd only been in Washington 12, 14 months, and my response was, "I'm delighted because that's where everybody's going. That's where the action is, and I'd love to go." I don't think I'm controlled by my wife, but I could never go home and look her in the eye with a new baby daughter and a three-and-a-half, four-year-old boy and say, 'Well, I've just volunteered to go to Vietnam.' But now that you've told me, when am I going?"

"You'll be going about the first of the year."

"Well, that's great."

I hung in there and was waiting to hear some more. I guess it was in November that I went over and said, "I've got to know when I'm going to Vietnam, on the first or not. And I mean this—I'm not trying to be, funny—for one reason. The family will stay right here in Washington. We're all set, thank God. We have no problems; my wife can take care of those children. We're all set; she has family. The only thing is, if I'm going, I'm not going to plant another hundred tulip bulbs because my wife couldn't care less. If I don't go, I want to have my tulips and my flowers come springtime." They laughed, but that was really a true statement. I wanted to prepare my household for my departure on the first.

"Yes, you're going on the first."

Well, I went home. I took some leave at Christmas, went to my wife's family down in North Carolina, and explained to them, "I'll be leaving, and I'll be gone for a year." Everybody was happy; nobody was upset about it. That was great.

"Good for you. Serve your country." I was supported by my family up in Altoona. They would look after my wife while I was gone for a year.

Now, let me go back to the initial announcement, "You're going to Vietnam."

"Oh, sure, love to."

"Come over and we'll talk about it." (This meant a trip to my detailer.)

"I'd love to."

I went to BuPers and said all the right things. As I was ready to leave, the detailer looked at me, and said, "Of course, you were requested by Admiral Zumwalt."[*]

I said, "Hey, wait a minute. Don't pump me full of that stuff. That's where I belong, that's where you're sending me, that's what I'm paid to do: have sword will travel, all the right things. But you don't have to pump me full of sunshine like that."

"Oh, no, your name and four other commanders are on the list."

I said, "Zumwalt doesn't know me. He couldn't request me. I saw him one time at the Army-Navy Country Club in 1958 when I was up there working for Admiral Mustin, and that's it."

Well, this detailer reached in and showed me a letter, and, by golly, there were five names on that list, in alphabetical order. I might add that they were all former DE skippers, as I recall—four of them out of CortRon 10, and myself out of CortRon 8, with O. K. Hallam. Then I saw that the letter was signed by R. E. Nicholson.[†] I said, "Oh, Commodore Nicholson. Now that makes sense. I see. He's getting all his DE skippers over there. Well, you said Zumwalt. Well, if Nicholson signs it, that's as good as Zumwalt." I said, "I understand perfectly." So now I was happy, because it was Dick Nicholson who was requesting us DE skippers come over, and that was fine.

In summation, after the first of the year, 1970, I was called and told, "Guess what?"

"What?"

"Billets have been cut. They cut 12,000 billets." I can even tell you whom I was going to relieve, Tom Kolstad, whom I know well, whatever he was doing at the time, but

---

[*] Vice Admiral Elmo R. Zumwalt, Jr., USN, served as Commander Naval Forces Vietnam/Chief of Naval Advisory Group Vietnam from 30 September 1968 to 14 May 1970.
[†] Captain Richard E. Nicholson, USN, was operations officer on the staff of Commander Naval Forces Vietnam.

the billets were cut.* The detailer said, "Tom Kolstad's coming home. He had no relief, and you're not going; you're staying here till next year. You'll do your three years in Washington." End of story.

Paul Stillwell: What was your reaction?

Captain Colbus: Fine. Fine. Some disappointment because I anticipated going over and becoming part of the action. At the same time, I really enjoyed that 963 program, and I'd get to see another year of it.

While I was there, I was told that because I'd commanded McCloy as a lieutenant commander, I would not command a destroyer as a commander. Now, I say that advisedly, because I always call them destroyers. I don't care of it's a DE or if it's an FF, it's a destroyer.† McCloy had everything a destroyer had on it—ASROC, two boats, etc. It did have 3-inch guns, so it wasn't a gunfire support ship. So the message I got was, "You've had your fun; that was your destroyer command. Just hang in there, young commander." Well, I understood that.

As far as what I was going to do next, I don't even remember what I had on any dream sheet. I guess in March of 1971, a year after the Vietnam thing, I got a call one day, and I was asked, "Are you seated?"

"Yes."

"Are you ready to go to your next tour?"

"Yes."

"Guess what it is."

"I don't know. You tell me."

"You're going to command USS Jonas Ingram."‡ I almost fell out of my chair.

I even get chills now when I think about it: "USS Jonas Ingram. Oh, a 931. Oh, I rode the ship. Oh, she's a Mayport ship. Oh! Thank you! Thank you!"

---

* Captain Tom I. Kolstad, USN.
† In 1975 the Navy reclassified its destroyer escorts (DEs) as frigates (FFs).
‡ USS Jonas Ingram (DD-938) was a Forrest Sherman-class destroyer commissioned 19 July 1957. She had a standard displacement of 2,780 tons, full-load displacement of 3950 tons, was 418 feet long, 45 feet in the beam, and had a draft of 20 feet. Her design speed was 33 knots. Following her ASW modification, she was armed with two 5-inch guns, an eight-tube ASROC launcher, and two triple torpedo tubes.

"Well, you can come pick your orders up in three weeks and start your household effects moving and what have you, because you'll be moving in June."

After I got the news, I called my wife, and I think I probably was in tears. "Guess what? I'm getting a destroyer." Well, she was delighted because she knew I was delighted. "Guess where?"

She said, "Newport, and we sold the house."

I said, "No. How about Mayport, right next to Jacksonville? You'll be down there with your sister, whom you go down to see every Christmas." This was fantastic.

So I went over to BuPers, hat in hand, walked in, got my orders, and said, "May I see the detailer?" I went in to see him. His foot was up on the desk as mine is now. He had it in a cast because he'd just broken it on a skiing trip. I went in and I said, "I want to tell you something. I can't thank you enough. I know you yourself didn't do it, but I've got to thank someone—the Navy, the CNO. I want to kiss somebody on the lips. I am just so delighted that you're giving me another chance. This is outstanding."

He said, "Sit down. I know you're kidding me."

I said, "No, why would I kid you?"

He said, "You're coming to complain, but you're setting me up."

I said, "You don't understand. Watch my lips. I have a destroyer out of Mayport. It just happens to be Jonas Ingram, and there's an attachment there."

He said, "Let me tell you something. You're the first sailor who has ever come into this place and thanked me or even said anything about being delighted. Everybody who comes over here, if you give them a 931, they're ticked off because they didn't get a DDG-2, a missile ship.* You give them a missile ship, they're unhappy because they didn't get a Coontz-class DLG. And if you give a guy a 2,200-ton ship today, he's all exercised because everybody wants something that they think is better."

I said, "Hey, a destroyer's a destroyer." And that was a real awakening to me. As I told you, when I was in the war college, I found out about people being competitive. I thought when you got in a destroyer, you just were so grateful that, boy, you marched off. if it happened to be at the top of the list, you did your best to keep it there. If it was at the bottom of the list, you worked to get it up. You had probably a better situation than the

---

* USS Charles F. Adams (DDG-2), first of her class, was commissioned 10 September 1960.

guy who took the one at the top of the list, which by the way, Jonas Ingram was. When I took command of Jonas Ingram, she had one casualty, and that was the ship's steam whistle. Absolutely immaculate, perfect ship.

Okay, let me tell you one more thing. We were in the Zumwalt era now.* When I went to get these orders that I talked about, as I walked in, they said to me, "By the way, Louis, we want you to know you have a black executive officer."

To which I answered, "Hey, that's great.'

They said, "Oh, cool it now. You don't have to be enthusiastic about it. You're overkill."

I said, "No, I'm not overkill. I'm thrilled."

"Are you more thrilled to have a black executive officer than you are to have a white executive officer?"

I said, "Oh, yes."

They said, "Why is that?"

I said, "In my Navy, the exec is the navigator. I sweat navigation. With a black navigator and a Jewish skipper, I'll put that son-of-a-bitch aground, and they'll give me a medal because no one's going to criticize us." They did just as you did; they laughed about it.

Well, by the time I got there, the executive officer had been relieved. I told you before that Terry Siple was the world's greatest executive officer. Now, I may sound insincere and incoherent, because Tom Anderson was the world's greatest executive officer—completely different type.† Tom had been there maybe three or four months.

Paul Stillwell: Was he the black officer or the one who relieved the black officer?

Captain Colbus: The one who relieved the black officer. I really never got to serve with this gent.

Paul Stillwell: Who was the skipper you took over from?

---

* Admiral Elmo R. Zumwalt, Jr., USN, served as Chief of Naval Operations from 1 July 1970 to 29 June 1974. During his tenure he introduced many personnel reforms, including increased opportunities for blacks.
† Lieutenant Commander Thomas A. Anderson, USN.

Captain Colbus: Don Metzler.*

Paul Stillwell: From what you say about the condition of the ship, I take it he was a hard act to follow.

Captain Colbus: No, he was an easy act to follow.

Paul Stillwell: Why?

Captain Colbus: When I went aboard ship, there was Don Metzler: beard, hair a little too long for my style, and a very casual guy. If Don hears this, he knows that I am speaking sincerely, because he knew that I was shocked. He would come to the ship in civilian clothes and change into his uniform. I didn't understand that. To me it was like a banker going to the bank in tennis togs and changing. That's fine. Well, after about two or three days, I guess he sort of picked up the feeling that I was a little, I guess, stiff-necked, and he told me that one of the things I ought to do is really get into this program of ombudsman. Sure. What I really ought to do was get myself a dashiki. I said, "What is that?"

"Oh," he said, "that's an African shirt." He didn't mention that he wore clogs, sandals. He said, "You'll find that everybody on the ship wears a dashiki, and you ought to have one too."

My answer to him was, "When I see every sailor wearing a yarmulke, a skullcap, I may think about going out and getting a dashiki. Until that time, you will see me in uniform aboard this ship." So that was the atmosphere in which I relieved. Don Metzler was a 4.0 sailor, and that was his style. We're talking about taking command of this great ship which was in such magnificent condition and a very happy ship, I might add. Happiness is a standard, it's a measure, and it was a happy ship. Now, the happiness in that ship was created by the skipper being a very mod man and working very closely with the crew.

---

* Commander Donald M. Metzler, USN.

For instance, during my first ten days there, I was approached by one very distraught signalman first class who was not allowed to leave the ship by a very tough, hard-nosed senior chief radioman who was right out of 1937. That signalman did not have the proper shoeshine. He didn't look ready to go ashore, so he was not permitted to go ashore. Now, this was from the chief to the first class, and—knowing that senior chief—it was probably done at the quarterdeck, where the chief was the officer of the deck. Boy, that first class was up at my door knocking: "Let me tell you what happened. I'm not allowed to leave the ship."

Of course, I backed the senior chief radioman. I was not going to get into one of these questions of who should leave the ship and who shouldn't leave the ship. We had high standards and if the chief was supporting them, fine.

Another day, about 1610, a young sailor, an 18-year-old deck force seaman came up to me in my cabin—or I might have been walking about, whatever—to tell me, "Do you know the chief is not letting us come up from cleaning the side, and here it is ten minutes after quitting time?" That's the way the ship ran. Everybody on that ship had direct access to the skipper.

Well, it didn't take but a week to ten days for me to get the word out, "This ship will operate through the executive officer. I have an open-door policy after you have checked with the chain of command. I love to walk the ship, you'll find me all over, but it isn't a complaint period. We don't have captain's calls on here." I laid down the law, and that included the ombudsman.

To continue, there was, as I thought, too much direct contact, not exercising the chain of command. The men in the chiefs' quarters in that ship were superb. We had three master chiefs on that ship, as I recall. When, all of a sudden, I turned the ship over to the exec and turned the ship over to the chiefs, they loved it. My predecessor worked through and with the crew and had everybody in that group happy. I worked the ship through the senior petty officers and the wardroom; now they were happy. So it was just a matter of how it was worked. We didn't have any problems.

The ombudsman came down to see me, and I might say that. my predecessor was most solicitous to the words of the ombudsman. I hit her between the eyes in my cabin, saying, "I appreciate what you ladies are doing. I think it's wonderful. I want you to know

I support you entirely. However, I don't need anybody to help me run my ship. This is my second destroyer command. I think everybody will prosper, and we're going to have a good relationship." And I let her know, "Any time you want to have a bake sale, the ship is yours. However, I don't want to hear calls that your husband's hours are too long," which had been done in the past. I just let her know from the very start.

Well, she walked out of there not too happy, because this was a complete change. While I was polite, while I was solicitous, I was not condescending, and that's exactly what I wanted to portray. Knock off this ombudsman coming to me three times a week to tell me what's going on in the ship.

Out of job fulfillment, whatever it was called, I was invited about a week later to an enlisted wives' club meeting, which was held right there at Mayport. My wife was invited as the adviser, I was invited as the new commanding officer. Now, I can eat like a field hand, and this was a potluck dinner. I went there, and if I didn't hit the line three times, I didn't hit it once. I mean, I didn't miss a trick. The way to a woman's heart is through her food. They say the way to a man's heart is through his stomach. These women went up to my wife and said, "Is he putting on, just trying to be nice?"

"Oh, no, that's the way he eats." I'm telling you, from that day on, I could do no wrong with those girls, and we had the best relationship. What I'm saying is, the entire thing was a flip-flop, but they saw that it was a good flip-flop. It was just a different way of doing business. So we continued and prospered.

Have we talked about Cadillac of the fleet? Have we talked about the house flag?

Paul Stillwell: No. Let's save those stories for the next meeting.[*]

Captain Colbus: Okay. Thank you.

---

[*] The discussion ended here so the interviewee and interviewer could attend a change of command ceremony that afternoon on board the aircraft carrier Coral Sea (CV-43).

Interview Number 3 with Captain Louis Colbus, U.S. Navy (Retired)

Place: U.S. Naval Institute, Annapolis, Maryland

Date: Wednesday, 19 December 1984

Interviewer: Paul Stillwell

Paul Stillwell: Captain, as we broke off the last time, you had just taken command of the Jonas Ingram. I know that was a high point in your career, so please tell me more.

Captain Colbus: We left off with my assumption of command on there and the, I would say, radical change from the crew and the ombudsman—I guess it was an ombudswoman—almost to the point of controlling the ship. Everything was done on there to satisfy the young sailor. Of course, I wasn't against that, but I immediately changed everything. Not immediately—that's not fair.

Let me talk about the first time it came out that things were going to be different. We steamed the ship to Barbados. The exec was Tom Anderson, who was an outstanding exec, an outstanding man, an outstanding friend—just everything. I was very fortunate in having Tom Anderson. He's retired now out in Moscow, Idaho, where he's a schoolteacher. Anyway, Tom Anderson and I came back to the ship at 1:30 one morning after a night's liberty in Barbados. As we went by the officers' pantry, there was a petty officer second class, a commissaryman, in there cooking. I looked in and said to the exec, "What the hell's that all about?"

The exec said, "I don't know, sir. I'll find out." I went up to my cabin and was about to shut the door and go to bed when the commissaryman second class came knocking on the door. His name was Cook.

"Captain, I've got to talk to you."

"What can I do for you, petty officer?"

"I got to talk to you."

"Have you talked to the exec?"

"Yes, sir, that's why I have to talk to you."

"I'm always open for business. What is it?"

He said, "Well, the exec ordered me out of the pantry, told me I couldn't come in there anymore. He really attacked me unfairly and tells me I have no business in the officers' pantry. If he continues like that, I'm not going to give the wardroom any more soups and desserts and condiments free."

As I recall, I think I did blow up. I really did. I tossed him out of there on his ear. If he thought the exec got on his case, I really did so. I didn't call the exec then, but the next morning before quarters, I got the exec up and said, "What was this last night about Petty Officer Cook?"

The exec told me exactly what had happened. Then I said, "On this ship we're not going to take anything for free. I have never heard of anything that gross. Square it away. You go out there, and we're going to start the chain of command like it's supposed to be. Officers do not live or eat from, off, or however you want to phrase it, the mess decks. When we get soup, we pay for it. We're going to run this thing and be purer than Caesar's wife."

"You mean that, don't you, Captain?"

I said, "You're damn right."

He said, "Thank you very much." And he marched off. I'm really just trying to give you a picture how most of the ships were running. It was a changing time, as you can imagine. This was September 1971.

We had our growing problems, because while my claim was that if a ship is run properly and you had things to do, you didn't need to talk about six-section liberty, you didn't have to give the ship away. Now, if we could provide four-section liberty and the next ship was giving three-section liberty, that's gamesmanship. We now have a better ship because we can do the job in a better manner with less people.

What happened in that era, in my opinion, is that the Zumwalt Navy—and I'll come out with it—the Zumwalt Navy wanted everybody to be a great ship. They wanted every ship to be outstanding, and that almost took away the competitive edge. So you always had to do something better or different than your sister ship. "I want to be in USS 'Never Sail' because they have early liberty on Friday and look how neat they are, and the waterline is great, etc., and that's really a great ship."

We work over here, 12 hours a day, seven days a week, and we're not in that kind of condition. So what I'm saying is I think the competition was made even more difficult in that time. I would say, and I'm proud of this, that we were very successful in Jonas Ingram by getting back the competition, by keeping it. By the way, it was an outstanding ship when I went there. That was one of the ships that all I had to do was keep it up there. I just had a different style. Instead of going to the young people and letting the young sailors bang on my door any time they wanted, the chiefs did it for me. Maybe that's a sign of being lazy, but it worked that way.

But getting back to Jonas Ingram, I recall an incident from about my third month in command. We were going in and out of Mayport on different assignments, and we were coming back from somewhere—no long deployment, two weeks or something like that. I went up on the forecastle, and I said to the gunner's mate there working on mount 51, "How about letting me wash this gun mount? I want to fool around with this gun mount. It's Saturday morning and I just love to take care of my automobile. A habit of mine is that when I'm home on Saturday morning, I come out and wash my gray car. Why don't you let me wash this mount?"

He gave me the sponge, and I just took a few swipes at it. He laughed. I said, "That's a fine mount." We got to talking. I wasn't going to do his job; that's something I learned from James Frank Hill, my first commanding officer, when I was an ensign. Don't do the young man's job because he's not going to come in and do your job. Everybody has a job. Anyway, we had a big kick out of that.

The next time we were in port, I brought back a can of Simonize, and I went up there and said, "Some mornings I Simonize my car. Have you ever thought of Simonizing this mount?"

And, lo and behold, he said, "No."

I said, "Well, it doesn't need to be painted. If you use Simonize, it'll not only be that much shinier, it'll probably protect it just as it protects my car." That thing took off. It was just a great success program. We were Simonizing the bulkheads on that ship. We did not wax the decks because that would have made them too slippery. But we actually were Simonizing the superstructure of that ship. That's how nifty it was. It had just come out of a very expensive ASW conversion. As I said last time, when I went aboard, the only thing that was inoperative on that ship was the ship's whistle, and that was corrected in no time when we got the parts. So all of a sudden, we've got this great ship being Simonized.

A while later we were out at sea again, and the boatswain came up to me and asked me, "Would you be offended if we put the ship's emblem on our new brow curtain?"

I said, "Well, no. That's where it should be."

"But we want to put in circles around that ship's emblem, "USS Jonas Ingram, Cadillac of the Fleet." My car was a silver and gray Cadillac. Well, I thought that was great. Do you know, from that day on until, I guess, that ship was decommissioned, it was known as the "Cadillac of the Fleet."[*] That almost, I would say, carried that ship, because when I saw her over in the Indian Ocean, she still had that same aura—Cadillac of the fleet.

We've talked about giving the ship back to the chief petty officers and about all these different things. I went up one day for one of my tours of the ship while we were at sea. I guess I don't know if I did the right thing or not, but I got a little penknife, and I went up on top of the gun mount, where there was a little piece of line whipping around, an Irish pennant. I went up there, and I trimmed that Irish pennant. Keep the ship neat. They knew I was a nut on Irish pennants.

Boy, the boatswain's mate second class who was in charge of that forecastle came running up: "Captain, please get down from there."

I got down and said, "What's the matter?"

"We'll do that."

I said, "Right."

He said, "Don't you ever go up there again, please, sir."

I said, "I understand. Why is that?"

He said, "You may fall and break your leg."

I said, "Well, how about your going up? You may fall and break your leg."

"Yeah," he says, "but you're going to take us home." They actually had instilled in them that the skipper was all supreme, and he was the guy who was going to get the ship back safely. That meant more to me—and I'm not talking about me personally. Really, the

---

[*] The destroyer Jonas Ingram was decommissioned 4 March 1983.

captain was sacred, and that's what these sailors believed. I learned that sailors really looked toward you, not only as a leader but as someone who was "going to get us home."

Paul Stillwell: Did you have any problems when you gave the responsibility and authority back to the chiefs, of having some young sea lawyer say, "Yes, but Z-gram so and so says thus and so"?[*]

Captain Colbus: I never found that to happen, and probably because of our chief boatswain on board, Joe Weaver. He was right out of the book. If you called Hollywood central casting and said, "Send me a chief boatswain's mate, United States Navy," Joe would have showed up. We're still in touch.

Let me give you an example. The chief was always about that ship. I can't remember going about that ship at any hour of the day, and I'm talking about 24 hours of the day, seven days a week, and though I never really saw Joe, Joe was always there. He ran that ship with an iron hand. He was also, of course, the chief master-at-arms. Why I say you never saw him was because he was all over the ship. Drugs were big in those days. We had just come in to the drug era, which just blew my mind. I did not understand it, and I'll admit it. I guess I still don't. The young people were just getting into drugs at the time, and we were becoming more lenient. That's another story. In those days, everybody had to come up front. It's just like the alcoholic, "Yes, I am an alcoholic," before you can attack the problem. In those days a realistic skipper had to say, "Yes, my ship has a drug problem."

I would say, "No, I don't have a drug problem," and, of course, everybody would say, "That skipper has his head in the sand." There was a gray-haired aviation admiral, ComFAirJax, who had a meeting of all the skippers over at his headquarters at NAS Jacksonville.[†] We all went there, and we were given the drug lecture—drug identification, that which had to be done; they gave us a good morning brief on drugs.

---

[*] Z-grams were consecutively numbered policy directives from Chief of Naval Operations Zumwalt that attempted to deal with such issues as enlisted rights and privileges, equal opportunity, and Navy families. Junior personnel viewed them much more favorably than did their seniors. See U.S. Naval Institute Proceedings, May 1971, pages 291-298.

[†] ComFAirJax—Commander Fleet Air Jacksonville. The Jacksonville Naval Air Station is adjacent to the fleet home port of Mayport, Florida, where Jonas Ingram was based.

Well, somehow during the course of this meeting, my name came up, and it was said, "Well, Captain Colbus is one of the skippers who insists he doesn't have a drug problem in his ship." They looked at me and they said, "How do you account for that?"

I said, "Chief Boatswain's Mate Joe Weaver doesn't allow it on board; he is very thorough in his searches. He does all of the things that we should be doing. We had success. It's the old story." Well, I guess I was almost booed out of there.

Oh, by the way, our squadron doctor was big on this thing. He was a long-haired, un-officer-like, brilliant physician. He related very well to these young people who were having drug problems. I knew that he had an apartment, which they called a pad, in Jacksonville, with the black light and the flashing lights and the whole nine yards. When he had a kid who was really in bad shape, he would take him home with him. He is a very commendable guy. I'm not criticizing the fact that he didn't live up to the image that I was used to, but I did respect him for the fine work he was doing. He was very liberal.

All of a sudden this young doctor stood up at the meeting, and he said, "The skipper's ship, Jonas Ingram, is in the squadron which I administer. And I will verify and agree with everything he says. He does not have a drug problem." Well, boy, that just took off. They wouldn't believe me, but they did believe this liberal who stood up and talked about it, and rightly so, rightly so. What I'm really saying is that Chief Joe Weaver was just everything he should have been. We had chiefs on there who walked about the ship, kept a taut ship, and I know it sounds old-fashioned, but it was a happy ship due to their individual attention.

That's when I learned that we were in an era that I talk about to my children today. I think that people—that, of course, includes sailors—want orderliness. That's the word I used to use. People want orderliness. I like orderliness in my life. I like to know that, in my particular case, 8:00 o'clock I go to quarters, and at 11:30 I stop for lunch. I like orderliness. I even used to give the pitch that we used to sing when we were kids, "This is the way we wash our clothes on Monday." Remember? "This is the way we iron our clothes on Tuesday." And all those things. You go to church or temple, you learn orderliness, the firmament, the creation, six days, that's orderliness.

I said these young people at that time in the '70s didn't know what orderliness was. They didn't see it in the home, because Mom and Daddy were now working. They didn't have a meal hour. It was just haphazard living. They sure didn't see it in the schools, because all you had to do was go to a school when the school bell rang, that was not an example of orderliness. Most of them had never been inside a church or a temple, so orderliness was gone.

So, by God, we took them out to boot camp, and they loved it. They liked boot camp. They all of a sudden learned about orderliness. They came aboard ship, and it was almost a complete change, back to the old way. So I said we had these kids mixed up. We took them out of the disorderly community, put them into an orderly situation, and then tossed them right back to a halfway. I claim that was the secret to that ship. They had exactly what they wanted—orderliness and toughness. They were tough.

Hey, I would get a sailor to mast and just about eat him up alive, did everything but physically attack him. The chiefs didn't like going to mast in those days because I could stand up there, and I used to say, "I'll put on my John Wayne act and tell a sailor, 'I'm so disappointed, just as I'm disappointed in my son. You've let me down, and I'm going to make you . . . .'" Really. A pattern. They knew what the consequences were when they erred. Now you, of course, tempered this. Just because it was a sailor's first time late didn't mean that I hammered him.

That ship had great people. The exec, outstanding. Chiefs, tremendous. Wardroom, too much talent on one ship. I felt embarrassed that they gave me too much. Those people didn't want to bring their problems up to me. They didn't want the old man to know that "I can't handle it." The chief didn't want the exec to know. The department heads didn't want the exec to know. The petty officers didn't want the chiefs to know. The attitude was, "I can handle this. I'm a leader. I don't need outside help." They tended to be very prideful about that.

When you take away their abilities to do these things, they're unhappy, the sailors are unhappy, and when they come up to see the old man who slaps them on the wrist, it becomes a pattern. If I may be crude, if you're in some lovely lady's arms at 4:30, 5:00 o'clock in the morning and it's cold up in Tiverton, Massachusetts, it takes a lot of willpower to get out, get on the bus, and ride to the ship for the 7:30 muster. Now, what are the consequences? I'll just lie here an extra couple of hours and get up when the sun's up and get down there at 1000. It won't be that difficult. If he knows that he's going to pay in money, if it's really serious, go to the brig for three days on bread and water, what are the consequences? My children do it and my sailors did it, and that's what I thought we had to do in the era of '71 to '73 when we were aboard Jonas Ingram.

Paul Stillwell: Let's talk about that talented wardroom.

Captain Colbus: Yes. Well, let's start off with the exec, Tom Anderson. Absolutely the finest ship handler I've ever seen. When we'd get in a tight spot, I'd call out, "Hey, Tom, you want to do this?" They all knew it, why not admit it? Tom would make the landings. He would bring it in.

Paul Stillwell: How did he compare with Terry Siple?

Captain Colbus: Oh, Terry Siple was not the ship handler. Of course, he was much younger then. Terry Siple was a young lieutenant. Terry Siple was much more the humanitarian. Tom Anderson was not mainly a humanitarian; he was a tough bird. He'd just come back from Vietnam, and I won't use the word "mean," but he was tough on the crew. He was hard on those chiefs. He was an officer who could look a chief in the eye and say, "You're wrong and you're fouling up and you'd better square away." He was a very, very—I hate the word—mature naval officer. Outstanding tactician, and again, a product of his environment.

He'd been on some of the great ships of our time. At that time the new DLGs had just come in, and he was in Wainwright. Pierre Vining, a great naval officer, his son's in the Navy today, was his teacher and skipper.[*] So Tom brought all these great attributes that he'd picked up. You don't just invent these things. You're not born with them. Tom was a very, very experienced, prepared, squared-away naval officer.

When it came time to have a fantail cookout or go over to the chiefs' club when we were invited, or have a crew's picnic, Tom was the first sailor to put on his Vietnam floppy hat, that Aussie-type hat with the flare on the side, a cigar, put his foot up, and get his

---

[*] Captain Pierre H. Vining, USN, commanded USS Wainwright (DLG-28) from 10 September 1969 to 2 July 1971.

guitar and become one of the boys. He had great ability, and he showed them that what he was doing wasn't because he wanted to do that; it was because he had to do it for the ship and the crew. And that crew really loved and respected him as much as I did.

When Tom Anderson left the ship, he and I were almost in tears. It was that close a relationship. We had children the same ages, both wives did very well; it was just a warm family relationship. When he left, I said, "Well, Tom, I hate to see you go, but maybe we'll serve again some day." That was in 1972. In 1975, I was ordered as a brand-new captain back to OpTEvFor. While I was there, he was on the PEB, Propulsion Examining Board, so here were the two families together again in 1975. I was a captain, and he was a commander. So Louis and Tom were together all the time.

Paul Stillwell: What do you recall about some of your other officers in Jonas Ingram?

Captain Colbus. Tom Yankura was the chief engineer.[*] I'm sure memory serves me correctly in saying Tom was a psychology major. He was the finest engineer that ever walked the deck of a ship, a leader of men, a sensitive individual, a sense of humor that you just couldn't beat. Tom Yankura was, I'd say, one of the mainstays of that ship. However, he almost had to compete with the ops officer, Fast Eddie Kaufman.[†] I think he's now in command of one of the DDGs in Charleston. Tom Yankura had an FF out of Charleston. But, anyway, these two brilliant naval officers were not only tacticians and operationally competent, they had a touch with the crew that you just never see. Very, very good with me. Now, they were very, very supportive of the previous way the ship was run, but they made the shift and never lost a beat. They could do it any way the skipper wanted it done, to their great credit.

We had another ops officer, Mike Gazarek.[‡] Mike Gazarek is the guy who taught me how to anchor a ship. He was on the bridge one day. He was a very, very demonstrative person—a very, very outgoing person. He almost pushed me away from the pelorus when I was steaming the ship to anchorage. He said, "Let me do this. Let me do

---

[*] Lieutenant Commander Thomas W. Yankura, USN.
[†] Lieutenant Edwin J. Kaufman, USN.
[‡] Lieutenant Michael J. Gazarek, USN.

this." And he did, and he did a better job than I know I could have done because he had some innovations there.

When it was all over, I shook my head and said, "Boy, I'm supposed to teach you, but jeez, Mike." And Mike just went on and prospered in that environment.

Paul Stillwell: Where had he learned that?

Captain Colbus: From his previous command. These shipmates were all well trained, and I think that's the whole thing. You know, by the time a fellow gets to be a lieutenant, he's been in the Navy seven, eight years. He's got some pretty good credentials, he's seen probably enough of a cross-section of commanding officers, and he's got negative learning too. You can't serve with all sweethearts; you've got to have an SOB in there once in a while, and, as I say, pick up some negative learning where you say to yourself, "I'll never do it that way." I was blessed with officers that had run the gamut and were very, very experienced.

In those days we were going down and doing a lot of patrolling off Cuba. Those sailors were very experienced at that. Surveillance ops were a big thing. But we're discussing the individuals.

Let me mention my supply officer, Dick Gudgen.* I've got to go back to the Pentagon. When we were in OP-03D with Tom Weschler, we had an office in the basement. The snack bar, if you know the Pentagon, was right around the corner. I went in the Pentagon snack bar every morning for a cup of coffee, a doughnut, whatever, and got to know the people in there pretty well. We had a very attractive girl who was there every morning as a customer. I got to flirting with her, and we became great friends. So it's Karen, my girlfriend. When she'd let me, I'd buy her a cup of coffee. One day she came in to my office and said, "May I ask a favor of you, Louis?"

"What's that?"

"I know that you're in the Navy, and I see the picture of a destroyer out there. My husband is a supply officer, and he's going to a ship."

"Oh."

---

* Lieutenant Richard A. Gudgen, SC, USN.

"I'd love to know about the ship. Can you find out?"

"That's easy. What ship is he going to?"

She said, "USS Jonas Ingram."

I said, "I served in that ship when I was a lieutenant; I've ridden that ship; I know all about that ship." I made phone calls while she was there and told her the ship was in the Philadelphia Naval Shipyard, it would be out of overhaul on this date, the homeport would be Mayport, etc., etc.

"Boy, that's great." About three weeks later, in came Karen to my office with this 6-foot, 4-inch handsome naval officer, lieutenant, Supply Corps. She said, "Louis, I want you to meet my husband Dick."

"Well, it's nice to meet you."

"Hey, I really appreciate what you did for me. Karen had the word before I did, and I'm just not going to worry about that."

So all of a sudden we had a nice thing going. I said, "Let me tell you something. I don't like supply officers, especially supply officers married to good-looking girls, so you better be careful." I said, again jokingly, "I may walk on your ship some day as your skipper, and you're going to be in big trouble."

So the day I walked on Jonas Ingram to report, do you know who was waiting for me on the quarterdeck? Dick was still the supply officer. He'd been there a year, year and a half. And, of course, that story was all about the ship. Dick and I just had a ball in that ship. We always called him "Richie" because I gave him that nickname. We had a movie at the time called Lovers and Other Strangers.* The theme through the movie was this fellow who'd always ask his son, "What's the story, Richie? What's the story, Richie?" The boy in the movie got married, got divorced. Every time he'd have a problem, the father would look at the boy and say, "What's the story, Richie?" To this day when we see Dick Gudgen, it's, "What's the story, Richie?"

Paul Stillwell: That was a good movie.

Captain Colbus: You remember it? Yes. He was an Italian chicken soup lover.

---

* Lovers and Other Strangers was a comedy released in 1970.

Paul Stillwell: In discussing these various individuals, let me ask how you dealt with a guy like Gazarek, who was so good that you have to give him his opportunities?

Captain Colbus: You give him his reins and you let him run with it. The navigator came in to see me one day. We were going into a port, and there was an obstacle that really didn't matter because it was in your shipping lane, in Europe somewhere. I remember he had laid down the track to leave that particular obstacle, marked by a buoy, to port, which was fine. But we had plenty of room on the other side to leave it to starboard. I looked at this, and he had it down to a gnat's eye. Absolutely perfect navigational brief. I said, "There's only one thing—I want to change. I want to leave that obstacle to starboard."

He looked at me and he said, "Yes, sir." And he changed his track a little bit. I guess about two or three days later he said, "For the record, why did you change that? I didn't see that it mattered."

"Oh, it didn't."

"Why did you change it?"

"To let you know that I'm the captain on here, and once in a while I like to do something." Well, that's the kind of officers we had, and that's how you gave those guys their reins.

Paul Stillwell: Let's talk about Europe. What was the ship involved in there?

Captain Colbus: We went in to the Sixth Fleet, in-chopped in Rota.[*] By the way, my commodore at that time was Captain Bob Hilton. He was riding my ship because he liked DD-931s, having commanded DD-937, USS Davis when I was exec in Basilone. So my commodore was no stranger to me. I ran things the way he had run things, so it was a natural match.

---

[*] "Chop" is short for change operational control. In this case, the ships were changing rom the operational control of Commander Second Fleet to that of Commander Sixth Fleet. The Jonas Ingram reported to the Sixth Fleet in January 1972.

When we arrived in Rota, the flagship was Springfield, and Com6thFlt was Jerry Miller.* Now, you talk about color and glamour and charisma and follow the leader, that was it. He had us over to his ship for breakfast and gave us probably the most inspirational pep talk that I have ever heard in my life: "Let's go get 'em, boys," He even got down to, "See, how do you like this uniform? Double-knit. I want you to know that that's the finest thing a sailor can do. We ought to all get down and get double-knits. Why not?" So he had one foot into the modern Navy and one foot, traditional Navy. He did a lot of fine things, inspired us, and off we went.

Our carrier division—and they were called carrier divisions then—was Commander Carrier Division Four, Rear Admiral Donald Engen.† He couldn't have been a better leader and commander. So here I was sitting with my commodore, a close personal friend, and I think he admired me as much as I admired him. I shouldn't use that word, but for lack of a better word. Admiral Engen—who today would be called a battle group commander, then called task group commander—was riding Franklin D. Roosevelt. He couldn't have been a better person and appreciated everything we did. The third, of course, in the chain of command was Jerry Miller. So we were going off to a great deployment. This was going to be the right way to do it.

We got under way late. It was late, after our briefings and turn-over. As we went around the corner there at Gibraltar, we were going through the strait at about 3:00 o'clock in the morning. We were going to go alongside Caloosahatchee for fueling. About that time this great, outstanding chief I referred to, Chief Weaver, came up with the chief hospital corpsman to tell me we had a very sick oil king.

"Oh?" I was then taking the ship alongside the oiler. The sick man was not able to get up and take his soundings as the petty officer first class in charge of the oil and water lab, and they had somebody else do it. It was determined that he was suffering from alcohol poisoning. When he came back from liberty, everybody said, "Ha, ha," he'd been drinking, which apparently he had. He went to bed. It turned out, in the aftermath, that he'd gone into the lab and started hitting the alcohol. He was drinking the alcohol that you

---

* Vice Admiral Gerald E. Miller, USN, commanded the Sixth Fleet from October 1971 to June 1973. His oral history is in the Naval Institute collection.
† Rear Admiral Donald D. Engen, USN. The oral history of Engen, who retired as a vice admiral, is in the Naval Institute collection.

aren't supposed to drink, with the big skull and crossbones on there. Now, they normally don't give that to a ship to carry just because of something like that, but in this case, NAS Jacksonville, which supplied us with those chemicals, didn't have denatured alcohol. It was regular alcohol.

The engineering master chief on the ship, Master Chief Winburn, had told everybody, "You guys think it's cute to hear these stories. Ain't kidding. This is it. Don't any of you fellows touch this." Well, this petty officer first class did just that. By the time we got him into the Stokes litter stretcher and transferred him by helicopter from Jonas Ingram to Franklin D. Roosevelt, he died. Well, you can imagine what a stigma this puts on a ship.

It was a Sunday morning, and we had services on the mess deck. Nobody had been to bed, but we were going to have services. Well, I went down and said what I had to say to my crew who had come to services. They knew we were going to talk about our departed petty officer. And I read to them a Jewish prayer that we use for mourners. There's not a word in there about death; it talks about their hallowed memory and good works, and it's a very moving prayer in English as in Hebrew. Well, I read that to them and told them, "We don't stop. We go on." I thought I'd said the right things. What can you say?

By the way, a couple of other sailors came forth and said, "We had drinks with the petty officer too." They'd put some alcohol in the Coca-Cola, and these young firemen were running scared and wanted medical attention. So I'd say by 9:00 o'clock Sunday morning, we had transferred, if memory serves me right, three young sailors in addition to the petty officer who died.

About 9:00 or 10:00 o'clock, I got the word that Admiral Engen was coming over by helicopter at 10:30. Boy, I knew that was it. Louis, cash it in. I can certainly understand this. It's been a great cruise, but he must think I'm running a zoo over here. Helicopter over the fantail, Admiral Engen came aboard, looked around, shook my hand, and put his arm around me. I figured, "Well, this is before he puts the knife in."

He said, "Let's go up to your cabin and talk."

"Yes, sir."

Paul Stillwell: Had you known him before?

Captain Colbus; Oh, yes. We transited with him and worked for him on the workup. By the way, Commodore Hilton was not on board at this time. He'd transferred to another ship. He was ship-hopping, as squadron commanders do. Anyway, Admiral Engen took me up in my cabin, and sat me down. I don't need to tell you that I was next to tears, and I was scared: "Why me?" All those things.

He looked at me and almost took me by the hand and said, "Louis, I was glad to see, as I came up to your cabin, that your crew is not demoralized. I could still see the spirit there. All I want you to know is, I'm behind you. And what can I do to help?" Whew. You just don't know what that meant. Boy, I practically grabbed him and hugged him, but my demeanor was a commander talking to an admiral.

I thanked him and said, "Would you join us for lunch?" He did, he came down, and we went on about our business. Very, very understanding, very supportive, because, hey, that's pretty serious. Where was my control?

Well, we had the investigation. I guess the outcome of that investigation was, "What more can you do when you trust the keys to a petty officer first class and he abuses that privilege?" Even his wife, back on the beach, understood. Of course, it was a tough time for the ship. We overcame it and went on to do some great things.

Let me tell you a fun story while we're there. We were out circling the Russians, doing our surveillance ops. In those days it was a big deal that we'd been at sea 32 days without a liberty port. That was big stuff. Today we do it 132 days and don't even bat an eye, but in 1972, that was a long time at sea. We got a message from Admiral Jerry Miller, saying, "You fellows have done a grand job; you're my heroes." He called us all that. We were all his heroes. He said, "How about liberty? You're due for a liberty port. Where would you like to go?" This was in a personal message to me.

Well, I got the exec, this outstanding exec, Tom Anderson, and said, "Tom, where do you want to take this ship?" Again, to tell you about the atmosphere, in that period it was not unusual to go out and take a poll of the crew as to where they wanted to go. I did not believe in that. My approach was, "I'll tell you where you go and then follow me and we'll have a good time." They knew that, so we never took a poll. But I did want to ask the exec, who'd been to Naples. We all knew Barcelona, we were over in the Eastern Med, and we really didn't want to get back too far away. Where could we go?

He said, "Well, when I was a lieutenant (j.g.) in USS Springfield, we went to the island of Mykonos."

"Where's that?"

"It's up there in the Aegean somewhere."

We got out a chart. Mykonos is 90 miles east of Athens. Fine. We put in our request, and it was granted. I'm going to say it was a Thursday morning when we arrived at Mykonos. It was absolutely the most gorgeous scene you've ever seen. Here was this Greek island with a mountain on the western end. On the eastern end was this gorgeous place—I guess you'd call it a fishing village. You could see four windmills, the gorgeous little clean square houses on the waterline, and then the seawall with the yachts inside.

Well, we knew we couldn't go inside, so I was going to anchor the ship. Mike Gazarek had taught me how to anchor this ship. I made a nice approach on the eastern end, the populated end of the island. I dropped the hook. I let the ship settle down. We were port side to the beach, with the ship's head facing east. The signalman called down to me, "Captain, look through your binoculars at those houses on the beach."

By this time the entire crew was on the port side of the ship. I raised the binoculars and looked through them at one particular house. It had two stories, had a roof with a little parapet, whatever you call it, around it. I saw topless girls hanging clothes on a line over there. Well, we had Mr. Roberts's long-glass liberty, whatever you want to call it.* My crew was going bananas. We didn't have enough binoculars to go around, but we were just having a grand time. About that time, out comes the putt-putt boat, and in it is a Greek Navy lieutenant. He had come there to be our liaison officer. We brought him on, we saluted, we did all the things.

He said, "This is not a good anchorage because come the wind, you're going to

---

* Mister Roberts was a book of fictional stories written by Thomas Heggen on the basis of his World War II experiences as a Naval Reserve officer. Published in 1946, it depicted life on board an imaginary cargo ship in which the officers and crew flouted rules and regulations. It was later made into a successful stage play and movie, both starring Henry Fonda. One of the scenes featured ship-bound sailors making "liberty" by using binoculars to look at nurses' quarters ashore.

blow down on that island. This is not a safe anchorage. I recommend you go to the western end of the island."

"Well, all right." We hadn't wrapped up the engines yet. I knew this was too good to be true. It was very close for the boat ride and good long-glass liberty. We picked up the anchor, turned the ship around, and headed west. We went, let's say, 2,000 yards, and dropped the anchor. Now we were in the lee of this mountain. He said, "Good anchorage. This is safe."

Now the starboard side of the ship was to the beach, but all we could see was beach and a lot of rocks over there. Then someone said, "Captain, look through your glasses at those rocks over there." Nude bathing. The damn place was covered with nude bathers.

I said, "Exec, when are you going to commence liberty?"

The exec said, "Commence liberty." We sent a swim party over there to the beach in our 26-foot motor whaleboat, and you wouldn't believe the time we had on that island. We had a very, very good time. Mykonos. Ideal. Travelogue. It's a spot for the tourists to arrive there at about 2:00 o'clock in the afternoon, come off the big cruise liners, do their walk about the town, and back on board. But at that time, May or June of '72, nude bathing was the thing. They had a couple of beaches all around the northwestern edge of this island. One bus took tourists back and forth, and it was a mecca for the jet set. They had them from all over. We became very popular on that island. My boys ended up bartending on those three days we were there. It goes on and on and on.

On Saturday night, I was called away from liberty and told there was a break-in of a grocery store/hardware store in this little shopping area. <u>Jonas Ingram</u> sailors did it, they were sure. Well, I went to the police station, and I told them, just as you would tell about your children, "I can guarantee you that it was not a U.S. Navy man because they're all my shipmates, and they were too well-behaved and too this, too that, absolutely. It's one of those hippies, it's one of those international guys. It's some of those bad guys who were backpacking through here that stole the two shotguns and the food out of that store." They believed me.

Sunday night we were wrapping up ashore, because the ship was leaving Monday morning at 8:00 o'clock. I got a call: "Come down to the police station." I got down to the police station, and there were two of my young firemen. Guess what? They had a room over the store that was robbed. As they were checking out, this sweet little old Greek lady, a very picturesque person, about 60-ish, real islander, went in to clean the room and found the two shotguns under the bed. These kids had gotten drunk, they had been ill in the room. The room was pretty much a mess, plus the two shotguns, and there are these two kids in there.

Well, do I have to tell you how embarrassed I was, how distraught I was? Here was another tragic moment in my ship's life. I shut the door and I said to them, "All you've got to do with me is level with me. You tell me the whole story, and I'm going to help you. I'm not going to protect you, but you deserve assistance. I'm going to give you that assistance."

Well, they told the whole story, too much to drink, etc., etc., "Yes, we did it."

"That's all I wanted to know. I'll do what I can."

Well, I got to take them back to the ship with me by promising they'd be delivered the next morning. The next morning I delayed sailing. I went back over with these two lads, and the ensign damage control assistant, who was their division officer. I called the judge, who was on an island about 20 miles to the south, which was headquarters for all this. He did speak English, and I started off with what little Greek I'd learned back in high school from my Greek friend. He thought that was great. I told him what I wanted to do. I wanted to leave my people—they had money to pay for any fines—and I was leaving the ensign. With this telephone call I was greasing the skids, so to speak. Well, the outcome of that was they went down there, they were chastised, they paid their money, and they got transportation to Athens, where we picked them up in a matter of days. So we did let that thing go by.

The point of the story is of course, that I filed the report, and then I got a message from Vice Admiral Jerry Miller to Commander Colbus: "What is the record of your culprits?" Because he told us when we in-chopped, "Know your sailors, and when you've got a problem, keep them off the beach. It's up to you."

My answer to him was not tongue in cheek; it wasn't flippant. But I told him—and this was, of course, a true statement, that if you wanted to find the apple-cheeked, Wisconsin fuzzy-faced kid who you'd take home with you to introduce to your daughter, you could take either of these two young men. And the money, the $270.00 one of them took with him to pay his fine, was taken from his locker, because he was saving up this money to buy his first-born child a gift. The child was due in three weeks.

All I got back from Jerry Miller was, "You are my hero." You just don't get that kind of senior support. Anyway, that was Jerry Miller.

Getting back to Mykonos, we took shipmates with us, damage controlmen from this sailor's division. They repaired any damage that had been boarded up. They found the glass, and they fixed it in better condition than it was originally. We went in and bought food for the wardroom out of wardroom mess funds, which are non-appropriated. We bought enough food to support the wardroom for the next two weeks. I remember buying my wife a hat, my daughter a gift. So we went over and supported this store and thanked this woman. We left there, I would say, in better shape than had that incident not occurred. In other words, it was a bad situation that Jonas Ingram made into a good situation.

Paul Stillwell: You turned a problem into an opportunity.

Captain Colbus: Yes, we did. They did. By the way, we went in there five or six more times. That became a regular stop for Jonas Ingram. For the third trip we had Commodore Hilton on board. He wasn't with us the first two times.

The second time, of course, I spread the word, "Hey, you have to go to this Mykonos." We did go back, we got to know everybody, and we were going out on yachts for trips around this island. We're talking about 92-foot yachts owned by whomever. The Revlon yacht had been in there; Onassis's yacht had been in there.[*] This was really a great, great place. My shipmates were well received, and everybody had their favorite place and took up with the Greek people very nicely.

USS Stribling went in with us, senior ship, on the second trip. When Stribling got there, that was another story. Now we had two U.S. destroyers; they just followed in our wake, and they had a great time.

When we left, Admiral Miller's second message to me was, "What's going on that everybody wants to go to Mykonos?"

---

[*] Aristotle Onassis was a super-rich Greek shipowner. In 1968 he had married the widow of President John F. Kennedy.

I can remember—I have it in my files somewhere—my answer to him was, "I have found the Garden of Eden without a fig leaf." It was well received and well accepted.

Paul Stillwell: Well, Admiral Miller has that kind of flair himself, so I think he could appreciate that.

Captain Colbus: What a great man. We tried to get Admiral Engen to go with us, and he tried, and he wanted to, but he just could never get away from his duties. But I took the commodore there. That was our homeport while we were there. We still hear from these people, and it's just a great place.

Paul Stillwell: That was the big detente period.[*] Can could talk about your operations in relation to Soviet ships?

Captain Colbus: Sure. We not only did surveillance ops down in Florida Straits, which occurred after our Med deployment, but while we were in the Med, the thing to do was go off and follow the Soviet fleet, a watch on watch. We would get these assignments. As I told you, we had just come off of 32-day trail. The modus operandi was to pick up the Soviet and stay astern of the ship and just observe it, and, of course, they would observe us. We learned a lot about each other, not only operationally but personnel wise.

We saw a lot of things on there that were unusual. They, of course, would go to anchorages. They didn't go ashore. They anchored the ship and then we'd circle the wagon, so to speak. I was never comfortable, because you would go sometimes three days and have a very nice, quiet time of it. On the third day, out of the clear blue sky, the Soviet skipper would make a crazy maneuver just to try to catch you, almost as if he wanted you to collide with him. So you had to be on your alert the entire time.

Commodore Hilton had been riding USS W. S. Sims, a DE out of Mayport. The skipper of Sims was a young lieutenant commander--I don't think he was frocked yet--named Gerrish Flynn.[†] He was an absolute genius, a brilliant individual, a true

---

[*] "Detente" was a word used at the time to describe the temporary easing of tensions between the United States and the Soviet Union. Vice Admiral Gerald Miller's oral history contains some excellent illustrations.
[†] Lieutenant Commander Gerrish C. Flynn, USN.

bachelor, and I'm proud to say when we ended up that deployment he was a good friend of mine.

With the commodore embarked, Gerrish Flynn in Sims got into one of these ship-shouldering situations. Sims had the right of way, the Soviet ship moved in on her. It was cat and mouse, I guess, for many hours. Gerrish was ingenious enough, or Bob Hilton was, to break out their television camera. (We'd just come into the closed-circuit TV era. The chaplains had a $2,000 unit, and they'd pipe their tapes through the ship.) He got this camera out and took films of the Soviet ship on the wrong side, on the right side, and he used his own ship as a reference point. The distance between ships was sometimes only 15 to 20 feet—not yards, feet. By the way, Commodore Hilton was fluent in Russian.

Well, of course, this was big news. Commodore Hilton carried those films back to the Pentagon at the time they were doing these Incidents at Sea negotiations with the Soviet at high level.* The Commodore Hilton/Gerrish Flynn film was shown, and apparently that was the clincher, so they made history. As Commodore Hilton was walking through the halls of the Pentagon with this film in hand, now done and on his way back to the Mediterranean, he was stopped and congratulated. He had made flag! So he came back as a flag selectee, and we went on to great things.

Paul Stillwell: Did the Soviets muscle in on your ship?

Captain Colbus: Oh, yes. I'd just come from the DD-963 program, where I'd studied but not seen these gas turbine ships. They're so reactive. Now I was up against a gas turbine Soviet ship, and he was imposing on me and infringing on me. All I wanted to do was keep a submarine in contact, which I happened to have at the time. The Soviet would come and get in front of myself and the sub, as he should.

Now, these 931s were the most powerful, highly maneuverable ships we had had up to that point, even more so than the DDGs, and that becomes a big discussion point between DDG skippers. The 931-class ships weren't completely automatic. The man was

---

* U.S. and Soviet officials signed the Incidents at Sea agreement in Moscow in May 1972. See John Erickson, "The Soviet Naval High Command," U.S. Naval Institute Proceedings, May 1973, pages 66-87, and David Winkler, "When Russia Invaded Disneyland," Proceedings, May 1997, pages 77-81.

in the loop there, and he controlled some of the things that were automatically controlled in the DDG-2s.

Anyway, my people were just very responsive, and we had a good, as I said, engineering team. We were running circles around that gas turbine ship. We were backing down, we were going left, right, and we didn't lose the submarine. We did this for about three hours, and I came up with the conclusion that either that Soviet skipper didn't want to maneuver his ship to really show it off, because he had me, or we got around him, or they weren't all that they were cracked up to be, or the ship wasn't fully functional that day. But we had a good three, three and a half hours of cat and mouse and, of course, we loved it, had a good time doing it, showing off our ship, and we ended up with a lot of good information.

Paul Stillwell: Do you recall what class of ship it was?

Captain Colbus: No, I really don't, but it was a gas turbine ship. I can almost remember the number.

Paul Stillwell: Let's talk about ASW in general. What other experiences did you have in Jonas Ingram?

Captain Colbus: Well, we did have an SQS-23 sonar on that ship, and I had come from an SQS-26 ship in McCloy, so when I was in a junior command, I had a bigger and more powerful, more modern sonar. It so happened that it was during this time that the technicians and the smart people came aboard and did some black box modifications to the sonar to give it a lot of additional abilities, characteristics, and capabilities. We were testing that the whole time we were there, and that proved to be very worthwhile.

We also as I said, had the ASW mod on that ship, which gave us an ASROC on the 02 level. It took away from the really classic destroyer lines, but it gave us a very, very great capability. We had ASROC. Of course, the original 931 didn't. We also had the foundation for a towed-array sonar. I didn't see that in my day; that came in the next overhaul. So we were a modern, up-to-date ASW ship. We were certainly exercised, and we also developed not a landing platform for a helicopter but a big area aft that provided us with a vertical replenishment capability.

Paul Stillwell: Was the emphasis at that point on active sonar tactics?

Captain Colbus: Oh, yes. Active. All active. Everything was active sonar, bigger and better.

Paul Stillwell: Can you draw a comparison in ASW capability between McCloy and Jonas Ingram?

Captain Colbus: Yes. Of course, Jonas Ingram went through a "mod," a modification that just took her out of the—I guess you'd call it out of the T model and put her right up into the supercharged model. McCloy, when she was commissioned and when I received her, had an SQS-26. Period. It had a steam generator, and it was the basic operational model. As we discussed, McCloy spent six months in the shipyard, where she was modified to become a SQS-26 AXR retrofit. That gave her the passive capability that the basic SQS-26 didn't have. So I saw that advance.

Then I went aboard USS Jonas Ingram, and she was given these modifications that advanced her. So what we're talking about is the advanced 23 versus the 26 AXR, and, of course, there was no comparison. We're talking about different frequencies, we're talking about different ranges, we're talking about capabilities that just weren't dreamed of in the ASW "mod" I had at that particular time. So as far as comparison, it was another world. However, the two did complement each other very nicely. In fact, at that time I am willing to say that the 23 worked better with Gerrish Flynn's ship, which was a 26 ship, than another 26 ship would have worked with Gerrish Flynn's ship. So we complemented very nicely.

Paul Stillwell: What do you recall about carrier task group operations?

Captain Colbus: Oh, my. Carrier task group operations. Don Engen, of course, was the task group commander, and I was shotgun for USS Franklin D. Roosevelt with one of the all-time greats, Captain Jack—Jack Youngblade.* Here we are back to Hollywood central casting, "Send me the skipper." Jack Youngblade would stand on the bridge of FDR, pulling on a Camel cigarette. He was right out of the book, a great naval officer, full of charisma. This whole crowd was fantastic, and I followed Jack Youngblade around the Med as his shotgun, stayed with him pretty much. Now, normally they'd have a missile ship, but I went along and was his, as I said, shotgun.

The other great ship we had was USS Leahy, a double-ender DLG.† The skipper of that ship was Roy Hoffmann.‡ If you mention that name to any sailor from the 1955 time frame on, he will just shudder, because this destroyerman's destroyerman, Roy Hoffmann, had the nickname of "Nails." He was the epitome of the destroyerman, the surface sailor, the man of the sea. "Nails" was absolutely letter perfect. Without a doubt—and this is my opinion—he is the finest ship handler we have ever seen. He would take any size ship anywhere and put it anywhere. He was also probably the toughest taskmaster we had at the time.

He ran that ship as a cruiser should be operated, not only at sea but in port. I mean, everything was perfect, spic and span, and I emulated him. I used to tell my crew, "I want to grow up and be just like Uncle Roy. Let's show 'Nails' we're going to keep up with him." Be it colors in the morning, be it going alongside the oiler, you just tried to emulate Nails Hoffman and USS Leahy. I knew him well enough to, in private, refer to him as "Nails." He was just a great senior officer to have around to keep a fellow like myself in tow. Great tactician.

Paul Stillwell: Was this the fellow who ran Market Time in Vietnam?

---

* Captain Charles John Youngblade, USN, commanded USS Franklin D. Roosevelt (CVA-42) from September 1971 to April 1973.
† The ships of the Leahy (DLG-16) class were known as double enders because they had missile launchers both forward and aft, whereas the later Belknap (DLG-26) class had a missile launcher forward and a 5-inch gun aft.
‡ Captain Roy F. Hoffmann, USN, commanded USS Leahy (DLG-16) from February 1971 to September 1972.

Captain Colbus: That's exactly the same man.

Paul Stillwell: I've talked to some of Admiral Zumwalt's people from Vietnam, and they said he's the epitome of a warrior.*

Captain Colbus: That's it. That's beautifully and eloquently and properly stated, yes. The epitome of a warrior. And a very, very tender man who under it all, when it came time, could be just as sweet a man as you could find. There were a lot of people who didn't know that because they didn't know Roy.

Paul Stillwell: No. They saw the "Nails" side of him.

Captain Colbus: And he would laugh at that nickname. He didn't trade on being a tough guy, but that's what people saw. That was fine. He and I did a lot of fun things together.

Paul Stillwell: Tell me about Sam Pearlman.† We haven't talked about him yet.

Captain Colbus: Sam Pearlman and I grew up together, and our careers had similar patterns. He had a cruiser; I had a desron. We both ended up in Norfolk together; we both retired in Norfolk. He now is out in Fullerton with Hughes Aircraft in an administrative operational job. A very brilliant man and a lot of fun. There are more sea stories about Sammy Pearlman than the law allows. He's one of the all-time characters of the Navy. Of course, I never worked for him, and I don't know if that's good or bad.

Paul Stillwell: Tell one or two of these sea stories.

Captain Colbus: Okay. My favorite sea story about Sam was when I had Jonas Ingram and he had Luce. We ended up in Augusta Bay. We went to a big evening cocktail party with all the Sixth Fleet admirals and skippers and commodores around. During a lull in the

---

* See the volume of Naval Institute oral histories on Admiral Elmo Zumwalt's staff officers.
† Captain Samuel Saul Pearlman, USN, retired in November 1982, a month before Colbus did.

conversation, with drinks in hand, I said to Sam, "By the way, Sam, I bring to you from Washington greetings and regards from a very good friend of ours."

He asks me, "Who is that, Louis?"

I said, "Admiral Frank Price, who was my boss in 03D."

"Ah."

"And your boss in the cruiser Long Beach."

To which he answered, "Let me tell you something, Louis. Frank Price is no friend of ours for two reasons. One, he's an admiral. Two, he's a gentile." Now, everybody heard this and that was a typical Sam Pearlman remark. He, I guess, realized how funny it was, looked around, laughed, and went on.

Another story when he was skipper of Luce. His weapons officer told me this. He said they were doing a gun shoot off Newport, and anybody who's a Newport sailor knows that's sometimes a lost cause. You go to sea and sit for days, waiting for the aircraft in the fog. They were steaming out there on this particular day and were waiting for a tug. It was a surface shoot. The tug was there, and after hours of being on station, waiting for the fog to break and what have you, the gun boss leaned over and said, "Captain, I don't think this is ever going to work. You just can't see a thing out there. This is ridiculous. I recommend we cancel the shoot."

To which Sammy yelled, "I'll tell you when the fog lifts. I'll tell you when it's time to run the exercise. You just listen to me. I wouldn't take any of your recommendations. As a matter of fact, cease fog signals. Batteries released." And they go on and on. As I say, he is a very good friend of mine. We went through lots of things together personally and, I guess, professionally. We went to oily rag school together and war college together.

Paul Stillwell: Any memories from your service in that ship other than the deployment? Back stateside, work on inspections, what have you?

Captain Colbus: When Jonas Ingram went to Sixth Fleet, we were the test bed, I might say, for the SMD, the Ships Manning Document for that particular class. Well, I got a lot of heat out of that. We had people on board from what's called MACLant in Norfolk—

Manpower, something, Atlantic. They're the people who come on with the pencil and do the time study and say, "What do you do, signalman?"

"Well, I go to the head and I get a haircut, and I have to eat and I have to sleep."

Then they would say to us, "You don't need that signalman. You need a quartermaster instead." This was, of course, the only way to go in the Navy, and MACLant was doing this study. I would be willing to say they weren't too well received.

They came aboard my ship and it was like coming to my home. "You're in my ship. I'm not here to criticize you, you were sent to do a job. You're part of the wardroom." And we had a lieutenant and a warrant officer who joined in with us and became part of our crew. We had four senior petty officers who became part of our crew, and we had a heck of a good time with these people. But let me tell you what the benefit was. Rather than fighting them, we joined them, and I was criticized back home.

"Sure, Louis is having a good tour over there, but who wouldn't, with MACLant on board, because if be has a fire controlman who breaks his foot and is taken off the ship, in no time they've got another fire controlman on there to take his place."

And I said, "Well, what's so bad about that?"

"It makes it too easy."

I said, "Whoa, whoa, whoa." I said, "We're always in three-section liberty under the toughest of times because we've got 100% manning. That's like somebody saying, 'Here's a million bucks. Enjoy it.'"

"'No, I can't do that because you're giving it to me.'" CruDesLant's personnel officer, Dick Dalla Mura, who is now a retired gent in Charleston, made that remark about it being too easy: "No wonder you're having such a good crew. We keep you pumped up with people."[*]

I acknowledged that and said, "Thank you very much," and went on to enjoy it.

Oh, one quickie. We had a gunner's mate first class, GM1 St. John. I don't know how we were lucky enough to get him, but there we were. He was as good as the men in chiefs' quarters. He was up in the gun mount one day dropping the breechblock, and he crushed his hand. We had a serious problem on our hands. One of the things I used to say was, "I won't hurt anybody, I won't maim anybody, and I certainly won't kill anybody."

---

[*] Captain Richard A. Dalla Mura, USN.

But here I've already told you we lost one man, and now we had a man who has a smashed thumb.

Well, the doctor looked at him, and we sent him to the carrier. They thought they might be able to save the thumb, but after a day or two, they said they'd send Gunner's Mate St. John up to Rhein Main in Frankfurt.* Well, he went off, and the outcome of that story was that he was up there, and after about four weeks, five weeks, he was all healed, and he was ordered back to the States.

He was almost arrested by the Army people up there and thrown in the brig, whatever Army people do to you, for being so disrespectful, not obeying orders, all these things. He said he would not go back to the States; he was going back to his ship. Magic. In other ships, sailors were fighting to get home; this crew, no, they were fighting to get back. So Petty Officer St. John made history at the Army hospital by almost going AWOL, as they call it, so he could get back to his ship in Naples.† And he did get back.

Paul Stillwell: How good a job did you do in keeping in touch with the families while you were on deployment?

Captain Colbus: I'm glad you asked that. We did a very good job. I told this story, but I guess it wasn't to you.

Okay, back to Mayport prior to deployment. It was time to get under way. We had this great wives' club, which I referred to, all done real well, and everybody was very, very happy with each other. I'll tell you what endeared the ship and the crew and everybody else. Did you ever hear of Dave Rosenberg?

Paul Stillwell: Yes, he's Mr. Culture.

Captain Colbus: Mr. Culture himself.‡ Cultural experience. Well, I knew Dave from my tour in BuPers and exercised my friendship and got Dave to come down and give his pitch

---

* Rhein Main is the name of a U.S. Air Force base in Germany.
† AWOL—absent without leave. The Navy equivalent for this term is UA—unauthorized absence.
‡ Rosenberg gave naval personnel demonstrations of the differing cultures they would encounter in foreign countries. Included in his repertoire was dressing up in native costumes.

at the family theater in Mayport. It was not just for Jonas Ingram but for all the deployers, and we invited the wives. Well, what a way to start the deployment.

Another thing that was very popular at the time, and rightly so, was that we must keep the families informed. Family-grams weren't anything new to me. Again, hey Mr. Zumwalt, I've been sending out family-grams ever since my first commanding officer taught me that. Take care of your people, make sure the families are cut in.

At that time it was allotments, allotments, allotments. Don't go off and depend on the mail. We still talk that way. And guess what? Sailors still go off and don't file allotments. Well, that wasn't going to happen in our ship. Everybody's allotment was going to be squared away. We did. We got under way, I think, on the sixth of January, 1972. We steamed with FDR to the missile and gun range in the San Juan area; we did all the things. By the first of February, we were in the Med, and a message came through from Commander Cruiser-Destroyer Flotilla 12, who was Ken Wallace.* Admiral Wallace had absolutely gone ballistic because in reading his message traffic, there were at least seven messages to Jonas Ingram concerning dependents' allotments. Wives had not received their allotments.

Well, we didn't understand this. I didn't understand it. Again, Bob Hilton was in my ship. He took the message, and he went back to Ken Wallace and said, "I witnessed the pre-sail briefings. I saw this ship do all these things. Don't ask me why in my entire squadron, Jonas Ingram has seven wives who didn't get an allotment the first of the month."

As it turned out, we had briefed these wives so well and told them exactly what to do, with the addresses and everything, that they reacted right away when they didn't get their allotments on the 30th of January. They went to GQ because we had influenced the men so much. These seven women, who were senior petty officers' wives, had had allotments, but the husbands increased the allotments. And when you change an allotment in the United States Navy, you now don't get the first change on the 30th; you get it on the first of the month. They had two days to stew and boil. Again, it turned out exactly right. The wives were told what to do, but they weren't told, "Instead of getting your new allotment on the 30th, you'll get it on the first," so that thing blew over very well.

---
* Rear Admiral Kenneth C. Wallace, USN.

That reminds me. Can I go back and tell another sea story?

Paul Stillwell: Sure.

Captain Colbus: Let's go back to Mayport in October of '71. It was, I'm going to say, the Wednesday before Columbus Day, which was a Monday. I remember it very well. I got a call from Ed Kelley, who was then my commodore.* Ed Kelley said, "Got to see you." Now, Ed Kelley and I go way back. We were old friends. Anyway, he called me over and said, "Can you get the ship together? Dog Smith died. [Smith was a very, very popular rear admiral in Jacksonville.] And we want to bury Dog Smith at sea. Can you do it?"†

"Yes, sir. When?"

He said, "Friday."‡

"Yes, sir. Let me go back, though, and check, because we're in a maintenance period, and I want to make sure. Let me check with my engineers." So I went back and met with the exec and the engineer. I said, "Can we get the ship together and go to sea Friday for a burial?"

Everybody said, "Yes, sir."

"Exec, can we get all the arrangements? Because this has to be first class, dignified."

"I've done this before. It's no problem."

"Good. You need me to tell you? Because I've done it too many times. Did it in McCloy, did it in all my other ships."

"No." The exec can handle the arrangements, the engineer can handle it too. That was Wednesday.

Thursday I had promised to take my then-six-year-old and three-year-old children to Saint Augustine, somewhere, wherever you go to see things that children want to see. Thursday I came in and I said to the exec, "Do you need me for anything?"

"No."

---

* Captain Edward G. Kelley, USN.
† Rear Admiral Daniel F. Smith, Jr., USN, retired from active duty in 1970. He died at the naval air station in Pensacola, Florida, on 5 October 1971.
‡ This particular Friday fell on the eighth day of the month in October 1971.

I said, "I'm going off to . . . " wherever we were going. "And I'll see you tomorrow morning, under way at 8:00 o'clock."

"Great."

Commodore Kelley came over about 2:00 o'clock to see how things were going for arrangements to get Dog Smith buried. He was delighted that I wasn't there. Now, you don't find that in many leaders today. And I should tell you that Ed Kelley made Nails Hoffmann look like a Sunday School teacher. Anyway, old Ed Kelley came over and was delighted. When I got back, I told my sailors early Friday morning, "We're only going out 60 miles. We'll be back here by 1430, 1500 and be on liberty at the normal time."

"Great."

We got under way, we did it, routinely, took the pictures, made up the book, X marked the spot on the chart. We were going to present this to the widow. As we were coming back to Mayport at about, I'm going to say, 1345—and Mayport's a very quick approach, it's about a 15-minute sea detail—we were running pretty fast as we were coming up. As we were coming up to the sea buoy, we requested permission to enter port, which is routine, as you know, aboard ship. We didn't hear any response. We entered the channel, made our first turn. We were coming in on course 255, right on the tower. We thought we were going to be in great shape here. Then we got a radiotelephone message, "What are your intentions?"

"Make the moor where I left my berth this morning."

"You do not have permission to enter port." Holy moly, Andy, I didn't ask questions, but I was really uptight, and I was also embarrassed, thinking, "What have I done?" I went in and turned around in the basin, because you can't turn in that channel, and went back out to sea.

I called and said, "Request permission to enter port."

"I need a clarification."

"What would you like me to do?"

"You have permission to enter port." Hmm.

So I turned around, came back in, and made the moor. It was now something like 1545, and I didn't keep my promise to my shipmates. I went over to port operations to find out why, after I was in the harbor, they didn't just chew me out.

Seaman Gronk was sitting at the watch officer's desk, and everybody else was gone; he was just following procedure. He didn't hear my request and figured I didn't have permission to enter port. He was told nobody comes in without permission, and he told me I didn't have it. I took that to mean go back to sea. Then, when I asked him, he said yes. If I'd have asked him in the channel, he'd have probably said yes. But, oh, you think that didn't go through the rooftops. That's when old Ed Kelley took a couple of round turns on the naval station. You never tell a ship to return to sea. If they violated something, you work it out afterwards. But that was a tough lesson. Of course, the harbormaster and all the officers were gone. It was Friday afternoon, and they'd left a seaman in charge. They forgot we were at sea.

Paul Stillwell: Sounds like Emmett Bonner and the movement reports.

Captain Colbus: I'm flattered you remembered that. Oh, yes. Emmett, may he rest in peace: "Does it matter, and who cares?"

Paul Stillwell: What do you remember about the burial of Admiral Smith?

Captain Colbus: The Smith family was invited to go along, of course, and the widow and a child or two elected not to. We went out and did the ceremony with the squadron chaplain. I thought it was done properly. Of course, I'm partial. We made up—as I'd done on two or three other occasions, on this ship and other ships—a black, leather-bound book of photographs, like a family album. Before going out, we bought one of these at the local stationery store, and you start off with the first page. In this case it was very neatly lettered by one of the shipmates who specialized in old English lettering. It told what it was, the date, the time. Then the first page under this isinglass cover was the chart. We actually cut the chart out where Admiral Smith had been buried at sea; there was a mark showing the latitude and longitude. As I would say, a memorial. And then we had the appropriate pictures, the honor guard, the wreath floating in the water. I thought it was the proper thing to do and could be used, I guess, as a memorial, like a tombstone.

On Monday, following that Friday we just talked about, it was Columbus Day. Admiral Ken Wallace, his wife, his aide, and I got in his staff car and we went over to call on Mrs. Smith. She was the most gracious lady whom I have ever met. I presented her with this picture book. She was most, most gracious and so sincere; she thanked the ship and wrote us a beautiful letter. She just made it a very, very warm family situation.

I might say that his daughter—and I'm not sure to this day if it was a daughter or a stepdaughter—was there. I think she was from Pittsburgh, a grown woman, 27, 28 years old, the best-looking, most elegant—under other circumstances, I would have really had some flirting to do with her, but under the circumstances, she came into the room with her mother and that's how I got to know this very beautiful woman. Both of them were gracious, charming, and thankful. And, of course, the crew just felt great when they got to read her fine words.

Paul Stillwell: How did the crew react during the burial itself?

Captain Colbus: Very serious, and you can see that in the pictures. I can see that picture now where, again, my friend, Boatswain's Mate Joe Weaver, with a pipe, very serious. I think that tells the whole story. They reacted as I would expect my family to react at such a solemn occasion. They did it with dignity, and everyone to a manjack was in proper uniform. We only needed a detail on the fantail, but they all came out to participate. I don't think I had a speaking part; the chaplain did all of that, so I was just a bystander. It was the crew's contribution to Admiral Dog Smith. Of course, before we got under way, we read the biography of this great naval hero and published it at quarters. He became a hero of our ship too.

Paul Stillwell: What else do you recall about your commodore, Ed Kelley?

Captain Colbus: When I was about to take command of <u>Jonas Ingram</u>, I went over to see my commodore. Ed Kelley sat me down and asked me the proper questions. By the way, I was with my predecessor, Don Metzler; I was just the relief at this point. As I said, Don ran a great ship. He was a great fan of Kelley's, and the two of them were fast friends.

Kelley was a very, very tough man. Once you got to know him, he was a father figure. He, by the way, was skipper of USS Blandy about '61 when USS Blandy held down a Soviet submarine for days—maybe 72 hours, something like that—and got a case of Jack Daniels. That's what CinCLantFlt at the time was offering. He was a famous destroyer sailor, an ASW gent in our circle, so it was a great privilege to serve with him.

I guess he had emphysema, smoked like a chimney. You couldn't get near that man that he wasn't smoking and always had this rough cough and the roughest, gruffest voice of any individual I've ever known. "Okay, Louis, glad to have you with us. What do you know about . . . ?" I answered all the questions. "You'll do fine. The only thing I'm sorry about is that you're not living on base out at Mayport." I'd bought a house a mile and a half from my sister-in-law in Jacksonville, 17 miles away.

"Well, Commodore," I said, "with my being gone, we are near my wife's sister. I like buying a house; it's a way to get ahead financially; I like house owning." I gave him the proper reasons for it.

"Well, that's too bad, because until you came, I could go out my back door, bellow, and have a meeting of all my skippers in ten minutes."

I said, "And that's the fifth reason I didn't want to come out here and live on the base." I don't know how I ever got away with that. He did not lose his cool. He just smiled and let me go.

The real story about Ed Kelley had to do with the time we went on a two-day operation to provide Delta services. We were providing a submarine with services, so we were the target. The sub would fire torpedoes at us. And while we were out there, we would get to fire a few ASROCs at the sub. And damn right, I was bragging about Jonas Ingram; we could do anything.

Well, we went out there for two days and did what we had to do. At one point we launched a torpedo, an ASROC. After it got in the water, the torpedo itself did what it was supposed to do, except the last number of yards it did not go negative and come to the surface. It bumped into the submarine! Now, that's serious. If the torpedo had gotten into the screws, it would have damaged them.

Well, of course immediately there was a big confab between the submarine skipper and myself. He said, "Hey, what's going on here? That torpedo dinged me." We were doing this by underwater telephone, which is a very difficult way to communicate. I was in sonar explaining myself, and I had the torpedoman first class with me. I was trying to explain to the sub skipper that, "We really don't program the torpedo, and yes, it was a malfunction. No, we have page so-and-so of such-and-such a manual that tells exactly what it didn't do. We would certainly like to recover that torpedo." We talked probably an hour on this underwater telephone as I explained why the torpedo physically kissed the submarine; no damage, but we were talking about it. Then we spotted the torpedo out there and were ready to recover it.

About that time, a radio messenger came to me and said, "I have a message from you. It's from the commodore." It was what we call a wire note, and it said, "Return to port immediately. Special assignment for USS Jonas Ingram. I know you'll be excited. Get on back." So we recovered the torpedo, we rang up flank speed, and we headed for Mayport. I think we were about 100 miles away. His next message was, "How are you in stores?"

"We're topped off. I do need another radar tube because this one's weak."

"You've got to have 45 days on board."

"Well, we do." And all this was just routine, administrative, logistics traffic.

At one time I said something about delivering stores tomorrow, and I got back, "Negative, negative, negative. Tonight, tonight, tonight."

As we approached Mayport from about ten miles out, it was now about 2000, and I gave an ETA, estimated time of arrival, I'm guessing now, of 2020. The navigator told me, "Ten miles to the sea buoy."

I gave him, "Very well."

At that same time, we got a report from combat that we were 16 miles from the sea buoy.[*] We were doing 27 knots at that point. So I ordered, "All engines stop," and I slowed down. We had a disagreement here. Were we 10 miles out, or were we 16 miles? I wasn't upset; I just wanted them to straighten it out. Well, we sorted all that out. The navigator was right; combat was incorrect. Fine. That's what it's all about, check and balance. So we took off again at flank speed.

---

[*] In this case "combat" refers to the combat information center, which was doing radar navigation as a backup to the visual navigation done on the ship's bridge.

We made the approach to the harbor entrance channel. As we looked up the channel, we saw lights that were absolutely ridiculous. Are we coming to Mayport? Stop again. I asked the navigator to have his men take a round of bearings. The answer was, "No, we're right, Captain. We don't know what that is up there." Well, we proceeded cautiously. As we got into the channel, we saw two little target submarines going up the channel, so we had to wait for them. By now it was probably 2040, but I decided not to send a change to my ETA because we were already in the channel.

Next we saw a dredge in the middle of the channel, which explained the strange lights. No one had ever notified us that there was a dredge in the channel; there was no notice to mariners. We got around that all right. Instead of charging in there and mooring, as we normally did, even at night because it's a good channel, we slowed down for all these variances. We didn't moor until probably almost 2115. I'd say we were an hour beyond our pierside ETA. I did not change it again, but I had requested permission to enter port.

We moored outboard of—I think it was <u>Stribling</u>, and Ed Kelley was standing on the quarterdeck of <u>Stribling</u> with hands on hips. I'll never forget it. But he was uptight all the time. He was a volatile individual. I turned to the exec and said, "Finish the moor, Tom. I'm going to go down and see what I can do for the commodore, find out exactly what's going on." We hadn't been told anything except return to port, be prepared to sail immediately. Maybe we were going to war. I came down as my quarterdeck was getting ready. They were about ready to put the brow between the ships. I said, "Evening, Commodore. How are you, sir?"

"Goddamn you, don't tell me good evening. There's nothing good about it. You've spoiled everything." And behind him was a large group of dependents. Now, it isn't normal for the dependents to come down to see the ship come in after a two-day evolution, so if all the dependents are there, I decided this must be some big, serious thing we were going out on. In the meanwhile, I got that blast from the commodore. Well, I didn't like it, and I was even more embarrassed that the dependents heard it. I could take it. Hell, Ed had yelled at me before. He came on board and said, "We're going right to your cabin."

"Yes, sir."

The dependents were there because when we picked up the spent torpedo, all the way back to our initial takeoff, we put it in the coffin. That's what we called the container.

So we reported back, "Torpedo's in the coffin, 27 knots, proceeding to port, ETA 2020." Don't ask me how the dependents heard that Jonas Ingram was returning to port with a coffin, and that we were called back and proceeding at high speed. So the dependents believed that somebody had been killed.

Ed was all exercised because I wasn't there on time. He came up to my cabin, and he started in on it, "Don't you ever countermand me. You asked me too many questions. When I tell you you're going, you're going. Now, tomorrow morning at 0800 you're sailing, and you'll have that cyclotron on board tonight. I want you out of here, etc., etc., etc., and don't you ever countermand me. You're going to catch these Soviets; they're down at the Caicos Passage, etc., etc., etc."*

I said, "Commodore, they won't be there for three days. We've got them located; we know where they're coming from. They won't be here for three days. If I get under way tomorrow at 0800 or I get under way tomorrow at 1600 or even the next day at 0800, I'm still going to be there in plenty of time, whether I proceed at six knots or 14 knots."

"Damn you, don't comment. I know how to run my squadron. You run your ship. I'm telling you you're out of here at 0800 in the morning."

"Yes, sir."

About that time, the exec came in and said, "Captain, unless you say otherwise, I'm going to start liberty to expire tomorrow morning at 0730."

Ed then cussed: "Don't you ever do anything like that. I didn't pull you back here for liberty. You talk to your skipper when I'm done with him, but you get out of here." He shut the door, and out he went.

It wasn't three minutes later that the engineer opened the door: "Captain, we're all doubled up. I've got the engines secured." He said, "I plan on fueling first thing tomorrow morning."

By now Ed was spastic: "No, no, no, you'll fuel tonight. You're leaving tomorrow morning. Doesn't anybody on this ship listen?" The commodore was beyond reason. Boy, I was really feeling mighty blue now. The engineer took off to fuel the ship. Commodore Kelley must have read me out till 2230 about my inability to run my ship properly. It was just a royal chewing-out.

---

* Caicos Passage is in the Bahama Islands in the Caribbean.

Oh, the other mistake of mine that he brought up was, "And why are you so goddamn late?"

"Well, sir, one time I wasn't sure where I was."

"Can't you navigate either?"

"Yes, sir, that's why I stopped. I don't want to go aground."

"Well, if you don't know this channel . . . "

And I said, "The other thing was, when I got here, I was not sure of the lights and I had to get a round of bearings because I was confused by the lights."

"I thought you used to take your ship into Key West."

"Yes, sir."

"Well, if you're confused here, how are you down in Key West? That's even worse."

I said, "Two different ports." I was losing everything with my boss.

Well, I left the ship about 0200, went home, and told me wife, "I'm under way tomorrow. I just came home to get some more gear." I must have laid down for a while, not feeling good, because I'm pretty sensitive. Even though I'm a big boy, I didn't like being chewed out like that. The whole crew knew what was going on. The dependents heard him say, "Goddamn you."

Back on the ship, first light, I went on board. I was just sitting there in the wardroom, waiting to get under way. I told Jody she could come down, say goodbye to us, watch the ship get under way with the little children. Well, by then all the dependents were there, because this was going to be perhaps a three-, four-month deployment; we didn't know. We were going to follow and monitor the Soviets in our waters. About 0715, Ed Kelley came on board, rushed into the wardroom, sat down with me, and had breakfast. You'd have thought he was my long-lost younger brother: "Boy, Louis, of all the ships in the United States Navy, you're the only one I could count on. When I needed you to plant Dog Smith, you did it for me. I'm so proud of your ship, I could always count on <u>Jonas Ingram</u>."

"Well, thank you, Commodore." I couldn't say anything else in the wardroom.

"Well, Louis, I'm going to get off so you can say goodbye. I know Jody's up in your cabin. She was coming as I was arriving, so I'll get off here." He went up to the cabin and kissed Jody and fussed over her, being the charming man he really was. As he walked out, in the passageway he put his arms around me and said, "Now, Louis, if there's anything you need, give me a call."

I said, "Listen, Ed, you've ruined me."

"What are you talking about?"

"You know what you did yesterday?"

"Well, I was a little upset."

"In front of my crew you goddamned me, in front of my dependents you made me look like a dummy. I've got no credentials with my crew. They think I'm some kind of a flop because of the way you behaved."

"Oh," he said, "I bet you're right."

I said, "You're damn right I'm right. What are you going to do about it?"

"Let me use your PA system." He went to the bridge, and that Boston Irishman got on that PA system for ten minutes. You'd have thought he was making a political speech. You'd have thought he was running me for President of the United States. He just erased everything he said the night before. He didn't refer to it, but he said, "When I need a ship, it's Jonas Ingram. When I need support, it's Jonas Ingram." And he mentioned my name once or twice. The man was perfect, just letter perfect. But that was Ed Kelley. Boy, he was outstanding. We just don't have officers like that anymore.

Paul Stillwell: Volatile, to be sure.

Captain Colbus: Volatile, short-fused. When I went to my cabin, my wife was in tears. Oh, that Boston Irish politician could bring tears to your eyes after kicking you and beating you around. Great guy. And then he was, of course, followed by Bob Hilton, and Bob Hilton was followed by Jean Fitzgerald.* Jean Fitzgerald was a unique individual. They were all unique, but this guy was a Zumwalt fan before that was popular, hair a little bit too long, very, very liberal, I mean liberal. Gorgeous wife.

Paul Stillwell: What did he think about your way of running the ship?

---

* Captain Jean Fitzgerald, USN.

Captain Colbus: He and I are the best of friends. I just talked to him the other day. Here's what he said to me in the wardroom one day: "Louis, in spite of being right out of 1937, you sure do run one magnificent ship." He said that while he was having lunch with us, almost a damnation with praise. "You're so old-fashioned, but I can't knock it because you're having success over here." So he didn't approve of the things I did, but, again, a great leader who turned me loose.

Paul Stillwell: I would suspect it was with some reluctance that you left that command.

Captain Colbus: Absolutely! I've got to tell you about Uncle Bill. I had a bachelor uncle up in Altoona, Pennsylvania. He was 76 years old and just dwelled on all his nephews and great-nephews. I called up there one day and said, "I'm getting the ship under way for the final time. When we leave Mayport, Uncle, how about coming along with me?" And he did.

To make a long story a little shorter, he came down to Jacksonville and boarded us. We had an airline ticket so he could fly back to Jacksonville from San Juan, which would be our first port of call, about three, four days out. Jody would meet him at the Jacksonville airport, entertain him, and get him on home. He got seasick on that ship. The first two days, that man was so seasick, I was beside myself. We had a young Jewish doctor on there. I forget his name; he was a temporary Navy man.

Uncle and he just got along fine. He looked after my uncle as if it were his personal uncle or even father. Poor Uncle Bill was just so ill, and he had been a heart attack victim. I can only remember one time he was getting a little better and the steward gave him some soft-boiled eggs. People were looking after him—you just can't believe it; he was one of these pied-piper individuals—all over the ship when he finally got around. But I remember him saying, "It sure tastes a lot better going down than it does coming up."

Anyway, we arrived at San Juan and showed him around the island. About the second day we were getting under way, proceeding to Gitmo, from Gitmo back to the Caribbean, then to St. Thomas. We were having a nice three-week cruise. Uncle Bill didn't want to leave the ship. In spite of everything, I kept him the entire time. In those days, the policy of three- to seven-day SecNav guest cruises were the norm.* I kept Uncle Bill on there for three weeks.

Of course, I gave him my cabin and I stayed in the sea cabin. We were very prompt and formal about the evening meals. One evening at 1800, we were gathered around the wardroom table. Uncle Bill normally sat to my left, but he wasn't there yet at two minutes to 6:00. I said, "All right, go ahead. Who has the buck tonight?" (The officer with the buck said the grace before the meal.)

The steward came up and said, "Can't start yet, Captain. Uncle Bill's not here." Well, we got a kick out of that. That was typical of the way he had the crew wrapped around his finger.

One day we were on the bridge while the ship was conducting gunfire support over in Culebra—watching, firing, just having a great time. And, of course, Uncle Bill was there, jumping every time the guns fired. I was trying to play John Wayne again with the glasses and not flinching when the guns went off. During a dry spell in gunfire support, I looked at him and said, "Well, Uncle, what do you think of that?"

He said, "Let me tell you something, kid. You may think you're a big shot now, but I can remember when I had to take you up in the ballpark and teach you how to drive an automobile. Don't show off for me." And he just turned and walked off the bridge.

All the crew said, "Yeah, yeah." They just loved it. When he left the ship, they manned the rail. And a month to the day he left the ship, he had a heart attack while he was driving his car, and died. But, boy, was he a hero in that ship. But I violated rules and regulations and kept him a little too long. Nobody cared. Looked the other way.

Paul Stillwell: Any final thoughts to wrap up the Jonas Ingram experience?

Captain Colbus: There are no final thoughts. It just goes on and on and on. Next to my wife and two children, I guess, Jonas Ingram—and I guess that if somebody ever pinned me down, maybe even more so than McCloy, but that's not fair. That's like saying one child—no, I have no final thoughts.

---

* SecNav—Secretary of the Navy.

Paul Stillwell: Okay. Where from there?

Captain Colbus: Bob Hilton insisted I go to Washington. I said, "I like it down here, and they're looking for post-command commanders, surface sailors to go to these carrier division staffs. I'd like to go over there, if I could. I'd stay here, not that I'm a nest builder, but I do have the house here."

"Well," he said, "you've got to come to Washington with me, and we're going to do great things together."

I said, "Well, thanks, Commodore."

I put on my dream sheet that I wanted to go over to CarDiv 6. That's where I went next. I reported over there about December 14, 1972, went aboard, and our cardiv commander was Rear Admiral Joseph P. Moorer, baby brother of big Tom.[*] I wasn't ready for that. Joe Moorer was, in my opinion, probably one of the all-time tough guys, who ran a very, very good show, had a lot of trust and faith in his people, allowed us a free hand. But, boy, you better not mess up, because Joe was quick to get into your business. I respected him. I feared the man a little bit, but that was a good tour.

Paul Stillwell: What ship were you in?

Captain Colbus: We went aboard Franklin D. Roosevelt.[†] I'm hesitating. Yes, I will tell this story.

My wife had always felt shortchanged because she never got to go to the ship for duty nights. She thought that was the greatest thing in the world, go to the ship and have dinner, watch a movie, play bridge, as all the JOs did. When she married me, I was already exec of a destroyer, so I didn't stand duty. Then I was very fortunate to immediately skip into being another exec, and two tours as a skipper.

---

[*] Admiral Thomas H. Moorer, USN, served as Chief of Naval Operations from 1 August 1967 to 1 July 1970. He was later Chairman of the Joint Chiefs of Staff from 3 July 1970 to 30 June 1974. His oral history is in the Naval Institute collection.

[†] USS Franklin D. Roosevelt was commissioned as CVB-42 on 27 October 1945. She was reclassified CVA-42 on 1 October 1952 and extensively modernized from 1954 to 1956. Among other changes, she received an enclosed hurricane bow and angled flight deck. Following the modernization she was 974 feet long, 110 feet in the beam, extreme flight deck width of 210 feet, maximum draft of 36 feet, full-load displacement of 62,000 tons, and rated speed of 33 knots. She could accommodate 70-plus aircraft.

Now that I was watch-standing aboard USS Franklin D. Roosevelt, Jody could have her wardroom nights. Jack Youngblade was the skipper. I hope he doesn't take offense at this story. My wife was all excited about, "I'm going to come down and have dinner in the carrier, in the wardroom. It's great." I hadn't been on there four or five days when it was time to have the duty and spend the night on the ship. In the meantime, I'd been having my meals in the flag mess. Now because it's a weekend, I think it was a Saturday, we secured the flag mess. As the duty officer, I was going to have my meals in the wardroom.

I had breakfast in the flag mess, because we were all in Saturday morning. I had lunch in the wardroom, and the cockroaches were so prevalent down there that I called Jody and said, "You can't come to dinner tonight. We've had a change; I have too many things to do." I made the appropriate excuses. I guess the point of my story is that the ship was cockroach-ridden. The ship was so old that my poor wife never did get to come aboard.

I mentioned that in passing to the skipper, and they had a heck of a good effort on there. But what I'm really talking about is the old Franklin D. Roosevelt. She had the very, very high knee-knockers.* If you think they're an obstruction in today's carriers, you should have been in that ship. And the ship was compartmented so that each boiler had its own compartment. There was no passage. She was very well built. I guess they'd call it impregnable. Anyway, that was our first flagship.

Then we went to USS Independence in 1973 for work-up.† Now I was on a relatively new carrier. That was a real experience. We rode all of the carriers in the Atlantic Fleet at one time or another.

Let me tell you about something that happened aboard Independence. How do you speak of this delicately? I will try. I discovered something about the urinals in the heads throughout the ship. These drains always have in the bottom a number of holes that form

---
* "Knee knocker" is a slang term for a hatch coaming that extends above the level of the deck. One has to pick up his foot and step over the coaming to get through the hatch, sometimes bumping his knee in the process.
† USS Independence (CVA-62), a Forrestal-class aircraft carrier, was commissioned 10 January 1959. She had a standard displacement of 56,300 tons, was 1,046 feet long, 130 feet in the beam, and had an extreme width of 252 feet. Her top speed was 34 knots. She was originally armed with eight 5-inch guns and could accommodate approximately 70-0 aircraft.

some sort of pattern. The pattern in <u>Independence</u> urinals was a six-pointed star. Well, this was an era of ethnic consciousness, so I wrote a very long, detailed tongue-in-cheek memo to Admiral Moorer. I called his attention to the fact that it was offensive to Jewish personnel to go into the heads aboard USS <u>Independence</u> because of this design in the drain system looked like a six-pointed Star of David.

I routed the memo through the chief of staff and the ops officer, and they sort of chuckled. I didn't know how it was going to be taken; it just was done. Within, I'd say, three days, I had a very formal, typed memo back from Rear Admiral Moorer that said he appreciated my interest, he appreciated the fact that I was looking after groups of people. He said he realized that in my particular area it was a matter of personal sensitivity. However, since this would reflect throughout the command, we must be alert to certain things.

He gave me about two pages of flowery dissertation as to how he appreciated it, and then another paragraph as to what he was going to do about this. He was going to let NavShips know exactly what the situation was, and he would task NavShips to make some arrangements for corrections. He said that I must also realize this would be a slow and expensive procedure, since shipalts take time.* Then he went into a discussion on that. The last paragraph, which was probably paragraph six or seven, said "It is appreciated that you have brought this to my attention, etc., etc., etc." He repeated himself. Then he went on to say, "I am embarrassed that I myself have not been able to observe this firsthand. At my last physical, I was told that I have a slight heart condition and am not allowed to lift anything heavy; therefore, I always sit down instead of using the urinal. Respectfully, Joseph P. Moorer."

Paul Stillwell: What can you tell me about that staff?

Captain Colbus: I was the plans officer and assistant ops officer. I'll go down the chain of command. Joe Moorer was the admiral. Tom Porcari, a famous black-shoe destroyer sailor, was the chief of staff, because we were now in this mirror image.† The aviators had

---

* Shipalt—ship alteration.
† Captain Thomas J. Porcari, USN.

black shoes as chiefs of staff and vice versa. The surface ops officer on the staff had always been a black shoe, but now the plans officer was also a black shoe. I was the first black shoe plans officer and assistant ops. The ops officer was the greatest, just a 4.0 individual, one of my dearest friends today, Ray Donnelly.[*] I was, I guess, maybe number six or seven in the pecking order.

Let's go to John F. Kennedy and Exercise Northern Wedding in the fall of '73.[†] We were getting a new cardiv commander. Joe Moorer and I had had our rounds. I had been chewed out by Joe publicly at the morning briefs, and I'm not going to say rightly so, but that was his prerogative. I'm a big boy; he was right. But Joe had been on me pretty tough in meetings, but on the bridge, we always got along. He could forget it very quickly. We were getting a new cardiv commander.

We got under way from being anchored in Glasgow, Scotland, and were told, "Do not return after the exercise. Don't go back to Norfolk. Go into the Mediterranean, because we're having problems in Israel," which turned out to be the Yom Kippur War.[‡]

Well, as we steamed through the Strait of Gibraltar at about 22 knots, with Sarsfield in tail, we got a new cardiv commander. Rear Admiral B. B. Forbes, Jr., came on board, quiet, unassuming, and with due respect to "Beetle," older-looking, a twinkle in his eye but that was it.[§]

As we were going in to the Med, we had a three-carrier task force, which was very unusual. They hadn't seen that, I guess, since World War II. As plans officer, I had to make up the battle organization, which I did. It wasn't ingenious; I just followed the book, a plan for this war plan. Well, I knocked on the door and went in. Admiral Moorer was sitting at his desk, and Admiral Forbes was sitting over in the corner talking.

---

[*] Captain Raymond D. Donnelly, USN.
[†] USS John F. Kennedy (CVA-67) was commissioned 7 September 1968. She was the last conventionally powered carrier built by the U.S. Navy. She has a standard displacement of 61,000 tons, is 1,048 feet long, 130 feet in the beam, and an extreme width of 268 feet. Her top speed is 30-plus knots. She can accommodate approximately 85 aircraft.
[‡] The Yom Kippur War started on 6 October 1973. Egyptian and Syrian forces began major coordinated ground offensives against Israeli positions, seeking to improve territorial claims in the wake of the Six-Day War of 1967. Supported in part by weapons supplied by the United States, Israeli forces counterattacked and drove back the Arabs. A cease-fire finally took effect on 25 October.
[§] Rear Admiral Bernard B. Forbes, Jr., USN. Forbes, who retired as a vice admiral, has been interviewed as part of the Naval Institute's oral history program.

I said, "Excuse me, may I get this message released?" I'd already chopped it through the ops officer and chief of staff.[*] I took it in, and just to be blunt, Joe didn't understand it. I thought I'd explained it to him. Fine, you don't understand it, other people aren't going to understand it. He's an admiral. "Well, Admiral, as you see, these three . . . "

"No, it doesn't make sense."

I won't go into the details, but it became one of those shouting matches: "Damn it, Louis, that's not clear. That's not good staff work. Has the chief of staff seen this?"

"Yes, sir."

"Did he understand it?"

"Yes, sir."

"How about Ray?"

"Yes, sir."

"There's something wrong here. I'm not going to put my name on this." While this going on, I was thinking that I was getting off on the wrong foot with this new admiral of mine. Because I'd started off with the right foot with Joe, and, as I say, this wasn't personal; this was professional. Well, I went out of there all glum. Ray went in with me, and we made Joe Moorer buy it, but I figured we were shot with Beetle Forbes.

Well, we had a very fine change of command there at sea in the cabin. Joe left, handed me my fitness report. It was glowing; it was love and kisses. He did not carry a grudge. The second day we were back in the Med, and Admiral Forbes got his people together. He said, "I'd like to find out exactly where we stand, and let me tell you about some of the things. First of all, I'm very candid. You will hear me speak to you, and you have to think as I think. I'll set the philosophy." He said all the right words: "In the confines of this cabin, you will know my innermost thoughts. If I think anyone out there is other than great, I'll let you know, so when you go over, you'll know from where you're dealing." He talked about this and that, and he said, "We all have our idiosyncrasies. One of the idiosyncrasies I have is spelling. I will not tolerate incorrect spelling, because Mary A. Litzinger, my eighth grade English teacher . . . " And he went on to a nice sea story

---

[*] Based on the original Hindi meaning of "stamp of approval," the Navy usage of "chop" in this sense is figurative rather than literal. Essentially, it means that a certain level in the hierarchy has signed off on a particular document.

about that. He said, "First of all, I've seen this Yom Kippur War spelled three or four ways, and the first thing we're going to do is find out how to spell Yom Kippur."

Well, my being Jewish, I put up my hand, and I spelled it for him. I guess he remembered me from two days earlier, this incompetent guy couldn't do anything right. He said, "Commander, how do you know that's the right one of the three choices we have?"

I said, "Well, because I'm the staff maven." Maven is a Yiddish word which I used all the time. It means to be an expert, self-appointed.

He never cracked a smile, he never said a word, but he nodded his head. Today if you ask him about it, Beetle will say, "I must have gone through every book, everything I could lay my hands on to find out. [It was not in the dictionary then.] It is not in the dictionary. I just couldn't believe it." And, of course, he went on to weave the tale of the staff maven after we became shipmates. Our headquarters, our staff flag mess, was very formal area, and finally it had a big hand-lettered sign, "Maven Haven," and he now had his staff maven. "What's my helicopter maven say?" This was after we got going. But those stories just go on and on.

This Beetle Forbes, the utmost gentleman and scholar, was loved, admired, and revered throughout the Navy. I stated just last Saturday at a big meeting that, "I have said it. I will give anybody $1,000—and I don't let my money go very easily—who could really look me in the eye without joshing, in all seriousness, and say, 'Well, let me tell you, Admiral Forbes is not perfect because . . .' Can't do it. Can't do it." The gentleman is a legend in his time. I tell you, you've got to talk to him.[*]

Anyway, we went into the Med fight the Yom Kippur War. Well, Admiral Forbes had a penchant, I guess is the word, for giving his staff members nicknames. We had 18 officers on that staff, and we were going to fight the Yom Kippur War right off Israel. Of 18 of his officers, I, as a commander, was Jewish. We had a lieutenant commander, Dick Sekuth, helicopter pilot, who was Jewish. And we had an ensign by the name of Abramowitz, who was Jewish.[†]

---

[*] Following the suggestion from Captain Colbus and others, Admiral Forbes was interviewed for the oral history program.
[†] Ensign Steven G. Abramowitz, USNR.

Now, three out of 18 in our Navy on a small staff like that, I think, is unique. It didn't take, I'd say, ten days till we became HH, MH, and JH—Head Hebe, Middle Hebe, and Junior Hebe. To this day he sees me as HH. The admiral has the greatest sense of humor of anybody I've ever been around, and I've been around some pretty humorous people, plus a very, very warm personality. You've heard that. You don't need that from me, but I'll tell you, he's also probably the quickest, not only in wit but in everything that I've ever been next to.

I could give you Yom Kippur War stories.

Paul Stillwell: Please.

Captain Colbus: We were in the Med for about three months during the Yom Kippur crisis. One day Admiral Forbes looked up at the mast, where his two-star flag flying from the truck in John F. Kennedy. However, instead of it being a nice two-star flag with five points he saw there was something wrong with it and asked me about it. We had changed the stars to six-pointed stars. He caught me one day on the flight deck of John F. Kennedy; he saw me from the flag bridge at 0-dark-100. I was down on the flight deck with a child's paint set—one of the hobby sets I'd found. He called out to me, "What are you doing?"

"Sending messages on those F-4s."* F-4s were leaving Norfolk, crossing the Atlantic, and transiting the Med. They were using the carrier for fuel stops before they went into Israel. The U.S. markings on them had all been painted out. Well, I was down there writing some very nasty Yiddish words on them. He just thought that was great.

What else did we do with the Beetle? He is a Humpty-Dumpty fan extraordinaire. Do you know who she is?

Paul Stillwell: No.

Captain Colbus: Humpty-Dumpty is the world's most renowned prostitute. She sits on a wall in Naples between the two big naval establishments out there. Ask anybody who's

---

*The F-4 Phantom II was a jet fighter built by McDonnell. It first entered fleet squadrons in 1961.

been to the Mediterranean about Humpty-Dumpty; they all giggle. There are T-shirts out, there are pictures of her, there are autographs—everything. It's Humpty-Dumpty memorabilia. You don't go to the Med without bringing something back. When he was chief of staff to the Sixth Fleet he became a big Humpty-Dumpty fan.[*] Humpty-Dumpty speaks seven languages because in her time there were seven invading armies. She's well past 60 now, well past her time. Oh, the woman's fabulous.

Later, when I was a desron commodore in 1977, Vice Admiral Forbes, who was Deputy CinCLantFlt at the time, had a very serious heart attack. I got the word immediately and found out that he was doing very well. While I was in Naples, I put on my business suit, got in one of those fine automobiles that they provided for us, and went to visit Humpty-Dumpty. Humpty-Dumpty isn't used to that. She is used to people going by and waving at her and maybe the kids catcalling to her, but she deals mainly with the truckers and the local Italians. I pulled right up to the wall, stopped, got out, shook hands, and said, "Do you speak English?"

"Un poco," whatever. She got in the car with me, and we started to negotiate. I had been to the exchange, and I bought a get-well card. I wanted her to sign it, "Humpty-Dumpty." In my pidgin Italian and in her little bit of English, I got the word to her that all she had to do was sign. How much would I pay? For 10,000 lira, she would make love and sign the card. Well, that went on for about 20 minutes. "No, that isn't what I wanted." I didn't want to make love; I wanted a signed card. I said, "Do you remember the Beetle who was here in 1969?" Well, she thought so. "You've heard of the Beetle. He's a friend of Admiral Pierre Charbonnet, a Frenchman, another famous U.S. admiral."

Finally I told her I was hurt in the war and couldn't make love; just sign. So for 2,000 lira, I got her to sign the card. She did not sign it "Humpty-Dumpty;" she signed it in her real name, which is Lina Pasquegali. Well, we sent that to the Beetle, and he knew he was the only United States naval officer who had an honest-to-goodness signed card, which he capitalized on throughout his entire confinement at the naval hospital. He still refers to that.

---

[*] While still a captain in the early 1970s, Forbes served as Sixth Fleet chief of staff under Vice Admiral Isaac C. Kidd, Jr. USN, and Vice Admiral Gerald E. Miller, USN.

We were talking about the Yom Kippur War with the Beetle. As I say, those stories go on and on. Maybe you now have the flavor of Admiral Forbes and his <u>modus operandi</u>.

Paul Stillwell: I'd be interested in what the plans officer did in that war.

Captain Colbus: Mainly stood watch. Mainly stood watch and reacted, because we had Sixth Fleet on scene, and we had CTF 60 on scene, who was Admiral Fox Turner at the time.[*] Sixth Fleet was Admiral Murphy.[†] Really the plans were patrol, alert, and provide a platform for the F-4s. As I said, we were in <u>John F. Kennedy</u>, and I can't say it was all that memorable or exciting; it was just a job. We left there and we were home in time for Christmas, I do remember that.

Paul Stillwell: What about interaction with Soviet ships? How much of that was there?

Captain Colbus: Well, we saw them. They were there, but nothing as dramatic as we'd done with <u>Jonas Ingram</u>, because we were minding our business doing the three-ship, three-carrier task group patrolling, sharing flight hours, and we saturated the area with airplanes. So it was really an air show. They had lots of flying; they had lots of interface with the three carriers and the three air wings.

But when you ask me what I did as the plans officer, I would say probably less than I did on a routine deployment because things were always changing on a routine deployment. We weren't changing. We were there, we were patrolling, we were sweeping, we were doing all the things that you'd expect the task force, in this case, a disposition, to do in a small area. When you get three carriers in a small area like the eastern Med, space becomes difficult to manage. As far as my plans, it was what areas, what the sweep would look like, and that was about it. But it wasn't that taxing.

---

[*] Rear Admiral Frederick C. Turner, USN, Commander Task Force 60, the attack carrier striking force of the Sixth Fleet. As a vice admiral, Turner later commanded the entire Sixth Fleet from September 1974 to August 1976.
[†] Vice Admiral Daniel J. Murphy, USN, commanded the Sixth Fleet from June 1973 to September 1974.

Paul Stillwell: Did you have a mission beyond just being there?

Captain Colbus: No.

Paul Stillwell: Were there any plans drawn up or contemplated that you would support the Israelis against the Egyptians?

Captain Colbus: I really wasn't at that level. I didn't know of them. Again, plans officer for that particular task group and that was about the size of it.

Paul Stillwell: So yours was more in tactical planning, would that be it?

Captain Colbus: Oh, absolutely, at that time. Exactly.

Paul Stillwell: Can you recall more about Admiral Moorer and his style of operation?

Captain Colbus: Oh, yes. Let me give you an example. We were going for a routine replenishment one morning. Our surface ops officer wasn't there, and I was filling in as surface ops. So I'd done most of the planning and the operations for that particular replenishment. I had the ships lined up about 0800 one morning, no question as to which side we were going. I think the oiler was Caloosahatchee.

I was the watch officer up on the bridge, standing flag watch. I called down to Admiral Moorer in the war room and went over the entire thing. I let him know exactly what we were going to do. I even gave him the order of the ships. About 0810, I got a call. One of the destroyers had a problem—a rig wouldn't work, something had happened. I had to change the order of ships. Well, I didn't have the time to go in and change all the charts I had prepared and would use for the 0830 briefing. As I was briefing him at 8:35, I said, "Admiral, this is not going to occur as I told you. Instead, we're going to do it in this order." And I started reversing the ships and putting in their numbers.

He came down with his fist and yelled, "Don't you ever B.S. me again," in front of everybody, including the carrier skipper. Instead of just correcting me or chastising me, he yelled at me. When the briefing was over and he went storming out of there, I was so damn mad, they told me that I looked like a thermometer; the blood went right up. You could see me turn red to the top of my bald head.

I immediately went to my boss, the ops officer, and said, "Captain, I'm going in to see the admiral. I want to straighten that out." I had it all planned as to what I wanted to say. "You think I'm incompetent and you think I'm kidding you, and you think that as a post-command commander I can't organize five destroyers, then you better get me relieved, because I can't work under those conditions. I've got to have your faith and trust. I can't prove myself." I had it all mapped out what I was going to say.

Ray Donnelly said, "Louis, let it lie. Don't worry about it."

"No, can't do that, sir. Need your permission."

"You've got it, but I'm advising you."

Went to the chief of staff, old Tom Porcari. Same thing: "I want to talk to the admiral."

Tom Porcari said, "I'm not telling you you can't, but as a personal friend that goes back 15 years, don't." Just the same words.

"No, I'm going in."

"Okay."

I went and knocked on the door. "Come in. Why, sit down. What can I do for you today? Let's have some coffee." That turned into one of the nicest, most pleasant hour chats I've ever had with the boss. He'd forgotten about the whole thing. He didn't want to ever talk about it again. He just let me know that, "Don't fool around with me, and advise me earlier. Don't catch me at a briefing." That was his whole message.

Paul Stillwell: What had he been so upset about?

Captain Colbus: That I told him something that wasn't so an hour later, and I didn't correct myself beforehand, I didn't correct my charts, and I wasn't there offering excuses: "Well, I came off the bridge and really was scraping to get ready for this." He was very understanding, very good with people too. I'm talking about the families. He had a great relationship with the wives.

Paul Stillwell: You mean of the staff people?

Captain Colbus: Yes. He could relate to them and was very quick to call us together to make awards, invite the family in, and make you feel like you were the biggest person in the world. He was very good at that. As I say, a quick temper and got what he wanted. Then, of course, Admiral Forbes was just the complete opposite, very soft-spoken, and his anger would be, "I'm very disappointed," which just crushed you. Joe could get your fighting blood up.

Paul Stillwell: Were there any instances where Admiral Moorer let you know he was the big boss's brother?

Captain Colbus: No, sir. No, no, no, no. No, in fact, that wasn't even discussed.

Paul Stillwell: I'm interested more in your job and the things you did on the staff.

Captain Colbus: Well, as I said, as the plans officer, I worked very closely with the surface ops officer. You don't just draw a line and say that's plans and that's ops. Our surface ops officer was one of the famous destroyermen of my era, a gent named Dave Oaksmith.* He was just a real fine shipmate who worked with us. His nickname was "the Troll." I was HH; Dave was the Troll. A troll was some kind of a Norwegian—what?—leprechaun, and Dave was one of those men who sort of look like a Norwegian leprechaun. He was the troll.

We had maintenance problems back then, and it was a big task. We did not have a material officer on the staff, so Dave was both surface ops and material. We did a lot of work in that area. As the plans officer, being the first in that series, I worked in surface ops with Dave Oaksmith. I relieved an aviator who had been the plans officer. We had a very, very outstanding aviator who was the air ops officer, Ken Russell.† We were working very closely with the NATO crowd at that time, going over to you name it in Europe with the

---

* Commander David E. Oaksmith, Jr., USN.
† Commander Kenneth B. Russell, USN.

NATO alliance. We were there. We were planning all these great NATO exercises, which would normally fall under my job.

I didn't resent it when Ken Russell tacitly became more plans than I. He would go to Europe and do the job, because he talked air, he knew air, he was an attack pilot, he had all the credentials. I'll tell you, the man was probably the most competent briefer I've ever been around. He had a very, very big, booming voice and would command your attention. He could tell you the grass is green, the sky is blue, and you'd take notes. In that relationship, he was doing all the travelling to Europe in making up the air plan, arranging air space, doing all the things that my predecessor had done, but Ken Russell jumped into it very nicely. Long-range plans almost became the intelligence officer's domain. He kept the long-range plans under lock and key. These were the plans passed on to us from higher authority.

In direct answer to your question, let's say we're going off to do a Northern Wedding exercise. I would get these top secret plans, I knew what the time frame was, I knew what we were practicing, and I would become the center of reference—the librarian: "Ken, you'll be launching your air strikes at such and such in accordance with so and so, because of that. And they will shoot in the destroyers because we have a mission for them on M plus five." That's exactly what it amounted to. You knew the plans, but you couldn't say that was purely plans, that's purely surface ops, that's intelligence. It was a conglomeration of all the disciplines, and I think we worked very well together.

We had actuality when we went to do the Yom Kippur unplanned thing, and then we had our NATO job that we did on three occasions, with both Joe and Beetle and then we also, of course, were responsible for the canned carrier work-ups. The first ten days you would do this, second ten days you do that, the third ten days you do the finale, crawl, walk, run. On the last day was the big launch, which was judged by a team of 40 people sent out from Commander Naval Air Force Atlantic. We called it ORI then, operational readiness inspection; now it's called ORE, operational readiness exercise.

Paul Stillwell: Do you have any specific memories from those work-ups and ORIs, any incidents that come to mind?

Captain Colbus: First of all, yes, of course. We went aboard each ship and started from scratch. We were pretty experienced by the time we did our third or fourth work-up. I don't mean it was automatic, but we were experienced and knew what to look for. We knew what to expect. We got to know the ship, because we interfaced daily with the captain. We were on the bridge, watched the captain. Within months you can see how Captain A works with carrier 1, and you see how Captain B works with carrier 2. It didn't take long to find out who were the key players. On some carriers, the exec doesn't come near the bridge; everything is the navigator, he's the powerhouse. You went to talk to the navigator when you wanted something done. In other ships, you went to see the exec. So that was one of the great things that I learned.

In carriers, we had, as I used to say, two kinds of naval officers as part of ship's company. There were those who wanted to be there because it was good for them. That included the captain, the navigator, and the exec. The other aviators on board didn't want to do duty on a "boat" but were doing so because they were ordered to. Then, of course, there were the black-shoes who were on board and sure as hell didn't want to be there either. They wanted to be on a fast destroyer. So it was an interesting group.

They used to tell me, "This is a very big platform. This is a big, big organization to manage. Don't expect on here what you expect on your destroyer. Yes, you can keep your destroyer squeaky clean, but not so here. No, no, no, no. I said, "You can do it easier here than there." Well, we would get into great debates; not operationally speaking, we're talking administrative. I'd say that as the skipper, all you've got to do is put out the policy, "I want a clean ship. I want all these things that we say make up a sharp ship, and you've got all this talent to execute it.

"Your department heads are all post-command commanders; many of them already captain selectees. Therefore, they have done command, they're not just feeling their way, they know how to command. They commanded an aircraft squadron where they managed and led people in airplanes. They can go down there and clean up an ops area in no time, where on a destroyer you're looking at jaygees, lieutenants, and if you're lucky, a lieutenant commander. They're feeling their way; they're learning as they go. Sure, I can do more myself, but on here you've got all this talent to help you."

The other thing I proposed at the time was make the exec of a carrier a black shoe who's had his destroyer command. Running this ship would be a piece of cake. What do you do about ascension to command? I give that up. I volunteer, and I realize I can never become the captain of this ship. Then in an emergency, the navigator will become the skipper. Poor plan, poor plan. Aviators didn't like it, and the black shoes liked it less.

Of course, in the air wing, I found that a fascinating organization. I just loved to hang around—and that's the only word for it, like you'd hang around a pool room when you were a kid—used to hang around the ready rooms. There is more activity there. We're very proud about the destroyer sailor and the macho. Boy, you get in those ready rooms, and there is nothing like it. Nothing like it. Fraternity—that word doesn't even touch it. Camaraderie—overworked. There's an ambience in a ready room that you just can't match anywhere.

Paul Stillwell: Did you feel a little jealous?

Captain Colbus: Sure. Always did. They called me a fighter pilot groupie. I was loyal to what I'd done and was, and I don't have to tell you I loved those ships I was in. Those fighter pilots and those attack pilots and all those pilots, there's something about them.

Paul Stillwell: How much of a difference does the skipper make in a carrier?

Captain Colbus: All the difference—as much as it makes in a minesweeper or it makes in a patrol boat, all the difference.

Paul Stillwell: You've said how he has all this great wealth of talent working for him. I would think that all that organization would have a momentum of its own, that maybe he wouldn't need to do all that much.

Captain Colbus: Well, as I said, so many of the jobs were not really coveted, so that many times these boys had to be inspired, maybe even kicked in the tail to go out and do it. If you'd asked me, I'd say the most complete, 360-degree, everything-the-right-way—and this is unfair to many of my other friends—the most complete carrier skipper I witnessed was Tom Watson, skipper of Independence.* The man was phenomenal. I think I have stamina; I'm a sleeper compared to him. The man was everywhere at once, without being dominating or domineering—just fantastic. Good on the bridge, good at mast, excellent in the crew's lounge. Anywhere the man went, he just had an air about him. As I say, I never saw him sleep and he never showed a sign of fatigue. That's not unusual among carrier skippers. You just can't praise them enough.

Paul Stillwell: There's a sort of natural selection process, that they probably wouldn't get there if they didn't have that talent, that trait.

Captain Colbus: We're skipping now, but we're talking about carriers and traits, what have you. I used to become very, very embarrassed by my destroyer skipper friends. Now I've done my squadron bit. Let's say I'm the chief of staff. A destroyer skipper would sometimes come to me, quietly back door or openly on the circuit or by official message about the scheduling: "You have us come alongside the carrier at 0600 to refuel," or some other such evolution. It wasn't that they were complaining; it wasn't that they were being no-can-do, because I think too much can-do can kill you just as much as no-can-do can ruin you. Then I would explain to these skippers. "Do you realize why you're scheduled at these times?"

And the skipper would say, "At 0600 we're just getting up, we're in the midst of breakfast, and we've got to break out the crew to handle lines." That's true. On a destroyer, you stop everything to fuel the ship because you've got to have all the people.

Paul Stillwell: Are you now talking about a time when you were a carrier group chief of staff?

Captain Colbus: Yes, but it was the same thing when I was a plans officer. I had more clout when I was a chief of staff, but the destroyer didn't understand why he had to do

---

* Captain Thomas C. Watson, Jr., USN, commanded USS Independence (CV-62) from 9 September 1978 to 28 May 1980.

these things at these odd hours. He was not an 8:00 to 5:00 sailor, but at the same time, I'd have to explain to him, "The carrier finished up flight ops last night at 0100."

"So why do they have to have us alongside at 0600? Why can't you make it 0800 or 0900?"

"Because they're starting flight ops again at noon again. They secure from flight ops, spot the deck, work the planes, do a myriad of things, and at first light, respot, pull in, move out. The only time they have to do it is at 0600, an hour where it won't interfere—not with their routine but with their operation." So you just can't take aboard what's going on in a carrier. I've been fascinated with them. Even after spending five and a half years in them, as I always said, an outsider who's been close enough to the problem to understand it but not accept it as routine as they do, I'm still mesmerized by the carrier.

Paul Stillwell: So in effect you were telling these skippers, "We didn't just set this time on a whim."

Captain Colbus: Yes: "Get off my back about scheduling [this was when I was a plans officer], and quit bitching about the dumb hours. Come over here and see what we're really going through." What I'm saying is it's a tough organization.

Paul Stillwell: How much, if any, black shoe/brown shoe rivalry was there in a staff like that?

Captain Colbus: Oh, there was a lot, but there in recognition of Joe Moorer, Beetle Forbes, Bob Dunn, Jim Service, and Jerry Tuttle, all those five admirals I worked for, there was never any discrimination. There was never anything that influenced whatsoever in fitness report time when it came time to ranking the black shoes versus the aviators. Very fair.

I'll tell you another thing—a black shoe can learn more on a carrier division staff than he can anywhere else. When you walk away from there, you're way ahead of your contemporaries. I have a lot of my young friends today who are doing their tours in carrier battle group staffs. They just do everything. If you want to get a taste of power projection ashore go to a carrier. If you want to find out about command and control, go to a carrier.

If you want to see complex operations and how it all comes together, go up in the back end of an E-2, and it's like watching your football game at home.* You aren't on the field playing; you're up there watching it, orchestrating it.

Paul Stillwell: You were fairly treated by the admirals. How were you treated by the aviation members of the staff itself?

Captain Colbus: Better than my own family treats me. As a matter of fact, maybe it's because I was just most recently with them, today I probably know more and interface more with my carrier acquaintances than I do with my destroyer buddies. Well, that's not really fair, but what I'm saying, in answer to your question, is that they just take you aboard, and you're one of them. They extend that camaraderie right out.

Paul Stillwell: The time we're discussing is the '73 period and even back to the time you were in Jonas Ingram, the racial unrest was really coming to the surface.

Captain Colbus: Sure was. There's a good Joe Moorer story of what happened. Fortunately, Joe Moorer went off one day in a helicopter down on the missile range in San Juan, the Caribbean area. He was over in USS Biddle. Ed Carter was skipper at the time, and Ed kept him busy that day going through a missile shoot.† That's the day Franklin D. Roosevelt, which was not in the missile shooting business, was off to the side as the admiral's flagship. She was flying airplanes as part of the missile action and what have you, but the ship itself was not a participant. So we were off here to the side, but we were, of course, launching aircraft, going through regular cyclical flight ops.

I'm going to say that 25 sailors sat across the bow of FDR and hindered flight ops until their complaints could be heard. I guess you could call it a strike. I wouldn't say it was a mutiny; that would be overkill. But it was certainly a strong protest, and only in that

---

* The E-2 Hawkeye is a propeller-driven carrier plane that has a look-down radar in order to track and manage the air picture from aloft.
† Captain Edward W. Carter III, USN.

time could that have occurred. The skipper was Jim Morin, who handled it beautifully; he did it on his own.*

Our chief of staff, Tom Porcari, sat in the war room. He watched the forecastle on remote television and did not get involved. Jim Morin came off the bridge, dealt with those men on the bow, and averted a very serious situation. You could say what you would have done if you had been there, but you had to see it. When we got back to the beach, of course, there was a big investigation. ComFAirJax, a distinguished gray-haired gent I'm thinking of, came over and conducted the investigation.

We really didn't see too much of the unrest that was so prevalent in that time frame. That's about the only thing that I recall as being a racial situation.

Paul Stillwell: What was the source of discontent?

Captain Colbus: I don't remember. Something about the mess deck, something about the hair style. It was so mundane, I don't even remember it.

Paul Stillwell: But no problems in Jonas Ingram?

Captain Colbus: Oh, no, no. I don't think any of the destroyers had problems in those days. Let me think a second. No, we were too busy doing our job, and everybody was too involved and too tight a crew.

I will say that Bob Hilton made a very, very profound observation to me in the Med, now that you asked. He and I were ashore one day, and he made an observation to me. It was about ships in general, but he noticed it in Jonas Ingram in particular. If you were in the mess decks during meal hours, movie call, musters, whatever, you would see our black sailors together in a group. Before movie call, they would get together. They were listening to the same music, talking the same dialect, and they were kidding in the same humor.

---

* Captain James B. Morin, USN, commanded USS Franklin D. Roosevelt (CVA-42) from April 1973 to December 1974.

However, when they left that quarterdeck and went into a bar, for instance, all of a sudden it was not that group in <u>Jonas Ingram</u>, but in the barroom it was <u>Jonas Ingram</u> people amongst the other sailors. That was a very, very profound and exact observation. So don't get concerned if you see ten black sailors together on the mess decks jiving and rapping. When they get ashore, they're now <u>Jonas Ingram</u> sailors. So it's just group identity. That was certainly not an incident, but that's exactly the way it was, and we can thank Bob Hilton for that observation.

Paul Stillwell: Do you think that the advent of the Zumwalt regime had helped defuse what might have been worse problems?

Captain Colbus: No, no, I really don't. As a matter of fact, I was saying at the time we promise too much and give too little. We made too many promises, especially. I used to use the example of the—hey, it just happened to be a black sailor who was put in the brig. I didn't say my crew was perfect. His problem was that he came in the Navy right out of the south side of Chicago. If I'd been writing a book, I'd have referred to him.

This sailor came in and just had been promised too much and mollycoddled too much. Somehow in his mind he thought that within six months aboard a ship after boot camp, he was going to be an ET3.* Well, six months later, he was chipping paint. He was a deckhand—and not a very good one at that—and didn't understand why we hadn't moved him up. He didn't even get to strike for signalman when he put in a chit.† He had to get in line. "You aren't that good yet." He understood that, but it took a lot of talking to that young man. He considered it an affront to himself personally, "Hey, I'm a man; I want to be up there too. Where's my chance? I was told so-and-so." Well, welcome to the real world.

But again, good, old-fashioned Joe Weaver, boatswain's mate leadership, where he's as tough with his sailors as Joe Moorer was with me, but guess what Weaver would do that evening after he might have been really tough on a sailor? Take him home and sit him down at his table and feed him "Now, I want you to see how my kids behave." And it

---

* ET3—electronics technician third class, a petty officer in the pay grade of E-4.
† A striker is a non-rated man who is in training for potential advancement to petty officer in a particular rating.

didn't matter—black, white, whatever.

Paul Stillwell: I don't think there's as much of that now as there was in the old Navy when Joe Weaver came up, is there?

Captain Colbus: As much what?

Paul Stillwell: Taking the guy home.

Captain Colbus: Oh, no. Let me tell you about my own disappointment as the commanding officer. You can't order it, and my shipmates were good. I think I've left you with the impression, I hope, that I had a very close, tight wardroom, and I loved each one of them. I was disappointed they weren't at my home more often, spontaneously. When I was a JO and it was a Friday night, I would take my date by Chas Sherwood's house and introduce her to him. I might have mentioned that. One Thanksgiving I said, "I've got a date."

"Sure."
"May I come by?"
"Oh, yes."
"What time is dinner?"
"Well, stay."

"No, we just want to come by." I went by to see the skipper. He knew my parents, because when they came to town, you paraded your parents by the captain. When your girlfriend came to town, you really looked to the captain.

As I used to tell Jody, "What are we doing wrong? They just don't come around?"

"Louis, they're not interested. They go off and do their own thing." Needless to say, things change. Today they all have pads, cars. That was always a disappointment to me. I say that because you mentioned Joe Weaver taking the young sailor home.

Paul Stillwell: Do you have a reaction to the Z-grams overall during those years?*

Captain Colbus: Well, I'm retired, and I'm sure Admiral Zumwalt doesn't need me to support him, but I never even read them. I don't think I ever read a Z-gram. The exec did. He was very attuned to that, as he should have been. No, I didn't read them. I didn't mean to be disrespectful, but I was going to run the ship in my style. You can't teach someone a style. I could tell you all my skippers--Joe Moorer, Beetle Forbes--opposites, like reading a psychology book. If page 12 is the way you're raising your child, you believe the author knows what he's talking about. If page 14 is off your path, you say, "That guy, what does be know about it?" That's to me what leadership is all about. You can't teach a leader a style. Well, I learned that early on amongst the JOs.

Paul Stillwell: Anything else to wrap up your tour of CarDiv 6?

Captain Colbus: Yes, sir. I can't tell you the Yom Kippur story with Beetle unless I finish that up with October 1974. Guess what? Same exercise, different name, Northern Atlantic, USS America. After what happened with Yom Kippur the year before, the staff was just ragging me something terrible, "Hey, we want to go home for Thanksgiving. Don't you let your cousins get us in another war."

Well, Yom Kippur is a fast day. We still had the three Jewish boys in the flag mess, MH, HH, and JH. We did organize an on-board Yom Kippur service. We even sent the helicopters out and rounded up all the Jewish lads in the task force, brought them on board, provided them services, didn't provide them anything to eat; that was easy. I told the flag mess that I would not be coming to dinner. I looked at my two associates. "Are you mates going to have dinner tonight?" Our final service of the day was at sundown, 1830. The flag mess meal was at 1800. Meanwhile, we had all these visitors from NATO on board. The three of us went to the chapel and conducted our service. There was a break-the-fast meal on the mess deck, which was a very nice gesture by the ship, but we

---

*Z-grams were consecutively numbered policy directives from Chief of Naval Operations Zumwalt that attempted to deal with such issues as enlisted rights and privileges, equal opportunity, and Navy families. Junior personnel viewed them much more favorably than did their seniors. See U.S. Naval Institute Proceedings, May 1971, pages 291-298.

went up to the flag mess for a saved ration.

I thought it was time for movie call. It was now about 1930, and I wanted to go in and see the movie, a quiet night at sea. I opened the door, and everybody was standing around the dinner table in <u>America</u>'s flag mess—very formal and dignified. It was a candlelight dinner. Well, we only have candlelight for special occasions such as dining in, dining out, VIP dinners, etc. Then I remembered that they had an air marshal on board. I had just cracked the door and saw all the officers standing around as if it was time to sit down. I shut the door, and the steward came around and said, "Commander Colbus, the admiral wants you."

I opened the door and said, "Yes, sir?"

Beetle said, "Come on, you're not too late. Come on in. We saved you a place." We went in and took our places at the table. This air marshal, a Brit, and another high-ranking NATO civilian were flanking the admiral. I took my seat down at this end, the other two Jewish officers filled in.

About that time, in came Jerry Sullivan.[*] Jerry Sullivan is an Irish commander, submariner. I say Irish because he was raised in Brooklyn and he understands any ethnic group around. Jerry can tell you all about it because he was raised in that environment. He came in from the admiral's side, had his long, black raincoat on, had a great big hat, a false beard. He looked and acted like a Hassidic Jew. The steward went over and flipped a button, and all of a sudden we heard "Fiddler on the Roof." Every staff officer picked his ball cap off the back of his chair and put it on backward as if he was wearing a skull cap, in honor of Yom Kippur.

This air marshal about went wild. All during the meal, he said to the admiral, "Those men are going to be offended. That commander down there, he won't tolerate this."

"Oh, he loves it. He loves it. HH, tell him about it." That's the kind of leader Beetle Forbes is, and that's another thing we had on the ship, but the visitors didn't understand it. The Brits sure didn't understand it. The NATO rep knew that in his country, which was Holland, you just didn't do those things in the war, didn't make fun of the

---

[*] Commander Gerald F. Sullivan, USN.

Jewish people. The staff's attitude was, "We're not making fun. We're saluting them." Which we understood, of course.

Paul Stillwell: Maybe there's a fine line there sometimes.

Captain Colbus: Perhaps. You have to know your audience, and you have to know your players.

I guess that would wrap up the CarDiv 6 stories, but as I say, they go on and on. I could talk about streakers, which were popular at the time. We had our streaking incidents.

Paul Stillwell: Mention the streaking incident, then.

Captain Colbus: I should. Let me talk about the pre-sail conference. We were going to Com2ndFlt headquarters to brief Admiral Stansfield Turner on the upcoming operation.* This was the first time we'd ever crossed the Atlantic with about a 20-mile front and submarines in direct support. Admiral Forbes was Turner's ComCarStrikeFor, CTF 401. That was the big NATO job, and as plans officer, I had written the op order, had done all the things I was supposed to do. I had this grandiose--not a plan, but an op order. There's a fine line, if you know the difference.

One morning we were not in the ship; we were sitting on the beach in our poor, humble headquarters in Mayport. There was the big carrier over there, and right alongside us on the opposite side of the pier was USS Sanctuary.†

Well, I was briefing Admiral Forbes as to what I wanted to do so he would sign the op order at the end of this two-hour brief. I must have been 15 or 20 minutes into the brief with the admiral seated in his chair, not swiveling, but doing what admirals do when they're listening. With his eye out the window, he caught sight of the quarterdeck of USS

---

*Vice Admiral Stansfield Turner, USN, commanded the Second Fleet from August 1974 to July 1975.
†USS Sanctuary (AH-17) was originally commissioned as a Navy hospital ship in 1945, then decommissioned the following year. She was recommissioned for service off Vietnam in the late 1960s, then decommissioned in 1971 for conversion to a dependents' hospital and commissary/Navy exchange. When she was recommissioned on 18 November 1972, the Sanctuary became the first U.S. Navy ship with a mixed crew of men and women.

Sanctuary, and he held up his hands. "HH, wait a minute. Who is that on the quarterdeck of Sanctuary?" I knew those people pretty well. These were the first women in a ship.

I got the glasses and said, "I think that's Ensign ..." whatever her name was and I used her name.

He said, "What do you think about those truck lights?[*] They're still on. Why don't you do something about it."

"Yes, sir."

Paul Stillwell: Right in the middle of a briefing.

Captain Colbus: Right in the middle of a briefing. So I went over and I picked up the phone, and I called Sanctuary. We could see all this from the flag space. Someone else answered, and then this ensign got on the phone, long glass under her arm. I said, "This is the SOPA duty officer. Your truck lights are burning," and hung up.[†]

Well, that poor woman started pacing the deck. She had no idea what I was talking about. We must have spent ten minutes watching that poor soul sweating the truck lights at 0920 in the morning. Finally I guess she talked to someone.

Now the brief was back on: "Where was I? Oh, yeah, okay."

Then I went back to it, and about 0950, the admiral asked, "Are you satisfied with this plan, HH?"

"Oh, yes, sir."

"You think it's a good one?"

"Yes, sir."

"Why don't I just sign it and we'll save time and trouble."

"Very good."

He signed it and we were out of there. It made me feel good that he had that kind of faith, made everybody feel good.

It wasn't a day later when we were going to brief Stansfield Turner, vice admiral, a brilliant man whom everybody knows about. I guess he's one of our more famous, if not

---

[*] This refers to red aircraft warning lights that are lit at the tops of masts at night.
[†] SOPA--senior officer present afloat.

most famous, admirals. I wasn't 15 minutes into my brief when he started on me. He started about the nittiest things, and he would ask questions. I wouldn't say two sentences that he'd get into me again. Now, whether he was doing this as part of his makeup or what, but I don't care who you are, that's going to rattle a commander.

"Yes, sir, you're absolutely right. However . . . " And when you have to explain yourself, you're coming from behind. Beetle Forbes sat there and let me swing for, I'd say, four or five of those questions.

Finally Beetle said, "Let me explain this to you, Admiral." And he got up and he--right to the point--did the whole thing. We thought he hadn't read the op order. Beetle was so quick that he saw exactly what Turner was homing in on. With his stars and his power of speech and his eloquence, he salvaged the whole thing. That showed another side of Beetle. Sure, he was joking around. Yes, he was kidding. But that was his way: "I'll sign it because I have faith in you." He had read it, he didn't need a brief, and he satisfied the most demanding of all admirals I've ever worked around, Stansfield Turner. That's the kind of leader he was. But I wanted to tell you more about this same situation.

We had this thing going with Sanctuary. In April 1974 Sanctuary went to Wilmington, North Carolina, to act as host ship for the Azalea Festival. While they are doing whatever you do on the ship, which was moored alongside, with all of the North Carolina dignitaries from the governor on down sitting out on the pier and watching the ship perform with the princesses and everything, a hospital corpsman third class, female, streaked. That was the big thing in those days.[*] She just streaked one end of the ship to the other. Well, of course, this was front-page news. While it was not right, everybody was grinning. Beetle had us rig up the biggest sound speakers you could actually find in the Mayport area, and we got that record, which was popular at that time, called "Don't Look Now, Ethel, it's the Streak." And as Sanctuary came steaming into Mayport, back home from the Azalea Festival in Wilmington, North Carolina, we played the record, full blast on the speaker system, "Don't Look Now, Ethel, it's the Streak." We had a lot of fun.

Paul Stillwell: Where did you go after that tour of duty?

---

[*] In the spring and summer of 1974, the short-lived streaking fad involved people all over the country who ran naked in public.

Captain Colbus: From that tour, I was fortunate enough to make captain. I left about the fifth of June in 1975, and Admiral Forbes left on, I'm going to say, the tenth of June. We both came to Norfolk, where he was the Deputy CinCLantFlt. However, he had a delay en route. He went via Sixth Fleet, where he was CTF 60 as an interim measure. There was a problem with one of the incumbents and reliefs, so he spent about three months over there.

I came up to Norfolk to ComOpTEvFor, Operational Test and Evaluation Force, to work for Admiral Bob Monroe.[*] My job there was a newly formed job, the 30 division, which was then called Ship Evaluation. I went there and found ten eager and aggressive officers who would go out and look ships over, ride ships, and make recommendations as to how they could better be arranged constructed, whatever. It was a new idea. This new division was a spinoff of the 70 division, and it was an indicator of times because we were now into the DD-963 world and the FFG-7 world.[†]

These were ships that were going to be op evaled before they were created, before they were accepted. We had never done that before for a ship class, and this was the way to go, so to speak. So we were looking at about 15 ship classes. One of them was Nimitz, which was newly commissioned, and our clout on there was almost nil, if any.[‡] Our job ranged all the way down to air-cushioned surface effect ships, those that were being built.

For instance, in Nimitz we'd go aboard and say that on the flag bridge there were inadequate communication equipments available: "We can't operate it because if you get in here, this is missing. There's no speaker over here." We went about the ship and made observations. I guess you'd call it the man-machine interface. Again, they could listen to us in Nimitz, if they wanted to, or they could ignore us, if they so chose. Now with FFG-7, we created mock-ups ashore, built the ship hands-on, and that was the genesis of that ship evaluation program.

---

[*]Rear Admiral Robert R. Monroe, USN, commanded the Operational Test and Evaluation Force from January 1974 to March 1977.
[†]The Navy eventually built 51 guided missile frigates of the Oliver Hazard Perry (FFG-7) class. The first of them was commissioned in December 1977.
[‡]USS Nimitz (CVN-68), the first of her class was commissioned 3 May 1975. She has a standard displacement of 81,600 tons, is 1,092 feet long, 134 feet in the beam, and an extreme width of 251 feet. Equipped with nuclear power, her top speed is 30-plus knots. She can accommodate approximately 90 aircraft.

As far as serving in OpTEvFor, I was really concerned because I didn't want to come to Norfolk. I wanted to go back to Washington into something similar to a follow-on to the 963. I guess wiser persons than I said that I could do the same thing with OpTEvFor. So I went there and, as I said, found a very, very interesting job. I was free to travel, a brand-new captain. I had these ten fine people working with me, so I didn't often have to put pencil to paper.

About the biggest job I had there in headquarters was answering the chief of staff on the squawkbox. He was a great person, a great naval officer named Captain Bob Crispin, a submariner.[*] He was a great puzzle player, word puzzles. He would call me up all the time and ask, "What does this mean?" He loved to do that. We had a good organization going there.

I learned much about our leader, Admiral Monroe, who is a known workaholic, but the man was so considerate. I remember him getting me in there, sitting me down on my initial arrival welcome, telling me that he had lots to do. He explained all the ins and outs and his charter from the CNO and the things he had to do, and depended upon us to support him. And he said, "What I don't want you to do is sit around waiting for me. We don't operate like that. What I will do, however, is feel free to call on you at any time. Now, that may be 2:00 o'clock in the morning, that may be Sunday morning at 3:00 o'clock, we just don't know. I work odd hours, I work long hours, hard hours." He explained all that.

And he said, "But you have a young family, you've just moved in a house, so I know you have other things to do. So on Saturday don't think you have to sit here and hold my hand, because I'm here on Saturday from 7:00 in the morning till 10:00 at night," which I thought was very considerate. Some of us took that guidance as he gave it, and others didn't believe it and hung around anyway. He was a very, very hard-working, fair boss, who did a lot while he was there.

It was a very tough row to hoe, because we ran into the different disciplines. If you're a project manager in Washington and you're given X number of months to produce a project to its finish, and you're a naval officer who's used to accomplishing things, your one goal in life is to get that project completed on time, in budget, and that's the way it is.

---

[*]Captain Robert E. Crispin, USN.

Well, we were the fly in the ointment, because we'd see something that wasn't right, had direct access to the CNO, went before the review boards, everything from the CNO review board to the defense acquisition board, and we'd just throw a wrench in the machine: "No, that is not ready because it was tested under ideal conditions, and that isn't the way we're going to use it." So we were not popular with the Washington community, yet people realized that Admiral Monroe was just doing his job.

That was a very interesting assignment for me, and I learned a lot about the Washington scene, the Washington politics, and got to watch Admiral Monroe, who is probably the most brilliant individual I've ever been around, quick. I was there ten months.

Paul Stillwell: How much work did you do on the Spruance class during that tour?

Captain Colbus: Well, we did a lot of work. We had a Spruance project officer. We'd get to visit Pascagoula and look at the ship and review the ship. The ship was already contracted for and being built, so I don't think this is the way it was supposed to be. I think we took more away from the ship for future use, especially in the FFG-7, than we contributed to the 963. The 963 was locked in cement in 1969, and I'm talking about 1975, so we were six years into production, and that's the word.[*] You're already producing it. What we hoped to do was influence ships of the '80s as to how they would be constructed, how we would interface man and machine. We did everything from habitability to technical equipment.

Paul Stillwell: Do you remember any specific things that you learned from that process?

Captain Colbus: Yes. I'm just trying to think quickly of all those gents who worked with us. As I said, we were not popular, because we sometimes carried a message that those people in Washington didn't want to hear. I can't think of anything specific at this very moment. I did a lot of traveling myself, went to a few of those DSARCs myself.[†] I got to

---

[*] USS Spruance (DD-963), lead ship of the class, was commissioned 20 September 1975.
[†] DSARC--Defense Systems Acquisitions Review Council.

do a lot of the briefings, such things as the OTO Melara gun in USS Talbot.* We interfaced with the entire ship. So what I could say is that I learned a lot about equipment, individual systems--and by the way, we were also thinking "systems." It used to be this piece here, that piece there; now it's a system, as in an airplane, and tie it all together. So I can't think of anything right now in particular.

Paul Stillwell: The reason for my question about Spruance is to ask how that related to your earlier experience. I would guess there was a fair amount of satisfaction in seeing a physical entity after being in on the conception stage.

Captain Colbus: No, it was just the opposite. The concept and the product were so apart that I was really, I guess, discouraged. Okay, you've now clued me. All right. When we looked at and evaluated at builders' time, April '69, Spruance was really a great ship. She had the latest of everything. As Admiral Weschler would say, "We're not going to gold-plate this thing. We're not going to build a Cadillac." But at the same time, we were looking at life-cycle costs, 20 years down the pike. Well, over the course of 20 years, if we save two U.S. sailors in billets aboard ship, it will cost us X number of dollars in retirement, benefits, salary, feeding, so on.

So you can run out a very, very fine analysis of how it paid to spend an extra, in this particular case I'm thinking of, I think it was an extra $14,000 to make the satellite navigation system plug into the entire program of the ship automatically, rather than have a man do it. Well, $14,000 wasn't that much money, therefore, we're going to have that which is going to save a quarter of a man-year, whatever, and this all adds up. When it came time to contract for the ship, $14,000 times 30, we were way over budget, very cost-conscious. All of a sudden, as I told you before, it's like buying an automobile. You know that if you buy radial tires, they're going to last 40,000 miles, but you've got to pay an extra $200.00 for them. At the time you don't have the $200.00. What do you do? You buy the regular standard tire and you know at 20,000 miles you're going to have to renew

---

* The Italian 76-millimeter OTO Melara gun became the basis for the U.S. Mark 75 3-inch/62 gun first tested in the USS Talbot (DEG-4) in 1974. The Mark 75 then became the standard gun in the FFG-7 class.

your tires. Though it's cost-efficient, you don't have the bucks, and that's what happened with the ship, in summation.

We had all these neat things that were really going to make it easy for maintenance. When I went aboard, I didn't see those things, the neat fabrics that were going to be on bulkheads and everything was going to be covered. I walked aboard in Pascagoula, the first time, went down on the second deck, and it looked like a regular destroyer.

Now, the habitability was there; don't get me wrong. It was gorgeous, it was big, it was air-conditioned, all those things. I'm talking about the little things. It no longer was going to be walking aboard, taking a damp sponge, and wiping down the bulkhead. Oh, no, there's the angle, there we are, sand soap, whatever. It was too costly to do all the things that should have been done, so that was a disappointment. Equipment wise, that was another story. Where a buck could be saved, it certainly was, and that was a disappointment to me, even though I understood it.

Paul Stillwell: Overall, how would you evaluate that class of ship?

Captain Colbus: In the words of Admiral Weschler, it's the greatest ship that ever has been built. If you think the 2,200-ton ship has served this nation well for 30 years, watch this ship, because the 2,200-ton destroyer grew into a 3,400-ton destroyer, as we loaded material into it.[*] Its weight went up and speed went down. You know the story of that. Still good ships, don't get me wrong; they served their purpose well.

Now, here was this new ship that was designed for space and weight, easy conversion, growth was there. Thirty years from now that ship will still be running strong and not look like it's been completely done over. It's built for change; it's built for the time. If you build a ship today and put in the weapons of today--I think we went through this in the 963 program--by the time you produce the ship, those weapons are obsolete and we're changing, changing, changing. Admiral Weschler had it all together. We're going to build this ship, and 30 years from now we're seeing that.

---

[*] The 2,200-ton destroyers were those of the Allen M. Sumner (DD-692) and Gearing (DD-710) classes, both built during World War II.

Paul Stillwell: So it was more a matter of being disappointed with details, it sounds like, than the overall result.

Captain Colbus: Exactly. Oh, yes, absolutely. The gas turbine was just fascinating. I was fortunate enough to have my squadron after this OpTEv tour, and got to ride the ships, watch them. Just beautiful.

Paul Stillwell: Let's talk about the FFG-7. That's another case of trying to save manpower. What was your involvement with that class?

Captain Colbus: Well, Admiral Weschler was gone, and Admiral Frank Price was there.[*] I guess I became his errand boy. I won't say his right hand, because he was a man who was very, very determined. He knew exactly what he wanted. He was good at giving direction and getting things done. I wouldn't flatter myself by saying I was his right-hand man, but I was pretty close to him working there in the Pentagon.

It was, I'm going to say, December 18, 1970, and it was a paper signed out by Packard, who was Deputy Secretary of Defense at the time.[†] It was about 1700 one evening when Admiral Price came back after being with Admiral Zumwalt. He got me and said, "Well, we're going to build a ship and it's going to be 3,500 tons, it's going to cost $45 million in today's dollars, and we've got to see this as our next project." It became the PF-109, which became known as "Price's Folly."[‡] Then it went into the FFG world.

Admiral Price was the man who was charged with bringing that ship in. It was similar to building a house: you have only so much money and so many people. He was a tough taskmaster. If he had ever given one iota, the ship would have just taken off. We had so much controversy within our own ranks. Forget the outside pressures and objections from the Congress and the shipbuilding community and whomever. There was

---

[*] Rear Admiral Frank H. Price, Jr., USN, was Director of the Ship Characteristics Division; Chairman, Ship Characteristics Board; and Program Coordinator, New Construction Destroyer Program.
[†] David Packard served as Deputy Secretary of Defense from 1969 to 1971. He was a co-founder of Hewlett-Packard Company and over the course of years held a number of positions, including chief executive officer and chairman of the board.
[‡] At the time the ship was classified as a patrol frigate, PF. In 1975, prior to the commissioning of the first ship, the class was redesignated FFG, guided missile frigate.

the question among our own sailors about single screw versus twin screw. Sonar--why doesn't it have a 26? That's the latest. Well, we've got enough 26s. Well, don't put a fish-finder on it. When it was first built, the ship went to sea without a sonar.

We had test plants, such as one in Philadelphia to test the gas-turbine engine. It was exactly one half of the 963 plant--two of the same engines instead of four. It had a bow thruster. Manpower was the big controversy. We really held that down. This ship would have two helicopters. How much ASW was it really going to do, how much AAW? And I still walk away with a very clear understanding that that ship was--and we used to argue about the word complement or supplement--I guess complement would be my choice--the 963. Spruance didn't have the missile capability but had the big sonar. Why put it all into one basket as we did with the DLG-26 class? Don't make them double-enders; we'd rather have two systems on two different platforms than a complete system on one platform. We're talking numbers. And that's the way the FFG was ginned up, and again, I believe rightly so.

Paul Stillwell: Did you work on that when you were in OpTEvFor?

Captain Colbus: Oh, yes, that was the one that came under our purview where we could put an op eval on it, and that's where we would go to look at the OTO Melara in Talbot and then be able to say, "This has been completely tested, and whether it's on the FFG-4 or FFG-7, it's the same gun. It'll work just fine." Controllable-pitch screws were under the testing on Barbey, a ship on the West Coast. John Fitzgerald, a young officer in my shop, was the test director. He gathered all these results, went to Philadelphia, observed the engine on the line, went to see the OTO Melara gun, looked at that screw on Barbey, and it all came together. We put those things into the ship, and then it became prototype. That was another big harangue in the halls of the Pentagon. Well, a prototype is just what it says. Build the ship, test it, and then start a production line. We didn't have the time, we didn't have that luxury. Fly before buy? Well, not with ships. So that became political.

Paul Stillwell: In a sense you were accomplishing that by testing the individual elements.

Captain Colbus: But powers to be didn't see it that way, and you can take either side. I don't mean who's paying you, but what's your job. And that's what I think is so great about the entire system. You're loyal to the job, and I think that keeps everything in balance. You take me and put me into a position where I'm going to probably be anti-PF-109--if I've been paid to be a critic of the ship, and I say paid, if that had been my job--I probably could have been a very rabid critic by saying the ship is going to grow regardless. So why don't we call it as it is?

Admiral Price would accept only--I think it was 188 persons on that ship, but we needed 192. That was only four, but then 192 becomes 197. It was always sneaking in, so another very strong pitch was that the number of people would be 188, and that's it. No, not one more. You can cut back but you can't add on. I think Admiral Price in his wisdom knew that when they put the LAMPS birds on there and when things really were shaken out, damn right that ship was going to grow in numbers.[*] That was not being dishonest, but if you'd have acknowledged it then, it would have taken off and then after it was commissioned, it would have taken off some more. So I'm talking about holding growth down. We held to those numbers--188 people, 3,500 tons, and $45 million.

Speaking of $45 million suddenly made me think of one thing that didn't get on the ship that I was pushing for and lost out. The single screw issue caused us to break out all the records from NavShips of all the ships from World War II that had damaged screws that prevented them from getting home, whatever. All of a sudden it wasn't the engine for backup; it was the screw. If you had one screw and that was gone, that was tough. If you had two screws, you could perhaps come home on one of those two. Well, if a torpedo was going to get you, it was going to get two as well as one, so that didn't fly. One screw is fine. We found out--I think I'm correct in recalling--that the only time screws were ever really damaged were in groundings, and you get both of them again. We had to prove that one screw would do the job. Of course, I'd just come from McCloy and thought that one-screw ships were just fine.

One other thing worth recounting in that FFG world is ASROC. Yes, the ship is an ASW platform because it has a sonar and it has LAMPS. How about an ASROC? Well,

---

[*]LAMPS, which stands for light airborne multi-purpose system, is an antisubmarine helicopter carried on board destroyers and frigates.

the ASROC competes with the LAMPS. Oh, no, it doesn't. Well, we hashed that around. Finally it became too expensive. Space, weight, dollars, people--many reasons for not putting ASROC in that ship. But I was an advocate of ASROC. What really queered the deal for putting ASROC in the ship was done with a study.

ASROC was designed as a long-range weapon. We made a study of all the ASROC firings that had occurred in the United States Navy, and it was shown that ASROC was not a long-range weapon; it was a short-range weapon. We had the over-the-side torpedo; therefore we didn't need ASROC. It was shown to me and proved by the smart people that ASROC was not a long-range weapon; it was a short-range, and we couldn't afford that kind of redundancy. They showed that all firings, as I just said, were at short range. I easily explained that away, but nobody wanted to listen.

I said that all these recorded firings were done by people such as myself who had been in command positions. About once a year we got to fire an ASROC for competition. Now, we were competitive so we wanted to beat out the other skippers in the squadron for that ASW E. One of the ways to do it was to get a good ASROC shot. So when I had the opportunity and I had everything prepped, and I had a submarine target at that long ASROC range, and I knew I had him for half an hour, I wasn't going to fire right away. I would wait to make sure my solution was perfect. I'd make sure that everything was lined up. By that time, we've got a short-range weapon. And that's when I really was disappointed in the analysis work. The figures were there, but what was behind the figures? We didn't get ASROC.

Paul Stillwell: Did you have any projects in which you were involved personally with Admiral Monroe?

Captain Colbus: Well, the FFG-7 mainly. We spent a lot of time together. He was very interesting to work for, also very frustrating, and I could tell him this to his face, because he knows it. We wrote up the brief that was going to go to the CNO and the Department of Defense for permission to continue with the ship. This was OpTEvFor's input, and it wasn't all bad, but it was, as we said before, piecemeal. I had, let's say, three or four weeks to prepare this brief to give to the higher-ups in Washington.

Admiral Monroe did not give it himself. I might give it, the project officer might give it, the test director might give it, whoever was most appropriate. Well, in this case, somehow it fell on to me. I didn't write it myself, but I certainly put some of the things in there, some of --I guess you'd call it my personality into it--my favorite items. It got up to Admiral Monroe. I bet you we had that to him a week to ten days in advance.

The day we were going to the Pentagon on a 0700 airplane to give this presentation--notice I didn't call it a pitch--presentation at 0900, we were still changing words as we got into the airplane. We were changing the slides as we were running up to the conference room. It just became a major crisis toward the end. That was typical of Admiral Monroe's modus operandi. The man was so exact, and he was a perfectionist. I used the word "workaholic" before. He was also a perfectionist to the point that everything that went out of OpTEvFor was absolutely letter perfect. I'm talking about I's dotted and T's crossed, and he personally saw to all that. The man worked; he set the example. The only thing you had to realize pretty soon was that the man was superhuman, and one couldn't keep up with him.

Paul Stillwell: What about the new technology things such as the hydrofoil and SES? What was your work on those?

Captain Colbus: Well, it was to go visit and get a handle on it, find out where it was. Those programs were just fledglings then. As I say, it was a great educational tour. I was only there from July 1975 till April '76 and just had enough time to get my feet wet in the programs, learn the characters, which was very important. You had to know your players. About the time I left, those air-cushioned vehicles were put on the back burner, as I recall, and now, of course, they're coming to the forefront again.

Paul Stillwell: You talked about your unpopularity with project managers and so forth. Do you remember specific cases of that?

Captain Colbus: No, not specifics. It was in general. I wouldn't say it was resentment on their part. It was just a case of our looking at the program from another point of view. The project manager, on the other hand, was fighting to get his program through, on budget, in a timely fashion. We were not interested in budgets and a timely fashion. We were interested in a good product. As a tester and an evaluator, it was going to take another six weeks to do this test right. No, we can't accept your figures because you're the developer and you have an interest in getting it through. So it was a tug of war, and I keep talking about this balance.

These were situations where our goals are different than your goals. You'll fix it when the ship is in the fleet. As I said, it's very similar, too, to the man who wants the radial tires but can't afford them, doesn't want to wait, wants that new car now, and bingo. I'll buy it now, and I'll get the radials next time.

Paul Stillwell: Do you recall combat systems or weapon systems rather than whole ships that you were specifically dealing with?

Captain Colbus: Well, again, we didn't deal with weapon systems. We dealt with the whole ship. For instance, there might be magnetic interference from putting this particular piece of gear in that particular place. The man who's developing the gun doesn't see that. The man who's coordinating the ship does. We had--and I'm safe in saying--the first land-based test site, a ship mock-up in Long Island. Sperry built this for the combat center in FFG-7. It was a living, breathing, feeling CIC.

You'd walk in there, and sometimes there were such things as move a knob, move a piece of equipment. Can the captain see what he's doing from his chair? No. Cant the chair a bit. That was my involvement in systems, especially in combat systems. But we were interested in the whole spectrum. We were interested in the individual advancements in the communications equipment. No longer were we sitting on a CW circuit.[*] We were now sophisticated. Again, the 60 division in OpTEvFor took care of all those electronic things, but we worked very closely so that we didn't have electronic interference. We wanted to make sure that it was all compatible.

---

[*] CW, or continuous wave, referred to a type of radio wave interrupted into the dots and dashes of the Morse code for the purpose of communication.

Paul Stillwell: And also that it could be operated by real people in the real world.

Captain Colbus: That's it exactly. Don't send us your chief engineer standing over the finest technician from Company X to operate that radar. Of course, he's going to operate it. He built it, he lived with it. I want to put Seaman Gronk on there, who's just fresh out of A school, and he's going to operate it.

Paul Stillwell: Any other aspects on OpTEvFor?

Captain Colbus: No, not at this time.

Paul Stillwell: Why was your tour only ten months?

Captain Colbus: I got there on July 6, 1975, my mother's birthday. I remember that because I was promoted to captain in Admiral Monroe's office. He promoted me and swore me in because my papers were there. We didn't frock in those days.* I could have been frocked at CarDiv 6, but I chose not to. You went and got your promotion.

On January 20, 1976, after I had been at OpTEvFor for eight months, I got a call from OP-03, Admiral Jim Doyle.† He told me I'd just been screened for major command and that I was going to leave in April. I should have been there probably a full year, and planned on being, but all of a sudden Dick Kinnebrew had to move on from DesRon 2.‡ They had a good notion that he was flag material and wanted him to move on, so I had to get down there and relieve him.

I told you before about Jonas Ingram and how I was so moved when BuPers called to tell me I was getting command. Well, I did cry that day about major command and ComDesRon 2. I called Jody: "Guess what? DesRon 2." Well, the first thing I did was get the organizational book out and see who was in DesRon 2. As I leafed through my

---

*"Frocking" a naval officer refers to the practice of allowing him to wear the insignia and assume the title for which he was recently selected. The officer does not receive the pay for the higher rank until a vacancy appears on the lineal list so he can be officially promoted.
†Vice Admiral James H. Doyle, Jr., USN, Deputy Chief of Naval Operations (Surface Warfare).
‡Captain Thomas R. Kinnebrew, USN, served as Commander Destroyer Squadron Two from May 1974 to October 1976. He eventually retired as a vice admiral in October 1985.

book, I saw Mullinnix in DesRon 2, and the skipper was Tom Anderson, who has been my exec in Jonas Ingram.* That evening, I called up the Anderson residence. I guess one of the boys answered, and I said, "Is your daddy there?"

When Tom came on the phone, he said, "Hey, Louis, what's doing?"

"Well, the first thing, Tom, you can knock off that Louis crap."

"What are you talking about?"

I said, "Well, I got the word today I got screened as ComDesRon 2, and I'll be your squad dog." We were both delighted.

I didn't get to relieve Dick Kinnebrew until October of '76, because between January, when I was selected for major command, and April, when I was detached, SOSMRC reared its ugly head.† Idaho Falls. And I say ugly head because that's the way we saw it, and that time turned out to be the best four months of my life.

Paul Stillwell: Some of your stories about that can be told on tape and some can't. So please tell the ones that can.

Captain Colbus: The ones that can. On our way there, we mustered in an airplane, and we took off with nine admirals and 15 captains. Of those 15 captains, eight were black shoes, seven were aviators. This was what we thought of as a hotshot group. The Navy was in a state of disrepair, and we were the 24 officers going to major commands. We would teach fleet people, starting at the top right on down, the proper methods of maintenance and operation of machinery, plants, whatever. Since we hadn't done a very good job of it, Admiral Rickover was going to show us how it was done in the wonderful world of nuclear engineering. No need to even try to think that we came out of there as nukes, but--and I said this when we left there--we learned so much from those nukes out there, and they didn't learn a damn thing from us, which is a sad experience. Where can I start out there?

---

*By 1976 Anderson was a commander.
†SOSMRC--Senior Officer Ship Material Readiness Course, held at the Naval Reactor Facility at Arco, Idaho. For a description, see David G. Clark, "SOSMRC: Steaming Along in the Desert," U.S. Naval Institute Proceedings, February 1980, pages 97-99.

Paul Stillwell: You could start with the curriculum.

Captain Colbus: Okay. The curriculum. Of the 24 naval officers, I guess I have to use myself as a low-water mark. I was the only one who didn't have some kind of an engineering background, be it two engineering degrees, master's degrees, as Admiral Bill Clifford had, or a Naval Academy background, where you graduate with a degree in engineering of some sort, or even a tour in an engineering plant.[*] We had one black shoe certified nuke, who'd gone through there as a lieutenant commander, and as I say, all these brilliant people and all of them technically competent, many with degrees in engineering.

I had no degree in engineering, and I'm not going to say I was ignorant of engineering spaces, but I certainly wasn't a technician. I knew to go to the engineering spaces, I knew where things were, I knew that was the boiler. I knew about the steam flow. So I resented everybody pointing to us in general, not me in particular, saying, "These officers don't know anything about engineering. We're going to make them smart."

The 24 of us were the first class at SOSMRC. They had a select group of instructors out there, and they were going to teach us. Now, these were, of course, nukes. We had nuclear submariners, we had nuclear surface folks there. These nukes and we students, I guess you might say, had a standoff. The first few weeks out there were what I guess would be termed a hell week.

First of all, it was a six-day week, no ifs, ands, or buts about it. On Saturday at 1730, you'd look around guiltily and think, "Boy, I would like to go to town for the evening. I wonder if we ever will." And I guess we did ease out of there. I guess it was on the third or fourth week, I looked at--I'll never forget--Admiral Tom Hughes, who was, I'd say, the character of the class.[†] I said, "This must be like being a plebe at the Naval Academy. Here we are standing around waiting for a car, Saturday evening, 1700. Tom, we're never going to make it for happy hour. We're like plebes."

The nukes, I think, felt the same way, because they had just moved out there with families, in the process of moving in, and they needed some time to get settled. Of course, the site is 65 miles from Idaho Falls. In that class, you lived at the site in a Butler building;

---

[*] Rear Admiral William F. Clifford, Jr., USN, who was Admiral Doyle's deputy in OP-03.
[†] Rear Admiral Thomas J. Hughes, Jr., USN.

you existed at the site. I know the only one who didn't live at the site was Admiral Tom Replogle, who had his wife and his two-year-old son Tommy out there.[*] So Tom, who by the way, I think, is a music or philosophy major, did very, very well out there; he represented music or philosophy majors very well. But he'd had some engineering experience.

But we all were required to have a residence in the town of Idaho Falls. We were given a per diem allowance. We were also given four station wagons, so six of us to a car, and that meant that was our transportation. Rickover had given us that amenity. We were racing back and forth on the weekends. Toward the end, a couple of people got more bold, and they were free to go in town each evening; however, we were discouraged from doing so. Toward the end I think there might have been a little back-off.

During the classroom sessions, I was just totally lost. As I said, I was the low-water mark. I'd say in our third day there, we were doing graduate chemistry. Well, I think I had chemistry in high school in 1948. Calculus--oh, what's that Studebaker sign? That's interesting. What's that? We're going to teach you to do that. Hey, I'm delighted. And it just went on from there. We had courses that I had no idea what was being said. And I must confess that I'm sure on some days by 2:00 or 3:00 in the afternoon, I'd just blank out, completely shut out because I was so frustrated. I didn't know what he was talking about, I'm not going to listen anymore, I'll get caught up tonight. And the other boys were very good about that. They would coach you right along.

When I talk about learning, I went out there with an empty glass and came away with a glass half full. Everybody else, maybe a half glass, three-quarters, whatever. But I feel I gained the most out of this school, and I was vocal about that. I felt so proud that all of a sudden I could take one of those HP-45 calculators and work it, not just add and subtract in a checkbook, but do all the functions it was supposed to do. When I went out there, I could not manipulate a slide rule. I'd never had an occasion to work a slide rule. Now I could do all these great problems. I could do boiler water chemistry on my calculator. Now I was going to navigate with this calculator. So I really felt good about all these things that had been taught to me.

---

[*] Rear Admiral Thomas H. Replogle, USN.

There were all kinds of feelings. Maybe the admiral felt, "This is a waste of my time. I'm a good engineer. I don't need this." But the discipline was there. The message was loud and clear. Improve the material conditions, and to do that, you fellows have to know. No longer will we accept a statement like, "Well, the valve doesn't work, let her blow," or bypass it. We were now exacting engineers. That really had an effect on me, as I can tell you when I get into the desron business. We'll have time to do that.

Anyway, one day near the very onset of the program, we were studying chemistry and logarithms, a big subject. After the class I went up to the young commander who was teaching. He was a nuclear engineer. I said, "How about these logarithms? You made the offer to help. Are you going to be around this evening for a while? I'd like to talk to you about logarithms."

"Well, what do you want to talk about?"

"I want to talk about logarithms."

"Well, what about logarithms?"

"Yeah, what about logarithms?"

He said, "What do you want to know, Captain?"

I said, "I want to know how to work a logarithm. I don't know what you mean. I can spell it but I can't do it."

He could not take aboard the fact that here was a 45-year-old Navy captain, apparently successful because he was going to a major command, who couldn't compute a logarithm and had no higher math. They never learned that there were people like me out there. I won't say he made fun of me, but he sort of looked down his nose at me.

In the physics class, same thing. Physics was a mystery to me. He might as well be teaching the course in Greek. The teacher was very brilliant, but he just glossed over that stuff.

Paul Stillwell: That he took for granted.

Captain Colbus: He took it for granted. I'd say something like, "Wait a minute. I want to see that incline and get that thing all over again, friction."

"Are you putting me on, Captain?"

"No, sir. I have never had a course in physics."

"Are you sure?"

"No, I'm not sure. Maybe at NROTC we had to take a semester, but that was 23 years ago in South Carolina. No, I don't remember anything."

He couldn't believe it. Both those instructors, who sort of made fun of me, were in my squadron a year later as skippers of ships. I never held it against them, and they knew that. No, it was all fun and games.

Okay, let me get into the biggie. I went out there, having heard the Rickover stories. When we got out there, I was just like a kid in a candy shop. Hey, this is great. Teach me. I want to learn. I will go home and be able to work a calculus problem. Just like the person who's learning to read, he's very proud of it. I made these remarks, wasn't embarrassed to say, "I couldn't do this before."

Well, the spy system out there was, I'd say, 24 hours away from Rickover's ear. He'd get a call every day from our civilian leader, a fellow named Duffy, who would say something like, "They're doing well, but this one admiral is balking at the system, a captain in there slept through two of the classes. Colbus says he's learning a lot even though he doesn't know anything."

It got to me that I was a subject of conversation, because somehow or other a memo was circulated from Admiral Rickover to Admiral Holloway, giving him a report on this, and I've seen it.[*] It named me for my enthusiasm and acknowledgement of being totally ignorant in the wonderful world of engineering and benefiting greatly from SOSMRC. That was not well received in the destroyer community because there was a great deal of contention. The CNO was going to improve material readiness. When you have a material readiness improvement program, go see Hymie. Hymie was saying, "See, I told you, you can't do anything right. I'll do it for you." Meanwhile, the black shoes are sitting back there--this is all ridiculous, and I think it's overkill--"Tell that officer who's enjoying it to go away. There's something wrong with him. We need him at sea more than we need him out there. Let his engineers worry about that." So there was this contention within the ranks, and it got to us loudly and clearly.

---

[*] Admiral James L. Holloway III, USN, served as Chief of Naval Operations from 29 June 1974 to 1 July 1978.

I was certainly not a Rickover fan, and that goes back--I won't go into those stories. They're a matter of record elsewhere. I understand that ours was the only class he did with this, and it was probably the only time he'd ever done it, and that was he sent us, via airplane, wooden boxes that would fill this room. The boxes contained his J-grams or Pink-grams, the J-grams being for his secretary Jean. These were all the things he would write. When we studied those, and we did, we tore them apart for an entire day.

Rather than being intimidating and frightening, it was absolutely awe-inspiring, how one man could know that much and be that powerful. He knew when Seaman Gronk didn't finish chapter three in his lesson book, and Gronk's skipper would get a call at 2:30 A.M. in his bedroom, at home, with Hymie on the other end. These were all true stories. All of a sudden, you realized, "Boy, that's control." Yes, it could be dangerous, but without putting that face on it, the admiral had absolutely total control, which required total devotion, hard work, full-time, ad infinitum. Any person who is that interested and that sincere and that devoted must be all right.

Paul Stillwell: Did you encounter him personally during your time there?

Captain Colbus: Yes, yes. That'll give you another flavor. We had done it all, we had been to our schools, we were about to take off on a two-week trip prior to completion. It included one week at Great Lakes, the hot plant, and a shipyard, and one week at sea practicing all these skills we had picked up: walk through the plant, identify steam leaks, correct them, etc. In my particular case, I was going to leave and I was going to Puget Sound. On Friday I was leaving the school, and on Monday morning, bright and early, I'd be at Puget Sound Naval Shipyard, visiting with Jim Nunneley and company to see how the shipyard operated.*

I threw a little personal in here and got my ticket arranged so I could swing by Portland, Oregon, on my way to Seattle, because I have a cousin in Portland. My ticket was for, let's say, 10:00 o'clock Friday morning. Everybody had a program. One man was going to Vegas, another man was going elsewhere. We were all taking off. Some were

---

*Captain James K. Nunneley, USN, commanded Puget Sound Naval Shipyard, Bremerton, Washington, from 5 June 1976 to 16 June 1979.

even taking off Thursday night. Well, we got the word on Wednesday, "Don't plan on leaving Friday morning. Think more of Friday afternoon, like late."

"Oh?"

"Admiral Rickover's coming out to talk to you personally. He's going to address you."

Well, we had our ups and down with him, because, for instance, this was the year of the Olympics with the little Comaneci girl.[*] This was the year of the Bicentennial. We wanted to watch the Comaneci girl, and we got special permission--and this is no kidding--to break out a television from a locked closet so 24 captains and admirals could sit around and see what was going on in the outer world on a Tuesday night.

Well, Mr. Smart Guy here, I thought I'd just sneak a little bit, and when we were all done watching her, I would just sit here and watch Johnny Carson.[†] It was that difference in time zones. The Olympics were over, everybody was gone, and I was sitting there. An instructor came in and turned that television off. I said, "I'll turn it off." No, it had to be put away that night. No Johnny Carson. And I really felt like a child. Everybody did.

For instance, earlier we wanted to go to Las Vegas. We did have a long weekend for the Fourth of July--that big Bicentennial weekend. In fact, Charlie Hunter, one of the aviators who is now an admiral, had arranged with AirLant to have a C-9 swing by and take us to Washington and bring us back.[‡] And it wasn't a junket just for us, because that C-9 flew cross-country all the time on schedule. Voted down. No, it wouldn't look right. We had to stay real close to home base. As I said, our senior man was Bill Clifford, and he had to play it very cozy, because I could see the politics involved here: the nukes versus the non-nukes, the CNO and Hymie Rickover against the OP-03, whatever.

Okay. Now we'd had these trying experiences, we were frustrated. We had seen the inner workings of the J-grams. "Admiral Rickover's going to come out and talk to you."

---

[*] The most acclaimed athlete of the 1976 Olympic Games at Montreal was a slender 14-year-old Romanian gymnast, Nadia Comaneci.
[†] Johnny Carson for many years was the host of NBC's "Tonight Show."
[‡] Captain Charles B. Hunter, USN. The C-9 Skytrain II, built by McDonnell Douglas, is a military version of the DC-9 civilian aircraft. The two-engine jet is 119 feet long, wing span of 94 feet, and gross weight of 110,000 pounds. It has a top speed of 576 miles per hour and a range of 2,500 nautical miles with 10,000 pounds of cargo. The payload is 90 passengers or 32,444 pounds of cargo.

Well, my attitude was, "To hear a man like that, it's worth an extra day, so I won't go see my cousin till Saturday." I changed my reservations for Saturday morning. One night was enough. I figured after hearing Rickover, I'd go hit the town of Idaho Falls, which was just a great liberty port. Boy, we learned a lot out there. It wasn't all nose-down-and-rear-end-up. When you did get to Idaho Falls, it was great.

Paul Stillwell: What made it great?

Captain Colbus: Oh, cowboy atmosphere, down home, country western. Everybody learned a whole new way of life. Plenty of good times and very friendly people. Of course, a great Mormon community, but, still, you don't have to smoke and drink to have a good time.

We were now waiting for the arrival of Admiral Rickover on our last day at the site. We were all packed out, and we had checked out of our apartments. I had a hotel reservation for Friday night, as everybody else did. He was going to be there about 1400. We were out at the site, had breakfast, looked around, and there was a good atmosphere. We were having fun now because we were on our way. At 1400 there was no Admiral Rickover. He showed up about 7:00 o'clock that night, kept us in waiting. That was fine. He walked in, looked at us, and he just started on his tirade.

First of all, we'd been told about the stand with the apples and the grapes that he required when he was in a cabin on a ship. Well, Ralph Bird was the skipper of the school at the time, a nuke captain, an admiral now, and Ralph Bird, of course, had done all these things.[*] The first thing Rickover did was scream, "Bird, get this crap out of here." That's the word he used; I'll never forget it: "Get this crap out of here." That's not a nice way to refer to food. But anyway, he did.

Then it started, "How many of you have been to war college?" We all raised our hands. "How many of you have been to a technical engineering school?" Maybe two raised their hands. "See?" Then he started cursing, "You goddamn people, you're all alike. You're nothing but politicians. You make your names in the bridge of the ship, but you can't get your hands dirty. If the ship doesn't steam, you're not going to get there to do all

---

[*] Captain Ralph G. Bird, USN.

your glamorous fighting so you can get promoted to higher rank." Oh, a 20-minute tirade. Boy, this man was living up to his reputation.

One of us made the mistake halfway through the tirade of closing his eyes. Man, he just homed in on him: "You don't like what I'm saying, you get the hell out of here." It was just fire and damnation. I had a great time. What a colorful gent. The message was there, though, "You owe it to your people, you owe it to the Navy, you owe it to all factions, learn that engineering plant, that's why you're out here. The fact you're out here is an admission that you've been negligent. Now you have a chance to correct your errors. Now, get the hell out of here."

Paul Stillwell: Did the school do you any good?

Captain Colbus: Absolutely. Oh, absolutely. I was always attentive to my engineer previously. He'd come up and talk to me, but he couldn't talk intelligently to me, "It's going to take me three hours, at least, more like five hours, to put a weld on that valve."

I'd be sitting up there and say, "Come on. Three hours? He's just doing that Middle Eastern training. He's going to tell me three to five hours and do it in ten minutes. Because I see them when they weld my car in a shop. That's it." I didn't know that it took all that preparation and all that ultrasound testing and all the things I learned. Now when he said three to five hours, I'd nod my head intelligently. He would show me a schematic, and I just politely answered, "Yeah, I trust you, it's your plant. I hope it's right. Thank you for the information." I didn't mean I was going to get in there and drive it. I was going to get in there and be able to intelligently understand what the chief engineer was telling me. That's what I gained out of it. I went out of there a little too eager, and especially when I got to USS <u>Mitscher</u>, but that's another story.

Paul Stillwell: Did they grade the class? Did you have competitive standings?

Captain Colbus: Yes, we certainly did, and there was no grade. You were one out of 24, and I am proud to say I never was--I don't think there was a 24 out of 24, because I probably would have been it if there had been. That's not fair. As I always said, I was never number one, but I was never number 24. I think one time I was 18 out of 24 and just delighted. Probably in physics I was 23, 22. But we really sort of took that all with a grain of salt because we realized--and my contemporaries were very, very understanding.

Tom Hughes was probably number one most of the time, because he was a real hard-working, down to pencil and paper man, who studied hard and played hard. On the weekends, we'd get away, but that man really put the hours in. If he didn't understand it, he didn't let it slip by. I have a lot of admiration for his tenacity. But I'm saying, here were these great engineering minds and very, very smart people, and then there were about three of us.

One officer--this might mean something to you--was slated to be skipper of USS Independence. He had finished up his deep-draft command in Norfolk, had his family out there on the West Coast because of many reasons, good ones, and they were not going to move him to the East Coast. Then he found out that he would not go to Independence upon graduating from this school, but he would be stashed another five or six months. He was still getting Independence, but there was going to be another delay.

So he'd had his deep draft, he had a stash at AirLant until this school, and now they told him he was going back to AirLant for another six-month stash. He made a call to BuPers and, I guess, AirLant and said, "Look, stash me, and I understand that, but stash me at AirPac so I can be on the West Coast, at least see my family because they're not moving east when I take command of Independence." And the answer was no, no, no.

I remember one day during an electrical quiz--we're not talking about positive and negative and grounds, we're talking about that high-class electricity that runs around the ship--I remember I think he put his pencil down, went and made a phone call, came back and said, "That's it." He, in plain words, quit. He all of a sudden figured, "I don't need this, but I'll put up with it. I want my carrier very badly, but when they say that I have to go to the East Coast just because the ship's there instead of the West Coast, where I'd like to be, plus this," and he left us. He was a fine officer, and we all understood that too.

Paul Stillwell: Had you had a preference in what your major command would be, or did you just take what was available?

Captain Colbus: No, I took what was available. Now, if you're a really neat guy--and we go back to my story when I got my destroyer--I have contemporaries who screened for major command and were very sure of themselves. Maybe they were good and they knew it better; whatever, they turned down a major command. They said, "I'll wait for something better, rather than just grab the first thing that comes along. I want a missile squadron. I don't want old ships. I don't want a squadron, I want a cruiser. I don't want a cruiser, I'll wait for a squadron." But, hey, when they told me I was going to DesRon 2, that was outstanding. It really was, too, the port I was in, the ships I knew.

Paul Stillwell: Please describe DesRon 2 and the ships that made it up.

Captain Colbus: I left Norfolk after about five days between school and command of DesRon 2. I flew to Palma, Majorca, to relieve Dick Kinnebrew. The flagship was USS Barney (DDG-6). It was a quick and dignified turn-over/relief, and the next day Dick was gone. I remember the night I relieved Dick, either Elmer Montgomery or Talbot was outboard. I should know that. This story will come out later. Anyway, the skipper of Barney and, I'm going to say, Elmer Montgomery went ashore that night.

With us was a man by the name of Smiley Chow, who's a very, very famous personage amongst Navy people. He was a Chinese gentleman who started off in the late '20s, early '30s, as a tailor in Shanghai and came to the States, where he made his fortune, and I mean a fortune. He just traveled around to see his old friends in the United States Navy.

Well, Smiley thought enough of Dick that he came over to attend the change of command ceremony. There weren't that many in Palma--the skipper, the two skippers, a lovely lady who worked for the USO, and her husband. It was a small ceremony, as I say, but very, very nice. We all went out that night on Smiley; he took us out to a farewell dinner at a very fine Chinese restaurant right there. The next morning we said goodbye to Dick Kinnebrew.

I was given the routine reports and nodded to all of this, and on the second day we got under way. We steamed to Gibraltar to join up with a big naval exercise. I'll think of the name of it in a minute, 50-some ships. Great review. When we arrived with my two ships, we were given station assignments. I immediately requested refueling, because I knew the ship was low and I didn't want to fool around. There was maybe 62% on one and maybe 70% on the other. But you don't like steaming around like that, especially with an oiler in company. And here we were, just steaming in these great columns with ships joining us, which I thought was a great time to fuel.

Boy, I got such a message from Admiral Carroll, CTF 60, that I figured my career was over, and, hell, I hadn't even started.[*] It said, "Why would you even consider joining this task force when your ships are low on fuel, you just came out of port?" The message just really took the wind out of my sails. Well, here you are, coming from behind. I went back to dear admiral and said, "If you look at the op order, it says you do not fuel ships in port because of (a) worry about spilling fuel, (b) time consuming, (c) cost, ad infinitum, when you know you're going to join up with an oiler. It's the easier way to do it. That's why we're here asking for fuel." He didn't accept that.

Paul Stillwell: No, because that showed him up.

Captain Colbus: And his staff. But, anyway, I got off to a bad start with Admiral Carroll. He was riding Nimitz, which was not an ASW carrier; she had no S-3s. So the ASW program was mine, and I got to play ASW screen commander, the whole nine yards. We had seven ships on that deployment, and again it was a mixed bag. Two or three of them were DesRon 2 ships, mixed up with DesRon 6, DesRon 4, and two cruisers. One cruiser was South Carolina, and the other cruiser was Josephus Daniels, with Clarke Chisum in command.[†]

Paul Stillwell: Those two cruisers weren't in your squadron.

Captain Colbus: Oh, no, those were in the group. But over there, they reported to and worked for the desron. Well, when Dick Kinnebrew was there, that was great because he

---

[*]Rear Admiral Eugene J. Carroll, Jr., USN, Commander Attack Carrier Striking Force Sixth Fleet; Commander Carrier Group Two.
[†]Captain Oscar Clarke Chisum, USN, commanded the USS Josephus Daniels (CG-27) from December 1975 to January 1978.

was the senior officer. Here I was, about a year-old captain, and here was Clarke Chisum, a seasoned senior captain, with Dick Kinnebrew gone. I'll never forget going to him with a message and asking if I might call on him via LAMPS helicopter off Montgomery. He answered, "Welcome any time, Commodore."

"Thank you, Captain." It was a Sunday morning. LAMPS came over, hoisted me off Barney, and took me to "Jack" Daniels. I boarded the cruiser and did as you're supposed to: walked up on this magnificent bridge, requested permission to come on the bridge. I'd known Clarke but not real well. He shook hands and welcomed me aboard; would I stay for lunch? "Absolutely, that's what I'm here for." And I said, "May I suggest three things? One, I can certainly work for you. I can live in this ship and be your squadron commander here under your guidance if that's what you'd like, since you are the senior destroyerman in the Sixth Fleet. Number two, I will be glad to go back to my ship and again work for you or do whatever, but not in your hair, back there in my own domain. Or, three, go in Barney, and I'll be the commodore and you be the captain and we'll play the game."

He said, "I'll take the third choice. You just don't worry about me. I'll be glad to." And it was just music from then on, and Clarke was a complete, total gentleman. I'd never met anybody like Clarke Chisum. What is it they say about an organization where rank has its place? If the senior is a gentleman, he will never think of it, and the junior, if he is a gentleman will never forget it. Well, he was the epitome. I did not personally use radiotelephones, but when it was time to detach Clarke, I'd do the unusual in deference to Captain Chisum's seniority and use the radio to say, "Request your departure. Would you please proceed to your next destination."

He'd come over. "Be glad to. Enjoyed working with you." And away he'd go. When he'd come back over, he'd say, "Request permission to join the group." And it was just fine. What a great officer, a real scholarly gent, a very cultured gentleman, and he just made the cruise very pleasant.

South Carolina was a nuclear cruiser; she was commanded by Captain Neel.[*] Though he was junior to Clarke, he was selected for flag during this deployment. He left

---

[*]Captain William C. Neel, USN, commanded USS South Carolina (CGN-37) from 15 April 1972 to 13 October 1976.

us, and we got a new skipper, and that was Captain Simonton.* So those were my cruisers. We did a five-month deployment over there and had a grand time.

Paul Stillwell: Describe some of the differences of having multiple ships under your command as opposed to just one, as was the case previously.

Captain Colbus: Chief staff officer was Dave Dean, the world's greatest trivia expert.† Boy, Trivial Pursuit wasn't popular then, but I'm sure he's the champion today. In fact, I've been trying to get in touch with him. He was a very experienced operational type. There were two young officers, lieutenants, Crash Calhoun and Paul Krupski.‡ Those gents had it all down pat. They were Kinnebrew-trained men and never missed a stroke. I'd hoped to say that it went as if Dick Kinnebrew hadn't even been there, because these officers worked for Dick, were trained by him, and did it all. So my contribution, I think, was to sit back, watch these officers prove what they could do, learn the ropes, learn the personalities, and make it all happen. Because we did detach.

My biggest job in that deployment was keeping peace between myself, my staff, and Admiral Carroll, among the ships and Admiral Carroll, whatever. I used to spend a lot of my time going over to the carrier to explain what was going on, everything from the count of torpedoes fired to fueling the ships, to whatever. So I would say that the running of the squadron was done in house, and as far as looking after the people above and keeping everything on a smooth, gracious level, I went over and did that with the CTF 60 staff and Carroll. As I said, Nimitz was an attack carrier, so they'd be off doing their thing while we were 60 miles away doing the ASW thing--not all the time, but 60% to 70% of the time.

Paul Stillwell: How much tactical control did you have?

---
*Captain Bennet S. Simonton, USN, commanded South Carolina from 13 October 1976 to 29 February 1980.
†Commander David T. Dean, USN.
‡Lieutenant Paul J. Krupski, USN.

Captain Colbus: Complete and total tactical control, which was a very nice way to go. All I had to do was give the guidance. As I said, these were all seasoned skippers who had been there about two months before I got there, so it was all very, very easy to do.

Paul Stillwell: Was there a satisfaction and enjoyment from that tactical control?

Captain Colbus: No, no, because my biggest problem was, "Oh, I could do this so much better if I could take command of this ship." I guess that's human frailty. I know I could have done more things with the ship than the skipper. That goes with the job and experience. I used to become very frustrated, thinking, "I wish I could moor this ship. This is terrible." Of course, you can't say anything. You sit there and bite your tongue. So that was an adjustment. And then, of course, you get into this, "Well, when I was in Jonas Ingram . . ." which, by the way, Bob Hilton used to do when he was embarked in Jonas Ingram as my squadron commander: "When I was in Davis, I would do this . . ."

I'd look at him and say, "That's a hell of a good idea, Commodore." And the next time I'd do it that way. Now, that wasn't being greasy; that was taking direction, suggestion. Some of my fellow skippers back in those Jonas Ingram days didn't do that. They didn't want to take direction; they wanted to run their own ships. Well, when does it become suggestion? When does it become direction? I remembered that, and I always had that in mind when I was in the squadron myself.

Paul Stillwell: How good were your skippers in picking up suggestions?

Captain Colbus: You notice I hesitate, so I guess it was a 50-50 answer. There was a lot of direction. I guess what I want to get into, though, is USS Mitscher. Mitscher was a famous basket case.* She'd been a basket case for ages. She was in the squadron, she was a late joiner, she'd done all these things, came in with leaking turbines. She had spent a lot

---

*USS Mitscher (DL-2) was originally commissioned as an all-gun destroyer leader on 15 May 1953. She was the first of a four-ship class with new 1,200-psi steam plants, and all were noted for having engineering problems. She was decommissioned for conversion to a guided missile ship in the 1960s, reclassified DDG-35 in 1967, and recommissioned on 29 June 1968. She was stricken from the Naval Vessel Register on 1 June 1978.

of the first two months of her deployment in a shipyard in Palermo. And this was all history that I'd learned back at SurfLant. Captain Kinnebrew went over it and explained it to me.

I didn't know the skipper that well, and I was pretty hot to trot, fresh out of oily rag school, thought I was a pretty hotshot destroyer sailor. By their giving me a squadron, they didn't deflate that any, so I didn't think anything of standing up there at a smart join-ups and when you came in, I wanted to see 25 knots; this coming in at 16 or 17 knots was for the sissies, and we were running a smart squadron.

I had watched Binks Leahy do this when I was in <u>Basilone</u>. I'd heard of Happy Harry, Hollywood Harry Alendorfer doing this when he had his squadron in the mid-1960s. These were the colorful leaders--you know, everything in formation, 25 knots. Things were a little different now. We had some FFs with the big sonar domes and the single screws. We had <u>Mitscher</u>, which was supposed to be old and tired and broken down, and it went on and on.

Well, I went aboard <u>Mitscher</u>. She was joining up one time, and it was the first time I'd seen <u>Mitscher</u>. She came limping in to station. I wanted the 25- and 27-knot approach to station, slow down to the 12-knot formation speed, and what's the next maneuver. Well, we didn't get that. I wasn't too kind. I think I said something to the skipper, went over to see him. We got talking, and I mentioned power plants and leaks and compression and all the things I knew about. I said, "Let's look at the plant."

Well, I walked down, and I can't remember if I cried or just went berserk. I'd never seen anything like this. It was a tea kettle of reserve fame; it was a rust bucket. I couldn't believe it. One didn't need Idaho Falls to see that there were problems. Well, we got back up in the skipper's cabin, and I let him know I just couldn't believe this. All the time I was thinking, "What did Dick Kinnebrew do? How did he put up with this?"

In retrospect--and I go ahead now about a year or two--I found out that you've got to know where they're coming from. I'm from Idaho Falls. Where is this spic and span polish? This young Gene Mosman had taken that ship from the pier, it hadn't operated in months, it was just there, and he brought it to sea and little by little chipped away at that thing, and each day he'd show improvement.[*]

---

[*]Commander Donald Eugene Mosman, USN.

For a sailor like me who came and didn't see the empty glass, saw the quarter-filled glass, I was very, very--I guess the word is intolerant. As I say to Gene when I see him today, "You're the skipper, you're the junior who taught the senior more than the senior taught the junior." Gene was just letter perfect. He never let me aggravate him; he never lost his patience with me.

Paul Stillwell: He educated you.

Captain Colbus: He educated me and got me back to the real world. I suddenly saw what Commander Mosman was doing, and he was just a hero. Because two years later, when he retired that ship, it was the star of SurfLant. He would take her to sea, run her up to flank speed, and do anything you wanted Mitscher to do. He worked with his crew in a low-key, effective manner that I was not in the position to appreciate at first.

We had a tough time with that ship. In Toulon over the Christmas season, I moved aboard the ship. I moved aboard--and I can say this now, and Gene knew it--I moved aboard to defend the skipper. Because Admiral Carroll saw the ship when it came limping in and went in the shipyard, but it still wasn't a fast-running destroyer. He was very, very harsh, because he, like me when I first saw Mitscher, did not understand or know what was being accomplished day by day, piece by piece.

Admiral Carroll was very harsh with that ship and extremely harsh with me, in that I wasn't more reactive to order it to overnight improvement. Well, Gene had taught me that, little by little, we were getting there. And they did. So I shifted my pennant to Mitscher from Barney in Toulon and spent the rest of the deployment in her. She came home a real fleet steamer, looked good, operated well, and Gene Mosman was one of those magic-touch persons. He just had that crew fine-tuned. If he had quietly said, "Let's go jump off the fantail while the ship's doing 25 knots," they'd have done it. They'd have done it.

That's another thing that you really appreciate when you're the squadron commander. It's like watching your children; each one is so different. Sometimes you wanted to go over and hug them. In fact, one day when we were back in Norfolk I was told by my boss, Admiral Walters, "Your trouble is you're too protective. You just can't let go of those destroyers. You're too protective of your skippers."[*]

"I think that's what I'm paid to do. I'll take care of them. We don't go out to the outside world and talk about what goes on behind the closed bedroom doors at my home; I'm certainly not going to broadcast what happens behind closed cabin doors." But they were a very, very tight group and a good group, and hard working. They were the world's unsung heroes, because the benefits sometimes just didn't meet the trying times. But we were going home with the good feeling of what those skippers accomplished, especially in Mitscher. She was the pride of the fleet at that time for what she accomplished.

Paul Stillwell: You got into some difficulty over her in a newspaper story, didn't you?

Captain Colbus: Oh, yes. Well, that wasn't the ship's fault; that was my fault. That happened November '77, when I came back to Norfolk after serving on a selection board in Washington. I'd been chosen to go up to Washington and sit on the major command selection, another great page in the career. Boy, I was going to find out what that was all about. I spent ten days there.

I'd been away from the ship and was coming home on Friday afternoon, probably 1500. I thought I'd just stop by the flagship before I went home, which was my first mistake. Just go on home, Louis. No, I went by Mitscher. By then she was the pride of the fleet, she looked good, she steamed well, and had a crew that you couldn't touch because they'd done it all themselves. Morale was sky high, and I was up there with them. The skipper came up, "Welcome home."

"Thank you. Good to be back. We'll hit it Monday. What's happening?"

"Well, right now I have George Wilson, the columnist, on board, and he's been with me all day looking the ship over. He's going to write an article for The Washington Post."

"Well, good."

"He wants to know if you'd have time to talk to him."

"Oh, absolutely. Love to."

---

[*]Rear Admiral Robert L. Walters, USN, Commander Cruiser-Destroyer Group Eight.

Well, he brought Wilson up and the PAO officer from SurfLant, Gene, and myself.* I think that was it. He asked me, "What's the condition of the fleet today?"

Well, I guess I gave him a dissertation. I know I gave him a dissertation of how we went to SOSMRC and how we saw improvement, the ship was a perfect example of can-do, high morale, effective. Well, somehow or other I got around to, "I'm sick and tired of reading about all the druggies and the long-hairs and all the bad boys. Did you see any in this ship?"

"Well, no, I didn't, Commodore."

"Well, good. Let me tell you why." Blah, blah, blah, X, Y, and Z. I read him the riot act as I would do in a bar. I said, "One of the things that young Gene Mosman is having a tougher time with leading his crew than I had with mine is that I could do all kinds of things that are no longer done. That was just five, six years ago. For instance, if I had a wimp, I'd write to his mama. I could feed him peanut butter for three days because he's such a baby.

"If Gene did that, why, the bleeding hearts would be all over him. What is that? Privacy Act, writing the parents, dehumanizing by feeding them peanut butter. He can't do that. So he has a very, very much tougher job because of the bleeding hearts. And the next time you come to town, or I'm going to send for you, Mr. Wilson, when I do one of my material and personnel inspections. You walk around a ship like this, and you want to grab and take home every shipmate and introduce him to your 17-year-old daughter, because that's how fine each sailor comes across."

"Thank you, Commodore."

"Wait. I'm not done. Let me tell you one more thing. You came down here, and I'm getting sick and tired of seeing the pictures of the ne'er-do-well that you just happen to snap outside the gate. Let's knock that off. Let's start taking pictures of my shipmates here or in any of my squadron ships."

"Thank you.'

Finally he left, thanked me, shook hands. That Sunday I went to Sunday School with my two children and got home at noon. The greeting from Jody was, "Well, you've done it."

---

*PAO--public affairs officer.

"What did I do now?" I didn't think I'd done anything to my wife.

She said, "Were you interviewed?"

"Oh, yes. How did you know?"

She said, "Admiral Read just called and wants you to call him right away. This is on the front page of The Washington Post."*

Well, I called up and finally got to see the article. It had, first of all, "The commodore of the Atlantic Fleet." Hey, I was not the commodore of the Atlantic Fleet. That offended people: "There he is down there telling people he's . . . " I didn't tell anybody that. And not only Admiral Read, but all of them wanted to know, "Who are these bleeding hearts? Where did you get that? Do you think I'm a bleeding heart?"

"No, sir. No, sir. I meant the Congress. I meant the people who make these ridiculous laws." I didn't say what I was thinking, which was, "However, if the shoe fits, wear it." No, I didn't do that, because they weren't bleeding hearts, they really weren't. So that was a bad scene.

At the time, poor Ted Kosmela, whom I guess we've talked about, was up in the psychiatric ward at Bethesda, undergoing a trying time caused by what had happened to him with his squadron, and we were old sea dogs from way back.† Anyway, he called to tell me he had a bed right next to him there in the psychiatric ward, had a cribbage board, good-looking nurses, and after reading the paper, I'd probably be up there with him. It worked out just fine.

Paul Stillwell: What was the outcome? Did Admiral Read cool off?

Captain Colbus: Oh, everybody cooled off, but you've got to watch yourself. You just don't get good press. I guess that goes without saying.

The other defense mechanism I had was, "Your public affairs officer was sitting there. You ask him what I said." They do take things out of context. I guess the best thing is just, "No comment." But I never lived with that. There's a good article in The Right

---

*Vice Admiral William L. Read, USN, served as Commander Naval Surface Force Atlantic Fleet from 1977 to 1979. He has been interviewed as part of the Naval Institute's oral history program. The article was published in November 1977.
†Captain Walter T. Kosmela, USN.

Stuff about naval officers being interviewed, how dull and drab, that they never commit themselves because they all run scared.

Paul Stillwell: We've talked about your liberty ports when you were in the carrier division and on the Jonas Ingram. What about when you were in the squadron command in the Mediterranean?

Captain Colbus: Well, same thing. Same type of fun and games, enjoyable, not so much time this deployment. It seemed we had more steaming hours. I'm trying to think of some of the highlights of some of our liberty ports. Oh, we had lots of fun. I did get to visit the Pope. We went to Naples and called on then-Admiral Turner, who was the four-star in command.[*]

We took the squadron into Naples for the 25th anniversary of NATO in the Mediterranean. It was a big ceremony that was conducted in USS Albany, which steamed down from Gaeta. She was Admiral Train's flagship; the skipper was Jim Storms.[†]

I remember going over to see Jim the first night in port. I went up to his cabin in civilian clothes. I guess I'd describe it as pushing my way in. The poor Marine didn't know who I was. I opened his cabin door, and he was in the head, shaving in his T-shirt. I didn't even say hello to him, I went over, jumped on the couch, put my feet up on the coffee table, and looked at him. I said, "Jimmy, we have come a long way. I'm sitting here in the flagship of Sixth Fleet, the skipper's cabin, feet up, and not really giving a damn what you think or what you care." And he laughed. Yes, we had come a long way, so that was a happy reunion.

We went from there to Gaeta because then the practice was that Admiral Train would bring all the Sixth Fleet ships into Gaeta for a day and a night, and he would personally get to know them. It was at his house that evening that I got to meet for the first time and talk to Admiral David Bagley, CinCUSNavEur, a very big, impressive, four-star

---

[*] Admiral Stansfield Turner, USN, served as Commander in Chief Allied Forces Southern Europe from September 1975 to March 1977.
[†] Vice Admiral Harry D. Train II, USN, commanded the Sixth Fleet from 5 August 1976 to 1 September 1978. His oral history is in the Naval Institute collection. Captain James G. Storms III, USN, commanded the guided missile cruiser Albany (CG-10) from 6 August 1976 to 17 November 1978.

gent.* And, of course, Admiral Train is soft-spoken, and I guess the word would be gentle. But here was this Bagley looking at me, and his cocktail chatter in the reception line was, "Well, Commodore, what do you do?"

"I'm Commander Destroyer Squadron Two."

"Well, I read that. I got that. But I want to know what the hell you do over there."

I said, "Well, I act as the commodore. I'm responsible for these six wonderful destroyer-cruisers."

"Well, I want to know what your duties are."

I said, "Whatever my staff tells me"

He said, "I want to talk to you tomorrow about this. You don't know what you do, so you and I are going to have a meeting."

The next day there was a luncheon in the fleet flagship. I went over there for lunch and sat down across from him and had about the most delightful two-hour conversation about destroyer ops that I've ever had in my life. After he got through with his blustery way, he said, "Tell me, really, what is going on over there?"

I explained to him how everything was ragtag in the destroyer force. Every six months the poor skipper looked to another commodore as his leader. This month it was ComDesRon 2. Then he'd go back to his home port of Charleston, in the case of whatever ship was from Charleston, and then he'd be with his regular squadron commander. Then his squadron commander would get under way, and some other squadron commander would be in charge. So this skipper had fitness reports from many short periods.

Well, we talked about that for two hours, and Bagley seemed to really all of a sudden appreciate that things were different in today's Navy than when he was a young commander, captain, running around in ships. I thought that was enjoyable, and I got to know that man. What an interesting gent he is. In fact, we kept the entire luncheon thing going; it was one on one. About 1400 I was excused, and he had all the Sixth Fleet admirals waiting out there to come up for a 1330 conference of some kind. And as I was leaving, Admiral Carroll looked at me, and I don't know if he was angry about being kept waiting while a junior was in there with the four-star--I don't know what it was, but he

---

*Admiral David H. Bagley, USN, served as Commander in Chief U.S. Naval Forces Europe and Commander in Chief U.S. Naval Forces Eastern Atlantic from May 1975 to August 1977.

looked at me, never batted an eye, and said, "You know such-and-such an incident in such-and-such a ship?"

"Yes, sir."

"Fire that skipper." Well, that was a direct order.

I said, "Oh, Admiral, you can't do that."

"I can do anything I want to. This is my task group." He was mad as hell. "I want him fired."

I said, "But there's more to the story than you know about. Please let me explain."

"I said fire him." And boom, off went the admiral. I went down to cabin of the Sixth Fleet chief of staff, who was Ted Parker.[*] I said, "Give me a piece of paper." And I must have sat there for an hour. I wrote Admiral Carroll a long explanation of what the real facts were in the case of USS Neversail. Somehow or other, I guess he either forgot about it or that went away. No more was said, and nothing was done. That was the atmosphere.

Paul Stillwell: What do you recall about your relationship during that period with Commander Norm Johnson?[†]

Captain Colbus: Well, that was the low point in my career, because I take great pride in all my shipmates, seniors, peers, juniors.

We were now back from the Med. We were a nine-ship squadron. The flagship was USS Dahlgren. I had never laid eyes on USS Dahlgren. I knew the skipper, Norm Johnson, by reputation. He had been exec of Jonas Ingram before I got there. I had met him at a dinner party before I was ComDesRon 2, and now he was in command of Dahlgren. He had just come back from a successful deployment to the Sixth Fleet. Our paths crossed, but we didn't see each other. He went to the Caribbean on a missile shoot when I returned.

We got to Norfolk on February 7, 1977. I remember that well, because Dick Kinnebrew called me when we got back to tell me that he was sorry he hadn't been down

---

[*] Captain John T. Parker, USN.
[†] Commander Wendell N. Johnson, USN, commanded USS Dahlgren (DDG-43) from October 1975 to June 1977.

there to meet me on the pier. He was then chief of staff for Carrier Group Eight, Admiral C. C. Smith, may he rest in peace.* He said he got so tied up because he'd just been notified the night before that he'd been selected for flag. I said, "Well, I understand your not coming down. Congratulations. Good."

So we'd been home about three weeks when my real flagship was arriving. I would get off <u>Mitscher</u> and let her go back to DesRon 26, where she belonged in the first place. She carried the DesRon 26 logo, not DesRon 2.

<u>Dahlgren</u> moored, and she was a barrel of problems. That's a two-hour story in itself. Having been to oily-rag school, I had a feel for this. She didn't look good, and she just looked neglected. Well, I realized she'd been operating hard, what have you, and there were a few discussions between the skipper and myself.

I made some suggestions, such as that he move off the ship so that in the evening the command duty officer could experience running it. The skipper was in Norfolk, and his family was in Washington. I told him, "It's good for the ship for you to get away, and it's good for you yourself to get away. This 24-hours-a-day, five-days-a-week is not a good situation."

He agreed but said he couldn't get a room in the BOQ. I called up Jimmy Pappas, the naval station exec, and got him a room.† He told me how great it was to get away in the evening in a nice new BOQ room. He even met some of his old buddies and had some discussions in the evening. So he was most pleased. Things were starting to come around. Later on, though, he remarked that I'd ordered him off his own ship.

The ship was home for a few weeks and then had to get under way. It got under way to be the consort for <u>America</u>. We were still celebrating our return from the Med, so I'd say it was three weekends after. I got a call one Saturday night at my next-door neighbor's, where we were having a party. I was told that I'd better come in and see the message traffic on USS <u>Dahlgren</u>. She was having all kinds of engineering problems, from contaminated lube oil to loss of feed water, to being limited in speed. She could do no good, and all <u>America</u> was doing was standing by helping her.

---

*Rear Admiral Carol C. Smith, Jr., USN. Later, as a vice admiral, he died on active duty on 14 October 1983.
†Commander Jimmy Pappas, USN.

That was when I figured it was time to act like a squadron commander, and I went out to my good friend, By Fuller, skipper of America, who had been in oily-rag school with me.* I asked him, "Request you release Dahlgren to return to port and if required, I will have another ship out there as soon as possible. If not, tomorrow, Sunday, I'll have a consort by Monday."

By came back and said no, they were done with ops, he could get along very well. He was returning to port on Tuesday, and Dahlgren would be detached to come home. Dahlgren came limping in on a Sunday. My material officer, Lou Harlow, and I went out by tug to board her.† He is a very, very brilliant engineer; he immediately diagnosed the problem, talked with the chief engineer, came up to see me on the bridge.

I had some problems on the bridge, in that I was not comfortable with regard to the navigation. I did not see what I call my fix with the DR, and I mentioned this to the skipper quietly, "Hey, let's get the ship fixed."‡ I'm talking about navigationally fixed. I made some suggestions there. The ship was proceeding in the channel without good navigational procedures. The captain later stated that I harassed him on the bridge of his ship when I became so concerned about navigation in restricted waters. He got the ship into port.

We had a big meeting that afternoon in the tender Puget Sound, which took Dahlgren alongside and started a massive corrective program. I immediately told the Dahlgren skipper, "Why don't we just get this ship fixed right? How about my getting you off the line for at least four weeks, get you a tender availability, help from the beach?"

He said, "That's exactly what I need." And that was it. There were many little stories that go along with that. The goal was to get Dahlgren repaired properly, no bandaids, but do it the way we talked about at oily rag school.

Well, it's a long, involved story, and we had all kinds of situations. We overcame them. The ship had some problems. One day they burned classified material over in the furnace. Secret material was left out unburned, and, of course, we had to run an

---

*Captain Robert B. Fuller, USN, commanded the USS America (CV-66) from 7 September 1976 to 17 April 1978.
†Lieutenant Louis F. Harlow, USN.
‡DR--dead reckoning (short for deduced reckoning) is a method of navigation whereby one plots a direction and amount of progress from the last well-determined position. The result, known as the DR position, amounts to the best estimate of one's actual position at a given time.

investigation. So all these things were picking on the ship. The ship didn't look good, but we hoped she was coming up. We worked very closely; I moved on the ship, and it just went on and on and on.

In summation, when it was time for the ship to get under way, she went to Gitmo and didn't do well. She had material things to do down there. She took corrective action, so we were still working on squaring Dahlgren away. I went to Gitmo to visit Dahlgren. Now we were into June, and I went to Silver Jubilee, the Queen's silver anniversary, 1977, in June and July.[*]

Anyway, to make a long story short, I wrote a fitness report that I think represented what I've just said here. I went into great detail, talked about many things that I thought reflected on this ship. That was never challenged. In fact, I sent a message on that fitness report to BuPers and to the skipper, saying that the fitness report will be viewed in anybody's eyes as other than favorable. I told the skipper, "I know you will probably want to comment on it, and I'm just giving warning because I know the 15-day time frame here." What I was saying was, "I want to make this stick. I am in Europe, the captain is in Gitmo, and others are in Washington, so stand by."

I never heard about that. Captain Johnson never challenged that report; he did, however, challenge me personally. Then I heard in August of that year from the Inspector General of the United States Navy, and I was taken before a one-man board of inquiry. Admiral Gureck, who'd commanded JFK, was the reviewing officer.[†] I knew him well; he is a real fine gent. He was embarrassed to, I think, have to see me eye to eye. I was embarrassed to go before him, plus have all my friends come out and talk about my character, because the accusation was that I was insensitive and used bigoted language. Now, when you look at the seven charges, each one gets an absolute, "Yes, sir."

"Did you . . .

"Yes, sir."

"Did you . . ."

"Yes, sir."

---

[*]Queen Elizabeth II of Great Britain had ascended to the throne in 1952 on the death of her father, King George VI.
[†]Rear Admiral William A. Gureck, USN.

Again, in what context? There were ethnic jokes, not slurs--jokes at myself, remarks to the skipper that were said to ease a situation about travel to Washington. I had called my chief staff officer a "Frog." He was French. These seven remarks didn't come out very well, and when it was all said and done, why, I was told that I was insensitive and I really should watch myself and get with today's modern program of the ethnic backgrounds of people.

Admiral Engen delivered a non-punitive letter to me.[*] He knew both me and my accuser, and he also was embarrassed. I think a little of the humor came into play here when he got me in there and sat me down. I really, even at this moment, was embarrassed that so many of my friends had to call--I'm talking about Ike Kidd, I'm talking about Bill Read.[†] Ike Kidd personally told me he had never had so many phone calls about anything in his naval career, and the word was, "Louis Colbus? Insensitive? A bigot? It's ludicrous, and we just laugh at it." He said he couldn't laugh at it, and I understood that. Anyway, when Don Engen called me in and told me the investigation was complete, Bill Gureck had to get on to oily rag school. In summation, what was going to happen was I was going to be given a non-punitive letter of caution, and he said, "How does that sit with you, Louis?"

I thought, again, to make light of it. They tell me humor covers up a bad situation. I said, "Well, I'll just go over to B'nai B'rith and let them and the NAACP work it out."[‡] Well, poor admiral, I thought he was going to have apoplexy right there when I said that. I immediately held up my hands and said, "Oh, no, no, no. I'm just making light of a very serious situation. No. If that's what's to be, that's what's to be, and all I want to do is put a lid on this thing." He thanked me for that, and it went away.

In my opinion, and you realize I am talking from my side, what happened later on was that Johnson's fitness report was for one of the 18 officers I was by then grading. I did not rank him number one of the 18, and I had reasons for that. He refuted, as I said, not the contents, but he refuted the report on the grounds of bigotry. Did I mention that Commander Johnson was black? I was personally accused of insensitivity, as I've said.

---

[*] Vice Admiral Donald D. Engen, USN, was Deputy Commander in Chief Atlantic Fleet.
[†] Admiral Isaac C. Kidd, Jr., USN, served as Supreme Allied Commander Atlantic, Commander in Chief Atlantic Command, and Commander in Chief Atlantic Fleet from 30 May 1975 to 30 September 1978.
[‡] NAACP—National Association for the Advancement of Colored People.

Now, months later, maybe the next year, he appealed the two fitness reports I had written, as well as the fitness report that Vice Admiral Rojo Adamson had written, saying, "While Commodore Colbus is new on the scene, relatively speaking, I've watched this ship do a nosedive for the past 18 months and what he says, I can certainly justify. I've seen it for 18 months."[*] His report was challenged at this later date. Both Rojo's and my fitness reports were removed from Norm's jacket and were replaced by one from Admiral Engen, who had been Deputy CinCLantFlt during this trying time.

Paul Stillwell: Hadn't you also made a remark in a light way toward Commander Johnson that he used against you later?

Captain Colbus: Oh, every remark I ever made, yes. Since you brought that up, I guess we'll talk about that. I went looking for the skipper of <u>Dahlgren</u> one Friday afternoon. My cabin was on the port side of the ship, and his was on the starboard side of this gorgeous ship that I called a light cruiser. I was told by somebody in the wardroom, "Oh, the skipper's gone to Washington for the weekend." I sort of grumbled, went up to my room, finished my work, and I left at 1600 or so.

The next Monday, when Norm came back, I said, "Hey, Norm, come on in here. I want to talk to you." I said, "I really felt foolish on Friday, and it isn't just me personally; it's the position. I didn't know you'd gone and I went looking for you. The ship shouldn't know that (a) I don't know you're not here and (b) I have to go looking for you. I didn't want that to be batted around. It's normal when you leave a ship and the senior's embarked to notify the senior. It's not a matter of really requesting; it's a matter of courtesy to request permission to leave the ship, especially if you're going off for the weekend."

He passed that off very nicely and said, "Oh, well, I never did that with your predecessor."

To which I snapped, "He's the curly-headed one. I'm the bald-headed one. Don't mix us up. Things have changed." And that wasn't referring to Dick Kinnebrew. Well, I don't like that kind of atmosphere.

---

[*] Vice Admiral Robert E. Adamson, USN, served as Commander Naval Surface Force Atlantic Fleet from 1975 to 1977.

The next Friday, at 11:00 o'clock, the skipper put his head in my cabin and said, "Request permission to leave the ship, sir."

"Yes, sir. You're headed up for Washington, I bet you."

He said, "Yes."

Now, I decided to make light of this also. I said, "Well, how you going up?" I was thinking about his personal car. I knew he drove an Oldsmobile; we talked about that. Or maybe he was going to take an airplane or ride with one of his buddies.

He said, "I'm going to go right out here and get a bus, which comes right down to the pier."

And I, again, in a light manner, asked, "You gonna ride in the front or the back?"

To which he answered, "You know, things have changed, and we groups are doing just like you fellows did. We've come out of the woodwork."

I said, "You're right. Right on. See you Monday. Have a nice weekend."

One of my charges in this Bill Gureck investigation was, "Have you ever asked the skipper if he rides in the front or the back of a bus?"

And the answer to Bill Gureck was, "Yes, sir."

Norm Johnson came to me when we were in the midst of making the ship well, alongside Puget Sound, about getting the human resources team on board. He said, "You know, that's one of our requirements."

I said, "Yes, but you know that requirement is a stiff one in that the whole ship stops, because you've got to get your chiefs in your chiefs' quarters and the officers in the wardroom. It's very thorough; it's a full five days. I like to do it coming back from the Med in Rota, which they'll do for us. But right now, priorities being what they are, you can't, I don't think, afford that kind of luxury during this four-week upkeep time. What you should do is make this ship a proud, operational fleet steamer. When we come back, we'll be at the crest, and then we can afford that. It's not a luxury it's just a matter of priority. We'll get them over here after your next success."

"You're absolutely right, Commodore. We'll do it later."

I said, "And besides, you want to talk about equal opportunity? I think you and I are the epitome of equal opportunity in this man's Navy."

"How's that, sir?"

"A Jew on the port side and a Jig on the starboard side. You can't beat that." He laughed and shook my hand.

So one of the questions from Admiral Gureck was, "Have you ever referred to Jigs?"

"Yes, sir." So as I say, it was a very, very bad time in context, out of context. I wasn't very smart, I guess. So that's the story.

Paul Stillwell: Eventually he wound up becoming a commodore.*

Captain Colbus: Yes, he's a very smart man and he has a lot to offer, and I don't say that just to be a Pollyanna. The man is brilliant. If the fitness reports were around, it would say where he is--I remember using the words--he is eloquent and elegant. He is cultured, well-groomed, and has many other attributes. He and I just had differences in how that ship should have been brought around, and it never happened, and that was reflected in my evaluation, which was interpreted back to me as bigoted and insensitive and I was picking on him.

As I said, I'm proud of the fact that I was pretty well known at the time, and it was all just ludicrous. But still, not nice. You don't like to get into those cheap-shot things. I give the man credit, he did know what he was doing and he is a good--what I call a good street fighter.

There were other incidents that should have alerted me that he was keeping book on me. At one skippers' conference, I asked, "Are you boys ready for lunch?"

He answered by saying, "I take umbrage to that." But then he'd do it to me. I saw that a Yeoman Johnson had reported on board. I asked Captain Johnson if Yeoman Johnson was a cousin, to which he answered, "He's not even a landsman," which is Yiddish for countryman.

Paul Stillwell: Do you think this inquiry and the letter hurt you any?

---

*Johnson was a fiscal year 1984 selectee for the rank of commodore; he eventually retired as a rear admiral in May 1989.

Captain Colbus: No. It was a non-punitive letter, and it went away. Some of my friends and associates said it did hurt. One very, very senior admiral told me I was the first dumb Jew he'd ever known. He said he thought I was smarter than getting into that trickbag. He also said I didn't use my strongest suit—people knowledge.

Other seniors said I was more hurt by an investigation I did on a ship grounding where I did some administrative foot-dragging to save the skipper. My boss, in retrospect, wanted a pound of flesh for the grounding, which caused us damage. In fact, that skipper was the best and very courageous to do what he did. Anyway, he was not punished, and I later heard I was not popular because I got him off.

As I stated at the beginning of this particular incident, this was the only low point of my career. If I had it to do over again, I would do a General George Patton and kiss the guy instead of slapping him. But I would be more politically attuned. My to-the-point, actual, factual fitness report didn't stick and blew up in my face. Meanwhile, everybody knew of this incident and was telling me I did the proper thing.

A cruiser skipper told me he'd conducted a boat drill at sea, utilizing Dahlgren's boat. He said it was so unsafe and appalling that after one and a half hours of attempts, the cruiser just put her boat in the water and effected the personnel transfer. One fellow commodore sent me a 25-page handwritten note telling me all the faults and problems in Dahlgren when he rode her. Then I saw that commodore's kudos messages and concurrent fitness report for his tour on board. When I next saw him and questioned his inconsistency, he just shrugged it off.

In fact, a black senior officer came up to me at the Norfolk BOQ during this trying time and shook my hand. He said he knew I was just doing my duty, and his community knew I was fair and not prejudiced. Anyway, nobody spoke up officially on my behalf. It was too sensitive an issue. Ike Kidd was known to have remarked, "Louie prejudiced? How could that be when Beetle Forbes, during his retirement, looked out over his audience and referred to his staff mates in CarDiv 6, specially 'Lou the Jew,' or better known as 'Head Hebe'?"[*]

---

[*] Vice Admiral Forbes retired 1 March 1977. His last tour of duty was as Deputy CinCLantFlt under Admiral Kidd.

Paul Stillwell: You mentioned the celebration over in England. What part did the squadron have in the Queen's Silver Jubilee?

Captain Colbus: By that time, John Dixon was ComCarGru 6 located in Mayport, my old Beetle Forbes organization.[*] I was told that I would go with a squadron of four ships, including the attack transport Francis Marion.

Paul Stillwell: She was along to provide boats.

Captain Colbus: She was to provide boats, and she was to provide berthing, in that it was both a midshipman cruise and a visit to Portsmouth for the Silver Jubilee.

John Dixon, being a carrier admiral, wished he had a carrier under his feet, but he embarked with his staff in Francis Marion and graciously turned the operation over to the DesRon 2 crowd. We just ran with it because it was a neat chance to train midshipmen, cross the ocean, visit Portsmouth, and, which we could talk about all day, visit Alborg, Denmark, for the Fourth of July festival. Alborg has the biggest Fourth of July, Independence Day celebration in the world. It pales anything in the United States.

Danes with U.S. connections and all the Danes in the U.S. who have homeland connections go back there for July Fourth. The celebration is held on a 40x2 acre tract of land right outside of Alborg. It's like World War II, VJ Day, and everything all rolled into one for the U.S. sailor. But we're talking about crossing, and we did that, and we had the group exercise for midshipmen, shot the guns, just did about everything and had a ball doing it. And Admiral John Dixon was most gracious in letting us do just that.

My favorite story about that crossing involved my good friend, Captain Pete Carr, aviator.[†]

Paul Stillwell: CO of Francis Marion.

---

[*] Rear Admiral John C. Dixon, Jr., USN, Commander Carrier Group Six.
[†] Captain Nevin P. Carr, USN.

Captain Colbus: CO of Francis Marion. He had all the midshipmen, and before we left, I asked him, "Hey, Pete, you want to play squads left and right with these great ships?" Oh, sure, he wasn't going to miss a trick. Got them lined up, and one day when we were doing squads left, somebody in Pete's ship did squads right, and his ship turned to the right, just like in the movies, while we were going left. Everybody giggled. No, don't touch the radio. That's fine. He doesn't need to be told he's going the wrong way. I later found out he didn't crawl all over the young OOD. We're there to train. I didn't jump on him for going the wrong way.

We were doing, I think, 10 or 12 knots. He turned that ship around and came steaming back into formation. He swung that ship into station as well as any destroyer would have done it. Big—as we called them, elephants, with an aviator in command, his first time to do tictacs, and boy, what a scene that was to see. Pete Carr had to absolutely be one of the top skippers of this era. He was very, very keen with young people, and you talk about a perfect man for a perfect situation, go over and meet the Queen and train the midshipmen, he was it. He went on to command Guadalcanal after that.

Paul Stillwell: I've met him because I had a reserve cruise in Francis Marion about two or three months before your trip to Europe.

Captain Colbus: Then you know of what I speak. Very, very fine gent, great deployment. My only disappointment was I didn't get to carry the Moths, little sailing craft. There was a group there in Norfolk that were very friendly with my boss at the time, Thor Hanson; one of the Moth sailors dated his daughter.[*] By the way, Dahlgren was supposed to be the flagship but didn't make it, so we took Conyngham instead.

These sailing boys came down to visit; they were going to put their Moth boats on the ship. We were going to stow them. I didn't have the stowage space. I went to Pete Carr and said, "May we stow them with you? All we're doing is carrying them over there because the group that sails Moths in Portsmouth, England, came to Norfolk for the centennial, therefore, we're going to take them back, reciprocate."

---

[*] Rear Admiral Carl T. Hanson, USN, Commander Cruiser-Destroyer Group Eight.

Well, everybody was happy, and I happened to mention it in my briefing, which was one of those dumb things. If you have any chance of there being a "No," don't ask; just do it. Then, if you do get a negative response after the fact, you can always say, "I didn't know that."

In briefing Admiral Dixon one day about what was going on, I said, "By the way, I'm proud to say that we're going to have aboard <u>Francis Marion</u>—and the skipper's been most cooperative—a dozen of these Moth boats so the civilian U.S. team that flies over can race them, and that's going to be part of our involvement."

Well, all of a sudden it became, "Do we have permission? Shouldn't we get permission?"

"Let's do it."

"What if we lose them? What if we break one?" All of a sudden we had these many questions. I guess if I had broken one or bent one, I'd have worried about that when we got there. All of a sudden, it became too complicated.

I went to Thor Hanson and said, "I don't know how I'm going to tell your friend, but we can't carry those boats. Maybe we can put them in an airplane." So I tried to get them in an airplane. No, that didn't work. We never did take the boats. But halfway over I got the word one day from—I guess it was Admiral Dixon in <u>Francis Marion</u>, "Do we have Moth boats?"

"No, sir."

"Are you sure?"

"Yes, sir."

"Are they in your ship?"

"No, sir."

It was just, "Did you do it? Did you do it behind my back?" I told him, no, we weren't going to do it. It all of a sudden became too big a deal, and I was sorry I asked or mentioned it.

Somebody back on one of the staffs had heard about this and said, "Well, there they are, out carrying Moth boats, going to get us in trouble with transporting things with the shipping lines and what have you." So maybe it was best I didn't take them. But that became a major, major cause celebre on the way over. "Where are the Moth boats?" I'll never forget that. And the sailing team had given me a nice send-off, and they weren't a bit unhappy because they realized the situation. So I know it wasn't any of them, but somebody on the staff picked this up and exercised it again.

Paul Stillwell: Was there a reception at which you got to meet the Queen?

Captain Colbus: No, I saw her but didn't meet her. I had too many other things to do in Portsmouth. In fact, we were so well received there and we had so much interplay in Portsmouth that during follow-on trips, hardly any of us ever went to London. We just stayed in Portsmouth.

Paul Stillwell: Any specific things to relate about the Denmark celebration?

Captain Colbus: Yes. When we went to Denmark, I was embarked in Conyngham. The skipper was John Leder, a true, genuine, bachelor—handsome devil.[*] We got there and this entire town had turned out to welcome the ship, and welcome it they did. They just didn't leave a stone unturned as to entertaining us, making us part of the group, and we had a very, very successful three or four days. We made lots and lots of friends over there. They dined and wined us to the point that we just never had a moment to ourselves.

Danes are most hospitable to begin with, and for a special occasion, they felt that they were obligated to us. They didn't think we were sent there as an assignment. We came there because we volunteered and we wanted to, which is, of course, fun enough. As far as anything in particular, it was just series of events after series of events. Dances, and everybody was taken care of, hotel rooms were provided. We were moored in downtown Alborg. We learned how to drink Aquavit, which is great stuff; I still keep a bottle of it at home.

We learned that the Danish community in the United States is very big, powerful, and wealthy enough to go over there once a year for this particular festival, and it all emanates out of a town in California. All these people who came to the United States have

---

[*] Commander John F. Leder, USN, commanded the USS Conyngham (DDG-17) from 14 October 1976 to 12 July 1978.

been very prosperous, mainly in the Midwest, with everything from dairies to nurseries. They've done well. The celebration always has a guest. The year before us, the featured speaker and center of attention was the Danish pianist Victor Borge. The year we were there, it was a Ford. He was one of the Fords from the Ford Motor Car family, a young fellow, 28 years old, who was the center of attention with his young wife. The following year it was Art Buchwald.[*] They get that kind of celebrity and that kind of attention.

When we got back that fall, we got a letter stating that 80 Danes were coming to the United States and they were going to make a tour. If I'd allow it, they would come to Norfolk. Reciprocity is the name of the game. I'd be delighted. We went off on our own. The squadron, with the ships that had been there, formed a committee, welcomed the Danes, and we brought them to Norfolk. They only spent a day and a night. They stayed in Williamsburg, and we bused them to Norfolk. These were 80 of the same folks we'd played with all summer.

We divided them up among ten destroyers, even though eight of the ships had never been to Alborg. We had all these people separated and then got them together in a group. We took them down and introduced them to the mayor and showed them Norfolk. In a ten-hour period we introduced them to Norfolk, Virginia Beach, and the Navy. They had lunch aboard the ships. We then went and spent the evening with them in Williamsburg, and they were gone the next day. We still get feedback. As a matter of fact, I bumped into somebody the other day who said, "Boy, we were over in Alborg last year and they're still talking about the Conyngham visit."

Paul Stillwell: Sounds like you made a good impression.

Captain Colbus: They made a good impression on us too. As I say, those kind of things just made deployments so great that sailors were dying to get on them.

Paul Stillwell: Are there any other of your skippers besides Commander Mosman that you would particularly like to discuss?

---

[*] Art Buchwald, who served in the Marine Corps in World War II, has for many years written a humor column that is syndicated in many newspapers.

Captain Colbus: I mentioned earlier that Tom Anderson had taken command of <u>Mullinnix</u> by this time. We had the best time together. He took the ship to Coastal Dry Dock and Shipbuilding Company in New York City, the old Brooklyn shipyard.* He did a magnificent job. That crew never lost its spirit, that crew never lost its camaraderie. They did move off the ship and they moved into a barracks up there.

I could give you a two-hour dissertation on what he did up there and accomplished as far as remodeling. About every six weeks or so, I went up there with my material officer to see him. They seemed to like it, and everything was going fine. The shipyard was pretty much, I would say, under test at the time as to what kind of product they were putting out. And they had some other ships up there. Tom did a magnificent job.

We had Saturday reviews up there, and I'd go up and stand there, and it looked like boot camp—the young <u>Mullinnix</u> sailors marching by with banners and halyards, taped music, an award ceremony, out on a grinder, in this old New York shipyard. I was so proud of <u>Mullinnix</u>, and I'd come back and rave about it. Well, it was time to have their LOE, light-off exam. Again, I went up, as I was charged to do, and they did very well.

Now I'm going to get into the shipyard. The founder, president, and number-one operating officer of that shipyard was Charlie Montanti. Charlie and I became big buds. I found out that Charlie was of a fine Italian background; his father had come to this country as an Italian shoemaker. He'd grown up as a poor boy and developed this great organization. He was very obviously a talented and successful businessman. When I got back, I went over to make my report to SurfLant. Someone asked me, "What do you think of this shipyard?"

So I described something I had seen myself. The president, Charlie Montanti, was walking through the shipyard, which is a dirty environment. He was in his very, very expensive business suit and kid shoes. Some yard bird comes running up to him, grimy, dirty, maybe 60 years old, grabbed him by the arm, and said, "Hey, Charlie, if you don't get me an operator down here to help me on that crane, you're going to have more problems because I can't keep up with it. I'm tired of talking about it. Where's my assistant?"

---

* This had previously been the New York Naval Shipyard in Brooklyn, closed in the mid-1960s as a Defense Department cost-cutting measure and made available to private industry.

The president turned to the yard bird and said, "I'll have him down there this morning." He turned to one of his aides, who was walking around with us and had a walkie-talkie, and said, "Make that happen." I checked on it. By noon, that man had it. I said to the man at SurfLant, "Now, when you have a shipyard that operates like that, you know it's successful."

Another thing, during the LOE for <u>Mullinnix</u>, we were all sitting in the wardroom, which had not been finished yet, waiting to learn the results. Charlie was sitting there with his walkie-talkie and two of his assistants. If you needed something, Charlie got it. That was pretty high-priced talent. And, as I said, they did well on the LOE.

What I'm leading up to is the ship transferred from Destroyer Squadron Two to Destroyer Squadron Six in Charleston. They were getting under way on the sixth of December 1978, and they weren't coming back to Norfolk; they were going to Charleston. On the 15th of December, the official change would occur when I would call Destroyer Squadron Six and say, "You've got the ship." Families had moved; everything was settled. The last weekend I was up in November, Tom took me up and showed me the unit commander's cabin. On there it said, "ComDesRon Two, Captain Louis Colbus, USN." He said, "You're going to ride this ship to Charleston with us, aren't you? I've got to take this ship with pride to my new home."

I said, "Oh, absolutely." Well, I went back and had no idea of doing anything but what I'd told Tom, and put in a TAD request.* It was on a weekend. I was going to go to New York Friday morning since they were getting under way, as I recall, on Friday afternoon. We were going to arrive in Charleston on Sunday. Anyway, it was a weekend journey.

About three days before it was to happen, I got a personal call from Admiral Bill Read. "Louis," he said, "I know that you want to go, and I know you like going to sea, but you have got to cut the umbilical cord on that ship. Let the skipper have the ship."

"But, but, but, but . . . "

"Louis, I'd rather you didn't go on that trip. Let him arrive down there with his new people and start anew and just cut the cord with you up here."

---

* TAD—temporary additional duty.

I went over to see him and explained to him, "Admiral, you just don't understand, but let me make you understand. It goes back." And I told him about the Jonas Ingram days. I said, "I'm vain enough to tell you that Tom wants me to go."

"No, he doesn't."

Hey, I didn't get to go, after I'd said three times, "Please, please, please." I had to call Tom, but I didn't tell him why. I just said, "Hey, Tom, I can't make it." And that was, I thought, a very, very insensitive thing. Tom wanted it, and I knew he wanted it, but I as the squadron commander had to comply with probably wiser feelings and decisions, so I didn't get to go on that ship.

The other disappointment I had was after young Grant Sharp brought USS King out of a very, very bad shipyard period in New Orleans.* The Navy brought King to Portsmouth, Virginia, and finished the overhaul. I worked very, very closely, and became, I'm glad to say, very good friends with young Grant Sharp. Grant took the ship to the Med on its first deployment. He was getting relieved over there, and he came back to me and said, "Hey Commodore, how about coming over and being the guest speaker at my change of command, which is in Ashdod, the Israeli port just south of Haifa?"

Well, of course, again I was elated, but this was going to cost big bucks for me to go over there. But before I even got my travel approved, I went down to see my rabbi and gave him my notes for my change of command speech. The first two paragraphs of it were going to be in Hebrew. Now, I can read Hebrew, but I can't translate it. So I got my rabbi to write out the first two paragraphs in Hebrew, and then I'd shift to English. They were going to have the mayor at the ceremony, along with other dignitaries, and I just thought, "Boy, this is going to be dynamite. This is going back to the homeland. We're going to dazzle them."

Then I got the call from Admiral Read: "You can't go. That's really not for you to do. You're not in the Sixth Fleet." I offered to pay my own expenses and go on no-cost orders. Again, no! So I was denied I'd say the privilege of going to Israel to do that. Grant never understood. He felt that I was reneging on him, but so be it.

---

* USS King (DDG-41) underwent an AAW upgrade in the late 1970s and was recommissioned in 1977. Following the recommissioning, Commander Grant A. Sharp, USN, served as the commanding officer from August 1977 to June 1979.

You asked about the skippers. Every one of them is an absolute genius. I could take each one of them and discuss his attributes. These skippers were highly selected and thoroughly screened. The toughest thing I had to do was separate the number one from the number three, because many times where one was strong in this suit, the other shined in another area. Nobody's perfect, but it's some selection process, really. What I always used to judge them by—and I told them this—do I want my son serving in your ship? And to a man, yes. Now, of course, maybe some more than others, but you'll teach more seamanship, that fellow will teach him more ethics, that fellow will teach him all.

Paul Stillwell: Is there one that you would single out as the top guy?

Captain Colbus: No, I couldn't do that. I've mentioned Gene Mosman. If I had it to do over again and could mold myself, I'd be a Gene Mosman—brilliant, low key, no nonsense, had a tremendous sense of humor, that kind of thing. Yes. Gene Mosman and John Carbone and I still meeting for social gathering, just for the three couples. (John commanded USS DuPont.)

Paul Stillwell: In World War II and in the '50s, destroyer divisions and squadrons were composed essentially of sister ships. You, on the other hand, had a very disparate crowd. Could you describe that?

Captain Colbus: That's because of the operational schedules today. Fewer ships, more operations, and you don't transit as a sister-ship squadron. You used to line up 762, 763, 764. They went to the yard together for three months, came out of the yard together, went to Gitmo together. Those were, as you said, a true squadron in spirit, in operations, in everything. You knew when your fellow skipper was going to come left. He didn't even have to pick up the radio and tell you. It was a symphony. This was what I explained to Admiral David Bagley when we were over there in Gaeta—that it ain't like that anymore. You can be told many, many reasons why that is so: squadrons are bigger, operations are longer, shipyard overhauls are now a year, and this goes on and on and on.

The attempt we made to bring it back into focus was a squadron realignment on April 8, 1978. DesRon 2, which had been to Europe and the Caribbean and done all the operational things with the commodore and flagship, all of a sudden changed. Now DesRon 2, DesRon 4, DesRon 6, and DesRon 10, and DesRon 12 became maintenance, training, and administration squadrons.

Now the commodore, instead of embarking on a ship and making up his squadron as best he could and going off and fighting the war and coming back, and then thinking about the shipyard, he stayed home and took care of the stay-at-home things. He went and talked to the wives when the ship was deployed. He was the center of contact. He was the fellow who'd been through three overhauls with the ship in Coastal Dry Dock, and he knew the idiosyncrasies and the weaknesses. When you do it enough, you get good at it. So it's a great concept. That was an attempt to put cohesiveness into the squadron again, and it has.

As I mentioned, when I was embarked in USS <u>Mitscher</u> as ComDesRon 2, the insignia on the deckhouse was ComDesRon 26. I didn't get exercised over that. But in today's world, you've got 17 or 18 ships in DesRon 2, and they carry the DesRon 2 logo. When they deploy now, they'll deploy with ComDesRon 22, a high-numbered squadron, but they still keep their logo and their identity. This also gives the operational squadron commander a great advantage. He's no longer running around the waterfront taking care of things that the squadron commander should care for, because it's common to all eight of his ships. He now sits in his flagship and reads his op order, he goes to the pre-sail briefings, he does the training routines at Dam Neck and Norfolk, and what have you, and he's purely concerned with operational items.

The low-numbered squadron, by the way, is a post-squadron/post-cruiser assignment, so it's really a bonus Navy command. He is the one who does all the things. The West Coast is not on this program yet. As I said, this has been around since April 1978, and was instigated between—I don't know who was the really pusher of it, but it was instigated between Ike Kidd and Bill Read. Bill Read called me to his office, because I was in port at the time, having just returned, and said, "What do you think of this idea?"

"I'm a status quo guy. I'd rather just keep things as they are."

"That's good. You keep that, but come to our meetings and work on this study group." And we did, and that's where we got that high-numbered, low-numbered concept.

For my aviators, it's the easiest thing in the world to explain. It was difficult for me to explain the concept to destroyer sailors, but I say to my aviator friends, "Here's the way it is. The high-numbered squadron commander is comparable to a CAG, the air wing commander, who's out there flying airplanes. The low-numbered squadron commander is like the FitWing, the fighter wing, the light attack, the medium attack wing aviator. He's at home doing everything that you have to do to get the planes ready to deploy. You're CAG if you're at sea, high number. You're FitWing if you're home."

"Right."

And the submariners understand it. That's the way submarines operate. Of course, they don't operate in a group as we do, but they have a stay-at-home comsubron who does all these things that the low-numbered desron now does.

Paul Stillwell: How did you manage to keep track of how your ships and skippers were doing when you weren't with them?

Captain Colbus: That's the task right there. Well, I guess it's like your child. You know what he's doing when he's away at college, and you know how well he's doing. You get reports, the grapevine, you knew him before he left, you know what to expect. It's not difficult. And the operational squadron commander is talking to you all the time. So it sounds difficult, but really, you can't put it on paper. It just happens.

Paul Stillwell: It works.

Captain Colbus: It works, yes. Of course, he gets a fitness report, too, if he's at sea for six months with this commodore. On a Med deployment, he'll get a fitness report, which is an input to the stay-at-home squadron commander. I've lost touch with what's involved there, but there's a good pipeline and a good feedback.

Paul Stillwell: What is your recollection of your boss, Rear Admiral Walters?

Captain Colbus: Well, I started off in the operational business with Thor Hanson, who, without a doubt, lives up to his background as a Rhodes Scholar. The man is so brilliant and perceptive that it's mind-boggling. At the same time, the man is so down to earth, so human, I can't believe it. If you wanted to pick the father of the year, look to Thor. If you wanted to pick the scholar of the year, look to Thor. If you want the admiral of the year, look to Thor.

Here's a perfect story about Thor Hanson. My brother-in-law, a true civilian newspaperman from Gastonia, North Carolina, was visiting us. We all ended up out at Dam Neck for a group party. CruDesGru 8 was having their annual Halloween party, and I took my brother-in-law, who is a wit and a very, very keen observer of people, being a newspaperman. We went out there and I was introducing him around. He just couldn't take his eyes off or his ears away from the country western singer, who was standing up on the stage with one foot up on a chair, a guitar, a ten-gallon hat, and a nice neatly cut Western style suit. I think he was singing "Tie a Yellow Ribbon," whatever, and these beautiful notes were coming out. My brother-in-law said, "Man, that has to be the best singer in the world. I've never heard of anything like that. Is he a pro from around here, or is he national? How do you get talent like that for a private party?"

I said, "He's neither. That's our admiral. That's Thor Hanson."

My brother-in-law, to this day, asks, "Whatever happened to Admiral Hanson?" When he met him, he expected to see an old, stiff, formal gent. No. He put his guitar down and came over, doing it all with a nice flair, not, "I'm here because I have to and I want to be one of the boys." He, of course, was one of our students out at Idaho Falls. In fact, he relieved Dick Nicholson as ComCruDesGru 8.[*]

Then he was relieved by Admiral Walters, who was my operational boss for a while. Then, as I say, we went to the high number, low numbers. Walters is a very, very brilliant engineer. He's also a missileer, and he certainly knows his ships. He took great pride in getting around each and every one of his ships on his surprise inspections. He loved to do them, for instance, on a Friday at 1600, and I used to shake my head and say,

---

[*] Rear Admiral Richard E. Nicholson, USN.

"Admiral, you say you're helping those people, but they don't need help on Friday afternoon. Let's be realistic."

"No, you don't understand. They really want me to come down there and see how well they're doing."

"Yes, sir. How about Tuesday at 1400?" He was very devoted, hard-working, and spent lots of hours. He kept a real tight rein on the ships. He had his cruisers that he directly commanded. He had two of us commodores here in Norfolk in the low-numbered squadrons, and then about three or four high-numbered all the time. He would have us to his Thursday briefings. As I say, he was very intimate with the ships, loved to come down, loved to see them, loved to go aboard them. He was quick to give guidance where it was needed, and could be very, very disappointed if one of us, one of the squadron commanders, wasn't on the scene first to correct whatever, which is only fair.

Paul Stillwell: Did you ever get him to change his schedule for surprise inspections?

Captain Colbus: I shouldn't say they were always on Friday. That happened maybe twice, but they were always around 1600, which is a good time, probably, to observe a ship. And then, in all fairness to him, he was very understanding, because I'll never forget when he went aboard <u>Richard E. Byrd</u>. <u>Richard E. Byrd</u> was one of the smart ships of the squadron, had a great reputation, had a skipper who was one of these water-walkers.

Paul Stillwell: Who was that?

Captain Colbus: He's ComDesRon 20 now—Bob Goodwin.* Now, Bob Goodwin was an officer whose leadership style, if I'd tell you about it without giving this prelude, you'd say, "What was he doing?"

I walked aboard the ship one day, and he was just a bundle of energy, a jumper. "Hey, that's great, let's go, Commodore. I want to take you up and show you so-and-so." We started walking up the starboard side of the ship, and there was an 18-year-old seaman standing there, scraping, cleaning, whatever. He snapped to attention, because they were

---

* Captain Robert L. Goodwin, Jr., USN.

well trained. He was standing there, and Bob came up, took him physically, and pushed him right into the bulkhead. "Look at you. You've got white socks on. Why do you stand here? Do you know you just embarrassed me in front of my commodore? Boy, what's he going to think I'm running over here—some kind of a ragtag outfit? Man, you just don't represent me well today."

That sailor was disappointed, and I was embarrassed. Five minutes later he came running after the skipper to show him his black socks. I had never seen anything like it. Bob Goodwin was the most, I guess, outgoing, you could say, and quick to react, never worried about, "I don't want the commodore to hear this, I don't want to embarrass anybody, him, me." And he was just so forthright and so open that he had that crew behind him like nothing I've ever seen.

Well, he brought the ship back after a very successful Med deployment, and Admiral Walters, about two days after he was in port, decided to visit the ship in one of these surprise inspections. I wasn't available; I was off somewhere. So he went to the ship with his ComCruDesGru 8 goon squad along with him. He had two material officers and an admin officer and his aide, so about four or five would hit the ship, go to a cabin or stateroom to change into overalls, and do an inspection. They did it that day, and there was no skipper on board. The exec was there, of course.

The admiral took that aboard, because he found everything so neat, except one 5-inch gun mount. I'll never forget that. Some grease was dripping in there, and he got all upset about that. But because they knew about it and because they had it logged and the gunner's mate was aware of it, they got all kind of kudos and "well done" and, "Boy, skipper, I'm glad to see you don't have to be on deck all the time." Let the exec run it. So it did have its positive feedbacks.

Paul Stillwell: Any more on the destroyer squadron to talk about?

Captain Colbus: Every time you ask me that, I could go on all day. But that's pretty much the flavor of the squadron. Good times, coming up in material condition, understanding at all levels, and lots of assets and lots of help being given from the tenders, from the shipyards, and all you had to do was ask for it, and it was then no disgrace being late getting under way.

There's a good comparison. When I drove my destroyer, I would get under way, and Admiral Jim Doyle pointed this out in one of his talks to us when we were between command and oily rag school. He said, "I'm just like you before I went to nuclear power school." (He went there, I think, as a commander.) He said, "I used to get my ship under way and just limp from casrep to casrep making the turns."*

I guess that's sort of maybe the way we all did it. For instance, I'd get under way with Jonas Ingram. Let's say we couldn't get a vacuum on number-two main. If we had a vacuum on number one, we said, "Fine, we'll go." Then going out the channel, miraculously somebody did something down there, then you had the vacuum, and by the time you were at the sea buoy, you had two screws turning. In this era, from '76 on, after the oily rag school, it was no disgrace to say, "I need a two-hour delay to fix a steam valve. I'm not going to get under way tomorrow because of so-and-so," which was good. You weren't perceived as a candy ass hanging back. At the same time, you were can-do, but not can-do to the point that you would get under way on one screw. And that's the way it should have been. So that was quite a big change in philosophy.

The other change in philosophy was ship handling. Now, you didn't ding ships anymore. It's not "ha-ha" at the club afterwards if you moored your ship and you took three stanchions down while you were doing it. I was raised in an era where World War II-trained men had become the commanding officers. They were all bravado and, "Watch me with my ship." If he'd ding something, as long as it wasn't serious, we called the damage controlman. The DC was up there, carried a torch with him, and that was it after a landing, fixing stanchions, waterways, whatever.

Then we got to the point we couldn't put a scratch on them. Again, I think there's a happy medium. Because I remember I used to get after my skippers pretty much about mooring, "They pay you to moor the ship. They pay him to run the plant. Let's do it." And I didn't mean he had to do it himself, but he had to prove himself as a competent ship handler. That really permeates the entire crew: "Boy, our skipper can really handle that ship." Of course, you let your other people do it, the training aspect of it.

---

* Casrep—casualty report.

Well, with people like Gene Mosman, I'd tell him, "Come on, Gene, you can do that. Why don't you do it yourself?" These are bigger ships. It's not "ha-ha" when you ding them anymore, and then the 963 skippers really had a lament about handling the ships themselves. I used to say, though, I wasn't in a position to say I'd done it. They said they really had problems doing it on their own without tugs and pilots. And I'm pretty much in agreement. Once you get tugs, get the pilots.

Now, there's a group of naval officers—old school, new school—who say there is nothing wrong with using tugs if you control them. Don't depend on an outside source such as a pilot. Well, if you get tugs—I never had much luck controlling tugs—use the pilot. But, anyway, that's where we stood.

Lots of times I went to bat for the fellow who was handling a ship. I'll refer back to Richard E. Byrd. She was making a moor when she was with StaNavForLant in Hamburg, Germany, and she raked the side pretty good. It was one of those. Within a matter of moments, an op immediate message was sent, calling it a collision. Well, I immediately went out and said I'd investigate it; I didn't have to go over, just give me a full report. Bob Goodwin knocked some stanchions down and, I think, put a ding in the torpedo deck. My personal message to him was, "That's one. I did three when I was in command. Don't try to beat my record," or something like that, which gave those skippers confidence. And that starts at the top.

I know since I've gone from the squadron, different admirals view it differently. If you put a ding in your ship, that was dumb; therefore, you're not exercising good judgment. Another thing, too, don't ding it so that you can't get under way, because we need you too much. We don't have substitutes. So we've become very, very cautious. As I say, I think there is a good, happy medium there somewhere.

Paul Stillwell: How was this kind of an ethic, if you want to call it that, communicated? Was it spread by word of mouth that it was no longer permissible to put dings in ships?

Captain Colbus: Yes, by word of mouth. It can also be the written policy. A senior would state, "I've had too many groundings, that goes without saying. We've spent too much time, effort, money on repairing ships for structural damage while coming alongside. Tugs are available. Use them." It may be that blunt. Then what are you going to do? If you're doing it yourself and you ding, ah-ha, I told you so.

Paul Stillwell: The reverse of it is the junior officers don't get as much experience and training.

Captain Colbus: Of course, you can also get people, and I call them non-seafaring people, who say, "What's the big deal about getting a ship under way? That's no big deal. That's why we have tugs and that's why we pay pilots." You don't understand the crew. It's an untapped reserve. That's my skipper up there. That's my exec. We're better ship handlers than USS "Neversail."

Paul Stillwell: Is it better to use the tug and pilot with the Spruances because they're so big?

Captain Colbus: Because they're so big and because they have that big sonar dome. They're very deep. On the other hand, they respond quickly. The screw operates at a constant speed, and movement occurs due to the pitch of the blades. There you may call it a propeller. On every other ship it's a screw. They have a reversible-pitch propeller. The propeller, of course, has vanes that close and the ship stops. It's like brakes. So it would be easier to move the ship 15 feet. It's more difficult to move a straight-stick destroyer.

Paul Stillwell: How did you wind up spending so much time in the Atlantic and so little in the Pacific during the course of your career?

Captain Colbus: Just good luck, I guess.

Paul Stillwell: Was that your preference?

Captain Colbus: No. In fact, that's a lament of my wife: "We know the East Coast. When I married you at Key West, it was a big deal. I enjoyed Newport. Thank God," she said, "not Charleston but Jacksonville." So I had duty and homeports on the East Coast. You're right. When we steamed around the world, we had a port call in San Diego, and that's about it.

Paul Stillwell: It's unusual.

Captain Colbus: I don't think so. He's an East Coast sailor; he's a West Coast sailor. I think it's probably more unusual finding a sailor who has done both.

Paul Stillwell: Oh?

Captain Colbus: Economies, travel funds.

Paul Stillwell: What was your dream sheet request after that?

Captain Colbus: I went to ComCarGru 8, but that wasn't what my first set of orders said. My orders said I'd be going back to OpTEvFor, which is a story in itself. It was said to reflect back to my insensitivity toward minority groups that one senior naval officer said that he didn't want me at sea, because I didn't know how to treat minorities. I think he was just coming from the record, he didn't know me. His attitude was, "Don't send him out to sea, and especially if I'm around, because we don't have room for people who aren't ethnically oriented."

I was supposed to go to sea duty with CarGru 4, and that was changed for a couple of reasons. Then no more sea duty for me, even though I wanted to go to a carrier group. I was told to go ashore, stay in Norfolk. I had put OpTEvFor for shore duty, but my first choice was a carrier group chief of staff. Com6thFlt, Admiral Watkins, was quoted as saying he didn't want a bigot in the Med.* He had been BuPers when I was on the carpet for Norm Johnson.† Therefore, no sea duty. I was asked if I wanted to go to Gitmo and be the training commodore down there.

---

* Vice Admiral James D. Watkins, USN, commanded the Sixth Fleet from 1 September 1978 to July 1979.
† Vice Admiral Watkins served as Chief of Naval Personnel from 10 April 1975 to 21 July 1978.

"That's fine. Love to."

"Well, go ask your wife."

"I don't have to ask my wife. You're talking to me."

"Your family has to move."

"My family, that's fine."

And Hi Gurney said, "Call me back in three days if your wife and you want to go."

I said, "I'm telling you right now I want to go." I told my wife we were probably going to Gitmo. Her reaction was, "Oh, great," but I never got a call back.

Anyway, when I was going to CarGru 4, this squadron realignment that we discussed came about, and they said I could stay there another year and a half. That was fine. Then it was also rumored, "Well, your friend doesn't think he did the right thing with your ethnic problem, doesn't think you should be at sea in command because you're going to ruin the image of the Navy." Then all of a sudden it was time to leave DesRon 2 after three years, and my orders came out to OpTEvFor. I was delighted and went over to see my predecessor. I was going to the 70 shop because 30, which I'd been in before, had by now disappeared. Ship evaluation was no longer in vogue; now it was surface systems. I was going to go to be that division chief, and that was fine. I went over to see Captain Baumgardner and said, "Yes, I'll be here to relieve you."*

"Great. Look forward to it. I'm going to be relieved in September. I'll be here."

One day I got a call from Rear Admiral Bob Dunn, who was ComCarGru 8; he had relieved C. C. Smith.† "What's this I hear, that you're going to OpTEvFor?"

"Yes, sir."

"Would you consent to come out and be my chief of staff?"

And I said, "Absolutely, but . . ."

He said, "There's no buts about it. I need you out here. We'll just cash in on your former carrier background and what you've done. So if you're willing, I'll get you over here, get your orders changed. You're coming."

"Thank you."

---

* Captain John S. Baumgardner, USN.
† Rear Admiral Robert F. Dunn, USN, served as Commander Carrier Group Eight from 19 May 1978 to 24 May 1980. The oral history of Dunn, who retired as a vice admiral, is in the Naval Institute collection.

Paul Stillwell: Did he know you?

Captain Colbus: Oh, yes. We'd been together in <u>Saratoga</u> when I was in Beetle Forbes's staff.

I got a call from Vice Admiral Gus Kinnear's office, and it said, "You're coming over to be in the aviation end again. And the admiral, if you have the time [all the nice words], would love to talk to you."[*]

"My honor. When?"

"Tuesday afternoon, 1300."

"Fine."

I went over, thought I'd get the nice treatment, cup of coffee, 20 minutes, if I was lucky, a pat on the fanny and out the door. He was there with me, I'd say it was over two hours, maybe pushing three, talking philosophy. This is the way it is. "Louis, we're glad to have you." I mean, it wasn't just pumping sunshine. It was, "This is the way it is in AirLant. This is what we're doing. Bob wants you. I'm delighted to have you." He really made me feel good.

And I'll never forget, as I got up to leave, I guess I just wanted to grab him and give him a kiss on the lips, and he wouldn't have liked that, a tough, rough guy. Instead, I told him, "Admiral, you just don't know how I appreciate the time, the opportunity, all those things. This is really a fine introduction. I'm going out there and I'm going to work my tail off. I'm going to work so hard to live up to all the things."

He said, "I wouldn't have had you over here if that is your reaction."

"Why is that?"

"Don't change a bit. You're here because of what you've done so far, and we want you here because of the way you are. Now, if you get out there and start busting ass and trying too hard, you're going to ruin it. Just do what you've always done. We want you for you."

"Right!" What a nice thought. And, of course, I was there for three years.

---

[*] Vice Admiral George E. R. Kinnear, USN, served as Commander Naval Air Force Atlantic Fleet from 31 March 1978 to 31 July 1981.

Paul Stillwell: He sounds like a psychology major.

Captain Colbus: Oh, yes. He's well known for his brilliance and charisma. The admiral is a self-made man, seaman in the Navy, all the way to four stars.

Paul Stillwell: You said he was talking philosophy. What did that include?

Captain Colbus: I'm talking about AirLant philosophy, what to expect; it's a different beat over here. You have to give up this number-one position. You don't mind being number two. No, no, not at all. How I see it from the top, where our Navy's going. There was no particular topic, but he discussed everything in general. It would have been a fine briefing for all the AirLant skippers, and he took the time out to do it with me individually, which I appreciated.

Paul Stillwell: When you say being number two, do you mean being a chief of staff as opposed to in command.

Captain Colbus: Exactly.

Paul Stillwell: What were some of your experiences with Admiral Dunn?

Captain Colbus: I've talked about all these people whom I admire, but Bob Dunn is truly special. I've said it before, and I say it now: Admiral Dunn is the most profound individual I've ever met. That includes clergy, family, anyone. He has a feel for things that is absolutely amazing. He can pick up on things that you just don't imagine he would even consider. He's not what you'd call a flamboyant man. He's a very friendly and open man. He has a temper that I saw maybe twice, nothing that you'd write home about. But let me give you an example.

    A reserve chaplain rabbi who was a good friend of mine, Bruce Kahn, came to see me one day.* We'd met in destroyer days; now he was here in Norfolk for active duty. He

---

* Lieutenant Commander Bruce E. Kahn, CHC, USNR.

was sitting in the cabin just shooting the breeze, having a good time, and in came Admiral Dunn. I said, "Well, Admiral, may I present my friend, Chaplain Rabbi."

Bob Dunn sat down, put his feet up, and said, "May I join the conversation?"

"Oh, yes, sir."

We talked a while, and I guess after about ten minutes of small talk, he said, "Rabbi, I never asked Louis this because I'm really embarrassed, but I know rabbi means teacher, so I want to ask you this . . ." He didn't say dumb question, but unsophisticated. He indicated that he was not conversant. "Let me ask you this question. You'll find, Rabbi, that between your music, literature, and your whatever . . ."

Bob Dunn asked Rabbi Kahn a question that caused the rabbi to sit there and look at Admiral Dunn with amazement. The rabbi was dumbfounded. He went over, grabbed Bob Dunn by the hand, and said, "If one of my congregants could ask that question, I'd feel I was complete. Where did you learn that kind of logic and background?"

"Well, I read a little bit."

Holy smokes. They got into an hour, hour and a half conversation on religion that was really high level. That's when I found out that Admiral Dunn reads a little. Fantastic, he really is.

Paul Stillwell: How was he at sea?

Captain Colbus: The minute you ask that, I see him sitting in combat, running the battle group. He'd sit in the admiral's chair in combat, with his left foot up on the chair by the heel, leaning on his right and smoking a cigar. He's not a great smoker but occasionally a cigar, a World War II-type battle group commander. He was completely relaxed, knew what was going on.

He really and truly exercised and proved what they then called the CWC concept. This was the composite warfare commander—do everything by negation. Everybody has his job: this sailor does EW, and that sailor does the ASW, and that sailor does this.[*] He would sit there and watch it, and when he didn't like something, he'd negate it or give it direction. He did just that. He knew every minute of every hour he was in there what was

---

[*] EW—electronic warfare; ASW—antisubmarine warfare.

going on. He had the air picture mentally as well as on the screen; he knew what the surface picture was; he sure had the intelligence in there. The man had everything at his fingertips and never opened his mouth unless it was to say, "Very well," or give a very concise bit of direction. Truly trusting, and trained his battle group to do just that. So in answer to how he was at sea, that's how he was. Great shipmate, great shipmate. Always pleasant during the meal hours, and just a great man to be around. All things to everybody.

Paul Stillwell: Describe your role as chief of staff in serving this admiral.

Captain Colbus: He called me in and welcomed me. I flew over to Rota, Spain, and relieved Don Cannell, who flew in from the ship, and we got together.* Again, I was chasing my carrier, Nimitz, just as I chased my squadron to Palma. I landed at the airport in Rota. The plane I flew in on was going to take Don Cannell to the U.S. We saluted each other, and I asked, "Got any guidance?"

"Yeah. Square away the uniforms and make sure the staff is always in the same uniform."

"Is that it?"

"Right."

"Got it."

I flew out to the carrier on a Sunday afternoon and landed. Bob was waiting right there to meet me, which I thought was very nice. He took me down to the mess and said, "Let's have dinner." I sat down, and there was a loafer's loop in my chair.† He pinned it on me, and we were going full speed. That evening, he told me, "I didn't bring you out here to retire, as I've seen many of your contemporaries do. You know I'll listen to everything you have to say. I want your experience, I want your input, and we're just going to do fine. Don't be afraid to step into the ops picture." That was it, and away we went.

He loved to get in a car and drive when we went ashore. He'd drive and I'd ride, and we'd go through, let's say, the French countryside on a Sunday afternoon when the ship was moored in Marseille. If you didn't get embarrassed by his knowledge and intimidated

---

* Captain Donald T. Cannell, USN.
† "Loafer's loops" is the sarcastic nickname for the aiguillettes worn by aides to high-ranking officers. They are loops of gold braid worn around the left shoulder, attached to shirt or blouse.

by it, he would just—and not to be a know-it-all—he'd spin yarns about the countryside, tell you the history of the area, take you up to the Basque. He has a wealth of knowledge. And not just knowledge for knowledge itself; that's why I used the word profound. He's say, "By the way, I read today in such and such a book. Do you really think that?" That kind of conversation.

That—if I may use the word—that romance lasted until his relief came aboard about a year later. That was Jim Service, the aviator's aviator, colorful, glamorous.* He was, again, a very trusting man, let his staff operate like a staff. He was more into my business than he was into anybody's. For instance, Bob Dunn looked to me to run the mess through the flag lieutenant. Now, Jim Service liked the good life and got into those details. He liked the ceremonial details. As I used to tell him at a later date, he had been exec of Independence, skipper of Independence, and now flag in Independence. He had a vested interest in that ship. It was a different situation, and we had a ball.

The first operation we went on in May of '80 was Boston's 350th birthday with Op Sail. Dynamite. Admiral Service's wife went with us, and she's as gracious as he is. We took Boston by storm. When we arrived, Admiral Service and Natalie went off and did their protocol. He had lots of commitments downtown—ceremonial things. I stayed pretty close to the ship, lived on the ship, and interfaced with a lot of different projects.

The rabbi chaplain whom I referred to, whom Bob Dunn had met when he first visited, was now a part of the staff. When he went on his annual two-week active duty, we had him assigned to the staff. We appreciated him very much as a staff chaplain; he contributed tremendously to everything. He'd explain things that other people just couldn't put into words. Anyway, Chaplain Kahn went to Boston with us, and he and Admiral Service became great shipmates. He came to my cabin after we moored to a pier on a Friday. He came over to me and told me very nicely—he always called me "Chief of Staff"—and even to this day I refer to him as "Rabbi." He asked me, "Why don't you call me by my first name?"

I said, "Because I didn't ever think I'd be high class enough to have a rabbi for a friend. I want to keep it in that context."

"Chief of staff."

---

* Rear Admiral James E. Service, USN.

"Yes, sir."

He said, "I need a favor."

"What's that?"

He said, "Chief of staff, you're going to temple with me tonight in uniform. That's an order from your rabbi, from your . . ."

"Yes. Right. Whatever you say."

We got suited up and went ashore; that started our tour properly. We went to the home of his seminary classmate—I call him the Paul Newman of the rabbi community. This man was Ivy League, blue-eyed, blond-haired, handsome, lovely wife, two gorgeous children. We went to his house for dinner. He was an administrative type rather than a preaching type.

We then went to the biggest congregation in Brookline, Mass.; that's like going to Miami Beach, New York, or Tel Aviv. Brookline has a big Jewish community. They had something like 1,800 families in this temple. Two rabbis were there, and we met with both. We went to Friday night Sabbath services. After the Friday night services, there was a community get-together in a social hall. It was just that—coffee, tea, cookies.

As we went into the social hall, there were the chaplain in uniform, myself in uniform, and three other rabbis. There was a group—and I'd heard about this—of about 50 people, children and families. These 50 people had just emigrated from the Soviet Union. A special Friday night Sabbath service had been conducted for these 50 Soviet Jews in this temple, but in a separate part because it was conducted in Russian.

Well, we walked in there, and this was the first interface the chaplain and myself had with these 50 Soviet Jews. You could see, almost as if it were staged, the fear, the fright, the surprise that they exhibited when they saw us. The word got back to us that these people were very fearful. One of their remarks was, "We left the Soviet Union to get away from this type thing, and now here they are again. The military. The police. Who are they? KGB? What's going on?"

"No, no, no. You don't understand. One's a rabbi."

"Now, come on."

"The other happens to be his boss, a Jewish fellow on the ship. See, he has four stripes, that rabbi has two and a half."

No, they didn't believe it. After 15 minutes of this, we finally got together and talked. They still didn't believe it. We did nice things, and . . .

Paul Stillwell: Did you have an interpreter?

Captain Colbus: Oh, yes. All this was being done through an interpreter. I said to the interpreter, "If these people really want to see how we live and what we do, send them down to the ship tomorrow, John F. Kennedy. She's moored right at the pier. You know where it is. Down there next to . . ."

"Oh, yes."

"If these people can, I'd love to host them on the ship tomorrow."

The following day, Saturday morning, I was sitting in the flag mess having breakfast, about 7:15. A messenger came up and said, "Chief of staff, a group of foreigners want to see you."

Whoops. They didn't speak English. I went to the quarterdeck. The interpreter was not there, and we started on a tour of the ship. The rabbi was still asleep. I said, "Get the rabbi. Get the chaplain. Get him up here." Well, I took them and toured the ship, and I'm very proud to say I was known in the ship, because I'm a ship walker. Every man we met came over and said, "Morning, chief of staff," or, "Good morning, Captain." It was just a pleasant atmosphere in that ship. These people were amazed.

Well, pretty soon the chaplain came on the scene. By showing these people the chaplain's insignia, the ten commandments on his sleeve, we finally convinced them that yes, he was a Jewish chaplain. We spent the entire morning touring the ship, took them into the flag mess for coffee and doughnuts. By 11:00 they were convinced. I grabbed a 15-year-old in there and through pidgin English, Russian, whatever, said, "Where do you come from?" He told me. I said, "My grandparents came from Lithuania. You know Lithuania?"

"Yes, Lithuania."

"That was just 100 years ago, when they came over. I'm named for my grandfather. You do right in this country, you can have my job. How old are you?"

"Fifteen."

"You can have my job in 30 years."

Paul Stillwell: His eyes got big.

Captain Colbus: Big! Those people were in tears when they left there. They were glad to be in America. They had a fright when they saw the two uniformed men in temple. So it worked out very well. We just had a fine time in Boston.

The city turned out for us. The ship was, by the way, part of Second Fleet. Admiral Service was not the senior officer since Com2ndFlt was present. But he delegated a lot to us.

Paul Stillwell: I'm sure that the ship was well received with the name John F. Kennedy.

Captain Colbus: We had 2,000 people on board for the day they had the sail-by. That was a real fine tour.

Paul Stillwell: Could you talk about some of the administrative duties as chief of staff?

Captain Colbus: Make it all happen. Interface with the ship, settle differences, let's say, between the ship's ops officer and maybe the staff ops officer, and there's a book in itself. Our staff ops officer, Ronald McKeown, Mugs McKeown.[*] The book Right Stuff describes Mugs McKeown. The man is a genius. He is absolutely a superstar. He's the most brilliant, talented, all-around wit, quick, ah! He's the fighter pilot's fighter pilot. "How was it that time you went over?"

"Oh, it was fine."

"What fight was that?"

"That was such and such."

"What did you do that day that you were talking about that date?"

"That's the day I . . ."

"What did you get the Navy Cross for?"

---

[*] Commander Ronald E. McKeown, USN.

"Bagged a couple of MiGs."

"When?"

"That day." Very casual about the whole thing. Colorful, too, proud, just perfect. What a shipmate! He was our ops officer, and he added more, I guess, to that entire battle group than any other individual. He was just well known, well liked, highly respected. He did everything with a flair and did it with ease; he wrote eloquently. The man's command of the English language is beyond comprehension. I mean, you had to sometimes cut out his $5.00 words because the admiral and I didn't understand them. We were even embarrassed to look them up in the book. He was our ops officer and had the complete confidence of Admiral Service. Mugs was not there when Admiral Dunn was there.

Anyway, we were in Boston, had a grand time, did everything from a visit and party at the top of the John Hancock building to lunch with the mayor, met the governor, etc. We got under way and went by a point of land whose name I've forgotten. I would guess there were 3,000, maybe 4,000 people at this point waving goodbye, cheering the Navy. My hat was worth, they tell me, $75.00 on the beach. A white hat was worth, I guess, $10.00, $15.00. A ship's baseball cap was $25.00. Anything with John F. Kennedy. In fact, sailors were saying, "Why do we go to the Med on liberty when we can come up here?" Lots of sailors returned to Boston from Norfolk. It was, I guess, one of the best liberties I've ever seen in my entire naval career, and the entire fleet was in port. I never heard of an incident ashore.

Paul Stillwell: Captain, we've talked about the first two flag officers under whom you served in the carrier group. The third one was Admiral Tuttle.[*] What do you remember of him?

Captain Colbus: I remember Admiral Tuttle from our Saratoga days, when Saratoga was a ship that was, I guess to bluntly put it, in trouble. Jerry Tuttle was CAG. I was plans officer for Beetle Forbes, as I previously discussed. I can't say I worked extremely close with him, but we certainly did interface in my plans job, my surface ops job, my staff job. I can remember talking to Jerry Tuttle many times. He's a very, very clever—and I say the

---

[*] Rear Admiral Jerry O. Tuttle, USN.

word respectfully—he was a very clever fellow then. He could take a situation and turn it around.

For instance, <u>Saratoga</u> broke down during our type training. The ship had to come in to the pier at Mayport. He flew in and arranged to get his airplanes into a naval facility, a landing area right there in Mayport rather than a flying field. He did this instead of taking them over to NAS Jacksonville. He set up tents for the air wing, maintenance people, and rented golf carts to get around.

The man was a genius. He never missed a stroke. I'd seen him through the years, talked to him when he came to visit Bob Dunn, and we had a nice conversation. Then, of course, I found out he was coming to relieve Jim Service. His reputation preceded him, and you can talk about it in front of him. He knows it. He is tenacious. He gets on to something, and he doesn't let go till it's done. He'll work it to the end.

Well, anyway, on came Jerry Tuttle: hard-working, not glamorous and charismatic in his own way. There are those who just love him—I'm one of them—and there are those who avoid him as much as possible. They fear him. I have never met a sailor—I'm talking about chief or below, that didn't think the world of Skipper Tuttle, Captain Tuttle, CAG Tuttle, Admiral Tuttle. He is a sailor's sailor. He trades on the fact that he's not one of these polished, highly educated, silver-spooned gents. He trades on the fact that he is an Indiana potato farmer who's very proud of his background—good, solid farm people.

Deep down, the man has a lot of feeling; he really does. I don't say it's there all the time. He sometimes has to remind himself of it, but when it's time, Jerry can be the most eloquent individual I've ever been around, and that includes all these others. The two times I saw that he did that, he worked at it very hard; I will say that. That's why I use the word tenacious.

The most eloquent I have ever heard him was when we took a Vietnam veteran's casket to sea for burial. It was in 1982 when we took the body to sea and buried him off <u>Independence</u>. Jerry was closely involved with the Vietnam POW-MIA program, and he became involved with that in his first flag job as Deputy DIA, Defense Intelligence Agency.[*] We took this body, with all the honors, embarked the sister of this deceased aviator, and went to sea off Fort Lauderdale. He did everything perfectly. I mean, he

---

[*] POW-MIA—prisoner of war/missing in action.

worked on that himself. He checked personally on every detail. He had me doing fourth-order minutiae work, but when that ceremony was conducted, it was letter perfect.

In addition to that, he got up and presented the eulogy. It was, I'd say, five minutes of the most moving words I've ever heard in my life; it absolutely should have been recorded and videotaped. I have a written copy of that at home. So that's what I'm saying about people who don't see that side of him; they just see this rough, tough, agile man who's going to take on the world, and nobody is going to push Jerry Tuttle around. And that's pretty much the way it is. And if Jerry were sitting here right now, he'd smile, maybe even kick at me. Good man.

Okay. He came aboard, and he and I were, as I say, old friends. Most of it is as it should be: knock off the first-name basis. He could call me what he wants, but he was the admiral, and away we go. As I said, we'd done all these great things with Jim Service, who was—and I don't want you to get the wrong idea, but he was the playboy by comparison. When Jim wasn't working, he was playing. I mean, that man did everything. He'd fly off the carrier and do all kinds of fun things. He'd go scuba diving. He liked the good life, and, as I said, a very polished, glamorous, parlor-room, I guess you'd call it, admiral.

And a hell of a good operator too. He just had the 360 degrees.

Jerry came on board and started working very hard, and there were lots of things that just didn't go right. For instance, the night before we were going to get under way on his first major exercise, which was a NATO exercise, we had a crisis. We were going back to Northern Europe in <u>Eisenhower</u>; this was the Northern Wedding series. That was in the fall of '81. Jerry had been with us for two or three months. The night before we were getting under way, the weather was terrible down at the pier in Norfolk.

Guess who was on board the carrier worrying about ships under way and what have you? The admiral was livid because I wasn't there, ops officer wasn't there, surface ops wasn't there, nobody was there. He had no support, and he started on that. We hadn't been at sea two days when he got us together in the war room and let us know—and I was among them—what he thought about our lackadaisical attitude and inattention to duty. And the way he phrased it, he was right. We were trusting the ships to look after themselves, but he was the task group commander, and he was on board, and when he was on board, you other jerks better be around. He added, "And if anybody doesn't like it, there's a COD tomorrow. And that starts with the chief of staff right on down. You be on that COD and get the hell off here. I'll run it myself, just as I did before getting under way."*

His tirade was effective. My approach was, "I just happen to think I'm a good sailor, and if that's the way he feels, I'm going to change his mind." All he got me to do was take a round turn on myself and the staff. We were going to support the admiral in his way. If that's what he expects, he's got it.

A few said, "I'm getting on that plane."

"The hell you are." And that kind of thing. Well, we got through that crisis.

We had a new surface ops officer. We had detached the other surface ops officer to his next duty station at my insistence. I said, "Admiral, you just can't keep this man forever. Send him off." Jerry wanted to keep both officers on board. Surface ops weren't going very well, we had some glitches, and Jerry was mad as hell that he'd let the experienced officer leave.

He got me in and just sat me down and told me, "Get the surface ops officer back here."

"Yes, sir. You realize he's on leave en route to his new job at Newport, where he's going to take over the OCS training. He's a captain."

"He doesn't care about that. His first duty is out here."

Well, we got him back and he came aboard, on the one hand flattered that the admiral needed him, on the other hand, what the hell, it certainly didn't reflect well on the incumbent. It just wasn't pleasant. Everything was done with great strain.

I've mentioned Mugs McKeown. Now, Mugs had served with Jim Service and it was just a honeymoon the entire year. We'd been to Perth, Australia, we'd been to the Indian Ocean, we'd done everything together. We were a team. Jerry Tuttle really resented us and our tales and sea stories of good times and the fun staff. Jerry was told by AirLant, "Boy, you sure know what you're doing. You got the best staff in the Atlantic Fleet." He was told that in all his briefings. Can do, they do everything well, and they're great.

---

* COD—carrier on-board delivery, an aircraft configured for carrier takeoffs and landings, dedicated to transporting personnel and cargo between ship and shore.

He didn't like that. It might have been great for the playboy, but not now. This is a working crowd. Knock off all that. Shore days are over. I thought that he would get over that. Well, he really didn't. We even got to talking about him being mercurial, up and down, up and down. The man could stay up for 48 hours working, and his measure of your loyalty was if you were at his side. You might just be sitting there looking at a scope, but stay with the admiral. I personally didn't do that. I'd tell him, "I do much better if I go turn in. Nothing's happening, it's 0100, I'm going in. See you in the morning."

I'd go to bed, get up at 0500 or whatever. Now, he never got on me for that, but he didn't understand how I could get my work done and do that. He became very, very concerned about loyalty. That was a big item with him: "Where is your loyalty? I'm not talking about personal; I'm talking about the staff. You're more loyal to others than you are to me." That was a rough, rough time. He really never turned Mugs McKeown loose, because Mugs could do anything in less time and do it better, but the admiral didn't use him in that mode. So these were unusual times for old CarGru 8.

I guess where Admiral Tuttle and I really had our face-off was one day when I was in his cabin talking about things in general. CAG came in and said, "Admiral, I'm here to tell you that this 24-hour-a-day flex deck is really running my people to the ground. The skippers don't want it to be known, because you'd say they're weak sissies, but they're tired. Their people are tired. We ought to really back off on these round-the-clock flight ops."[*]

Tuttle about threw him out physically, and he did get him out verbally: "I don't have time. I'll teach you boys how to fight. You're all too well rested looking, too good looking, you're going to get some lines in your face like me. I'll show you how to fight a ship. When it comes to war [and, of course, he was right], you're not going to have the luxury of getting all the rest you need."

Well, that enters into what I call "Do you have to practice being miserable?" As CAG went out, I said, "Let me ask you something, Admiral. Really, I'm close to those squadrons. You can't and I can go into their ready rooms regularly. You know that. I have mid-rats with them, I watch movies with them. Those aviators are tired. They're

---

[*] CAG—commander carrier air group. A carrier air group comprised all the planes assigned to the ship. The air group commander was the senior pilot in a flying billet, as opposed to being part of ship's company. In 1962 the Navy began using the term CVW, carrier air wing, in place of carrier air group, but the abbreviation CAG is still often used to denote the air wing commander.

starting to slow up. They'll be sitting there dozing in their chairs. They're not the bright lads that we started out with. We've already had one plane go over the side after he was on deck because he didn't keep his brakes on with a pitching deck."[*]

Well, he lighted into me. The door was open. He lighted into me like nothing you ever heard. Who the hell do I think I am coming out of my box, a black shoe? "You may know those destroyers, but you sure don't know my airplanes. And I'll tell you when they're tired. You just side with those fliers." I mean, this was a real harangue.

After it was over, I closed the door and looked him in the eyes. I got angry and went to a first-name basis, "Jerry, you've got to listen. You're not understanding CAG." Then he took off on me again and told me I was wrong. Then I said, "Jerry . . ." First-name basis again. He knows now it's personal, not professional. And he lighted into me again. After it was all over, I hung my head and said, "Well, Admiral, you're absolutely right." Now, he's three years younger than I. I said, "That's why you're the young admiral and I'm the old captain." And I got up almost as if to drag myself out in disgrace.

Well, that was it. "Come on back, let's talk about it." All you had to do was get to the man's inner feelings. He knocked off flight ops, but it took that—what do you call it?—almost emotion. You're young and I'm old, and I guess I don't know what I'm talking about. I had him. And every time I wanted something from the boss, it was, "You're right again. I keep forgetting."

"No, no, I didn't mean that, Louis. You're probably right. Let's consider it."

Also, any man who is as much a family man as Jerry is and that sensitive to other people's families has to be a good fellow. Yes, he's tough and it's not just a facade, but he has another side that a lot of people don't know. Another thing, too, is he is so knowledgeable. He's done it all. He's flown the airplane, he's been the CAG, and he hasn't forgotten a thing. And he is just a hard worker. Then the animosity went away, and all of a sudden the staff molded. He's like all great leaders. A year later, he called me in and said, "See what I've done? See how that staff is? That's a staff. They're great," without saying, in the parenthesis that I see, "due to my leadership." But that's fine. We all have an ego.

---

[*] Mid-rats is short for midnight rations, which are essentially mini-meals for those who go on watch around midnight or are otherwise still awake then.

Paul Stillwell: How was Admiral Service at sea? You've talked about the other two.

Captain Colbus: Admiral Service at sea was, as I've said before, knowledgeable, interested, concerned about the administrative details and how the ship was performing inside. I worked very closely with the carrier's exec. Admiral Service was also interested in that. I don't mean more interested than his other duties, but he was interested in the mess decks. He was interested from a morale standpoint: "Here's what we did in Independence. I had the chief master-at-arms . . . " Lay that on the exec. Right. He was more interested in the details of running the ship than the other flags because of his involvement, not just in Independence but in all the ships.

Paul Stillwell: How was he on the big picture?

Captain Colbus: Very, very understanding, very knowledgeable, and again, he used his staff. He wasn't an "I'll do it myself" admiral.

Paul Stillwell: He was the admiral when those two Libyan planes were shot down.[*]

Captain Colbus: But he wasn't ComCarGru 8. He was CTF 60 then, and he was aboard Nimitz.

Paul Stillwell: So you weren't involved in that?

Captain Colbus: No, no. He was over there with Howard Burdick as his chief of staff.[†]

Paul Stillwell: Please talk about the contrast between the way the aviation people protect each other and the surface people. I think the Ranger case is a good illustration there.

---

[*] On 19 August 1981 two U.S. Navy F-14s shot down two Soviet-made SU-22 aircraft of the Libyan Air Force that had attacked them in airspace above the Gulf of Sidra, claimed by Libya but held by the United States to be international waters.
[†] Captain Howard F. Burdick, USN.

Captain Colbus: When you get in trouble in the surface community, and I don't care who you are, and I think this has been for the last—I've observed it the last 15 years. If you get your hands dirty in the surface community, you don't see a lot of support. We don't ding ships, we sure don't ground ships. Except in one case, I recall, we saved a man on a grounding, but that's the exception to the rule. Normally speaking, the reaction is, "Son, you messed up." I haven't seen any real, "Let's band together and help old So-and-so. Everybody makes a mistake." It's either, "The dummy deserved it," or, "Too bad it happened."

The aviation community is just opposite, and I go back to Jerry Miller, whom we talked about earlier, going into the Med that morning in Springfield. His direction was, "Now, I'm not wishing anybody bad luck. I'll tell you what I can't do and what I can do. Collisions, I might be able to help you; I've had one myself, I know all about that. Forget groundings. I can't do anything for you on that. You should know that stuff's there. We understand. But let me worry about your problems. Share them with me. I'm here to help." And he did, as I think I illustrated.

Let's go back to this surface community thing. As I said, I've had my hands dirtied at times, and it can wear off, but nobody really comes out and strongly says, "Let's band together." I can name shipmates of mine, with great careers, and they did maybe one careless thing, and they knew they'd had it. When we were in the Indian Ocean, we got to know the carrier Ranger pretty well. We came back and we were in Norfolk right after the Ranger had a very tragic death up on the flight deck. This young sailor had been taken out of the brig, exercised, exhausted, laid down on the deck, dehydrated, and the poor soul died. Big investigation. That's a story in itself, which I'm not familiar with, but that was the scene.*

We had a big meeting aboard the flagship in Norfolk, and I think all the airdale flag community was there. It was just about flag selection time; the admirals' board was in

---

* On 14 April 1981, 21-year-old Airman Recruit Paul Trerice died of heat stroke and cardiac arrest on board the aircraft carrier Ranger (CV-61). He had been doing exercises in hot, humid weather after being confined to the ship's brig for previous infractions. As a result, the ship's commanding officer, Captain Dan A. Pederson, USN, received a letter of censure, and several enlisted crew members were court-martialed. For details, see Time, 25 May 1981, page 30.

session. I can remember the guidance given when we concluded the meeting. We were talking about things in general, and one of the admirals said, "Well, don't forget, gentlemen, we do what we can. I don't know what that is, but the least we can do is hope, wish, maybe even pray that our good friend, skipper of <u>Ranger</u>, is not condemned and is able to make flag on this go-around, and that the tragic incident on his ship certainly won't ruin his brilliant career. We need him in the flag community."

I think that tells the whole story. Those boys really get together, they really band together, and I don't mean this as a slur; it's just a difference. Aviators understand. I've read in an article that they're like the Israeli Navy. You're going to make mistakes and you're going to learn by those mistakes, and they're not going to condemn you for those mistakes.

I guess the other thing I always talk about is that I used to get very upset aboard the destroyers, where everybody musters on the quarterdeck when it's time for an evolution, time for a visit, the commodore, the captain, the exec. Then there's poor Ensign Benson standing there doing nothing but watching all these senior officers running about, making sure that the sweepdown is occurring, making sure that the sideboys are exercised.

I think we should turn all that over to Ensign Benson, as it was to me when I came to the Navy, and let him run it. The four-star visitor who is coming down will understand if Ensign Benson fouls up. That's part of learning, that's part of training, but he's going to do it on his own. He'll hear about it when he fouls up and he's going to get a critique, because I'd rather let him do a 3.8 job on his own than me, as the captain or commodore, come down and do a 3.99 job. This was the feeling I tried to instill. Let the young people do their jobs—as long as it's not going to jeopardize the ship.

It's not navigation. You can't train in that. You've got to be there all the time; you can train while you're doing it. And the other, of course, is down in the engineering spaces or when you're actually picking up the boat seamanship. I'm talking about life-threatening evolutions, we don't train primarily, but our experienced boat people do it while the juniors observe. If Com So-and-so is coming on board and one of the sideboys is not perfect because I wasn't there to inspect them, the ensign and the chief are going to pay for it. That's what I mean about the difference. Aviators in their ships might make a little error.

Oh, well, the breaks of naval air. And that's good. I don't mean they're careless and they don't give a damn, but it's part of their training.

Paul Stillwell: We've been talking about your deployments to the Mediterranean. Did you have anything else to say on Indian Ocean ops?

Captain Colbus: The Indian Ocean operation, as I said, was probably the best deployment of my career. We got out there in the middle of the Indian Ocean, and we were there for Christmas of '80 and New Year's of '81. That ship actually took on board an ambience, whatever you want to call it, of true Christmas spirit. If it sounds cornball, it wasn't at the time. You'd walk around that ship—now, they'd been at sea, let's say, two months.

Paul Stillwell: What ship was this?

Captain Colbus: This was USS Independence. Tom Shanahan was our skipper.[*] Jim Service was the flag embarked. Walking through that ship, you'd have a seaman come up, an airman, whatever: "Sir, you have to stop by our workspace. My mama sent me the best cookies and we're having a little party and we're going to share it." Christmas music on the PA system, a Christmas show, and that was it, but it was a true Christmas spirit, true "Let's get together" and we were a family. I'm talking about 5,000 people.

The other thing is that the Chief of Chaplains, Ross Trower, came out to spend Christmas with us and brought with him Captain Chaplain Ecker, who was his executive assistant.[†] They just toured the battle group, and that was a great, great event. They cared enough to sacrifice their own time, and we really appreciated it. That meant a lot to that ship in the battle group.

Also, we had two lovelies—two dancing girls from Las Vegas who came out and spent ten days with us. They were backed by their band of four or five non-military types, all good lads. We brought them on board, gave them cabins, and each day we'd take them

---

[*] Captain Thomas E. Shanahan, USN, commanded USS Independence (CV-62) from 28 May 1980 to 5 December 1981.
[†] Rear Admiral Ross H. Trower, CHC, USN, served as the Navy's Chief of Chaplains from June 1979 to August 1983. Captain Robert J. Ecker, CHC, USN.

to a different destroyer via helo. They gave us about three shows on the ship. They'd come down, grab Jim Service, take him up on the stage, put a long-hair wig on him, and sing songs. That was really a great time. Those little ladies came on that ship, both of them good-looking, both of them dancers, both of them from Las Vegas, what I'd call Las Vegas showgirls. They found their way around that ship. There was never a moment's hesitation. They were treated as if they were the sailors' sisters. I mean it. None of the smart-aleck catcalls. They could go anywhere they wanted to go, and they were welcome. I can give you all kind of sea stories about that, but that was really a great deployment.

Of course, we went to Perth for four or five days. That was worth any time on station. I'd never been to Australia. Most of us hadn't, and that's a book in itself—what we did and how we were received. I talked about Boston. I don't want to say Boston paled by Perth; it's just apples and oranges. We had a great time. The people were just what you'd expect. It was very much like San Diego in appearance and climate, and the sailors took to the beach and the beach took to us. No problems, no incidents. USS Independence and the cruiser Harry E. Yarnell.

There's something about Jim Service's style. The carrier was anchored in the Swan River. The cruiser was moored to the pier. To make things easy, Admiral Service shifted his flag to Harry E. Yarnell, and we did all our business on the cruiser. A nice touch. I went out to the carrier daily. We all stayed ashore, but that was a nice way to do things. We did the same thing when we went to Mauritius and we had a DDG-2 in there, USS Charles F. Adams. We shifted the flag to Adams. You could live over there in the unit commander's cabin, which I did.

Paul Stillwell: That cruise in a carrier group sounds like a good way to wind up a career. Are there any final thoughts that you want to add on this whole experience that we've been talking about?

Captain Colbus: That's too big an order to fill. I've got to tell you one finish story on that carrier as to what the environment was. You had asked me, "How did the aviators take to you?" Well, I told you I was hanging around the ready rooms. Right before we went on this deployment, I'd flown in the S-3, I'd flown in the E-2, I'd flown in an A-6 one time.

When I was down in VF-33's ready room, an F-4 squadron, one day, the skipper, Freddie Vogt, came up to me and said, "Hey, chief of staff, you're always hanging around the ready room and you're one of the boys. How would you like to go for a flight? You've never flown with us."[*]

I said, "In an F-4? In a fighter? I can't believe it."

"Oh, yeah."

Well, they checked me out, had the day set, suited me up. Of course, all my buddies said, "You're crazy. You don't have to do that."

"No, I want to do it." They put me in the back of the F-4, launched us, and we went up. The pilot's nickname was "Hun." We chased clouds, we dog fought, we did everything. He put 5 G's on me, and I'd just pass out but didn't throw up. We came back just about sundown, made our trap, and I was elated. I was just like a little kid. Hey, I have just been in a fighter airplane. Launched, chased, refueled, recovered. As I got out of that airplane, there was a sea of faces. Every swinging man jack who was on the flight deck crew was up there, all these hard-working sailors, 18, 20 hours a day, dirty, grimy from dragging the tie-down chains, mechanics, ordnancemen. They were all out there looking at me as I got out and walked through the group.

"How was the flight, chief of staff?"

"Hey, it was great."

They asked all the nice questions. Down in the ready room, I was getting out of my flight gear, and Freddie came in and said, "How was it?"

"It was so great I can't believe it and that's it."

"Are you ready to go up again?"

I said, "Oh, no, I couldn't do that."

He said, "Oh, you didn't like it?"

I said, "You didn't hear me. I loved it, but let me tell you why I can't go up." I said, "Here I am, so to speak, the fat cat, I've never done a thing for naval aviation, I've never turned a bolt on that airplane, and I get to ride in that airplane. And there are all those hard-working men who would give their eyeteeth to go up. Did you see them standing around there? I felt so bad. I stole the ride."

---

[*] Commander Frederick H. Vogt, USN.

He said, "No, no, you don't understand. I thought you understood. They know that there are too many of them to go up. They're never going to get a chance to go up. The fact that you don't have to go up and you went up and enjoyed it shows that you have faith in them and their maintenance and all their procedures. That was the greatest morale boost you could have given those boys."

"Are you kidding, Freddie?"

"No." I was going up at least two, three times a week with those lads after that. That's the kind of spirit you see over there. There's no jealousy, they understand each other, and it's because, I guess, of that tight work they do. A unique group.

But you asked me for a summation. I do have a statement to make. When you retire, you realize how you were smart enough, lucky enough, and good enough to have lived like that for 30 years. So it's not a matter of it's all over; it's just, "Boy, was I lucky." Because there's no group like it and all my good civilian friends—God bless them—they are nice and all that, but I really feel that anybody who gets to do 30 years is just fortunate, and you have to do it to fully appreciate it.

Well, one more statement, and I used this last Sunday with a group. Where else can a man go into a profession that pays him well, rewards him in all other areas, and it parallels his religious beliefs? I think we talked about that today earlier; at least I was thinking of that. Where else do you deal in integrity, care of your fellow man? My main purpose here is morale; the purpose is not the bottom line. If you're even slightly religious, all the tenets of your religion go absolutely in parallel with a career in the Navy. That would about sum up what I think 30 years is all about.

Paul Stillwell: I can see you're fortunate to have had that experience, and I'm fortunate that you've shared it not only with me but with people who will read and enjoy these reminiscences of yours in the future.

Captain Colbus: You know I enjoyed it. I'm not going to say I was embarrassed by it, but again, I am, because everybody could come up here and tell you the same story, just in different words, and I appreciate the opportunity. You're doing great work, and I'd like to read more about what you have. Maybe when I retire retire, you'll let me come back and leaf through it.

Paul Stillwell: Thank you.

Captain Colbus: You're welcome.

Index to the Oral History of Captain Louis Colbus, U.S. Navy (Retired)

Acadia, USS (AD-42)
Destroyer tender that in 1967 provided valuable repair services to the evaporators on board the destroyer escort McCloy (DE-1038), 209-211

Adamson, Vice Admiral Robert E., Jr., USN (USNA, 1944)
In 1977 wrote a concurring endorsement on an unfavorable fitness report Colbus submitted on Commander Wendell N. Johnson, 344

Africa
Visits to in the late 1950s and early 1960s by ships of the U.S. South Atlantic Force, 88-98

Aircraft Carriers
In the early 1970s different carriers had different internal administrative organizations, 292-294; surface warfare officers can learn a good deal from their service on carrier battle group staffs, 295-296

See also: Carrier Division Six; Carrier Group Eight; America, USS (CVA-66); Dwight D. Eisenhower, USS (CVN-69); Independence, USS (CVA-62); John F. Kennedy, USS (CVA-67); Franklin D. Roosevelt, USS (CVA-42); Ticonderoga, USS (CVA-14);

Albany, USS (CG-10)
In the late 1970s, as Sixth Fleet flagship, was the site of a NATO anniversary celebration, 337-338

Albert T. Harris, USS (DE-447)
Destroyer escort that in the mid-1950s operated out of Newport, Rhode Island, 18-19, 22-23, 35-36, 39-40, 123; school ship for the sonar school at Key West, Florida, 20-27, 31-32, 34-35, 44-45; Walter J. Czajkowski was an impressive chief boatswain's mate in the crew, 21-23; towed the destroyer escort Tabberer (DE-418) after she collided off Block Island with the submarine Diablo (SS-479), 27; officer of the deck training, 27-28; Lieutenant Isaac Nelson Franklin was a demanding executive officer, 29-31, 39; port visits to Havana, Cuba, 32-34; gunnery exercises, 35-38; had a basic 600-PSI steam propulsion plant, 38-39; officers of the deck stood watches on a bridge exposed to the weather, 39; practiced North Atlantic convoy operations, 39-40; formal mealtime practices, 45-47; visit in the mid-1950s to Nassau in the Bahamas, 47-49; officers from various commissioning sources, 66; in 1957 won the squadron Battle Efficiency E, 67; characteristics of enlisted men in the crew, 67-70; yard period in 1956 at the New York Naval Shipyard, 69; leadership qualities of junior officers, 110; in the mid-1950s one of the officers was Lieutenant

Bill Myers, who had gone into surface ships after a midair collision as an aviator, 113-114; in the early 1960s was reactivated as a result of the Berlin Crisis, 134-135

Alcohol
Since people couldn't drink in South Carolina, except in private clubs, in the early 1950s, NROTC midshipmen were pleased to be able to join such clubs, 17; in the mid-1950s the crew of a Scottish merchant ship entertained officers from the destroyer escort Albert T. Harris (DE-447) by serving whiskey from the ship's cargo, 47-48; alcoholic chief quartermaster in the crew of the destroyer Basilone (DD-824) in the mid-1960s, 68; in 1972 a crew member of the destroyer Jonas Ingram (DD-938) died of alcohol poisoning, 250-251

America, USS (CVA-66/CV-66)
Celebration of Yom Kippur in October 1974 by Jewish personnel on board the ship, 300-302; operated in the late 1970s with the guided missile destroyer Dahlgren (DDG-43) when that ship was having engineering problems, 340-341

Anderson, Lieutenant Commander Thomas A., USN
Fine individual who served in the early 1970s as executive officer of the destroyer Jonas Ingram (DD-938), 234, 238-239, 245-246, 252-254, 267, 273-274, 317; in the mid-1970s commanded the destroyer Mullinnix (DD-944), 317, 353-354

Anderson, Captain William L., USN (USNA, 1926)
Submarine officer who ran the NROTC program from 1952 to 1955 at the University of South Carolina, 3-5

Antarctica
Site of high-altitude nuclear weapons tests conducted near in late 1958 by Task Force 88 during Project Argus, 73-79

Antiair Warfare
Spectacular gunnery exercise in the mid-1950s performed by the destroyer escort Albert T. Harris (DE-447), 35-36

Antisubmarine Warfare
In the mid-1950s Key West, Florida, was the site of a Navy sonar training school, 20-21, 26-27, 31-32, 34-35, 43-45; in the late 1950s Escort Squadron 12 operated as part of hunter-killer groups out of Quonset Point, Rhode Island, 55-56; use in the 1960s of the antisubmarine rocket (ASROC) as a weapon in exercises, 172; ASW upgrade around 1970 to the destroyer Jonas Ingram (DD-938), 259-260, 312-313; in the early 1970s the Jonas Ingram was involved in exercises with a submarine off Florida, 271-274

Argus
See: Project Argus

ASROC
Use in the 1960s of the antisubmarine rocket as a weapon in exercises, 172; was part of the ASW upgrade put in the destroyer Jonas Ingram (DD-938) around 1970, 259-260; used in the early 1970s by the Jonas Ingram during ASW exercises off Florida, 271-272, 312-313; in the early 1970s was considered but not used in the Oliver Hazard Perry (FFG-7)-class frigates, 312-313

Astronauts
In late 1965 the destroyer Basilone (DD-824) was involved in the recovery of Gemini astronauts in the Atlantic, 166-167

Atkinson, Lieutenant Commander Wilton L., USN (USNA, 1945)
Held court in the wardroom in 1959-60 while serving as skipper of the destroyer escort John R. Perry (DE-1034), 118

Australia
In the early 1980s the aircraft carrier Independence (CV-62) visited Perth, 385

Bagley, Admiral David H., USN (USNA, 1944)
In the late 1970s, as CinCUSNavEur, visited with Colbus in Gaeta, Italy, about the role of Destroyer Squadron Two in the Sixth Fleet, 337-338, 356

Bahamas Islands
Visited in the mid-1950s by the destroyer escort Albert T. Harris (DE-447), 47-49; site of filming of the movie Flame of the Islands, 48-49

Bainbridge, USS (DLGN-25)
New nuclear-powered frigate that in the early 1960s had a most gracious skipper, Captain Ray Peet, 144-146

Band, U.S. Navy
A number of band members were killed in February 1960 when a plane carrying them crashed in Brazil, 85-87

Barney, USS (DDG-6)
In 1976 served as flagship for Commander Destroyer Squadron Two, 327, 329, 333

Basilone, Gunnery Sergeant John, USMC
World War II Marine for whom the destroyer Basilone (DD-824) was named, 164-165; in the mid-1960s his relatives went to Newport, Rhode Island, to visit the namesake destroyer, 165-166

Basilone, USS (DD-824)
In 1965 visited Norfolk and held a wardroom party, 65; alcoholic chief quartermaster in the crew, 68; in the mid-1960s Commander Robert E. L. Stokes, Jr., was the commanding officer, 163-164; in 1958 went aground off Fort Story, 164; in 1965

members of the Basilone family went to Newport, Rhode Island, to visit the ship, 165-166; in late 1965 was involved in recovery of astronauts in the Gemini program, 166-167; in January 1966, as part of Destroyer Squadron 12, deployed from the East Coast to the Vietnam War, 167; the crew was beefed up for deployment, 167-168; in the mid-1960s Commander Robert Stokes was a demanding skipper, 169-171, 173-174, 183-185; liberty in Taiwan, 169-170; use of a drone antisubmarine helicopter, 170-172; in 1966 provided shore bombardment of South Vietnam, 172-174, 184-185; replenishment at sea, 174-176; provided plane-guard and escort service for the aircraft carrier Ticonderoga (CVA-14), 175-177; port visit to Hong Kong, 179-181; visited a variety of ports in completing a cruise around the world, 181-182, 185-186; operational chain of command, 182; relationships among the ship's officers, 183

Bates, Rear Admiral Richard W., USN (Ret.) (USNA, 1915)
In the late 1940s and early 1950s, he worked under the auspices of the Naval War College to conduct analytical studies of World War II naval battles, 41-43

Bath Iron Works
In the late 1960s was involved in the DX/DXG destroyer design development competition, 218-219

Beach, Captain Edward L., USN (USNA, 1939)
As commanding officer of the oiler Salamonie (AO-26) in the 1957, performed a fine piece of ship handling in recovering a man overboard, 61-62

Beecher, Commander John D., USN (USNA, 1952)
In the late 1960s served in OpNav on the staff of the DX/DXG destroyer development project, 214-215

Belgian Congo
Visited in the late 1950s by Commander U.S. South Atlantic Force and members of his staff, 91

Berlin Crisis
As a result of this crisis in the early 1960s ships were reactivated and Naval Reservists recalled to active duty, 129-130, 134-136

Biddle, USS (DLG-34)
In the early 1970s was involved in missile exercises in the Caribbean, 296

Bird, Captain Ralph G., USN (USNA, 1956)
In 1976 ran the Senior Officer Ship Material Readiness Course in Arco, Idaho, 324

Bonner, Captain Emmett P., USN (USNA, 1939)
Exceptionally capable officer who in 1957-58 commanded Escort Squadron 12 during various operations, 53, 56-64, 71; in 1963-64 commanded the cruiser Oklahoma City (CLG-5), 60; was a protege of Rear Admiral Lloyd Mustin, 77-79

Boston, Massachusetts
　　In May 1980 had a visit from the aircraft carrier John F. Kennedy (CV-67) to celebrate the city's 350th birthday, 371-375

Boston Naval Shipyard
　　In the late 1960s updated the sonar equipment on board the destroyer escort McCloy (DE-1038), 188-189, 203-204, 207

Brady, Lieutenant Commander Robert E., USN (USNA, 1949)
　　Quiet, reserved officer who in the early 1960s commanded the destroyer escort John R. Perry (DE-1034), 120, 122, 125-127; personal qualities, 122

Brink, Captain Frederick W., CHC, USN
　　In 1967, while serving as ComCruDesLant force chaplain, engaged in a humorous exchange of letters with Colbus, the Jewish lay leader of the destroyer escort McCloy (DE-1038), 192-193

Britannia, HMS (British Royal Yacht)
　　In the mid-1950s visited Nassau in the Bahamas with Princess Margaret on board, 48-49

Brown, Lieutenant Robert S., USN
　　Killed in February 1960 when the plane carrying the U.S. Navy Band crashed in Brazil, 86-88

Burdo, USS (APD-133)
　　High-speed transport that in the summer of 1951 made a midshipman training cruise to Europe, 9-13

Bureau of Naval Personnel
　　In 1950 matched Colbus with an available NROTC billet at the University of South Carolina after none was available at Penn State, 1-2; work in 1963-64 of Pers-A31, the plans and policy branch in writing billets, 140-145, 150-151, 154, 155; the branch provided stewards' billets to serve the presidential yacht, White House, and former President Dwight Eisenhower's farm in Gettysburg, Pennsylvania, 141; provision of billets for the Naval Home in Philadelphia, 142-144; review of recent Hollywood films before releasing them to the fleet, 146; discussion in the early 1960s of slating various flag officers into billets, 147-148; in 1964 several people served as judges of the Miss BuPers beauty pageant, 148-149; duplicity in reporting to Congress on billets in various shore stations, 151-152; BuPers in the early 1960s was able to get the best people to serve there and gave them good assignments afterward, 153; use of computers in the early 1960s, 154; long working hours for those stationed in the bureau, 156; in late 1969 considered Colbus for assignment in Vietnam but did not send him because of budget cutbacks, 230-232; in 1971 assigned Colbus to command the destroyer Jonas Ingram (DD-938), 232-234

Burial at Sea
In October 1971 the destroyer Jonas Ingram (DD-938) buried the remains of Rear Admiral Daniel F. Smith, Jr., off Florida, 267-270; in 1982 the carrier Independence (CV-62) conducted a burial off Florida, 376-377

Caney, Captain Lawrence D., USN (USNA, 1943)
In the late 1960s was deputy head of the DX/DXG destroyer development program in OpNav, 213-214, 221, 229

Cannell, Captain Donald T., USN (USNA, 1953)
In the late 1970s served as chief of staff to Commander Carrier Group Eight, 370

Cape Town, South Africa
Visited in the late 1950s by ships of the U.S. South Atlantic Force, 88-89, 94-95

Carr, Captain Nevin P., USN (USNA, 1953)
Commanded the attack transport Francis Marion (LPA-249) in 1977 when she served as flagship for a squadron of U.S. Navy ships that went to England to help celebrate the Silver Jubilee of Queen Elizabeth II, 348-350

Carrier Division Six
Value of Colbus's previous Naval War College experience in the 1960s in doing staff work, 162; in the early 1970s Rear Admiral Joseph Moorer was division commander, 279-282; at that time the carrier Franklin D. Roosevelt (CVA-42) was flagship, 279-280, 296-297; work-up period in 1973 on board the carrier Independence (CVA-62), 280-281; officers on Admiral Moorer's staff, 281-282, 290-291; Mediterranean deployment on board the carrier John F. Kennedy (CVA-67) in 1973 during the Yom Kippur War, 282-288; early 1970s participation in NATO exercises, 290-291, 300-304; in the early 1970s conducted operational readiness inspections of different ships in the work-up phase, 291-293

Carrier Group Eight
Operations of in the late 1970s and early 1980s, 294-295, 369-387; in 1978-80 Rear Admiral Robert Dunn commanded the group, 366, 368-371; in the early 1980s the commander was Rear Admiral James E. Service, 371, 374-377, 379, 381, 384-385; later group commander was Rear Admiral Jerry O. Tuttle, 375-380

Carroll, Rear Admiral Eugene J., Jr., USN
As Commander Task Force 60 in 1976 made things difficult for Commander Destroyer Squadron Two, 328, 330, 333, 338-339

Carter, Captain Edward W. III, USN (USNA, 1951)
In the early 1970s commanded the frigate Biddle (DLG-34) during missile exercises in the Caribbean, 296

Charleston, South Carolina
 In 1961 the destroyer escort John R. Perry (DE-1034) went to Charleston for updating of the sonar dome, 116-118; in the early 1960s was the homeport for the nuclear-powered frigate Bainbridge (DLGN-25), 144-146

Chisum, Captain Oscar Clarke, USN
 In the mid-1970s, while in command of the cruiser Josephus Daniels (CG-27), was gracious in his dealings with Colbus, 328-329

Chovan, Quartermaster First Class George, USN
 In the early 1960s was a skilled navigator on board the destroyer escort John R. Perry (DE-1034), 117

Clifford, Rear Admiral William F., Jr., USN (USNA, 1948)
 Was the top-ranking student in 1976 when the first class went through the Senior Officer Ship Material Readiness Course, 318, 323

Coastal Dry Dock and Shipbuilding Company, Brooklyn, New York
 In the late 1970s did overhaul work on the destroyer Mullinnix (DD-944), 353-354; working style of the president, Charlie Montanti, 353-354

Colbus, Captain Louis, USN (Ret.)
 Boyhood in the 1930s in Altoona, Pennsylvania, 1; education of, 1-2, 7-8, 16; parents of, 1-2, 6-7, 61-62, 71-72, 152; as an NROTC midshipman from 1950 to 1954 at South Carolina and Penn State, 2-17; served from 1954 to 1957 in the destroyer escort Albert T. Harris (DE-447), 18-50; served in 1957-58 on the staff of Commander Escort Squadron 12, 50-72; temporary duty in late 1958 on the staff of Commander Task Force 88 for nuclear weapons testing, 73-79; as flag secretary, 1958-60, to Commander South Atlantic Force, 79-106; wife of, 95, 127-131, 136, 138, 140, 152, 156, 159, 161-162, 186, 194, 198, 230, 233, 237, 246, 275-277, 279-280, 299, 316, 335-336, 364-366; in 1960 took the general line course at the Naval Postgraduate School, 106-116; served 1961 to 1963 as executive officer of the destroyer escort John R. Perry (DE-1034), 109, 116-140; in 1961 met and married Jody Rierson, 127-130; duty in 1963-64 in the plans and policy branch of the Bureau of Naval Personnel, 140-157; in 1964-65 was a student at the Naval War College, 156-163, children of, 159-160, 163, 166, 230, 267, 275; in 1965-66 served as executive officer of the destroyer Basilone (DD-824), 163-187; from 1966 to 1968 commanded the destroyer escort McCloy (DE-1038), 187-213; from 1976 to 1979 commanded Destroyer Squadron Two, 212-213, 316-317, 327-365; from 1968 to 1971 worked in the destroyer development program in OpNav, 213-230; in late 1969 was briefly considered for a billet in Vietnam, 230-232; in 1971-72 commanded the destroyer Jonas Ingram (DD-938), 232-279, 331, 362; from 1972 to 1975 served on the staff of Commander Carrier Division Six, 279-296, 300-304; from 1979 to 1982 served as chief of staff to Commander Carrier Group Eight, 293-295, 366-387; in 1975-76 served on the staff of Commander Operational Test and Evaluation Force,

305-316; in the spring and summer of 1976 attended the Senior Officer Ship Material Readiness Course in Idaho, 317-326

Colbus, William
An uncle of Louis Colbus, he played baseball for the armored cruiser Washington in World War I, 2; had an enjoyable visit to the destroyer Jonas Ingram (DD-938) in the early 1970s, 2; 277-278; died shortly after his visit, 278

Collisions
In the mid-1950s the destroyer escort Tabberer (DE-418) collided off Block Island with the submarine Diablo (SS-479), 27; in 1961 the destroyer escort John R. Perry (DE-1034) collided with a merchant ship in San Juan, Puerto Rico, 130-133

Commercial Ships
In 1961 the destroyer escort John R. Perry (DE-1034) collided with a merchant ship in San Juan, Puerto Rico, 130-133

Communications
Voice radio used for maneuvering in a 1957 exercise en route Canada, 51-52; ComSoLant radio communications in the late 1950s with South American nations, 84-85, 105-106; use of ham radio by an officer's wife in late 1962 to learn the movements of the destroyer escort John R. Perry (DE-1034), 138-139; attempts to miniaturize communications equipment in the Spruance (DD-963)-class destroyers, 225-226

Computers
Use of in the early 1960s by the Bureau of Naval Personnel in recording and changing billet assignments for various commands, 154

Congress
In the early 1960s the Bureau of Naval Personnel sometimes engaged in duplicity in reporting to congressional staffers how many billets were at a given shore station in the Washington, D.C., area, 151

Conyngham, USS (DDG-17)
In 1977 made a cruise to Northern Europe in connection with the Silver Jubilee of Queen Elizabeth II, 349-352

Crispin, Captain Robert E., USN (USNA, 1948)
In the mid-1970s served as chief of staff to Commander Operational Test and Evaluation Force, 306

Cruiser-Destroyer Force Atlantic Fleet
In 1967 the force chaplain conducted humorous correspondence with Colbus, who was the Jewish lay leader on board the destroyer escort McCloy (DE-1038), 192-193; objections concerning several problems the McCloy experienced in 1967

during the course of a NATO deployment, 198-202; in the early 1970s monitored manpower studies on board the destroyer Jonas Ingram (DD-938), 263-264

Cuba
In the mid-1950s the destroyer escort Albert T. Harris (DE-447) made port visits to Havana, 32-34, 101; in the early 1960s Guantanamo Bay was the site of training for the crew of the destroyer escort John R. Perry (DE-1034), 122-126; Guantanamo was the training place in the early 1960s for ships of Escort Squadron 12, 134-136; in October 1962 the John R. Perry and other ships deployed to the area of Cuba to support the quarantine of the island, 136-137; U.S. destroyer patrols off the island in 1972, 138; in 1967 Guantanamo provided training for the crew of the destroyer escort McCloy (DE-1038), 211-212

Cuban Missile Crisis
In October 1962 the destroyer escort John R. Perry (DE-1034) and other ships deployed to the area of Cuba to support the quarantine of the island, 136-137

Czajkowski, Chief Boatswain's Mate Walter J., USN
Colorful individual who served on board the destroyer escort Albert T. Harris (DE-447) in the mid-1950s, 21-23, 213

DX/DXG
See: Destroyer Development Program (DX/DXG)

Dahlgren, USS (DDG-43)
In the late 1970s, Commander Wendell N. Johnson filed a complaint of racial insensitivity against Colbus following a critical fitness report on Johnson's performance while in command of the Dahlgren, 339-347; engineering problems, 340

Dailey, Captain Robertson C., USN (USNA, 1939)
Served in the late 1950s as operations officer for Commander South Atlantic Force, 76, 82; in the early 1960s gave Colbus a book about the 1923 Honda disaster, 116

Dalla Mura, Captain Richard A., USN (USNA, 1951)
In the early 1970s served as ComCruDesLant personnel officer, 264

Damon, Captain Arthur H., Jr., USN
Engaged in a bit of gamesmanship in the mid-1950s while commanding the destroyer Fechteler (DD-870) during a gunnery exercise, 36-37; as training officer in the early 1960s at Guantanamo Bay, 122-126; in the mid-1950s accompanied Colbus on liberty, 123; wife of, 123-126

Darby, USS (DE-218)
Destroyer escort that went through refresher training in the early 1960s after being reactivated as a result of the Berlin Crisis, 134

Davidson, Lieutenant Commander Charles H., USN
In the mid-1960s served as executive officer of the destroyer Basilone (DD-824), 165

Davis, USS (DD-937)
In early 1966, as flagship of Destroyer Squadron 12, deployed to Vietnam, 167

Dealey (DE-1006)-Class Destroyer Escorts
Capabilities of this class, which went into service in the 1950s, 205

Dean, Commander David T., USN (USNA, 1961)
Trivia expert who served in the mid-1970s as chief staff officer to Commander Destroyer Squadron Two, 330

Denmark
In the summer of 1977 a group of ships from Destroyer Squadron Two visited Alborg, 348, 351-352

Des Moines, USS (CA-134)
In 1957 was involved in an exercise with destroyer escorts while en route Canada, 51-52, 54-55

Destroyer Development Program (DX/DXG)
In the late 1960s and early 1970s developed the Spruance (DD-963) and Virginia (CGN-38) classes, 213-215; organizational structure for the program, 215-217; design competition among various defense contractors, 218-221; the design contained margins for future growth, 222-223; Litton built an enlarged facility for construction of the Spruance (DD-963)-class destroyers, 223-224; land-based training facility for the ships' crews, 224-225; attempts to miniaturize communications equipment in the class, 225-226; satellite navigation capability was deemed too expensive, 226-227; concerns on habitability and labor saving, 227-228; the four guided missile versions were originally designed for Iran and later became the Kidd (DDG-993) class in the U.S. Navy, 228-229

Destroyer Squadron Two
As commodore in the late 1970s, Colbus emphasized smart appearance for the ships of the squadron, 212-213; included the destroyer Mullinnix (DD-944), commanded by a former shipmate of Colbus, 316-317; in the late 1970s made a Sixth Fleet deployment, 327-333, 337-339; in the late 1970s the guided missile destroyer Mitscher (DDG-35) had serious engineering plant problems, 331-334; some of the squadron ships went to England in 1977 to help celebrate the Silver Jubilee of Queen Elizabeth II, 348-350; visit to Alborg, Denmark, 348, 351-352; in the late 1970s the ships often operated separately, 356; in 1978 was redesignated from an operational squadron to one that focused on maintenance and training, 357

Destroyer Squadron 12
　In January 1966 became the second East Coast destroyer squadron to deploy to Vietnam, 167-169

Destroyer Squadron 24
　In 1965-66 encountered a number of problems as the first East Coast destroyer squadron to deploy to Vietnam, 167

Diablo, USS (SS-479)
　In the mid-1950s collided off Block Island with the destroyer escort Tabberer (DE-418), 27

Dimitrijevic, Captain William Joseph, USN (USNA, 1932)
　In the late 1950s served as chief of staff for Project Argus and later for Commander South Atlantic Force, 76, 97

Disciplinary Problems
　In the 1950s, on board ship, infractions were dealt with at the lowest possible level to try to keep them from command attention, 10-12; difficulties between sailors and local police in the mid-1950s in Key West, Florida, 23-24; incorrigible sailor who in the mid-1960s served on board the destroyer escort Albert T. Harris (DE-447), 69; in 1972 two crew members from the destroyer Jonas Ingram (DD-938) committed a robbery on the Greek island of Mykonos, 254-256; in April 1981 a crew member of the aircraft carrier Ranger (CV-61) died of heat stroke and cardiac arrest after physical exertion in connection with being punished, 381-383

Dixon, Rear Admiral John C., Jr., USN (USNA, 1949)
　In 1977, while he was Commander Carrier Group Six, commanded an expedition to England to help celebrate the Silver Jubilee of Queen Elizabeth II, 348-350

Donnelly, Captain Raymond D., USN
　In the early 1970s served as operations officer on the staff of Commander Carrier Division Six, 282, 289

Donnelly, Lieutenant Richard F., USN
　Dedicated officer who in 1960 was the top student in the Navy's General Line School, 112

Doyle, Vice Admiral James H., Jr., USN (USNA, 1947)
　As DCNO (Surface Warfare) in 1976 told Colbus he had been screened for major command, 362; talked about the importance of shipboard engineering, 362

Drones
　In 1966 the destroyer Basilone (DD-824) successfully operated the drone antisubmarine helicopter (DASH), 170-172

Drugs
In the early 1970s strong vigilance by Chief Boatswain's Mate Joe Weaver prevented drug problems on board the destroyer <u>Jonas Ingram</u> (DD-938), 242-243

Duncan, Rear Admiral Charles K., USN (USNA, 1933)
Personable, effective officer who served in the early 1960s as head of Pers-A in the Bureau of Naval Personnel, 146-147, 150-152

Dunn, Rear Admiral Robert F., USN (USNA, 1951)
From 1978 to 1980 served as Commander Carrier Group Eight, 366, 368-371; viewed by Colbus as a very profound individual, 368-371

<u>Dwight D. Eisenhower</u>, USS (CVN-69)
In the fall of 1981 participated in a NATO exercise in Northern Europe, 377-378

Ecker, Captain Robert J., CHC, USN
In 1980-81 visited carrier battle group ships operating in the Indian Ocean, 384

Education
In the late 1940s and early 1950s, Colbus studied at Penn State and South Carolina, 1-2, 7-8, 16; in the late 1960s the Program for Afloat College Education was instituted on board the destroyer escort <u>McCloy</u> (DE-1038), 189-190

Eisenhower, President Dwight D.
His visit in early 1960 to South America was marred by the crash of a plane carrying the Navy band, 84-86; in the early 1960s the Bureau of Naval Personnel provided stewards' billets to serve the former President's farm in Gettysburg, Pennsylvania, 141

Elizabeth II, Queen
Destroyer Squadron Two and other U.S. Navy ships went to England in 1977 to help celebrate the Silver Jubilee of the Queen's coronation, 348-351

<u>Elmer Montgomery</u>, USS (FF-1082)
Destroyer Escort that in the mid-1970s deployed to the Sixth Fleet as part of Destroyer Squadron Two, 327, 329

Engen, Vice Admiral Donald D., USN
Fine leader who in the early 1970s commanded a carrier task group in the Mediterranean, 250, 257, 261; visited the destroyer <u>Jonas Ingram</u> (DD-938) after a crewman died of alcohol poisoning, 251-252; as Deputy CinCLantFlt in the late 1970s delivered a non-punitive letter of caution to Colbus for remarks considered racially insensitive, 343-344

England
See: Great Britain

English, Quartermaster William, USN
   In the mid-1960s served in the navigation team of the destroyer Basilone (DD-824), 175

Enlisted Personnel
   Lot of veterans in the crew of the high-speed transport Burdo (APD-133) in 1951 during a summer training cruise, 9-12; Chief Boatswain's Mate Walter J. Czajkowski was a colorful individual who served on board the destroyer escort Albert T. Harris (DE-447) in the mid-1950s, 21-23; characteristics of enlisted men in the crew of the Albert T. Harris, 67-70; in the mid-1960s on board the destroyer Basilone (DD-824), 68; billet justification in the early 1960s by the Bureau of Naval Personnel, 140-141, 154-155; retired personnel at the Naval Home in Philadelphia, 142-144; high cost of living for enlisted personnel stationed in the Washington, D.C., area in the early 1960s, 152; increase in the late 1960s in pay and allowances, 152; in the early 1980s Colbus flew in the back seat of an F-4 based on board the aircraft carrier Independence (CV-62) to demonstrate his confidence in the maintenance work of Fighter Squadron 33 maintenance personnel, 386-387

Equator Crossing
   In the summer of 1953 on board the battleship Missouri (BB-63), 15

Escort Squadron 12
   In the mid-1950s destroyer escorts from the squadron provided services for the sonar school in Key West, Florida, 20, 26-27, 31-32, 34-35, 44-45; officers from the various ships gathered in clubs ashore to talk shop, 25-26; weekend liberty in Havana, Cuba, 32-34; in 1956-57 Commander Joseph M. McDowell served as squadron commodore, 35-36, 50-51; operations on a midshipman training cruise to Canada, 51-55; in 1957-58 Commander Emmett P. Bonner served as squadron commodore, 53; the squadron was disbanded in 1958 when the ships were mothballed, 53-54; in 1957-58 Commander Emmett P. Bonner was commodore, 53, 56-63; operation in ASW hunter-killer groups from Quonset Point, Rhode Island, 55-56; deployment to the Mediterranean in the late 1950s, 58, 61-64, 71-72; awarding of the Battle Efficiency E, 66; competition among the various ships, 66-67; the squadron was reactivated in the early 1960s because of the Berlin Crisis, 129-130, 134-136

F-4 Phantom
   In the early 1980s Colbus delighted in the opportunity to ride in the back seat and get a sense of the airplane, 386-387

Families of Servicemen
   In the mid-1950s crew members of the destroyer escort Albert T. Harris (DE-447) brought their families on board for meals on duty days, 46, 48

Fechteler, USS (DD-870)
Skipper Art Damon employed some gamesmanship in the mid-1950s while conducting gunnery training, 36-37

Ferguson, Colonel Edwin C., USMC
Marine officer who ran the NROTC program from 1948 to 1952 at the University of South Carolina, 3

Fighter Squadron 33 (VF-33)
In the early 1980s Colbus flew in the back seat of an F-4 based on board the aircraft carrier Independence (CV-62) to demonstrate his confidence in the maintenance work of the squadron's maintenance personnel, 386-387

Fitch, Vice Admiral Richard G. A., Royal Navy
In 1967 commanded HMS Berwick during a multinational NATO exercise, 194-195; met his future wife in Lisbon, 194-195; in the 1980s commanded antisubmarine forces, 195

Fitness Reports
While commanding Task Force 88 in late 1958, Rear Admiral Lloyd Mustin was exacting in his preparation of officer fitness reports, 78; in the late 1970s, Commander Wendell N. Johnson filed a complaint of racial insensitivity against Colbus following a critical fitness report on Johnson's performance while in command of the guided missile destroyer Dahlgren (DDG-43), 339-347

Fitzgerald, Captain Jean, USN
In the early 1970s was liberal in viewpoint while serving as a destroyer squadron commander, 276-277

Flynn, Lieutenant Commander Gerrish C., USN
As commanding officer of the destroyer escort W. S. Sims (DE-1059) in 1972, was involved in a "shouldering" incident with a Soviet ship in the Mediterranean, 257-258; sonar capability of his ship, 260

Forbes, Rear Admiral Bernard B., Jr., USN (USNA, 1945)
Colorful individual who served in the early 1970s as Commander Carrier Division Six, 282-286, 290-291, 300-304; in the mid-1970s served as Deputy CinCLantFlt, 286-287, 305

Forrest Sherman (DD-931)-Class Destroyers
Much more appealing esthetically than the later Spruance (DD-963) class, 229; comparison of the engineering plants in the ships with those in Charles F. Adams (DDG-2)-class ships, 258-259; added capabilities for the ships with the ASW upgrade, 259-260

Fort Lauderdale, Florida
In the early 1960s was the site of port visits for the destroyer escort John R. Perry (DE-1034), 127-129

Francis Marion, USS (LPA-249)
Attack transport that in 1977 served as flagship for a squadron of U.S. Navy ships that went to England to help celebrate the Silver Jubilee of Queen Elizabeth II, 348-350

Franklin D. Roosevelt, USS (CVA-42)
In 1972 a petty officer from the destroyer Jonas Ingram (DD-938) died on board this carrier after suffering alcohol poisoning on board his own ship, 250-251; task group operations in 1972 in the Mediterranean, 261; deployment work-ups in the Caribbean, 266; in the early 1970s served as flagship for Commander Carrier Division Six, 279-280, 296-297; racial protest on board in the early 1970s when the ship was operating in the Caribbean, 296-297

Franklin, Lieutenant Isaac Nelson, USN
In the mid-1950s was a demanding executive officer of the destroyer escort Albert T. Harris (DE-447), 29-31, 36, 39-40; in 1958 as a BuPers detailer, he got Colbus some staff assignments, 72

Gaeta, Italy
In the late 1970s was the site of a gathering of Sixth Fleet ships, 337-339

Gallery, Rear Admiral Daniel V., Jr., USN (USNA, 1921)
Colorful, hard-of-hearing flag officer who was an institution in Puerto Rico in the late 1950s while serving as Commander Caribbean Sea Frontier, 103-104

Gardes, Captain Alfred W., Jr., USN (USNA, 1937)
In the early 1960s was in Puerto Rico as commodore of an amphibious squadron, 131

Gazarek, Lieutenant Michael J., USN
Fine officer who served in the early 1970s as ops officer on board the destroyer Jonas Ingram (DD-938), 246-247, 249, 253

Gemini Program
In late 1965 the destroyer Basilone (DD-824) was involved in the recovery of Gemini astronauts in the Atlantic, 166-167

General Dynamics
In the late 1960s was involved in the DX/DXG destroyer design development competition, 218, 220

General Line School
In 1960, this course at Monterey, California, provided sort of an advanced NROTC training in naval subjects, 106-110, 112-114; competition among classmates, 107-108, 112; description of instructors, 108-109; social life for the line school students, 114-115

Germany
Hamburg was the site of an oil spill in the late 1960s by the destroyer escort McCloy (DE-1038), 199-200; mooring accident in Hamburg in the late 1970s by the guided missile destroyer Richard E. Byrd (DDG-23), 363

Gibbs & Cox, Inc.
In the late 1960s was involved in the DX/DXG destroyer design development competition, 218-219

Goodwin, Captain Robert L., Jr., USN
Energetic officer who in the late 1970s commanded the guided missile destroyer Richard E. Byrd (DDG-23), 360-361; damaged the ship during a moor in Hamburg, Germany, 363

Great Britain
Destroyer Squadron Two and other U.S. Navy ships went to England in 1977 to help celebrate the Silver Jubilee of Queen Elizabeth II, 348-351

Greece
The island of Mykonos served as a popular liberty spot in 1972 for the crew of the destroyer Jonas Ingram (DD-938), 253-257; in 1972 two crew members from the Jonas Ingram committed a robbery on Mykonos, 254-256

Grischy, Lieutenant John S., USN
In the mid-1950s served as executive officer of the destroyer escort Albert T. Harris (DE-447), 19

Guantanamo Bay, Cuba
In the early 1960s was the site of training for the crew of the destroyer escort John R. Perry (DE-1034), 122-126; training place in the early 1960s for ships of Escort Squadron 12, 134-136; provided training in 1967 for the crew of the destroyer escort McCloy (DE-1038), 211-212

Gudgen, Lieutenant Richard A., SC, USN
Fine officer who served in the early 1970s as supply officer on board the destroyer Jonas Ingram (DD-938), 247-248

Gunnery-Naval
During a summer cruise in 1953 the battleship Missouri (BB-63) fired her 16-inch guns, 14-15; exercise in the mid-1950s for the crew of the destroyer escort Albert T.

Harris (DE-447), 35-36; exercise in the mid-1950s on board the destroyer Fechteler (DD-870), 36-37; in 1966 the destroyer Basilone (DD-824) provided shore bombardment of South Vietnam, 172-174, 184-185; gunfire exercise in 1972 by the destroyer Jonas Ingram (DD-938), 278; in 1974 the destroyer escort Talbot (DEG-4) was used as a test platform for the 76-millimeter OTO Melara gun, 307-308, 311

Gureck, Rear Admiral William A., USN

In the late 1970s conducted a one-man inquiry on Colbus in connection with complaints of racial insensitivity made by Commander Wendell N. Johnson, commanding officer of the guided missile destroyer Dahlgren (DDG-43), 342-343, 345-346

Guy, Captain Robert S., USN

In 1966 was the commodore of Destroyer Squadron 12 when it deployed from the East Coast to Vietnam, 167

Habitability

As a factor in the design of the Spruance (DD-963)-class destroyers and Virginia (CGN-38)-class cruisers, 227-228, 309

Hallam, Captain Orval K., USN

As Commander Escort Squadron Ten in the late 1960s was involved in responding to complaints about one of his ships, destroyer escort McCloy (DE-1038), 200-201

Hamburg, Germany

Site of an oil spill in the late 1960s by the destroyer escort McCloy (DE-1038), 199-200; site of a mooring accident in the late 1970s by the guided missile destroyer Richard E. Byrd (DDG-23), 363

Hanson, Rear Admiral Carl Thor, USN (USNA, 1950)

In 1977 commanded Cruiser-Destroyer Group Eight when a group of his ships went to England to help celebrate the Silver Jubilee of Queen Elizabeth II, 349-350; assessed as a brilliant, versatile man, 359

Harl, Musician First Class Richard D., USN

Killed in February 1960 when a plane carrying the U.S. Navy band crashed in Brazil, 86-87

Havana, Cuba

In the mid-1950s the destroyer escort Albert T. Harris (DE-447) made port visits to this city, 32-34

Hedgehog

Antisubmarine weapon used in the mid-1950s on board the destroyer escort Albert T. Harris (DE-447), 32, 34-35

Helicopters
In 1966 the destroyer Basilone (DD-824) successfully operated the drone antisubmarine helicopter (DASH), 170-172; origin in the late 1960s of the LAMPS helicopter program for antisubmarine warfare, 214-215; use of LAMPS in the Oliver Hazard Perry (FFG-7)-class frigates, 312

Hill, Lieutenant Commander James Franklin, USN
In the mid-1950s served as commanding officer of the destroyer escort Albert T. Harris (DE-447), 19-23, 25-28, 33, 48; duty in the early 1960s in the Washington, D.C., area, 140

Hilton, Captain Robert P., USN
In early 1966 served as commanding officer of the destroyer Davis (DD-937) when she deployed to Vietnam, 167; in 1972 used the destroyer Jonas Ingram (DD-938) as flagship when he was a destroyer squadron commander, 249, 252, 256, 266, 276, 297-298, 331; also used the destroyer escort W. S. Sims (DE-1059) as flagship, 257-258; in 1972 tried to get Colbus to serve in Washington, D.C., 279; observed to Colbus that the black sailors in the crew of the Jonas Ingram tended to hang out together on board ship but not ashore, 297-298

Hoffmann, Captain Roy F., USN
Tough-minded officer who in the late 1960s served in country in Vietnam and in the early 1970s commanded the guided missile frigate Leahy (DLG-16), 261-262

Holloway, Admiral James L., Jr., USN (Ret.) (USNA, 1919)
In the early 1960s served as governor of the Naval Home in Philadelphia, 142-144; very formal in manner, 147

Holloway, Admiral James L. III, USN (USNA, 1943)
As Chief of Naval Operations in 1976, received a memo on Colbus's enthusiasm as a student in the Senior Officer Ship Material Readiness Course, 321

Honey Fitz
Presidential yacht that in the early 1960s was based at the Washington Navy Yard and manned by naval personnel, 141-142

Hong Kong, British Crown Colony
Popular liberty port for U.S. Navy ships during the Vietnam War, 179-181

Honolulu, Hawaii
In 1966 was the site of a memorable evening on the town for Colbus, 178-179

Hughes, Rear Admiral Thomas J., Jr., USN
In 1976 was a top-notch student in the Senior Officer Ship Material Readiness Course, 318, 326

Independence, USS (CVA-62/CV-62)
In 1973 Colbus wrote a humorous memo about the pattern of drain holes in the ship's urinals, 280-281; in the late 1970s Captain Tom Watson did a fine job as commanding officer of the ship, 293-294; commanded in the mid-1970s by Captain James Service, 371, 381; in 1982 conducted a burial at sea off Fort Lauderdale, Florida, 376-377; in 1980-81 operated in the Indian Ocean, 384-387

Indian Ocean
The U.S. Navy conducted aircraft carrier battle group operations in the region in the early 1980s, 384-385

Ingram, Vice Admiral Jonas H., USN (USNA, 1907)
Created a highly favorable impression in South America when he was stationed there in World War II, 81

Inspections
Personnel inspections in 1951 on board the high-speed transport Burdo (APD-133), 11-12; as Commander Cruiser-Destroyer Group Eight in the late 1970s, Rear Admiral Robert L. Walters liked to conduct surprise inspections of ships, 359-361

Intelligence
Collection of information in the late 1950s, when ships of the U.S. South Atlantic Force visited Africa, 97, 100

Investigations
Inquiry following a collision in the early 1960s at San Juan between a merchant ship and the destroyer escort John R. Perry (DE-1034), 132-133; in the late 1970s Rear Admiral William Gureck investigated the charge that Colbus had made racially insensitive remarks to Commander Wendell N. Johnson, 342-343, 345-346

Iranian Navy
Four guided missile versions of the Spruance (DD-963)-class destroyer were originally designed for Iran and later became the Kidd (DDG-993) class in the U.S. Navy, 228-229

Italy
Naples was the site of a 1957 nightclub incident that involved naval officers from the Sixth Fleet, 62-64; in the 1970s a well-known madam in Naples had the nickname "Humpty-Dumpty," 286-287; NATO celebrations in the late 1970s in Naples and Gaeta, 337-338

Jamaica
In the early 1960s Montego Bay was a liberty attraction for reservists on active duty, 134-135

John F. Kennedy, USS (CVA-67/CV-67)
In the autumn of 1973 deployed to the Mediterranean during the Yom Kippur Arab-Israeli War, 282-288; in May 1980 visited Boston to celebrate the city's 350th anniversary, 371-375

John King, USS (DDG-3)
Both the ship and her crew had a smart appearance in 1967 under the command of Commander Ted Kosmela, 211-212

John R. Perry, USS (DE-1034)
As executive officer in the early 1960s Colbus briefed crew members on retirement pay provisions, 109; in 1961 the ship went from to Charleston for updating of the sonar dome, 116-121; top-notch appearance, 119; training in Guantanamo, Cuba, 122-126; operations in the early 1960s in the Bermuda-Florida area, 127-129; in 1961 went through an overhaul at Norfolk, which became the ship's home port, 129-130, 133-134; in 1961 collided with a merchant ship in San Juan, Puerto Rico, 130-133; joined recently reactivated ships for training at Guantanamo, 134-136; role in October 1962 in support of the quarantine connected with the Cuban Missile Crisis, 136-139; use of ham radio by an officer's wife in late 1962 to learn the ship's movements, 138-139; playing of bugle calls on the general announcing system, 213

Johnson, Rear Admiral Wendell N., USN (Ret.)
In the late 1970s, while in command of the guided missile destroyer Dahlgren (DDG-43), filed a complaint of racial insensitivity against Colbus following a critical fitness report, 339-347

Jonas Ingram, USS (DD-938)
Destroyer that deployed to South America in the late 1950s, 81; visit to Africa as part of the South Atlantic Force, 91-93; in 1972 patrolled off the island of Cuba, 138, 274-276; her ASW modernization made her less appealing esthetically than she had been originally but more capable operationally, 229, 259-260; was in fine material condition in 1971 when Colbus took command, 234; restoration of the chain of command and strong discipline, 235-240, 243-245; improperly handled provisions for the wardroom mess, 238-239; smart appearance of the ship, which was nicknamed the "Cadillac of the Fleet," 240-241; strong leadership provided by Chief Boatswain's Mate Joe Weaver, 242-243, 298-299; talented group of officers on board, 245-249; deployment in 1972 to the Sixth Fleet, 249-265; in the early 1970s Captain Robert Hilton was embarked as commodore, 331, 249, 252, 256, 266, 276, 297-298, 331; one crew member died of alcohol poisoning, 250-251; liberty on the island of Mykonos in the Aegean, 253-257; in 1972 two crew members from the ship committed a robbery on Mykonos, 254-256; maneuvers in the vicinity of Soviet ships in the Mediterranean, 257-259; comparison of the ship's engineering plant with those in the Charles F. Adams (DDG-2)-class ships, 258-259; carrier task group operations in the Mediterranean, 261; in 1972 served as test bed for the ships manning document for her class, 263-265; Gunner's Mate St. John returned to the ship after hospitalization in Germany for an injured hand, 264-265; prior to Sixth

Fleet deployment, the crew heard a lecture from David Rosenberg on the culture of the Mediterranean area, 265-266; pay allotments for dependents, 266; in October 1971 buried the remains of Rear Admiral Daniel F. Smith, Jr., at sea off Florida, 267-270; hit a submarine with a torpedo while providing target services, 271-274; navigation uncertainties while returning to home port, 272-273, 275; in 1972 made a cruise to the Caribbean, 277-278; in the early 1970s the black sailors in the crew tended to hang out together on board ship but not ashore, 297-298; junior officers in the 1970s didn't visit the skipper's home as much as junior officers of other ships had done in the 1950s, 299; can-do spirit in engineering, 362

Joseph P. Kennedy, Jr., USS (DD-850)
In October 1962 sent a boarding party to check out the Soviet-chartered cargo ship Marucla as part of the Cuban Missile Crisis, 137

Josephus Daniels, USS (CG-27)
Cruiser that in the mid-1970s operated as part of the Sixth Fleet in the Mediterranean, 328-329

Kahn, Lieutenant Commander Bruce E., CHC, USNR
Chaplain who in the late 1970s and early 1980s had temporary duty on the staff of Commander Carrier Group Eight, 368-369, 371-374; visit to a temple in Brookline, Massachusetts, 372-373

Kaohsiung, Taiwan
In 1966 was an enjoyable liberty site for the crew of the destroyer Basilone (DD-724), 169-170

Kaufman, Lieutenant Edwin J., USN
Fine officer who served in the early 1970s as operations officer on board the destroyer Jonas Ingram (DD-938), 246

Kelley, Captain Edward G., USN
In the early 1970s commanded a destroyer squadron based at Mayport, Florida, 267-276; tough, demanding style of leadership, 271-276

Kennedy, President John F.
Visited Navy ships in Florida in late 1962 in connection with the Cuban Missile Crisis and got wet paint on his hand, 139; the Bureau of Naval Personnel provided stewards for the White House, and one remained with Mrs. Kennedy after her husband was assassinated, 141

Key West, Florida
In the mid-1950s was the site of a Navy sonar training school, 20-21, 26-27, 31-32, 34-35, 43-45; popular liberty attractions, 20, 24-26, 34; difficulties between sailors and local police, 23-25; in late 1962 served as logistics base for ships involved in the quarantine of Cuba, 138-139; the job of the base commander, Rear Admiral R. Y.

McElroy, became a lot busier than it had been with the advent in late 1962 of the Cuban Missile Crisis, 140

Kidd, Admiral Isaac C., Jr., USN (USNA, 1942)
As CinCLantFlt in the late 1970s disagreed with charges that Colbus was prejudiced, 343, 347; in 1978 had a hand in realigning the functions of Atlantic Fleet destroyer squadrons, 357-358

Kidd (DDG-993)-Class Destroyers
Four guided missile versions of the Spruance (DD-963)-class destroyer were originally designed for Iran and later became the Kidd class in the U.S. Navy, 228-229

King, USS (DDG-41)
In the late 1970s deployed to the Mediterranean after having a difficult shipyard period, 355

Kinnear, Vice Admiral George E. R. II, USN
As ComNavAirLant in the late 1970s had a long meeting with Colbus about serving as a carrier group chief of staff, 367-368

Kinnebrew, Captain Thomas R., USN
Prior to October 1976 served as Commander Destroyer Squadron Two, 316-317, 327-330, 332, 339-340; selected for flag rank, 340

Kirk, Lieutenant Commander George Griswold Ely Kirk, USN (USNA, 1947)
Colorful officer who in the early 1960s commanded the destroyer escort John R. Perry (DE-1034), 116-120, 122-130; aggressive ship handling, 117; fondness for liberty, 118-119; was skipper in 1961 when the John R. Perry collided with a merchant ship in San Juan, Puerto Rico, 130-133

Korean War
In the early 1950s Naval ROTC midshipmen at the University of South Carolina were eager to get into action, 15-16

Kosmela, Commander Walter T., USN (USNA, 1952)
As commanding officer of the destroyer John King (DDG-3) in 1967, ensured that his ship and crew had a smart appearance, 211-212; in 1968 worked in OpNav on a destroyer development program, 212, 214; hospitalized in the late 1970s at Bethesda, 336

LAMPS
Origin in the late 1960s of this ASW helicopter program for surface combatants, 214-215; use of in the Oliver Hazard Perry (FFG-7)-class frigates, 312; use of in 1976 in the Sixth Fleet for transportation, 329

La Rocque, Captain Gene R., USN
As chief of staff for Commander Destroyer Flotilla Six in 1961 was very helpful to those who served in destroyers, 118, 127

Leahy, USS (DLG-16)
In the early 1970s operated in the Mediterranean under a tough skipper, Captain Roy F. Hoffman, 261

Leave and Liberty
In 1951 when the high-speed transport Burdo (APD-133) was on a midshipman cruise to Europe, 12; in the mid-1950s around Newport, Rhode Island, 19-20, 40-41; in the mid-1950s in Key West, Florida, 23-26, 34; in the mid-1950s the destroyer escort Albert T. Harris (DE-447) made port visits to Havana, Cuba, 32-34; at Nassau in the Bahamas in the mid-1950s, 47-49; Naples, Italy, was the site of a 1957 nightclub incident that involved Sixth Fleet officers, 62-64; attractions in the late 1950s at Palma, Majorca, sometimes included movie stars, 71-72; in the late 1950s in Africa, 89-91, 94-95; in 1960 in San Francisco, 106-107; social life in Carmel, California, in 1960 for students from the General Line School, 106-107, 114-115; in 1961 in Charleston, South Carolina, 119; in the early 1960s in Fort Lauderdale, 127-129; in the early 1960s in Montego Bay, Jamaica, 134-135; in 1965 sailors from the destroyer Basilone (DD-824) had a great time when they visited Raritan, New Jersey, home of the Basilone family, 165-166; in 1966 in Kaohsiung, Taiwan, 169-170; in 1966 Olongapo in the Philippines was a wild and wooly place for sailors, 177-178; in 1966 Colbus had a memorable evening on the town in Honolulu, 178-179; in 1966 in Hong Kong, 179-181; in 1972 on the Aegean island of Mykonos, 253-257; in the early 1970s the black sailors in the crew of the destroyer Jonas Ingram (DD-938) tended to hang out together on board ship but not ashore in Mediterranean ports, 297-298

Liberia
Visited in the late 1950s by ships of the U.S. South Atlantic Force, 90

Linder, Lieutenant Commander James B., USN (USNA, 1949)
In the early 1960s served as aide to the Chief of Naval Personnel, Vice Admiral William Smedberg, 147

Litton/Ingalls
In the late 1960s was involved in the DX/DXG destroyer design development competition, 218-220; Litton built an enlarged facility for construction of the Spruance (DD-963)-class destroyers, 223-224

Logistics
Support provided at various ports in the late 1950s to ships of the South Atlantic Force, 104-105

Luce, USS (DLG-7)
In the early 1970s was commanded by a colorful officer, Commander Sam Pearlman, 262-263

Luciano, Charles "Lucky"
Gangster who in 1957, in a Naples nightclub, mistakenly believed that Colbus was Yul Brynner, 62-64

Macon, USS (CA-132)
Heavy cruiser that in early 1960 deployed to South America as flagship of the South Atlantic Force, 81, 84-88

Majorca
Liberty attractions at Palma in the late 1950s sometimes included movie stars, 71-72; in 1976 Palma was the site of the change of command for Destroyer Squadron Two, 327

Manpower
In the early 1970s the destroyer Jonas Ingram (DD-938) served as a test bed for the ships manning document on billet needs, 263-264

Margaret, HRH (British Princess)
In the mid-1950s visited Nassau in the Bahamas on board the royal yacht Britannia, 48-49

Marine Corps
From 1948 to 1952 Colonel Edwin Ferguson provided a strong influence as professor of naval science in the South Carolina NROTC program, 3; in 1957 Brigadier General Ralph Rottet mistakenly believed he met Yul Brynner in a Naples, Italy, nightclub, 63-65

Mauritius
Visited in the late 1950s by ships of the U.S. South Atlantic Force, 99-100

Mayport, Florida
In the early 1970s served as home port for the destroyer Jonas Ingram (DD-938), 267-273

McCloy, USS (DE-1038)
In 1967 the ship took part in NATO exercises, 49-50, 190-191, 193-197, 207; updating of sonar equipment at the Boston Naval Shipyard, 188-189, 203-204, 206; implementation on board of the Program for Afloat College Education, 189-190; Colbus's role as the ship's Jewish lay leader, 192-193; difficulties with the engineering plant, especially a shortage of fresh water, 193, 206-211; shipyard period in Norway, 198-199; oil spill in Hamburg, Germany, 199-200; controversy over payment for a shipboard reception in Hamburg, 200-201; in the late 1960s the ship was blessed with a talented group of commissioned officers and chief petty

officers, 203; ship handling difficulties imposed by the addition of a large sonar dome, 204-205; belonged to a class of ship not produced in quantity, 205; received repairs in 1967 from the destroyer tender Acadia (AD-42), 209-211; methods to save labor in keeping the ship clean, 227-228; equipment and weapons capability, 232

McComis, Lieutenant Charles W., USN
Well-heeled mustang officer who saved his money in World War II and in 1960 was a student in the Navy's General Line School, 110-112

McDowell, Commander Joseph M., USN (USNA, 1938)
Served in 1956-57 as Commander Escort Squadron 12, 35-36, 50-52; in 1957 requested Colbus for his staff, 50-51; McDowell was difficult to get along with, 51-52

McElroy, Rear Admiral Rhodam Yarrott, Jr., USN (USNA, 1935)
As base commander at Key West, Florida, in the autumn of 1962, during the Cuban Missile Crisis, his job suddenly became a lot busier than it had been, 140

McKeown, Commander Ronald E., USN (USNA, 1961)
In the early 1980s served as operations officer on the staff of Commander Carrier Group Eight, 374-375, 378-379

Mediterranean Sea
See: Greece; Italy; Majorca; Sixth Fleet, U.S.

Metzler, Commander Donald M., USN
Modish officer who commanded the destroyer Jonas Ingram (DD-938) in the early 1970s, 235, 270

Miller, Vice Admiral Gerald E., USN (USNA, 1942)
Popular leader in the early 1970s while commanding the Sixth Fleet, 250, 252, 255-256, 382

Mississinewa, USS (AO-144)
Fleet oiler that in 1967 was unsuccessful in trying to provide fresh water to the destroyer escort McCloy (DE-1038), 210

Missouri, USS (BB-63)
Battleship that in the summer of 1953 made a midshipman training cruise to South America, 12-15

Mitscher, USS (DDG-35)
Guided missile destroyer that in the late 1970s had considerable problems in the engineering plant, 331-334; subject of a 1977 article in The Washington Post, 334-336

Monroe, Rear Admiral Robert R., USN (USNA, 1950)
In the mid-1970s worked long hours while serving as Commander Operational Test and Evaluation Force, 305-307, 313-314

Montego Bay, Jamaica
In the early 1960s was a liberty attraction for reservists on active duty, 134-135

Moorer, Rear Admiral Joseph P., USN (USNA, 1945)
In the early 1970s served as Commander Carrier Division Six, 279-283, 288-291, 296-297; wrote humorous response to a tongue-in-cheek memo from Colbus, 280-281

Morin, Captain James B., USN
In the early 1970s did a fine job of handling a racial protest on board his ship while in command of the aircraft carrier Franklin D. Roosevelt (CVA-42), 296-297

Mosman, Commander Donald Eugene, USN
In the late 1970s provided fine leadership as commanding officer of the guided missile destroyer Mitscher (DDG-35), 332-335, 356, 363

Movies
The 1955 Republic Pictures film Flame of the Islands was made in the Bahamas while the destroyer escort Albert T. Harris (DE-447) was there, 48-49; in the early 1960s the Bureau of Naval Personnel reviewed new Hollywood films before releasing them to the fleet, 146; filming in Hong Kong in 1966 for the movie The Sand Pebbles, 179-180

Mozambique
Visited in the late 1950s by ships of the U.S. South Atlantic Force, 90-93

Mullinnix, USS (DD-944)
New destroyer that deployed in the late 1950s as part of the South Atlantic Force, 104-105; much more appealing esthetically than the later Spruance (DD-963) class and even converted versions of her own class, 229; in the late 1970s had a shipyard period in Brooklyn, 353; in 1978 transferred from Destroyer Squadron Two to Destroyer Squadron Six and changed homeports, 354-355

Music
A number of members of the U.S. Navy Band were killed in February 1960 when a plane carrying them crashed in Brazil, 85-87; in the 1950s and 1960s Newport, Rhode Island, was the site of annual jazz festivals, 162-163

Mustin, Vice Admiral Lloyd M., USN (USNA, 1932)
In late 1958 commanded Task Force 88 during high-altitude nuclear weapons tests in the Antarctic, 73-79; was a smart, tough, exacting taskmaster, 77-78; very skilled operationally, 79

Mykonos Island
    Greek island that served as a popular liberty spot in 1972 for the crew of the destroyer Jonas Ingram (DD-938), 253-257; in 1972 two crew members from the Jonas Ingram committed a robbery on Mykonos, 254-256

NATO
    See: North Atlantic Treaty Organization (NATO)

NROTC
    See: Naval Reserve Officer Training Corps (NROTC)

Naples, Italy
    Site of a 1957 nightclub incident that involved naval officers from the Sixth Fleet, 62-64; in the 1970s a well-known madam in Naples had the nickname "Humpty-Dumpty," 286-287; in the late 1970s was the site of a NATO anniversary celebration, 337

Nassau, Bahamas Islands
    Visited in the mid-1950s by the destroyer escort Albert T. Harris (DE-447), 47-49; site for the filming of the 1955 movie Flame of the Islands, 48-49

Naval Academy, Annapolis, Maryland
    Comparison in the 1950s of academy midshipmen with their NROTC counterparts, 5-6, 12, 16; football players joined a 1953 summer training cruise when it was partly over, 15

Naval Home, Philadelphia, Pennsylvania
    Billet justification in the early 1960s when Admiral James L. Holloway, Jr., ran this haven for retired naval personnel, 142-143

Naval Postgraduate School, Monterey, California
    In 1960 the general line school course provided sort of an advanced NROTC training in naval subjects, 106-110, 112-114; social life for the line school students, 114-115

Naval Reserve, U.S.
    When destroyer escorts were reactivated in the early 1960s as a result of the Berlin Crisis, they were manned by reservists, 134-135

Naval Reserve Officer Training Corps (NROTC)
    In the late 1940s Colbus tried to join the program at Penn State University, but instead went to the University of South Carolina, 1-2; operation of the programs from 1950 to 1954 at South Carolina and Penn State, 3-18; comparison in the 1950s of Naval Academy midshipmen with their NROTC counterparts, 5-6, 12, 16; scholarship benefits, 6; summer training cruises in the early 1950s, 8-15

Naval War College, Newport, Rhode Island
Site of World War II analytical work conducted in the late 1940s and early 1950s by Commodore Richard Bates, 41-43; competition among students during the 1964-65 school year, 158-160; subject matter of courses, 159-162; war gaming, 160-161

Navigation
In 1961, as navigator of the destroyer escort John R. Perry (DE-1034), Colbus was cautious as a result of reading a book about the 1923 Honda disaster, 116-117; difficulty for the destroyer Basilone (DD-824) in 1966 while operating off the coast of South Vietnam, 172-173, 175, 226; satellite navigation capability was deemed too expensive for the Spruance (DD-963)-class destroyers, 226-227; uncertainties about position when the destroyer Jonas Ingram (DD-938) in the early 1970s was returning to her home port of Mayport, Florida, 272-273, 275

Neel, Captain William C., USN (USNA, 1954)
In the mid-1970s commanded the cruiser South Carolina (CGN-37) during operations in the Mediterranean, 329-330

Netherlands Navy
Operated in 1967 as part of a multinational NATO squadron, 193

Newport, Rhode Island
In the early 1950s served as a base for Atlantic Fleet destroyer and destroyer escort operations, 18; liberty opportunities in the area, 19-20, 40-41; in the 1950s Jewish personnel attended the Touro Synagogue, a famous historical landmark in Newport, Rhode Island, 41; people of the Naval War College in the mid-1950s, 41-42; local atmosphere in the mid-1960s, 162; in the mid-1950s was the site of jazz festivals, 162-163

See also: Naval War College, Newport, Rhode Island

News Media
In 1977 Colbus did an interview with writer George Wilson of The Washington Post concerning personnel in his destroyer squadron, 334-336

New York Naval Shipyard
Site of a yard period in 1956 for the destroyer escort Albert T. Harris (DE-447), 69

Nicholson, Captain Richard E., USN (USNA, 1948)
As operations officer on the ComNavForV staff in late 1969, requested Colbus and several other former destroyer escort skippers for the staff, but budget cutbacks precluded the assignment, 230-232

Nimitz, USS (CVN-68)
In the mid-1970s, when the ship was newly commissioned, she received a visit from representatives of the Operational Test and Evaluation Force, 305; in the autumn of 1976 was involved in Sixth Fleet exercises, 328, 330

Norfolk Naval Shipyard, Portsmouth, Virginia
In the early 1960s was the site of an overhaul for the destroyer escort John R. Perry (DE-1034), 129-130, 133-134

North Atlantic Treaty Organization (NATO)
In 1967 conducted naval Exercise Matchmaker in Northern Europe, 49-50, 190-191, 193-197, 207; social aspects of the exercise, 197-198; in the early 1970s Carrier Division Six was involved in NATO exercises in the Mediterranean, 290-291; in 1974 Carrier Division Six participated in a North Atlantic NATO exercise, 300-301; briefing in the spring of 1974 for a crossing-the-Atlantic exercise, 302-303; in the late 1970s celebrated anniversary of NATO in the Mediterranean, 337; in 1981 Exercise Northern Wedding was conducted in Northern Europe, 377-378

Norton Sound, USS (AVM-1)
Missile test ship that fired nuclear weapons as part of Task Force 88 in late 1958 during high-altitude tests near Antarctica, 73-75

Norway
In 1967 the destroyer escort McCloy (DE-1038) visited this country during the course of a NATO exercise, 190-191; shipyard work for the McCloy while in Norway, 198-199

Nuclear Propulsion
In the early 1960s on board the nuclear-powered frigate Bainbridge (DLGN-25), 144-145; in the late 1960s was considered too expensive for the Spruance (DD-963)-class destroyers but was used for what became the Virginia (CGN-38)-class cruisers, 215-217

Nuclear Weapons
High-altitude tests conducted near Antarctica in late 1958 by Task Force 88 during Project Argus, 73-78

Nuessle, Rear Admiral Francis E., USN (USNA, 1932)
In the mid-1960s served as deputy and acting president of the Naval War College, 158; had the playful nickname of "Admiral Hershey," 159

Oaksmith, Commander David E., Jr., USN
In the early 1970s served as surface operations officer and material officer on the staff of Commander Carrier Division Six, 290

Officer Candidate School
   Graduates who served in the destroyer escort Albert T. Harris (DE-447) in the mid-1950s were excellent officers, 66

Oil Fuel
   In the late 1960s the destroyer escort McCloy (DE-1038) had an oil spill in Hamburg, Germany, 199-200

Oklahoma City, USS (CLG-5)
   In the mid-1960s Captain Emmett P. Bonner did a fine job of handling the cruiser during a visit to Saigon, South Vietnam, 60

Oliver Hazard Perry (FFG-7)-Class Frigates
   Strict cost-saving measures were used in the early 1970s when the ships were designed, 310-312; testing of planned elements in other ships, 311; Colbus considered growth inevitable, 312; combat center mockup was built by Sperry while the ship was being developed, 315

Olongapo, Philippines
   Wild place where sailors much enjoyed liberty during the Vietnam War, 177-178

Operational Test and Evaluation Force
   In the mid-1970s the newly formed ship evaluation division visited various ships to make recommendations for improvements, 305, 307-308, 311-315; Rear Admiral Robert Monroe, the force commander in the mid-1970s, was a perfectionist who worked extremely long hours, 306-307, 313-314; in 1974 the destroyer escort Talbot (DEG-4) was used as a test platform for the 76-millimeter OTO Melara gun, 307-308, 311

PACE
   See: Program for Afloat College Education

Palma, Majorca
   Liberty attractions in the late 1950s sometimes included movie stars, 71-72; in 1976 was the site of the change of command for Destroyer Squadron Two, 327

Pay and Allowances
   In the early 1950s for Naval Academy and NROTC midshipmen, 5-6; in 1960 a junior officer had a relatively meager salary on which to pay for entertainment, 115; substantial increase in the late 1960s for enlisted personnel, 152-153; in the Vietnam War servicemen received extra pay for hazardous duty, 180; problems with dependents' allotments during the 1972 Mediterranean deployment of the destroyer Jonas Ingram (DD-938), 266

Pearlman, Captain Samuel S., USN
   In the early 1970s commanded the destroyer Luce (DLG-7), 262-263

Peet, Captain Raymond E., USN (USNA, 1943)
Gracious officer who in the early 1960s served as the first skipper of the nuclear-powered frigate Bainbridge (DLGN-25), 144-146; in the late 1960s was the original head of the DX/DXG destroyer development program, 216, 222

Pennsylvania State University, State College Pennsylvania
In the late 1940s and early 1950s provided undergraduate and postgraduate education to Colbus, 1; Colbus tried to enter the NROTC program there in the late 1940s but found no seats available, 1; Colbus did a year of graduate work at the university in 1953-54 and was then commissioned in the Navy, 1-2, 16-18; Colbus's father attended the university early in the century, 33

Pensions
In the early 1960s Colbus learned the provisions of the Contingency Option Act for providing continuing benefits to survivors after a service member dies, 109

Perth, Australia
Visited in the early 1980s by the aircraft carrier Independence (CV-62), 385

Philippine Islands
Liberty for Navy men in 1966 in Subic Bay and Olongapo, 177-178

Pocono, USS (AGC-16)
Served in 1957 as flagship for Marine Brigadier General Ralph Rottet during a deployment to the Mediterranean, 62-64

Porcari, Captain Thomas J., USN
In the early 1970s served as chief of staff to Commander Carrier Division Six, 281, 289, 296-297

Price, Rear Admiral Frank H., USN (USNA, 1941)
In the early 1970s was the subject of comments by a former shipmate, 263; in the early 1970s headed the Navy program for what eventually became the Oliver Hazard Perry (FFG-7) class, 310-312

Program for Afloat College Education (PACE)
In the late 1960s was instituted on board the destroyer escort McCloy (DE-1038), 189-190

Project Argus
In late 1958 Task Force 88 conducted high-altitude nuclear weapons tests, 73-79

Propulsion Plants
In the mid-1950s the destroyer escort Albert T. Harris (DE-447) operated a basic 600-PSI steam plant, 38-39; difficulties in the late 1960s with the plant on board the destroyer escort McCloy (DE-1038), 193, 206-209; selection in the late 1960s of gas

turbines for the Spruance (DD-963)-class destroyers, 216-217; comparison of the Forrest Sherman (DD-931) steam plants with those in Charles F. Adams (DDG-2)-class ships, 258-259; gas turbines for the Oliver Hazard Perry (FFG-7)-class frigates, 311; in the mid-1970s the Navy established the Senior Officer Ship Material Readiness Course in Idaho to provide engineering training to officers who were not in the nuclear program, 317-321; in the late 1970s the guided missile destroyer Mitscher (DDG-35) had serious engineering plant problems, 331-334; engineering problems in the late 1970s on board the guided missile destroyer Dahlgren (DDG-43), 340-341; can-do spirit in the early 1970s about operating with the plant on board the destroyer Jonas Ingram (DD-938), 362

Prostitution

In the late 1950s in Mozambique, 92-93; in the 1970s a well-known madam in Naples had the nickname "Humpty-Dumpty," 286-287

Puerto Rico

In 1961 the destroyer escort John R. Perry (DE-1034) collided with a merchant ship in San Juan, 130-133; in 1967 the destroyer escort McCloy (DE-1038) received repair services in San Juan from the destroyer tender Acadia (AD-42), 209-211

R6D Liftmaster

Navy transport plane that crashed in Brazil in February 1960 and killed nearly all on board, 86-87

Racial Issues

Segregation in the early 1950s in South Carolina, 17; apartheid for sailors who in the late 1950s went to the Union of South Africa, 88-89; racial protest in the early 1970s on board the aircraft carrier Franklin D. Roosevelt (CVA-42), 296-297; in the early 1970s the black sailors in the crew of the destroyer Jonas Ingram (DD-938) tended to hang out together on board ship but not ashore, 297-298; Colbus believes that under the regime of Admiral Elmo Zumwalt, CNO in the early 1970s, black sailors were promised too much and given too little, 298; in the late 1970s, Commander Wendell N. Johnson filed a complaint of racial insensitivity against Colbus following a critical fitness report on Johnson's performance while in command of the guided missile destroyer Dahlgren (DDG-43), 339-347

Radar

In the early 1960s the Bureau of Naval Personnel had to ensure a supply of trained personnel to operate and maintain various radar systems, 154

Radio

Voice radio used for tactical maneuvering in a 1957 exercise en route Canada, 51-52; ComSoLant communications in the late 1950s with South American nations, 84-85, 105-106; use of ham radio by an officer's wife in late 1962 to learn the movements of the destroyer escort John R. Perry (DE-1034), 138-139; attempts to miniaturize communications equipment in the Spruance (DD-963)-class destroyers, 225-226

Ranger, USS (CV-61)
In April 1981 a crew member died of heat stroke and cardiac arrest after physical exertion in connection with being punished, 381-383

Read, Vice Admiral William L., USN (USNA, 1949)
As Commander Naval Surface Force Atlantic Fleet in 1977, questioned an interview Colbus did with The Washington Post, 336; in 1978 prevented Colbus from making a trip to Charleston on board the destroyer Mullinnix (DD-944), 354-355; in 1979 prevented Colbus from attending a change of command in Israel for the guided missile destroyer King (DDG-41), 355; in 1978 realigned the Atlantic Fleet destroyer squadrons to divide functions between readiness and maintenance, 357-358

Reddick, Ensign Pat, USNR
In the mid-1950s served on board the destroyer escort Tabberer (DE-418), 26-27

Refueling
In the late 1950s ships of the South Atlantic Force depended on stops in port to take on fuel rather than getting it at sea, 104-105; replenishment of the destroyer Basilone (DD-824) in 1966 off Vietnam, 174-176; large carrier task group replenishment in the Mediterranean in the early 1970s, 288-289

Religion
In the 1950s Jewish personnel attended the Touro Synagogue, a famous historical landmark in Newport, Rhode Island, 41; in the mid-1960s Commander Robert Stokes, skipper of the destroyer Basilone (DD-824), was quite religious, 160-161; when he commanded the destroyer escort McCloy (DE-1038) in the late 1960s Colbus also acted as the ship's Jewish lay leader, 192-193; in the early 1970s several Jewish officers served on the staff of Commander Carrier Division Six, 283-285; celebration of Yom Kippur in October 1974 by Jewish personnel on board the aircraft carrier America (CVA-66), 300-302; in the late 1970s Rear Admiral Robert Dunn, ComCarGru 8, had a long religious discussion with a visiting Jewish chaplain, 368-369; in 1980 the chaplain visited a Jewish temple in Brookline, Massachusetts, 371-373; in 1980 Soviet Jews visited the aircraft carrier John F. Kennedy (CV-67) in Boston, 373-374

Replogle, Rear Admiral Thomas H., USN
In 1976 was a student in the Senior Officer Ship Material Readiness Course at Arco, Idaho, 319

Richard E. Byrd, USS (DDG-23)
Guided missile destroyer that in the late 1970s had a very energetic skipper in Commander Robert Goodwin, 360-361; damaged in the late 1970s while mooring in Hamburg, Germany, 363

Rickover, Admiral Hyman G., USN (Ret.) (USNA, 1922)
In the mid-1970s established the Senior Officer Ship Material Readiness Course in Idaho to provide engineering training to officers who were not in the nuclear program, 317, 321-323; delivered a tirade when he spoke to the students at SOSMRC, 324-325

Rottet, Brigadier General Ralph K., USMC (USNA, 1934)
Commanded a Marine task force in the Mediterranean in 1957 and mistakenly believed he met actor Yul Brynner, 63-64; daughter of, 65

Rowlands, Ensign Warren L., USN
Was commissioned through the NROTC program at South Carolina in 1953 and subsequently became an FBI agent, 3-4, 18

Royal Navy
In the mid-1950s the royal yacht Britannia visited Nassau in the Bahamas with Princess Margaret on board, 48-49; participation in 1967 in NATO naval exercises, 49-50, 194-195

Russell, Commander Kenneth B., USN
In the early 1970s served as air operations officer on the staff of Commander Carrier Division Six, 290-291

SOSMRC
See: Senior Office Ship Material Readiness Course (SOSMRC)

Saigon, South Vietnam
In the mid-1960s Captain Emmett P. Bonner did a fine job of handling the cruiser Oklahoma City (CLG-5) during a visit to Saigon, 60

Sailing
A plan to carry Moth sailboats to England on board the attack transport Francis Marion (LPA-249) was turned down because of a concern for damage, 349-351

Salamonie, USS (AO-26)
Fleet oiler whose skipper, Captain Edward L. Beach, performed a fine piece of ship handling in the Mediterranean in 1957 to recover a man overboard, 61-62

Sanctuary, USS (AH-17)
Dependent support ship that in early 1974 had inexperienced women crew members, 302-303; during the Azalea Festival in Wilmington, North Carolina, in 1974 one of the crew members ran naked from one end of the ship to the other, 304

Sanders, Captain Viola B., USN
In the early 1960s served as director of the WAVES, 148-149

San Francisco, California
In 1960 was the site of enjoyable liberty for Navy people, 106-107

San Juan, Puerto Rico
In 1961 the destroyer escort John R. Perry (DE-1034) collided with a merchant ship in San Juan, 130-133; in 1967 the destroyer escort McCloy (DE-1038) received repair services here from the destroyer tender Acadia (AD-42), 209-211

Saratoga, USS (CVA-60)
In the early 1970s Commander Jerry Tuttle arranged for the air group to operate ashore when the ship had a breakdown, 375-376

Sarsfield, USS (DD-837)
In late 1962 President John F. Kennedy got wet paint on his hand when he visited this destroyer in Key West, Florida, 139

Semmes, Vice Admiral Benedict, J., Jr., USN (USNA, 1934)
Aloof individual who served in the mid-1960s as Chief of the Bureau of Naval Personnel, 148-149

Senior Office Ship Material Readiness Course (SOSMRC)
Established in the mid-1970s at Idaho Falls to teach engineering to senior shipboard officers, 7, 317; curriculum, 318-321, 325-326; demanding schedule for students, 318, 322; living conditions for students, 319, 323; visit by Admiral Hyman Rickover, 323-324; recreation in Idaho Falls, 324

Service, Rear Admiral James E., USN
In the early 1980s served as Commander Carrier Group Eight, 371, 374-377, 379, 381, 384-385

Sharp, Commander Grant A., USN (USNA, 1960)
In the late 1970s took command of the guided missile destroyer King (DDG-41) after she'd have a difficult shipyard period, 355

Sherwood, Lieutenant Commander Charles, USN
Fine leader who in the mid-1950s commanded the destroyer escort Albert T. Harris (DE-447), 28-30, 35-37, 39, 180, 299

Ship Design
Various firms competed in the late 1960s to develop the design for the DX/DXG destroyer, 218-221; the Spruance design contained margins for future growth, 222-223; problems with putting in modern communications and navigation equipment in the Spruance class, 225-227; concerns for habitability and labor saving, 227-228; in the early 1970s there was great emphasis on cost saving in the design of the Oliver Hazard Perry (FFG-7)-class frigates, 310-311

Ship Handling
Training on board the destroyer escort Albert T. Harris (DE-447) in the mid-1950s, 20-21, 26-29; in the mid-1960s Captain Emmett P. Bonner did a fine job of handling the cruiser Oklahoma City (CLG-5) during a visit to Saigon, 60; as commanding officer of the oiler Salamonie (AO-26) in 1957, Captain Edward L. Beach performed a fine piece of ship handling in recovering a man overboard, 61-62; in the early 1960s Lieutenant Commander G. G. Ely Kirk was an aggressive ship handler while commanding the destroyer escort John R. Perry (DE-1034), 117-118; Lieutenant Commander Bob Brady's skill in the John R. Perry, 122; difficulties imposed by a sonar dome added in the late 1960s to the destroyer escort McCloy (DE-1038), 204; Captain Roy Hoffmann was a very capable ship handler in the early 1970s while commanding the USS Leahy (DLG-16), 261; by the late 1970s there was less tolerance than previously for damage caused by poor ship handling, 362-364

Shore Bombardment
In 1966 the destroyer Basilone (DD-824) provided shore bombardment of South Vietnam, 172-174, 184-185

Simulators
In the mid-1970s Sperry built a mockup of the combat center for the Oliver Hazard Perry (FFG-7)-class frigates, 315

Siple, Lieutenant Commander Terrence E., USN
Brilliant individual who was commissioned in 1960 following enlisted service, 187; in the late 1960s was executive officer of the destroyer escort McCloy (DE-1038), 188, 189-191; liberal viewpoints, 188; missed ship's movement in Norway, 190-192

Sixth Fleet, U.S.
In 1957 Escort Squadron 12 made a cruise to the Mediterranean, 61-64; in 1972 the destroyer Jonas Ingram (DD-938) deployed to the Med, 249-254; Vice Admiral Gerald Miller was a morale-building leader as fleet commander, 250, 252, 382; in 1972 two crew members from the Jonas Ingram committed a robbery on the Greek island of Mykonos, 254-256; in the early 1970s U.S. warships maneuvered in the vicinity of Soviet ships, 257-259; carrier task group operations, 261; prior to the ship's deployment in 1972, the crew of destroyers heard a lecture from David Rosenberg on culture in the Mediterranean, 265-266; in the autumn of 1973 the aircraft carrier John F. Kennedy (CVA-67) deployed to the Mediterranean during the Yom Kippur Arab-Israeli War, 282-288; in the autumn of 1976 the ships of Destroyer Squadron Two operated as part of the fleet, 327-333, 337-339; in the late 1970s, Vice Admiral Harry Train, the fleet commander, hosted a visit by fleet ships to Gaeta, Italy, 337-338

Smedberg, Vice Admiral William R. III, USN (USNA, 1926)
As Chief of Naval Personnel in the early 1960s, had a major role in slating flag officers into various billets, 147-148; enthusiastic personality, 149; his son was also a naval officer, 150

Smith, Rear Admiral Daniel F., Jr., USN (Ret.) (USNA, 1932)
   In October 1971 the destroyer Jonas Ingram (DD-938) buried his remains off Florida, 267-270

Smith, Rear Admiral Norman M., CEC, USN (Ret.) (USNA, 1906)
   In the 1950s served as president of the University of South Carolina after retirement as Chief of the Bureau of Yards and Docks, 4-5

Sonar
   In the mid-1950s Key West, Florida, was the site of a Navy sonar training school, 20-21, 26-27, 31-32, 34-35, 43-45; the SQS-4 provided an upgrade in sonar capabilities in the 1950s for the destroyer escort Albert T. Harris (DE-447), 34; in 1961 the destroyer escort John R. Perry (DE-1034) went to Charleston for updating of the sonar dome, 116; in the late 1960s the sonar equipment on board the destroyer escort McCloy (DE-1038), was updated, 188-189, 203-204, 206; part of ASW upgrade around 1970 to the destroyer Jonas Ingram (DD-938), 259-260

South Africa, Union of
   Visited in the late 1950s by ships of the U.S. South Atlantic Force, 88-91, 94-95

South Atlantic Force, U.S.
   Was reestablished in late 1958 after a hiatus of some years, 62-63, 76, 79-80; had no permanently assigned ships, 79-80; made various goodwill visits, 80-99; in the late 1950s and early 1960s Trinidad served as a base for Commander South Atlantic Force, 80, 84-85, 101-103; provided training in the late 1950s to South American ships in company, 82-83; relationship of the flag secretary with other staff officers, 93-94; logistic support in various ports, 104-105

South Carolina, University of, Columbia, South Carolina
   Operation of the Naval ROTC program in the early1950s at the university, 2-17

South Carolina, USS (CGN-37)
   In the mid-1970s operated as part of the Sixth Fleet in the Mediterranean, 329-330

South Vietnam
   In the mid-1960s Captain Emmett P. Bonner did a fine job of handling the cruiser Oklahoma City (CLG-5) during a visit to Saigon, 60

Soviet Navy
   In 1972 Soviet ships in the Mediterranean maneuvered in the vicinity of U.S. warships, 257-259; "shouldering" incident with the U.S. destroyer escort W. S. Sims (DE-1059), 257-258

Soviet Union
   In 1980 Soviet Jews visited the aircraft carrier John F. Kennedy (CV-67) in Boston, 373-374

Space Program
In late 1965 the destroyer Basilone (DD-824) was involved in the recovery of Gemini astronauts in the Atlantic, 166-167

Sperry Corporation
In the mid-1970s built a mockup of the combat center for the Oliver Hazard Perry (FFG-7)-class frigates, 315

Spruance (DD-963)-Class Destroyers
Resulted from the DX/DXG destroyer development program in the late 1960s and early 1970s, 213-215; selection of gas turbines for propulsion, 216-217; design competition among various contractors, 218-221; the design contained margins for future growth, 222-223; Litton built an enlarged facility for construction of the class of destroyers, 223-224 land-based training facility for the ships' crews, 224-225; attempts to miniaturize communications equipment in the class, 225-226; satellite navigation capability was deemed too expensive, 226-227, 308-309; concerns for habitability and labor saving, 227-228, 309; the four guided missile versions were originally designed for Iran and later became the Kidd (DDG-993) class in the U.S. Navy, 228-229; the boxy appearance was dictated by the need to house gas turbine machinery, 229; reviewed in the mid-1970s by the Operational Test and Evaluation Force, 307-308; ship-handling considerations, 364

State Department
Involvement in the late 1950s in U.S. Navy ship visits to various nations, 97

Stephan, Rear Admiral Edward C., USN (USNA, 1929)
Served 1958-60 as Commander U.S. South Atlantic Force, 72, 79, 81-84, 86, 88, 91, 93-100; personal characteristics, 73, 76, 81, 84, 95-97; work with Admiral Jerauld Wright in setting up the command, 79-80; unpleasantness about the Navy Band playing at his daughter's wedding, 87; wife of, 96; post-retirement routine, 103

Stokes, Commander Robert Edward Lee, Jr., USN
Served in the mid-1960s as commanding officer of the destroyer Basilone (DD-824), 65, 163, 169-171, 173-175, 183; demanding style as skipper, 169-171, 173-174, 183-184; was passed over twice for captain but was eventually selected after serving in Washington, D.C., 185-186

Storms, Captain James G. III, USN
In the late 1970s was commanding officer of the Sixth Fleet flagship Albany (CG-10) during an anniversary celebration in Italy, 337

Subic Bay, Philippines
In 1966 provided repairs to a damaged catapult on board the aircraft carrier Ticonderoga (CVA-14), 177

Sullivan, Commander Gerald F., USN
In October 1974 was involved in a Yom Kipper stunt on board the aircraft carrier America (CVA-66), 301

Surface Force, Atlantic Fleet
In 1978 the type commander, Vice Admiral William L. Read, realigned Atlantic Fleet destroyer squadrons and divided functions, 357-358

Swank, Lieutenant John A., USN (USNA, 1945)
Naval aviator who was admired in the early 1950s while serving as a Naval ROTC instructor at Penn State University, 18

Tabberer, USS (DE-418)
Destroyer escort that served in the mid and late 1950s as flagship of an escort squadron, 26-28, 66-67; collision with the submarine Diablo (SS-479), 27; modifications to the ship's original design in the 1950s to accommodate a squadron commodore and his staff, 66-67

Tactics
Antisubmarine maneuvers practiced in the mid-1950s by ships at the sonar school in Key West, Florida, 26-27, 31-32, 34-35, 44-45

Taiwan
In 1966 Kaohsiung was an enjoyable liberty site for the crew of the destroyer Basilone (DD-724), 169-170; provided tender availability, 181

Talbot, USS (DEG-4)
In 1974 was used as a test platform for the 76-millimeter OTO Melara gun, 307-308, 311

Tarawa, USS (CVS-40)
Aircraft carrier that was part of Task Force 88 in late 1958 during high-altitude nuclear weapons tests near Antarctica, 73-74

Task Force 88
In late 1958 conducted high-altitude nuclear weapons tests near Antarctica, 73; makeup of the task force, 73-79

Thearle, Lieutenant William James, USN (USNA, 1955)
Served in the late 1950s and early 1960s served as aide to Rear Admiral Lloyd Mustin and Rear Admiral Charles Weakley, 120-121

Ticonderoga, USS (CVA-14)
Operations in 1966 off the coast of Vietnam, 175-177; a problem with a catapult in 1966 required a speed run to Subic Bay for repairs, 177; port visit to Hong Kong, 179

Torpedoes
    A malfunctioning torpedo fired by the destroyer Jonas Ingram (DD-938) during an ASW exercise in the early 1970s hit a submarine, 271-274

Train, Vice Admiral Harry D. II, USN (USNA, 1949)
    In the late 1970s, while serving as Commander Sixth Fleet, hosted a visit of fleet ships to Gaeta, Italy, 337-338

Training
    Midshipman summer cruise to Europe in 1951 on board the high-speed transport Burdo (APD-133), 9-12; summer cruise to South America in 1953 on board the battleship Missouri (BB-63), 12-14; in the mid-1950s Key West, Florida, was the site of a Navy sonar training school, 20-21, 26-27, 31-32, 34-35, 43-45; training of junior officers in the 1950s on board the destroyer escort Albert T. Harris (DE-447), 20-23, 27-29; provided in the late 1950s by the U.S. South Atlantic Force to South American ships in company, 82-83; refresher training at Guantanamo Bay in the early 1960s for the crew of the In the early 1960s was the site of training for the crew of the destroyer escort John R. Perry (DE-1034), 122-126; for the crew of the destroyer Basilone (DD-824) in 1966 while deploying to Vietnam, 167-168 land-based training facility for the crews of the Spruance (DD-963)-class destroyers, 224-225

Trinidad
    In the late 1950s and early 1960s served as a base for Commander South Atlantic Force, 80, 84-85, 101-103; local social structure in the late 1950s, 101-102; political unrest was led by Eric Williams, 102-103

Trower, Rear Admiral Ross H., CHC, USN
    In 1980-81 visited carrier battle group ships operating in the Indian Ocean, 384

Turner, Vice Admiral Stansfield, USN (USNA, 1947)
    As Commander Second Fleet in 1974, received a briefing from Commander Carrier Division Six on a planned NATO exercise in the Atlantic, 302-304

Tuttle, Rear Admiral Jerry O., USN
    In the early 1970s was air group commander on board the carrier Saratoga (CVA-60), 375-376; in the early 1980s served as Commander Carrier Group Eight, 376-377

Uniforms-Naval
    Looked sharp in 1951 for personnel inspections on board the high-speed transport Burdo (APD-133), 11-12; in the mid-1950s officers on board the destroyer escort Albert T. Harris (DE-447) had to wear their blues while standing bridge watches, 39

VF-33
    See: Fighter Squadron 33 (VF-33)

Van Arsdall, Rear Admiral Clyde, J., Jr., USN (USNA, 1934)
As Commander Cruiser-Destroyer Force Atlantic Fleet in 1967 was not as concerned as his subordinates were over some problems the destroyer escort McCloy (DE-1038) experienced during a NATO deployment, 201-202

Venezuela
Visited in the 1958, a time of domestic political upheaval, by ships of the U.S. South Atlantic Force, 98-99

Vietnam War
In January 1966 Destroyer Squadron 12 became the second East Coast desron to deploy to Vietnam, 167-169; in 1966 the destroyer Basilone (DD-824) provided shore bombardment of South Vietnam, 172-174, 185-185; carrier operations, 175-177; in late 1969 the Bureau of Naval Personnel considered Colbus for assignment in Vietnam but did not send him because of budget cutbacks, 230-232

Virginia (CGN-38)-Class Cruisers
In the late 1960s nuclear power was considered too expensive for the Spruance (DD-963)-class destroyers but was used for the Virginia (CGN-38) class, 215-217

Vogt, Commander Frederick H., USN
In the early 1980s, as commanding officer of Fighter Squadron 33 on board the aircraft carrier Independence (CV-62), encouraged Colbus to fly in the back seat of an F-4 Phantom, 386-387

Wallace, Rear Admiral Kenneth C., USN (USNA, 1943)
As Commander Cruiser-Destroyer Flotilla 12 in 1972, was concerned with pay allotment problems of the destroyer Jonas Ingram (DD-938), 266; visited Mrs. Daniel F. Smith, Jr., in October 1971 after her husband was buried at sea off Florida, 270

Walsh, Lieutenant Commander Thomas W., USN (USNA, 1944)
In the late 1950s served as commanding officer of the destroyer escort Tweedy (DE-522) during a deployment to the Mediterranean, 63

Walters, Rear Admiral Robert L., USN (USNA, 1949)
As Commander Cruiser-Destroyer Group Eight in the late 1970s, said Colbus was too protective of the ship skippers in Destroyer Squadron Two, 333-334; liked to conduct surprise inspections of ships, 359-361

War Games
Played in the mid-1960s at the Naval War College, 160-161

Washington Post, The
    In 1977 Colbus did an interview with writer George Wilson of this newspaper concerning personnel in his destroyer squadron, 334-336

Watkins, Vice Admiral James D., USN (USNA, 1949)
    As Commander Sixth Fleet in the late 1970s was quoted as saying he didn't want Colbus serving under him, 365

Watson, Captain Thomas C., Jr., USN (USNA, 1954)
    From 1978 to 1980 did an outstanding job as commanding officer of the aircraft carrier <u>Independence</u> (CV-62), 293-294

Weakley, Rear Admiral Charles E., USN (USNA, 1929)
    Gentlemanly officer who in 1960-61 served as Commander Destroyer Force Atlantic Fleet, 120-121

Weaver, Chief Boatswain's Mate Joseph, USN
    In the early 1970s did a fine job of discipline on board the destroyer <u>Jonas Ingram</u> (DD-938) and prevented drug problems, 242-243, 250; took some sailors home for dinner, 298-299

Weschler, Rear Admiral Thomas R., USN (USNA, 1939)
    In the late 1960s ran the DX/DXG destroyer development program in OpNav, 212-215, 217, 222-223, 225-226, 228-229, 308-310; difficult man to work for, 214-215

Williams, Eric
    Racist dictator who came to power in Trinidad in the 1960s, 103

Wilson, George
    In 1977 interviewed Colbus about the men of Destroyer Squadron Two for an article in <u>The Washington Post</u>, 334-346

Wright, Admiral Jerauld, USN (USNA, 1918)
    As CinCLant in the late 1950s, conferred with Rear Admiral Edward C. Stephan about plans for use of the U.S. South Atlantic Force, 79-80

<u>**W. S. Sims**</u>**, USS (DE-1059)**
    Destroyer escort that in 1972 was involved in a "shouldering" incident with a Soviet ship, 257-258; sonar capability, 260

Yankura, Lieutenant Commander Thomas W., USN
    Fine officer who served in the early 1970s as chief engineer on board the destroyer <u>Jonas Ingram</u> (DD-938), 246

Yom Kippur War
   In the autumn of 1973 the aircraft carrier John F. Kennedy (CVA-67) deployed to the Mediterranean during the Arab-Israeli War, 282-288

Youngblade, Captain Charles John (USNA, 1949)
   In the early 1970s was skipper of the aircraft carrier Franklin D. Roosevelt (CVA-42) during Sixth Fleet operations, 261, 280

Zumwalt, Vice Admiral Elmo R., Jr., USN (USNA, 1943)
   In late 1969 Colbus was selected for Zumwalt's staff in Vietnam but did not go because of budget cutbacks, 230-232; perception that competition among ships dropped off in the early 1970s when he was CNO, 239-240; effect of Z-grams on board the destroyer Jonas Ingram (DD-938), 242, 298, 300; as CNO placed great emphasis on cost saving in the design of the Oliver Hazard Perry (FFG-7)-class frigates, 310

www.ingramcontent.com/pod-product-compliance
Lightning Source LLC
Chambersburg PA
CBHW080623170426
43209CB00007B/1502